Foundations of Economics

Third Edition
David Begg

Foundations of Economics
Third Edition

David Begg

The **McGraw·Hill** Companies

London Boston Burr Ridge, IL Dubuque, IA Madison, WI New York
San Francisco St. Louis Bangkok Bogotá Caracas Kuala Lumpur
Lisbon Madrid Mexico City Milan Montreal New Delhi Santiago
Seoul Singapore Sydney Taipei Toronto

Foundations of Economics Third Edition
David Begg
ISBN-13 9780077114237
ISBN-10 007711423X

 **Education**

Published by McGraw-Hill Education
Shoppenhangers Road
Maidenhead
Berkshire
SL6 2QL
Telephone: 44 (0) 1628 502 500
Fax: 44 (0) 1628 770 224
Website: www.mcgraw-hill.co.uk

British Library Cataloguing in Publication Data
A catalogue record for this book is available from the British Library

Library of Congress Cataloging-in-Publication Data
The Library of Congress data for this book has been applied for from the Library of Congress

Acquisitions Editor: Kirsty Reade
Development Editor: Hannah Cooper
Marketing Manager: Marca Wosoba
Senior Production Editor: Beverley Shields

Produced for McGraw-Hill by MCS Publishing Services Ltd, Salisbury, Wiltshire
Text design by Hard Lines
Cover design by Ego Creative
Printed and bound in Spain by Mateu Cromo

First Edition published in 2001 by McGraw-Hill Education
Second Edition published in 2003 by McGraw-Hill Education

ISBN-13 9780077114237
ISBN-10 007711423X

For Jenny

Brief Table of Contents

Detailed Table of Contents

Preface

Useful foundations need to be reliably up to the job, help you understand the rest of your life, and be fun enough to make you want to bother.

Foundations of Economics is specially designed for students studying introductory economics in a single term or semester. The book streamlines the arguments that make its parent text *Economics* 8/e the 'student's bible' for economics (BBC Radio 4).

Foundations of Economics covers only the core topics but trains students to think for themselves, using a wide range of data and examples, and offers authoritative commentary on topical issues.

Learning by doing

Few people practise for a driving test just by reading a book. There is no substitute for finding out if you can actually do a hill start. We give you lots of examples and real-world applications in order to help you master economics for yourself. Try to do the examples at the end of every chapter, and compare your answers with those we give at the end of the book.

Don't read on 'cruise control', highlighting a few sentences and gliding through paragraphs that we worked hard to simplify. Active learning is much more efficient. When the text says 'clearly', ask yourself 'why' it is clear. See if you can construct diagrams before you look at ours.

To assist you in working through the text, we have developed a number of distinctive features. To familiarize yourself with these features, please turn to the Guided Tour on pages xi–xii.

Key changes to the third edition

The third edition has been completely rewritten to meet the needs of today's busy students, on whom pressures are greater than ever. It includes:

◆ Extended case studies in every chapter, and interesting examples of economics in action, encouraging readers to view economics as practical and illuminating;
◆ More extensive coverage of microeconomics, now expanded to seven chapters, providing a clearer, and more even paced, introduction to demand, supply, and markets;
◆ Reordering of macroeconomics section, beginning with growth, cycles, and issues, before introducing analysis and explanations;
◆ Simplification of aggregate supply and inflation dynamics;
◆ New streamlined layout, fewer analytical diagrams.

More than ever before, the third edition of *Foundations of Economics* incorporates extensive feedback from students, lecturers, and teachers, in order to deliver the ideal learning support for a single-term introduction to economics.

Guided Tour

Learning outcomes present the key concepts that you should understand when you have finished this chapter section.

Key terms are highlighted where they first appear in the text, so that you can note the new term and the definition that accompanies it.

Boxes and case studies provide examples, illuminating ideas, and theories presented within the chapter and offering an insight into how economics applies to the real world.

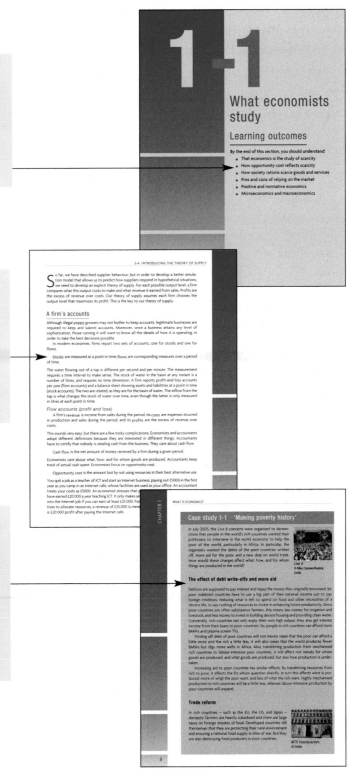

1-1

What economists study

Learning outcomes

By the end of this section, you should understand:

- That economics is the study of scarcity
- How opportunity cost reflects scarcity
- How society rations scarce goods and services
- Pros and cons of relying on the market
- Positive and normative economics
- Microeconomics and macroeconomics

3-4 INTRODUCING THE THEORY OF SUPPLY

So far, we have described supplier behaviour, but in order to develop a better simulation model that allows us to predict how suppliers respond in hypothetical situations, we need to develop an explicit theory of supply. For each possible output level, a firm compares what this output costs to make and what revenue it earned from sales. Profits are the excess of revenue over costs. Our theory of supply assumes each firm chooses the output level that maximizes its profit. This is the key to our theory of supply.

A firm's accounts

Although illegal poppy growers may not bother to keep accounts, legitimate businesses are required to keep and submit accounts. Moreover, once a business attains any level of sophistication, those running it will want to know all the details of how it is operating, in order to take the best decisions possible.

In modern economies, firms report two sets of accounts, one for stocks and one for flows.

Stocks are measured at a point in time; flows are corresponding measures over a period of time.

The water flowing out of a tap is different per second and per minute. The measurement requires a time interval to make sense. The stock of water in the basin at any instant is a number of litres, and requires no time dimension. A firm reports profit-and-loss accounts per year (flow accounts) and a balance sheet showing assets and liabilities at a point in time (stock accounts). The two are related, as they are for the basin of water. The inflow from the tap is what changes the stock of water over time, even though the latter is only measured in litres at each point in time.

Flow accounts (profit and loss)

A firm's revenue is income from sales during the period, its costs are expenses incurred in production and sales during the period, and its profits are the excess of revenue over costs.

This sounds very easy, but there are a few tricky complications. Economists and accountants adopt different definitions because they are interested in different things. Accountants have to certify that nobody is stealing cash from the business. They care about cash flow.

Cash flow is the net amount of money received by a firm during a given period.

Economists care about what, how, and for whom goods are produced. Accountants keep track of actual cash spent. Economists focus on opportunity cost.

Opportunity cost is the amount lost by not using resources in their best alternative use.

You quit a job as a teacher of ICT and start an Internet business, paying out £5000 in the first year as you camp in an Internet cafe, whose facilities are used as your office. An accountant treats your costs as £5000. An economist stresses that you could have earned £20 000 a year teaching ICT. It only makes sense to move into the Internet job if you can earn at least £25 000. For you can earn a revenue of £25 000 is a mere £20 000 profit after paying the Internet cafe.

CHAPTER 1   WHAT IS ECONOMICS?

Case study 1-1   'Making poverty history'

In July 2005, the Live 8 concerts were organised to demonstrate that people in the world's rich countries wanted their politicians to intervene in the world economy to help the poor of the world, particularly in Africa. In particular, the organisers wanted the debts of the poor countries written off, more aid for the poor, and a new deal on world trade. How would these changes affect what, how, and for whom things are produced in the world?

Live 8
© Mike Clasase/Reuters/Corbis

The effect of debt write-offs and more aid

Debtors are supposed to pay interest and repay the money they originally borrowed. So, poor indebted countries have to use a big part of their national income just to pay foreign creditors, reducing what is left to spend on food and other necessities of a decent life, to say nothing of resources to invest in enhancing future productivity. Since poor countries are often subsistence farmers, this means less money for irrigation and livestock, and less money to invest in building decent housing and providing clean water. Conversely, rich countries not only enjoy their own high output, they also get interest income from their loans to poor countries. So, people in rich countries can afford more BMWs and plasma screen TVs.

Writing off debt of poor countries will not merely mean that the poor can afford a little more and the rich a little less, it will also mean that the world produces fewer BMWs but digs more wells in Africa. Also, transferring production from mechanised rich countries to labour-intensive poor countries, it will affect not merely for whom goods are produced, but also how production is undertaken.

Increasing aid to poor countries has similar effects. By transferring resources from rich to poor, it affects the for whom question directly. In turn this affects what is produced: more of what the poor want and less of what the rich want. Highly mechanised production in rich countries will be a little less, whereas labour-intensive production by poor countries will expand.

Trade reform

In rich countries – such as the EU, the US, and Japan – domestic farmers are heavily subsidised and there are large taxes on foreign imports of food. Developed countries tell themselves that they are protecting their rural environment and ensuring a national food supply in time of war. But they are also destroying food producers in poor countries.

WTO headquarters
© Corbis

8

Graphs, tables, and figures are presented in a simple and clear design to help you understand key economic models and to absorb relevant data.

Recaps sum up the ideas that have been discussed in each chapter, reviewing the concepts and topics that you should now comprehend.

Review questions provide questions and problems to test your understanding of the material.

Solutions to exercises are available at the end of the text so you can check your progress.

Technology to enhance learning and teaching

Online Learning Centre

A range of supplementary teaching and learning resources has been developed to accompany the new edition and area available on the Online Learning Centre website for the textbook.

Resources for students include:

- **Twelve chapter-by chapter student tests** enable students to test their understanding of each chapter online.
- **Case studies and applications** provide contemporary examples demonstrating economics in action.
- **Web links and further reading resources** allow students to research companies, government, and academic sources and journals online.
- **Glossary of key terms:** a complete glossary of economics terms and definitions to aid revision of the important ideas and concepts from the textbook.

Also available for lecturers:

- **Twelve chapter-by-chapter lecture presentations** summarize the key concepts from each chapter, for use as presentations in lectures and seminars or as student handouts.
- **Chapter-by-chapter lecturer manual** offers a synopsis of each chapter and teaching suggestions for presenting the material from the book on a one-semester module.
- **600 test questions in a test bank platform**, to create tests, assessments, and exams based on the textbook.

- **All figures from the text** available to download, to enable lecturers to manipulate, print, and present the graphs and diagrams to students.

To access these resources and further updates, visit the Online Learning Centre website at www.mcgraw-hill.co.uk/textbooks/begg.

Lecturers: Customise Content for your Courses using the McGraw-Hill Primis Content Centre

Now it's incredibly easy to create a flexible, customised solution for your course, using content from both US and European McGraw-Hill Education textbooks, content from our Professional list including Harvard Business Press titles, as well as a selection of over 9,000 cases from Harvard, Insead and Darden. In addition, we can incorporate your own material and course notes.

For more information, please contact your local rep who will discuss the right delivery options for your custom publication – including printed readers, e-Books and CDROMs. To see what McGraw-Hill content you can choose from, visit www.primisonline.com.

Study Skills

Open University Press publishes guides to study, research and exam skills to help undergradute and postgraduate students through their university studies.

Visit www.openup.co.uk/ss to see the full selection of study skills titles, and get a **£2 discount** by entering the promotional code **study** when buying online!

ACKNOWLEDGEMENTS

Acknowledgements

The authors would like to thank all those students, former students, and lecturers who have made suggestions on how we should revise the third edition. We are grateful for the usual highly professional support from the editorial and production team at McGraw Hill, particularly Hannah Cooper, Kirsty Reade, and Caroline Prodger.

The publishers would like to thank the following reviewers who provided their comments and suggestions for developing the new edition of this book:

Fran Alston, Napier University

Dean Garratt, Nottingham Trent University

Lester Hunt, University of Surrey

Roger Fitzer, University of Surrey

Rob Watkins, Kingston University

Paul McVeigh, Leeds University

Douglas Chalmers, Glasgow Caledonian University

We would also like to thank all contributors to the Online Learning Centre website resources, in particular Lester Hunt of the University of Surrey who has updated the content for the new edition, and Richard Godfrey of the University of Wales Institute, Cardiff, for the creation of student and lecturer test questions.

1

What is economics?

1-1

What economists study

Learning outcomes

By the end of this section, you should understand:

- ◆ That economics is the study of scarcity
- ◆ How opportunity cost reflects scarcity
- ◆ How society rations scarce goods and services
- ◆ Pros and cons of relying on the market
- ◆ Positive and normative economics
- ◆ Microeconomics and macroeconomics

Economics is much too interesting to be left to professional economists. It affects almost everything we do, not merely as students but as parents, voters, and workers. It influences climate change, whether we can make poverty history, and the resources we have to enjoy ourselves.

The formal study of economics is exciting because it introduces a toolkit that allows a better understanding of the problems we all face. Everyone knows a smoky engine is a bad sign, but sometimes only a trained mechanic can give the right advice on how to fix it.

This book is designed to teach you the toolkit and give you practice in using it. Nobody carries a huge toolbox very far. Like Swiss army knives, useful toolkits are small enough to be portable but have enough proven tools to deal both with routine problems and nasty surprises. With practice, you'll be surprised at how much economic analysis can illuminate daily living.

Every group of people must solve three basic problems: what goods and services to make, how to make them, and who gets them.

Economics is the study of how society decides what, how, and for whom to produce.

Goods are physical commodities such as steel and strawberries. Services are activities such as massages or live concerts, consumed or enjoyed only at the instant they are produced. If you attended Live 8, you enjoyed a service. If you made a video of it, the video is a good that can be enjoyed later when your friends come over.

Society has to resolve the conflict between people's limitless desire for goods and services, and the scarcity of resources (labour, machinery, raw materials) with which goods and services are made. Economics is the analysis of these human decisions, about which we aim to develop theories and test them against the facts.

As a student, you can afford the necessities of life – a place to live, food to eat, a brilliant textbook – and some extras, such as summer holidays and visits to clubs. You are richer than some people, poorer than others. Income distribution across people is closely linked to the 'what', 'how', and 'for whom' questions. Table 1-1 shows that in poor countries, average income per person is only £285 a year. In the rich industrial countries, income per person is £17 162 a year, 70 times larger. For whom does the world economy produce? Mainly, for the 15 per cent of its people in the rich industrial countries. What is produced? What people in those countries want to buy!

	Country group		
	Poor	Middle	Rich
Income per head £	285	1275	17 162
% of world population	41	44	15
% of world income	4	15	81

Table 1-1   World population and income
Source: World Bank, *World Development Report, 2003*

The large differences in incomes between groups reflect *how* goods are made. Poor countries have little machinery, and their people have less access to health and education. Workers in poor countries are less productive because they work in less favourable conditions.

Income is unequally distributed within each country as well as between countries, and this affects *what* goods and services are produced. In Brazil, where income is unequally distributed, rich people can afford domestic servants who work for low wages. In egalitarian Denmark, few people are sufficiently rich to afford to hire servants.

Box 1-1   At your service

Although it may surprise you, most output is services, and this sector's share of national output continues to grow. In rich countries, agriculture is usually less than 2 per cent of national output. Manufacturing is rarely over 25 per cent. Manufacturing plus mining gives us total industrial output, usually around 30 per cent of national output. The remaining 70 per cent is services (banking, transport, communications, tourism, entertainment, defence, education, health).

How can transport be a service? Making a plane is an act of manufacturing, but using a plane is a service. Thus Boeing is a manufacturer but British Airways provides services. If you miss the flight, you don't get the service.

Next time you hear about the loss of jobs in manufacturing, remember that in rich countries it is only a small part of national output, and still in trend decline. More and more of manufacturing is being outsourced to cheaper locations in the global economy.

Percentage of national output	Japan	France	UK
Agriculture	2	2	1
Industry	33	26	27
Services	65	71	72

Source: World Bank, *World Development Report*

Scarcity and opportunity cost

Economics is the study of scarcity. When something is so abundantly available that we get all we want, we don't waste time worrying about what, how, and for whom it should be produced. In the Sahara, there is no need to worry about the production of sand.

For a **scarce resource**, the quantity demanded at a zero price would exceed the available supply.

When resources are scarce, society can get *more* of some things only by having *less* of other things. We must *choose between* different outcomes, or make trade-offs between them.

The **opportunity cost** of a good is the quantity of *other* goods sacrificed to get another unit of *this* good.

As a country, we can have more education only if we have less of something else, perhaps less defence or less food. Governments may make these tough choices, but markets also play a role.

Box 1-2   Scarcely a hospital bed

After 2001, Gordon Brown and Tony Blair committed Britain to a substantial rise in government spending on health care. Yet real, inflation-adjusted, government spending on health had already risen by a third in the 1990s. Why did people want even more money spent on health?

First, we are all living longer. Older people need more health care. Second, medical advances have led to successful but very expensive treatments. Making these available to some people reduces the resources left for others. With an ageing population, health spending must rise *faster* than national output if people are to get the same standard of care as in the past. And to get every new treatment, however expensive, health spending has to rise *much faster* still. To pay for this within a National Health Service, taxes would have to rise a lot.

The real issue is *scarcity*, on what taxes to spend our limited resources? Do we have fewer teachers and televisions in order to pay taxes and divert more resources to health? If not, we can't avoid rationing health care. This rationing can be done via markets (charging for health care so people choose to have less) or by rules (limiting access to treatment). Society's decision affects what is produced, how it is produced, and, dramatically in this example, for whom it is produced

The role of the market

A **market** uses prices to reconcile decisions about consumption and production.

Markets and prices are one way in which society can decide what, how, and for whom to produce. During the British beef crisis, caused by fears about mad cow disease, pork prices rose 30 per cent while beef prices fell. This provided the incentive to expand pig farming, and stopped too many shoppers switching to pork until the new piglets were ready for market.

How might resources be allocated if markets did not exist?

In a **command economy**, government planners decide what, how, and for whom goods and services are made. Households, firms, and workers are then told what to do.

Central planning is complicated. No country has ever made all decisions by central command. However, in China, Cuba, and the former Soviet bloc, there used to be a lot of central direction and planning. The state owned land and factories, and made key decisions about what people should consume, how goods should be made, and how much people should work.

Imagine that you had to run the city where you live. Think of the food, clothing, and housing allocation decisions you would have to make. How would you decide how things were made, and who got what? These decisions are being made every day in your own city, but chiefly through the mechanism of markets and prices.

The opposite extreme from central planning is a reliance on markets in which prices can freely adjust. In 1776, Adam Smith's *The Wealth of Nations* argued that people pursuing their

5

self-interest would be led 'as by an invisible hand' to do things in the interest of society as a whole.

In a **free market economy**, prices adjust to reconcile desires and scarcity.

Hoping to become a millionaire, you invent the mobile phone. Although motivated by self-interest, you make society better off by creating new jobs and using existing resources more productively. In a free market, people pursue their self-interest without government restrictions. A command economy allows little individual economic freedom, since decisions are taken by the state. Between these extremes is the mixed economy.

In a **mixed economy**, the government and private sector interact in solving economic problems.

The government affects economic activity by taxation, subsidies, and the provision of services such as defence and the police force. It also regulates the extent to which individuals may pursue their own self-interest. All countries are mixed economies, though some have freer markets than others, as Figure 1-1 shows.

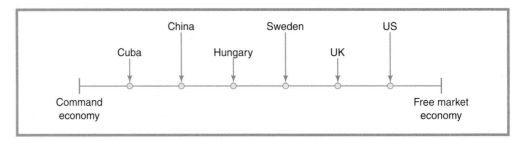

Figure 1-1 Market orientation

Box **1-3** Poor marx for central planners

During 1989–91, the Soviet bloc abandoned Marxist central planning and began transition to a market economy. The Soviet bloc grew rapidly before the 1970s, but then stagnated. Economic failure brought down the Berlin Wall. Key difficulties that emerged were:

♦ **Information Overload** Planners could not keep track of all the details of economic activity. Machinery rusted because nobody came to pick it up, crops rotted because storage and distribution were not co-ordinated.
♦ **Bad Incentives** Complete job security undermined work incentives. Since planners could monitor quantity more easily than quality, firms met output targets by skimping on quality. Without environmental standards, firms polluted at will. Central planning led to low-quality goods and an environmental disaster.
♦ **Insufficient Competition** Planners believed big was beautiful. One tractor factory served the Soviets from Latvia to Vladivostok. But large scale deprived planners of information from competing firms, making it hard to assess managerial efficiency. Similarly, without electoral competition, it was impossible to sack governments making economic mistakes.

Positive and normative

Positive economics deals with scientific explanation of how the economy works. Normative economics offers recommendations based on personal value judgements.

Positive economics aims to explain how the economy works, and thus how it will respond to changes. It formulates and tests propositions of the form: if cigarettes are taxed, their price will rise. In this sense, positive economics is like natural sciences such as physics, geology, or astronomy.

Many propositions in positive economics are widely agreed to be correct. As in any science, there are some unresolved questions where disagreement remains. Research in progress will resolve some of these issues, but new issues will arise, providing scope for further research.

Normative economics is based on subjective value judgements, not on the search for objective truth. Should resources be switched from health to education? The answer is a subjective value judgement, based on the feelings of the person making the statement. Economics can't show that health is more or less desirable than education. However, it can answer the positive question of what quantity of extra health could be achieved by giving up a particular quantity of education.

Micro and macro

Economics has many branches. Labour economics deals with employment and wages, urban economics with housing and transport, monetary economics with interest rates and exchange rates. However, a different classification cuts across these branches.

Microeconomics makes a detailed study of individual decisions about particular commodities.

For example, we can study why individual households prefer cars to bicycles and how firms decide whether to make cars or bicycles. Comparing the markets for cars and for bicycles, we can study the relative price of cars and bicycles and the output of these two goods.

However, in studying the *whole* economy, such detailed analysis gets very complicated. We need to simplify to keep the analysis manageable. Microeconomics offers a detailed treatment of one part of the economy – for example what is happening to cars – but ignores interactions with the rest of the economy in order to keep the analysis manageable. However, if these wider interactions are too important to be swept under the carpet, another simplification must be found.

Macroeconomics analyses interactions in the economy as a whole.

To be able to study the economy as a whole deliberately simplifies the individual building blocks of the analysis. Macroeconomists don't divide consumer goods into cars, bicycles, TVs and iPods. Rather, they study a single bundle called 'consumer goods' in order to focus on the interaction between household shopping sprees and firms' decisions about building new factories.

Case study 1-1 'Making poverty history'

In July 2005, the Live 8 concerts were organised to demonstrate that people in the world's rich countries wanted their politicians to intervene in the world economy to help the poor of the world, particularly in Africa. In particular, the organisers wanted the debts of the poor countries written off, more aid for the poor, and a new deal on world trade. How would these changes affect what, how, and for whom things are produced in the world?

Live 8
© Mike Cassese/Reuters/
Corbis

The effect of debt write-offs and more aid

Debtors are supposed to pay interest and repay the money they originally borrowed. So, poor indebted countries have to use a big part of their national income just to pay foreign creditors, reducing what is left to spend on food and other necessities of a decent life, to say nothing of resources to invest in enhancing future productivity. Since poor countries are often subsistence farmers, this means less money for irrigation and livestock, and less money to invest in building decent housing and providing clean water. Conversely, rich countries not only enjoy their own high output, they also get interest income from their loans to poor countries. So, people in rich countries can afford more BMWs and plasma screen TVs.

Writing off debt of poor countries will not merely mean that the poor can afford a little more and the rich a little less, it will also mean that the world produces fewer BMWs but digs more wells in Africa. Also, transferring production from mechanised rich countries to labour-intensive poor countries, it will affect not merely for whom goods are produced, and what goods are produced, but also how production is undertaken.

Increasing aid to poor countries has similar effects. By transferring resources from rich to poor, it affects the *for whom* question directly. In turn this affects *what* is produced: more of what the poor want, and less of what the rich want. Highly mechanised production in rich countries will be a little less, whereas labour-intensive production by poor countries will expand.

Trade reform

In rich countries – such as the EU, the US, and Japan – domestic farmers are heavily subsidised and there are large taxes on foreign imports of food. Developed countries tell themselves that they are protecting their rural environment and ensuring a national food supply in time of war. But they are also destroying food producers in poor countries.

WTO headquarters
© Corbis

Case study 1-1   *Continued*

The WTO exists to negotiate and implement agreements on the rules and tariffs governing international trade. In the last 50 years, the WTO has agreed many reductions in import tariffs, but has yet to secure agreement to cut trade protection of farmers in rich countries.

Poor countries rely a lot on agriculture. If they cannot sell their output in rich countries, their produce fetches only low prices, trapping poor farmers in poverty. Worse still, if they raise agricultural productivity by better seeds, irrigation, or mechanisation, they simply bid down the price of their crops, because they have to sell even more agricultural food output to the same poor countries as before.

Suppose the rich countries now allow imports of foreign food on equal terms with those enjoyed by farmers in rich countries. Now African farmers can sell in London and Paris. This has two effects. Food prices fall in London and Paris, where food is now less scarce. But these prices still greatly exceed the prices African farmers previously received when selling only in poor countries. So European consumers are better off (lower food prices) and African farmers benefit (much higher prices than before for their output).

This argument applies whatever the barriers faced by African farmers. It does not matter whether these are import duties into rich countries or subsidies by rich countries to their own farmers. Trade reform has to eliminate both if African agriculture is to prosper, and that might be the largest single contribution that the rich countries could make to ensuring sustainable improvements in the world's poorest countries. Without trade reform, neither aid nor debt relief is likely to make poverty history.

1-2

How economists think

Learning outcomes

By the end of this section, you should understand:

- ◆ Why theories deliberately simplify reality
- ◆ Nominal and real variables
- ◆ How to build a simple theoretical model
- ◆ How to interpret scatter diagrams
- ◆ How 'other things equal' lets key influences be ignored but not forgotten

I t is more fun to play tennis if you can serve, and cutting trees is easier with a chainsaw. Every activity or academic discipline has a basic set of tools, which may be tangible, like the dentist's drill, or intangible, like the ability to serve in tennis. To analyse economic issues we use both models and data.

A **model** or **theory** makes assumptions from which it deduces how people behave. It deliberately simplifies reality.

Models omit some details of the real world in order to focus on the essentials.

An economist uses a model as a traveller uses a map. A map of London omits traffic lights and roundabouts, but you get a good picture of the best route to take. This simplified picture is easy to follow, yet provides a good guide to actual behaviour.

Data are pieces of evidence about economic behaviour.

The data or facts interact with models in two ways. First, the data help us quantify theoretical relationships. To choose the best route we need some facts about where delays may occur. The model is useful because it tells us which facts to collect. Bridges are more likely to be congested than six-lane motorways.

Second, the data help us to test our models. Like all careful scientists, economists must check that their theories square with the relevant facts. The crucial word is *relevant*. For several decades the number of Scottish dysentery deaths was closely related to the UK inflation rate, but this was a coincidence not the key to a theory of inflation. Without any logical underpinning, the empirical connection eventually broke down. Paying attention to a freak relationship in the data increases neither our economic understanding nor our ability to predict the future.

Economic data

To gather evidence, we can study changes *across* groups or regions at *the same point in time*; or for a single group or region *over time*. Table 1-2 shows a *cross-section* of unemployment rates in different countries in 2005, while Table 1-3 shows a *time-series* of UK house prices between 1960 and 2004.

Canada	Italy	France	UK
7	8	10	5

Table 1-2   Unemployment by country, 2005 (percentage of labour force)
Source: OECD, *Economic Outlook, 2005*

	1960	1980	2000
House price (£'000s)	2.5	27.2	124.7
Consumer price index (2000 = 100)	7.4	39.3	100.0
Real price of houses (2000 £'000s)	33.8	69.2	124.7

Table 1-3   UK house prices (average price of a new house)
Source: ONS, *Economic Trends*

The average price of a new house rose from £2500 in 1960 to £124 700 in 2000. Are houses really 50 times as expensive as in 1960? Not once we allow for inflation, which also raised incomes and the ability to buy houses.

Nominal values measure prices at the time of measurement. **Real values** adjust nominal values for changes in the general price level.

In the UK the consumer price index (CPI) measures the price of a basket of goods bought by a typical household. Inflation caused a big rise in the CPI during 1960–2000. The third row of Table 1-3 calculates an index of real house prices, expressed as if the CPI had always been at the level it attained in the year 2000. It shows how house prices would have changed if there had been no general inflation in the price of goods as a whole.

An **index number** expresses data relative to a given base value.

Comparing 1960 and 2000 but allowing for inflation, real house prices tripled, from £33 800 to £124 700. Most of the rise in nominal house prices in the top row of Table 1-3 was actually caused by inflation.

Box 1-4   Millionaires galore

One in every 500 adults in Britain is now a millionaire. The Lottery created only a handful of Britain's 85 000 millionaires. It's mainly just the effect of inflation. The table below shows how much an old-fashioned millionaire would be worth at today's prices. Being a millionaire gets easier all the time.

£1 million in prices of year:	2000	1988	1978	1968	1948	1938
= £ million in 2000 prices	1	2	4	11	22	43

Source: ONS, Economic Trends; UN, Economic Surveys of Europe

Economic models

After a career in business, you become head of the London Underground. The Tube is losing money. You want to change the level of fares to get more revenue. Revenue is the P, the price of a Tube fare multiplied by Q, the number of passengers. You can set the fare, but what determines the number of passengers?

The number of passengers will fall if the Tube fare is higher, but will rise if passengers have more income to spend. You now have a barebones model of the demand for Tube journeys. It depends on Tube fares and income.

Higher Tube fares *add* directly to revenue, by raising P and hence revenue per passenger, but also *reduce* revenue by reducing Q as fewer people take the Tube. Theory alone can't tell you the best fare to maximize $P \times Q$. The answer depends on how much Q falls when you raise P.

Some empirical research may establish the facts. Experimental sciences, including many branches of physics and chemistry, conduct controlled experiments in a laboratory, varying one input at a time while holding constant all the other relevant inputs. However, like astronomy and medicine, economics is primarily a non-experimental science. Astronomers can't suspend planetary motion to study the earth in isolation, and doctors rarely poison people just to see what happens. Similarly, economists don't create 50 per cent unemployment to see if wages will then fall.

Most economic data are collected while many of the relevant factors are simultaneously changing. We need to disentangle their separate influences. To make a start, we can pick out two of the variables in which we are interested, pretending the other variables remain constant.

A **scatter diagram** plots pairs of values simultaneously observed for two different variables.

Figure 1-2 measures the Tube fare on the horizonal axis, and Tube revenue on the vertical axis and plots a scatter diagram in which each point represents a different year. It is pretty clear that years of low fares are also years of low revenue. Through the scatter of points, Figure 1-2 draws a line in the position that best fits the points, showing the *average* relation between fares and revenue during the period. It seems that higher fares *cause* higher revenue, but we should not jump to conclusions. Incomes also rose a lot in the last few decades, and our theory tells us that higher incomes let people afford to use the Tube more.

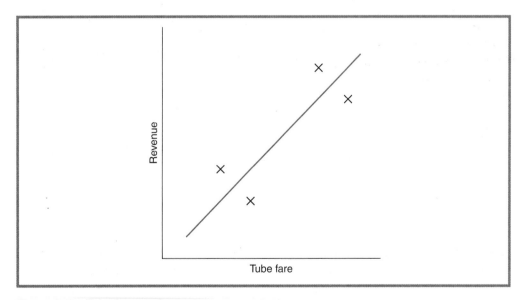

Figure 1-2   Tube fares and revenues

Other things equal

When one 'output' is affected by many 'inputs' we can always draw a two-dimensional diagram relating the output to *one* of the inputs, treating the other inputs as given. Moving along this line shows how the highlighted input affects the output. However, if any *other* input changes, we need to show this as a shift in the relationship between output and our highlighted input.

CHAPTER 1

Other things equal is a device for looking at the relation between two variables, but remembering other variables also matter.

Figure 1-2 can be interpreted as saying that higher Tube fares cause higher revenue only if no other important input to the passenger decision was changing. If income also rose significantly, we need to redraw the diagram.

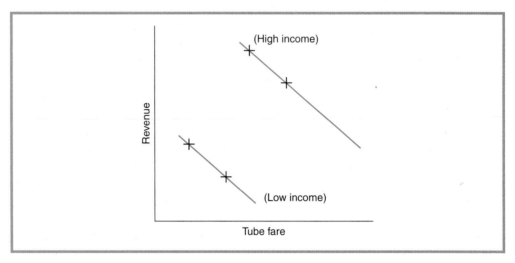

Figure 1-3   How income affects tube passengers

Figure 1-3 replots Figure 1-2 to take account of changing income, a change in one of the 'other things equal' implicitly assumed when drawing a diagram relating revenue only to Tube fares. We now draw one line corresponding to points when income was high, and another line through points when income was low.

In this example, replotting the diagram reverses our previous conclusion. Other things equal, higher Tube fares *reduce* revenue. In Figure 1-2 this effect was obscured by the simultaneous effect of rising income.

Case study 1-2   Why let drug dealers get rich?

Chicago economist Gary Becker won the Nobel Prize for Economics for applying the logic of economic incentives to other facets of human behaviour, from divorce to drug policy. Here is an example of how economics can inform supposedly 'non-economic' aspects of social policy.

Prohibition of alcohol gave the US Al Capone but failed to stop drinking. In Becker's judgement, 'The end of Prohibition was a confession that the US experiment in banning drinking had failed dismally. It was not an expression of support for heavy drinking or alcoholism.' Becker's solution for drugs is to legalise, boost government tax revenue, protect minors, and cut out organized crime's monopoly on supply. UK policing has begun to stop arresting people smoking cannabis in public, switching police resources

Case study 1-2 *Continued*

into the combat of hard drugs like cocaine and heroin. UK cannabis seizures in 2000 were only half those of 1997. As supply rose, the price on the street slumped.

In 2002, the UK government experimented with decriminalization of soft drugs. Perhaps they will eventually be legalized. With 1500 tonnes consumed annually in the UK, if an excise duty of £3 a gram was introduced, it would raise up to £5 billion a year in tax revenue. It would also reduce the £1.4 billion currently spent enforcing anti-drugs laws, and the £1.5 billion cost of drug-related crime. Enough to pay for the Olympics twice over!

Not only would it provide the Treasury with serious tax revenue (which it is perfectly happy to gather for other drugs such as alcohol and tobacco), by legitimizing competition between private suppliers it would eliminate the high revenues enjoyed by drug gangs who use violence to control their monopoly of supply, taking advantage of their monopoly position to charge enormous prices for drugs. We do not see gang wars fought over the tobacco monopoly because there is legal competition between tobacco producers that prevents a monopoly being established.

Economics is not the only social science that matters. Sociology, psychology, and political science also yield vital insights into human behaviour. For example, society may wish to assert its strong disapproval of some drugs by outlawing to signal our collective social disapproval. Even when society decides such issues are important, economics can help establish the price of such policy decisions. Would voters agree that cannabis should be outlawed if they knew that this policy costs taxpayers around £8 billion a year?

Sources: G. S. Becker and G. N. Becker, *The Economics of Life*, McGraw-Hill, 1997; The *Observer*, 8/7/01

1-3

How markets work

Learning outcomes

When you have completed this section, you should understand:

- ◆ Demand and supply
- ◆ Equilibrium in a market
- ◆ How markets resolve what, how, and for whom things are produced
- ◆ Price controls

Some markets (shops, fruit stalls) physically bring together the buyer and seller. Other markets (the Stock Exchange) operate through intermediaries (stockbrokers) who transact business on behalf of clients. E-commerce is conducted on the Internet.

These markets perform the same economic function. Prices adjust to equate the quantity people wish to buy and the quantity people wish to sell. By making the price of a Ferrari ten times the price of a Fiat, the market ensures that the output and sale of Fiats greatly exceeds the output and sale of Ferraris. Prices guide society in choosing what, how, and for whom to produce.

To think about a typical market we need demand, the behaviour of buyers, and supply, the behaviour of sellers. Then we can study how a market works in practice.

Demand is the quantity buyers wish to purchase at each conceivable price.

Demand is not a particular quantity but a full description of the quantity buyers would purchase at each and every possible price. Even when food is free, only a finite amount is wanted. People get sick from eating too much. As the price of food rises, the quantity demanded falls, other things equal.

Supply is the quantity sellers wish to sell at each conceivable price.

Again, supply is a full description of the quantity that sellers would like to sell at each possible price. Nobody would supply anything at all if the price was zero and they got no revenue from sales. At higher prices, people are able and willing to supply more. The quantity supplied rises.

The **equilibrium price** clears the market. It is the price at which the quantity supplied equals the quantity demanded.

Suppose the price is below the equilibrium price. With a low price, the quantity demanded is high but the quantity supplied is low. There is a shortage, or *excess demand*, a shorthand for the more accurate statement 'the quantity demanded exceeds the quantity supplied *at this price*'.

Conversely, at any price above the equilibrium price, the quantity supplied is high but the quantity demanded is low. Sellers have unsold stock. To describe this surplus, economists use the shorthand *excess supply*, meaning 'excess quantity supplied at this price'. Only at the equilibrium price are quantity demanded and supplied the same. The market clears. People can buy or sell as much as they want at the equilibrium price.

Is the market automatically in equilibrium? Suppose the price is initially too high. There is unsold stock and excess supply. Sellers have to cut the price to clear their stock. Cutting the price has two effects. It raises the quantity demanded, and reduces the quantity supplied. Both effects reduce the excess supply. Price cutting continues until the equilibrium price is reached and excess supply is eliminated.

Conversely, if the price is too low, the quantity demanded is large but the quantity supplied is small. With excess demand, sellers run out of stock and charge higher prices. Prices rise until the equilibrium price is reached, excess demand is eliminated, and the market clears. Prices adjust until equilibrium is reached, after which things settle down at that level.

By behaving in this way, prices help resolve the basic questions of economics – what, how, and for whom goods are produced. The goods (and services) produced are those that people are prepared to buy at the equilibrium price, which is also necessary to induce producers to supply those goods. Until recently, most households could only envy the plasma screen TVs they occasionally saw in airports or TV newsrooms. At the price that they cost to produce, there was little household demand apart from that from popstars and footballers' wives. However, technological advances, affecting how plasma screen TVs are made, are steadily reducing the equilibrium price, making them increasingly affordable. In 1985, mobile phones had yet to arrive. By 2000, almost every student had one. Lower prices had brought them within everyday reach.

Price controls

Price controls may be floor prices (minimum prices) or ceiling prices (maximum prices).

A price control is a government regulation to fix the price.

Price ceilings may be introduced when a sharp fall in supply occurs. Wartime scarcity of food would mean high prices and hardship for the poor. Faced with a national food shortage, a government may impose a price ceiling on food so that poor people can afford some food.

Suppose, due to a shortage of wheat and flour, the equilibrium price of a loaf of bread would have been £15. Not a good time to be a student or a pensioner. To try to help out, the government imposes a price ceiling of £2 a loaf. Compared with the equilibrium, the quantity demanded is now much higher, but, at £2 a loaf rather than £15, bakers are bound to want to produce even less.

With a higher quantity demanded but a lower quantity supplied, there is now excess demand, long bread queues, and two outcomes. The lucky people who manage to buy a loaf at £2 get cheaper bread than before, but with fewer total loaves for sale, some people actually get less than before. Also illegal markets emerge as bakers find willing buyers for bread at prices above the legal price ceiling of £2.

Whether or not this system is 'fairer' than the free market system depends in part on how society responds to this bread rationing. If everyone abides by the rules, bread may be distributed more evenly across people than in a free market when the advantage of being rich would be enhanced in times of food scarcity. However, it is also possible that bread rationing becomes corrupt, and bakers favour their friends or take bribes. Since excess demand means that some people may get nothing, it is possible that it is always the poor and the disadvantaged who get nothing. In an effort to avoid this, ceiling prices may be accompanied by government-organized rationing, to ensure that available supply is shared out fairly, independently of ability to pay. Provided the government itself is not corrupt, this may be a reasonable compromise in times of acute food shortage.

A *ceiling price* aims to reduce the price for consumers. Conversely, a *floor price* aims to raise the price for suppliers. A national minimum wage is a floor price for labour. If this is set above the equilibrium wage that would equate the quantity of labour supplied and demanded in a free market, the minimum wage will have two effects. It will raise the quantity of labour that workers wish to supply, but reduce the quantity of labour that firms wish to demand. There is excess supply of labour, total work falls, but the fortunate workers who obtain work will earn a higher wage than they would have done in a free market.

Many governments also set floor prices for agricultural products, and then buy up the excess supply unwanted by the private sector. European butter prices are set above the free market equilibrium price as part of the Common Agricultural Policy. European governments have bought massive stocks of butter that otherwise would have been unsold at the floor price. Hence the famous 'butter mountain' – and of course it has been necessary to prevent African producers accessing the EU agricultural market to take advantage of these artificially high food prices.

Case study 1-3   Green piece

Our planet is running out of rain forests and fish stocks. Environmental campaigners, such as Greenpeace, aim to raise awareness and encourage voters to demand that their politicians take action to save the planet before it is too late.

Why do we manage the environment so badly? An economist's response is 'because we don't price the environment like other commodities'. The market 'solved' the problem of scarcity in the 1970s when oil producers in OPEC (Organization of Petroleum Exporting Countries) collectively restricted oil production in order to make oil more scarce, inducing users to outbid each other to buy the oil that was available for sale. The figure shows the dramatic rise in the (inflation-adjusted) price of oil during 1973–80.

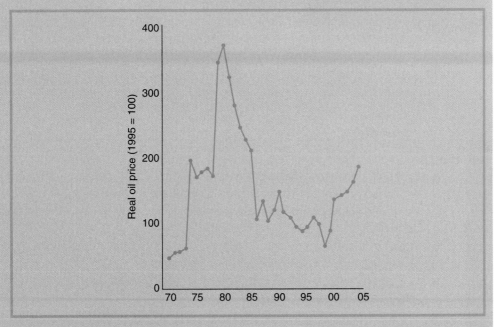

The real price of oil, 1970–2004
Source: IMF, International Financial Statistics

But the high price did not stick for long. Users of oil found ways to use less – buying smaller cars, insulating their houses better, moving closer to their jobs to reduce commuting distances; and non-OPEC oil producers – firms such as Shell, BP, and Exxon – increased their exploration activity and found it worthwhile extracting oil from deep

Case study 1-3   *Continued*

fields previously considered too expensive. Why not price the environment, encouraging people to look after it?

Until now, the reason has been technology. Anyone can walk in a field, dump rubbish after dark, pump chemicals into a river, or drive down a public street. Gradually, however, electronic monitoring of usage is getting easier and cheaper. It will then be possible to treat the environment as another commodity to be marketed. This will give rise to a vigorous debate about the 'what, how, and for whom' questions.

We know how to charge cars for using a particular street at a particular time. A smart card in the car could pick up signals as it passed various charge points. The driver would get a monthly bill like an itemized phone bill. Rush-hour traffic would pay more when congestion was severe. The 'for whom' question could also be addressed. Residents could get a flat-rate annual payment, in exchange for supporting road pricing. Pricing the environment has a big advantage. It introduces a feedback mechanism, however crude, so that when society makes mistakes an alarm bell rings *automatically*. The price of scarce things rises.

In April 2005, the *Sunday Times* reported that UK transport minister, Alasdair Darling, was going to conduct trials of a national system of road charging that would see drivers paying up to £1.40 a mile, replacing existing taxes such as the annual tax disc that motorists must purchase. Many economists think that a 'carbon tax' on emission of the gases that induce climate change will eventually become an important part of the solution to global warming.

Recap

- Economics analyses what, how, and for whom society produces. The central economic problem is to reconcile the conflict between people's unlimited wants and society's limited ability to make goods and services to meet these demands.

- Industrial countries rely extensively on markets to allocate resources. Prices reconcile production and consumption decisions.

- In a command economy, central planners decide what, how, and for whom things are produced.

- Modern economies are mixed, relying mainly on the market but with a big dose of government intervention.

- Positive economics studies how the economy actually behaves. Normative economics makes prescriptions about what should be done.

- Microeconomics gives a detailed analysis of particular activities. Macroeconomics focuses on the entire economy, but simplifies the building blocks in order to keep track of the main interactions.

- A model is a deliberate simplification of reality.

- Data or facts suggest relationships to be explained. Having formulated theories, we use data to test our hypotheses and to quantify the effects implied.

■ Index numbers express data relative to a base value. The consumer price index is the average price of things bought by consumers. Inflation is the annual growth rate in the CPI.

■ Nominal (current price) variables are valued at the prices when the variable was measured. Real (constant price) variables adjust nominal variables for changes over time in the general level of prices.

■ Scatter diagrams plot the relation beween two variables. A line through these points shows their average relationship, other things equal. If a relevant 'other thing' changes, we need to plot data separately for the different subperiods.

■ Demand is the quantity that buyers wish to buy at each price. Other things equal, the lower the price, the higher the quantity demanded. Demand curves slope down.

■ Supply is the quantity that sellers wish to sell at each price. Other things equal, the higher the price, the higher the quantity. Supply curves slope up.

■ The market clears, or is in equilibrium, when the price equates the quantity supplied and the quantity demanded. At this point, supply and demand curves intersect. At prices below the equilibrium price, excess demand (shortage) then raises the price. At prices above the equilibrium price, excess supply (surplus) then reduces the price. In a free market, deviations from the equilibrium price are self-correcting.

■ An effective price ceiling must lie *below* the free market equilibrium price. It then reduces the quantity supplied, raises the quantity demanded, and creates excess demand. An effective price floor must lie *above* the free market equilibrium price. It then reduces the quantity demanded and raises the quantity supplied, creating excess supply. The government may buy up this excess supply.

Review questions

1 How are the problems, what, how, and for whom settled within your own family?

2 Which of the following are scarce? (a) water in the desert, (b) water in a rainforest, (c) economics textbooks, (d) hours a day for work, rest, and play.

3 An economy has five workers. Each worker can make four cakes or three shirts. (a) How many cakes can society get if it does without shirts? (b) How many shirts can it get if it does without cakes? (c) What is the opportunity cost of making a shirt?

4 Which statements are positive and which are normative? (a) Taxing cigarettes reduces the quantity sold. (b) Cigarettes should be highly taxed. (c) Brits earn more than Jamaicans. (d) Jamaicans should work harder. (e) All Africans earn high salaries.

5 If markets are so good, why do sergeant-majors give orders rather than buying military services from private soldiers?

6 Society abolishes higher education. Students have to find jobs immediately. If there are no jobs available, how do wages and prices adjust so those who want jobs can find them?

7 At the start of the twenty-first century, Europeans are richer than Africans. Give three reasons for this, and propose one policy change that could help close the gap.

8 The table below shows a student's annual income and the number of times that she visits a club each year. (a) Plot a scatter diagram. (b) Try to fit a line through these points. (c) Suggest a relation between income and clubbing. (d) Which causes which?

Income £	1000	2000	3000	4000
Number of club visits	17	23	32	38

9 You are hired as a fancy consultant to advise on whether the level of crime is affected by the fraction of people unemployed. (a) How would you test this idea? What data would you want? (b) What other-things-equal problems would you bear in mind?

10 If economics can't conduct controlled laboratory experiments, can it be a science? Can all sciences conduct controlled experiments?

11 Use the data of Table 1-3 to plot a scatter diagram of the relation between nominal house prices and the consumer price index. Is this a time-series data or cross-section relationship?

12 Chelsea Football Club charge high prices to get into the ground to watch a game. Why can they charge such high prices? Does this mean that if they charged higher prices, even more people would want to come?

13 Why are these statements wrong? (a) The purpose of a theory is to let you ignore the facts. (b) People have feelings and act haphazardly. It is misguided to reduce their actions to scientific laws.

14 Given the data for CDs below, find the equilibrium price and quantity.

Price	10	12	14	16	18	20
Quantity demanded	10	9	8	7	6	5
Quantity supplied	3	4	5	7	8	9

15 What is the excess supply or demand when price is (a) £12? (b) £20? In which case would you have a long queue at the music shop?

16 Suppose the government raises the minimum wage a lot. What effects do you expect to see in the market for workers? Will employment rise or fall? Could trade unions still be in favour of the policy? Is it likely employers would favour the policy?

17 Why are these statements wrong? (a) Manchester United, being a more famous football club than Wrexham, will always find it easier to fill their stadium. (b) The European 'butter mountain' shows how productivity can be improved when farmers are inspired by the European ideal.

Answers on pages 341–342

2 Demand

2-1

The demand curve

Learning outcomes

By the end of this section, you should understand:

- ◆ That demand describes the behaviour of buyers
- ◆ How price affects the quantity demanded
- ◆ How demand curves illustrate this behaviour
- ◆ The shape of demand curves

I n 2000, the Mayor of London, Ken Livingstone, introduced a congestion charge of £5 a day to drive into central London. Subsequent studies concluded that the effect of this had been to reduce demand for road use in London by up to 20 per cent. This success led the mayor to raise the charge to £8 in 2005. But price is not the only determinant of demand. In the week after the terrorists first bombed London in July 2005, traffic congestion increased sharply as commuters took to their cars rather than get on buses and Tubes while TV footage of bomb blasts was fresh in their minds. Demand depends on more than the price of the good or service itself. We need to develop a framework in which to think things through.

In this chapter we explore demand, the behaviour of buyers, in detail. Chapter 3 will discuss supply, the behaviour of sellers. Combining the analysis of demand and supply, we can then deepen our understanding of how markets work.

Demand is the quantity buyers wish to purchase at each conceivable price.

Demand is not a particular quantity but a full description of the quantity buyers would purchase at each and every possible price. We can show this relationship between price and quantity demanded as a *demand curve, DD* in Figure 2-1.[1] The vertical distance measures the price of the good or service. The horizontal distance measures the corresponding quantity demanded. Thus, each point on *DD* indicates a price and corresponding quantity demanded at that price.

A **demand curve** shows the quantity demanded at each possible price, other things equal.

Even when bread is free, only a finite amount is wanted: beyond 1000 loaves a week, everyone is stuffed with bread and can't eat any more. As the price of food rises, the quantity demanded falls, other things equal. In Figure 2-1, this corresponds to moving *along* the line DD – leftwards and upwards – buying less and less bread as the price is increased, until

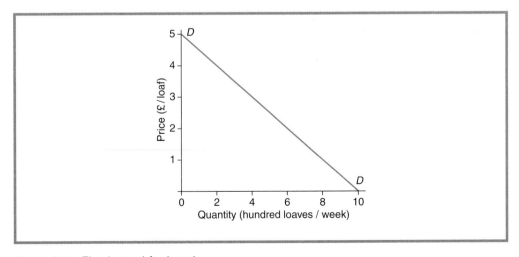

Figure 2-1 The demand for bread

[1] Depending on the way in which buyers react to changes in prices, a demand curve may be a straight line as shown in Figure 2-1 or a curve whose slope gradually flattens out as we move along it to the right. Either way, the key thing is that it slopes downwards, indicating that lower prices increase quantity demanded.

buyers demand no bread at all once the price reaches £5 a loaf. We can use a similar figure to think about the congestion charge. Think of the vertical axis as measuring the congestion charge (the price of using London roads), and the horizontal axis as measuring the extent of vehicle traffic in London. Initially, drivers did not have to pay any direct charge for using London streets. They paid for petrol, but there was no additional fee for driving down Oxford Street rather than going round London on the M25 ring road. So drivers simply used London streets as much as they wanted. They were free. With a zero price, daytime demand for London streets exceeds the capacity of London streets to cope with this amount of traffic.

Figure 2-2 shows the demand curve DD for daytime car use in London. Initially, with no congestion charge, the outcome is at point A. Traffic is heavy and Piccadilly Circus is congested because the quantity of car and lorry trips demanded is so large. Introducing the congestion charge at the level CC shown in Figure 2-2 raises the price of car use, and moves buyers up the demand curve from A to B. As a result, traffic falls from point A to point E. The purpose of the congestion charge was therefore to make people demand less use of London streets, and in so doing to reduce congestion, allowing traffic to flow more freely. How much a given price increase reduces the quantity demanded depends principally on how easily buyers can find alternative goods and services that perform a similar function. With brilliant public transport available, a modest congestion charge on cars might induce large numbers of people to switch to buses. The demand curve DD for car travel is then relatively *flat*, showing that small price rises reduce the quantity demanded a lot. If public transport is unreliable, slow, and dirty, a big rise in price of road use may reduce the demand for road use by only a little. We would then draw a *steep* curve DD to show that car use is fairly insensitive to the level at which the congestion charge is set.

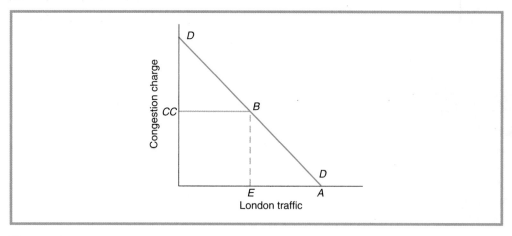

Figure 2-2   The demand for London road use

If higher prices make demanders move upwards *along* a given demand curve, how then do we represent the surge in demand for car travel after the London bomb explosions on public transport?

2-2

Behind the demand curve

Learning outcomes

By the end of this section, you should understand:

- ◆ Other determinants of demand
- ◆ When demand curves shift

O ther things equal, lower prices are accompanied by higher quantities demanded, and vice versa. But prices are not the only determinant of demand. Other things do not always remain constant. We now study three other influences: the price of related goods, the income of buyers, and tastes or preferences of buyers.

1 **The price of other goods** *Higher* bus fares may *raise* the quantity of car travel demanded at each possible price of car use. In everyday language, buses are a substitute for cars. Higher prices for substitutes for cars make people switch towards more car use. Conversely, petrol and cars are not substitutes but complements. You can't use a car without using fuel. A *rise* in the price of petrol tends to *reduce* the demand for cars since it raises the price of using a car.

A rise in the price of one good raises the demand for **substitutes** for this good, but reduces the demand for **complements** to the good.

Most goods are substitutes for each other. If the price of food rises, you will generally demand a little less food and a little more entertainment. Complementarity is usually a more specific feature (CD players and CDs, coffee and milk, shoes and shoelaces). If CDs become more expensive, fewer people will bother to buy CD players.

2 **Consumer incomes** When incomes rise, the demand for most goods rises. Typically, richer consumers buy more of everything. Compared with what you demand, David Beckham and Richard Branson buy more cars, more restaurant meals, more holidays, larger houses, and more legal advice. However, there are exceptions. You probably buy more pot noodles and use more launderettes than they do.

For a **normal good**, demand rises when income rises. For an **inferior good**, demand falls when income rises.

Most goods are normal goods. As we have got richer over the last 100 years, we have bought more food, more travel, and more household goods. Inferior goods are cheap, low-quality goods that people would prefer not to buy if they could afford to spend a little more. Students buy cheap cuts of meat but graduate to steaks when they get a good job. David Beckham does not have to take his clothes to a public launderette. He can afford to install expensive washing machines at home and employ people to make sure his house runs smoothly.

3 **Tastes** Tastes or preferences of consumers are shaped by convenience, custom, and social attitudes. The fashion for the mini-skirt reduced the demand for textile material. The emphasis on health and fitness has increased the demand for jogging equipment, health foods, and sports facilities but reduced the demand for cream cakes, butter, and cigarettes.

So why did people switch into London car use after the London bombings? Not because the price of car use changed (there was no cut in the congestion charge). The additional quantity of car use demanded was *not* a movement downwards along a given demand curve *DD* in response to a lower price of car use. The only other possibility was that the bomb blasts *shifted* the *entire* demand curve *DD* to the right, leading to greater car demand. Figure 2-3 shows this as a shift from the original demand curve *DD* to the new demand curve *D'D'*. At any price (a given vertical distance), buyers now wish to purchase a higher quantity (larger horizontal distance) than before. In particular, at the original congestion charge, *CC*, the quantity demanded now rises from *E* to *G*.

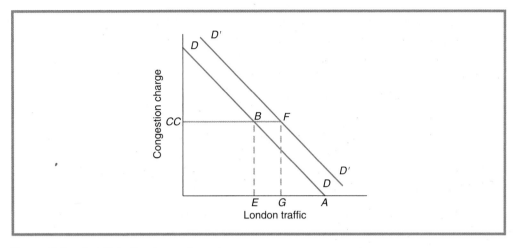

Figure 2-3 A shift in the demand curve

Changes in the price of the good (or service) move us *along* a *given* demand curve: other things equal, higher prices reduce quantity demanded. But other things do not always remain fixed. When they change, we have to shift the entire demand curve. Changes in other determinants of demand (changes in the price of substitutes or complements, changes in incomes, or changes in tastes) *shift* the demand curve. Such changes that *increase* demand *shift* the demand curve to the *right* (from *DD* to *D'D'* in Figure 2-3). Such changes that *reduce* demand *shift* the demand curve to the *left* in Figure 2-3 (for example, think of beginning with the demand curve *D'D'* but then shifting to *DD*).

When the bomb blasts raised the demand for London car use from *DD* to *D'D'*, which of the 'other things equal' behind the demand curve *DD* had then changed? There was no significant change in consumer incomes immediately after the bombing, so it must have been one of the other two potential channels.

We can reflect the consequences of the bombing as a rise in the effective price of using public transport (not because fares rose but because the danger to users increased). A rise in the price of a substitute for car use led some people to switch from public transport into greater car use in London. Alternatively, we can tell ourselves that consumer tastes changed. People thought cars more strongly preferable to buses than they had before. Both approaches lead us to the right answer about what happened to the behaviour of Londoners. The demand for car use increased. At any level of the congestion charge, the effect of the bombing would have been to make people switch towards greater car use than before. The entire demand curve shifted to the right in Figure 2-3.

To sum up, the quantity demanded reflects four things: its own price, prices of related goods, incomes, and tastes. We could draw a two-dimensional diagram relating quantity demanded to any one of these four things. The other three would be the 'other things equal' for that diagram. In drawing demand curves, we always choose the price of the commodity itself to put in the diagram with quantity demanded. The other three things become the 'other things equal' for a demand curve.

Why single out the price of the commodity itself to plot against quantity demanded? Because, once we add supply, we can show the self-correcting mechanism by which a market reacts to excess demand or excess supply, by changing the *price* to restore equilibrium. We want to show how quantities are affected by prices as the market does its job. But when one of the other important determinants of demand changes, we have to show these as shifts in the demand curve. Things that increase demand shift the entire demand curve to the right (more quantity at any price). Things that reduce demand shift the entire demand curve to the left (less quantity at any price).

Here is a chance to see if you have understood. Try completing Table 2-1, describing what happens to the demand curve for UK higher education in response to each of six important events.

	Demand curve for UK university places	
Event	Shifts right	Shifts left
1 UK top-up fees abolished		
2 Other EU countries raise university fees		
3 UK gets richer		
4 Young people lose faith in education, volunteer instead for a lifetime of service in Africa		
5 Bill Gates subsidizes all UK university places		
6 An earthquake destroys five UK universities		

Table 2-1   Shifts in the demand curve (please tick the appropriate box in each line)
(answers on page 36, but complete the table before skipping to the answers!)

Case study 2-1   One little piggy went to market

The 1996 BSE crisis led to a temporary collapse in the demand for British beef. The demand curve for beef shifted downwards rather like the demand curve for Tube journeys shifted downwards after the 2005 bomb blasts in London. In the latter case, London commuters switched from the Tube to their cars. In the former case, a few beef eaters decided this was the moment to become vegetarians, but most continued to indulge their taste for meat by switching to eating chicken and pork.

Questions for discussion:

1   What do you think happened to the demand for pork, and hence to the price of pork?
2   How would you expect pork farmers to have responded?
3   What effect should this then have on pork prices?
4   And in turn on beef prices?

The nice thing about historical case studies from the real world is that we can actually look at what happened next, and whether or not it is consistent with the theory we have been developing. Let's start with the theory. When consumers switched from beef into pork demand, this should have bidden up the price of pork but bidden down the price of beef. If you were a farmer, this would have reduced the incentive to continue supplying beef, but increased the incentive to supply pork. You went out and bought

Case study 2-1   *Continued*

lots of piglets to fatten up, but when these piglets were later brought to market in a glut – all your farming friends having also decided that they should get into pig farming – the large increase in pork supply might actually have outstripped the increase in pork demand that had been caused by the BSE scare in the first place. Also if beef farmers eradicated disease, and confidence returned, beef prices should have been expected to recover as beef demand was restored. If consumers gradually switched back to beef, they might even start abandoning pork at the very time that the glut of piglets matured into marketable pigs.

This account gives some idea of the ebb and flow of prices as markets adjust to swings in supply and demand. But is this really what happened? We can look at historical UK data to examine the answer.

The left-hand figure below shows how the real prices of beef and pork evolved after 1996. In each case, for convenience, we set the 1996 price at 100 and express subsequent prices relative to this baseline. Initially, pork prices soared as our theory predicts. But then they reverted to earlier levels again. Since 2002, pork prices have climbed once more. Beef prices fell, as our theory predicts, but by 2002, beef prices had made up all the ground they had lost when BSE led to the collapse of demand in 1996.

The right-hand figure helps us understand these price movements by showing what was happening to supply and production. As expected, we see the dramatic fall in beef production as animals were slaughtered. Even by 2003, the quantity of UK beef production had not recovered its pre-1996 levels. This partly explains why beef prices eventually recovered – despite the fact that some consumers were permanently turned off beef – a corresponding permanent fall in beef supply made beef sufficiently scarce that the price recovered.

The right-hand figure also shows that surge in pork production. Farmers responded to high pork prices by increasing pork production by nearly a third. But demand for pork could not be sustained at that level. As the price of pork fell back after 1997 (left-hand diagram), farmers stopped rearing pigs and by 1998 the volume of pork coming to market was also in steep decline.

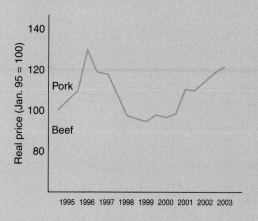

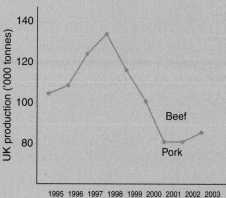

2-3

Measuring demand responses

Learning outcomes

By the end of this section, you should understand:

- ◆ The price elasticity of demand
- ◆ The revenue effect of a price change
- ◆ Why bad harvests help farmers
- ◆ The income elasticity of demand
- ◆ Inferior, normal, and luxury goods

The price responsiveness of demand

When a price cut has a large effect on quantity demanded, we say that the demand for the good is *price elastic*. Consumers are very responsive to prices. When the same size of price cut has a small effect on quantity demanded, we say that demand is *price inelastic*. Consumers are not very responsive to prices.

The **price elasticity of demand** measures the *responsiveness* of quantity demanded to price.

When demand is elastic, a 1 per cent price cut raises quantity by more than 1 per cent. Hence total spending by buyers (and hence total revenue of sellers) increases. Quantity rises more than prices fall. Conversely, when demand is inelastic, a 1 per cent price cut leads to a rise in quantity by less than 1 per cent. For such goods, a price cut reduces consumer spending and producer revenue. Quantity rises less than prices fall. In the intermediate case between elastic and inelastic demand, we say that demand is unit elastic: a 1 per cent fall in prices induces exactly a 1 per cent rise in quantity, leaving spending by buyers and revenue of sellers unaffected.

Why do we care whether demand is elastic or inelastic? We look first at an example about farmers. Suppose a harvest failure reduces by 30 per cent the crop supplied to market. Since the demand elasticity for food is low – people need to eat and if necessary can sacrifice holidays and nights out – it may take a price rise of 60 per cent to reduce quantity demanded by 30 per cent in line with the lower supply. However, if prices rise twice as much as quantity falls, farmers' incomes will *rise* when the harvest is *bad*! Conversely, a bumper harvest that adds 30 per cent to the quantity of food being sold at market may require a 60 per cent price reduction to induce buyers to buy all this extra quantity. Farmers will then make *low* incomes when the harvest is *good*. This paradox only arises because the demand for food is inelastic – it takes large price changes to induce small changes in quantity demanded.

Box 2-1   What determines demand elasticities?

The elasticity of demand depends on consumer taste. If everyone must have a mobile phone, higher phone prices have little effect on quantity demanded. If mobile phones are thought a frivolous luxury, the demand elasticity is much higher. Psychology and sociology help explain why tastes are as they are. Taking these tastes as given, the easier it is to find a substitute that fulfils the same need, the higher is the demand elasticity.

If the price of *all* cigarettes rises, addicted smokers buy cigarettes anyway. However, if the price of a single brand of cigarettes rises, smokers switch to other brands to meet their nicotine habit. Thus, for a particular cigarette brand the demand elasticity is quite high, but for cigarettes as a whole it is low. Similarly, if all clubs raise ticket prices, dedicated football fans will probably pay up reluctantly. But if Manchester United alone raise prices, as people feared after the Glazer takeover in 2005, some supporters might switch to other clubs and some supporters of visiting clubs might choose not to make the trip.

Similarly, when Mercedes has 10 000 cars for sale but 20 000 customers eager to buy at the current price, knowing the price elasticity of demand for Mercedes cars lets its executives in Stuttgart work out how much they can raise the price while still selling all the cars that they have produced.

Price, quantity, and revenue

Reducing the price P boosts the quantity demanded Q. The effect on sales revenue, $P \times Q$, depends on how quantity responds to price cuts. When demand is elastic, quantity rises by more than the price falls, so revenue rises. When demand is inelastic, price cuts lower P more than it boosts Q. Hence revenue falls.

In Table 2-2, demand for Stella Artois is elastic but demand for beer as a whole is inelastic. Falls in the price of Stella alone raise spending on Stella by increasing its sales a lot, whereas falls in the price of all beer reduce spending on beer. Table 2-3 relates these results to demand elasticities.

Price	Stella		All beer	
P	Q	$P \times Q$	Q	$P \times Q$
2	5	10	30	60
1.5	10	15	32	48
1	20	20	34	34

Table 2-2   Price changes, spending, and revenue

	Price elasticity of demand		
Change in total spending caused by	Elastic (e.g. −3)	Unit-elastic (−1)	Inelastic (e.g. −0.3)
Price rise	Fall	Unchanged	Rise
Price cut	Rise	Unchanged	Fall

Table 2-3   Demand elasticities and spending changes

By collectively restricting oil supplies, the oil-producers' organization OPEC made oil prices soar from $13/barrel in 1998 to $28/barrel in 2000. This raised oil producers' revenue since oil demand was *very* inelastic. Oil users had few alternatives to oil in the short run. Cuts in oil supply caused a big price rise and vast revenue gains for OPEC members.

Case study 2-2 Good news! A bad harvest!

There's an awful lot of coffee in Brazil, which supplies a big share of the world market. In 1994, a frost in Brazil wrecked the 1995 harvest. The table below shows what happened to coffee exports from Brazil. As a result of the crisis, world coffee prices (measured in US dollars) more than doubled from 90 cents per pound weight to 210 cents/pound. This price increase reflected not a rise in demand but a fall in supply to the world economy. The second row of the table below shows the sharp drop in Brazilian exports, which by 1995 were 20 per cent

Coffee harvesting in Brazil
© Ricardo Azoury/Corbis

below their level of 1993. What happened to Brazilian export revenue from coffee? It *increased* by 70 per cent, despite the 'bad' harvest and lower export quantities. The demand for coffee is inelastic–very inelastic. New Yorkers, and many other coffee addicts, cannot do without their coffee fix.

Brazilian coffee exports 1993–95		1993	1995
P:	Price (US cents/pound weight, 1995 prices)	90	210
Q:	Export quantity (1990 = 100)	113	85
P × Q:	Export revenue (P × Q)	10 200	17 900

Source: IMF, *International Financial Statistics*

This case study illustrates a general result. If demand is inelastic, farmers earn more revenue from a bad harvest than from a good one. The demand elasticity is low for many components of our staple diet, such as coffee, milk, bread, tea, and meat.

When demand is inelastic, suppliers *taken together* are better off if supply falls. However, if a fire destroys the crop of a single farmer, that farmer's revenue falls. Lower output from a single farm has almost no effect on supply. The market price is unaffected. The unlucky farmer sells less output at the same price as before. The individual producer faces an elastic demand – consumers can switch to the output of similar farmers – even if the demand for the crop as a whole is very inelastic.

This sharp contrast between the individual and the aggregate is sometimes called the *fallacy of composition*. What is true in the aggregate need not be true for individuals, and vice versa.

Short run and long run

In the *short run*, customers may be unable to adjust much to changes in prices. For example, when fuel prices rise, people still need to drive their cars and heat their houses, so there is little immediate change in the quantity of fuel demanded. However, as time passes, smaller cars can be designed and built, and people can move back into city centres to save commuting costs. In the *long run*, the demand for fuel is more elastic.

This result is very general. Even if addicted smokers can't quit when cigarette prices soar, fewer young people start smoking. In response to a price increase, quantity demanded gradually falls as time elapses.

Event	Demand curve for UK university places	
	Shifts right	Shifts left
1 UK top-up fees abolished	Demand curve shifts *neither* left nor right – reducing the price of UK university education moves us downwards along the original demand curve. Quantity demanded increases, but only because the price fell	
2 Other EU countries raise university fees	The demand curve for UK university education shifts to the right. At each and every price, the quantity of UK university places demanded is larger than it would have been before	
3 UK gets richer	At any price, people demand more UK university places than before, demand curve shifts right	
4 Young people lose faith in education, volunteer instead for a lifetime of service in Africa		Change in tastes reduces demand for UK university places, demand curve shifts left
5 Bill Gates subsidizes all UK university places	Price falls and moves downwards along a given demand curve – unless the fact that Bill is cool after his Live 8 appearance means more young people become interested in university, in which case the change in tastes also shifts the demand curve to the right	
6 An earthquake destroys five UK universities	Loss of universities is a change in supply not a change in demand. If greater scarcity then drives up the price, this moves people up a given demand curve. If the loss of university professors implies that total income falls, this may shift the demand curve down (but not by much – professors don't get paid a lot)	

Answers to Table 2-1 (page 30) Shifts in the demand curve

The effect of income on demand

Having studied changes in prices, we now study changes in income. For the moment we neglect saving, and assume higher income is all spent. This tends to raise the quantity demanded of most individual goods. However, quantities demanded don't all change by the same amount, so budget shares change with income.

The **budget share** of a good is the spending on that good as a fraction of total consumer spending.

Table 2-4 shows the UK budget shares of food and services (personal and leisure activities such as eating out and going to the theatre) between 1992 and 2002. Real consumer spending rose over the period. The budget share of food fell, but the budget share of services rose. If the prices of all goods do not change, spending on a good changes only because quantity demanded changes. To show how sensitive quantity demand is to changes in income, we calculate the income elasticity of demand.

		Percentage budget share	
	Real consumer spending (2001 £ bn)	Food	Services
1992	378	12	48
2002	614	9	50

Table 2-4 Budget shares, 1992–2002

Source: ONS, UK National Accounts

The **income elasticity of demand** measures the percentage increase in quantity demanded when income rises by 1 per cent, other things equal. It is positive for a **normal** good, but negative for an **inferior** good.

Thus, when income rises, the quantity demand rises for all normal goods. For the few exceptions called inferior goods, quantity demanded actually falls when income rises. Inferior goods are low-quality goods. Poor people buy fish fingers and polyester shirts. With more income, they buy seafood and comfortable cotton shirts. Higher income reduces the demand for fish fingers and polyester shirts.

We also distinguish luxury goods and necessities.

A **luxury good** has an income elasticity above 1. A **necessity** has an income elasticity below 1.

All inferior goods are necessities, since their income elasticities of demand are negative, and hence below 1. However, necessities also include normal goods whose income elasticity of demand lies between 0 and 1.

As income rises, the budget share of inferior goods falls: income rises but quantity demanded, and spending on the good, fall. Conversely, the budget share of luxuries rises when income rises. A 1 per cent rise in income raises quantity demanded (and hence spending on luxury goods) by over 1 per cent. Finally, higher income *reduces* the budget share of normal goods that are necessities. A 1 per cent rise in income raises quantity demanded by less than 1 per cent, so the budget share falls.

Luxury goods are high-quality goods for which there are lower-quality, but adequate, substitutes: Mercedes cars not small Fords, foreign not domestic holidays. Inferior goods are low-quality goods that people readily abandon as they get richer. Necessities that are normal goods lie between these two extremes. As incomes rise, the quantity of food demanded rises, but only a little.

Table 2-4 showed that services are luxuries whose budget share rose with UK income after 1991. Food is not a luxury; its budget share fell as income rose. Nor is it an inferior good. At constant prices which adjust for the effects of inflation, during 1992–2002 real food spending *increased* from £45 billion (12 per cent of £378 billion) to £55 billion (9 per cent of £614 billion).

Table 2-5 summarizes the demand responses to higher income, holding constant the prices of all goods. Lower income has the opposite effect.

Good	Income elasticity	Quantity demanded	Budget share	Example
Normal	Positive	Rises		
Luxury	Above 1	Rises more than 1%	Rises	BMW
Necessity	Between 0 and 1	Rises less than 1%	Falls	Food
Inferior	Negative	Falls	Falls	Bread

Table 2-5   Demand responses to a 1% rise in income

Income elasticities are vital to business and government in forecasting the changing pattern of consumer demand as the economy grows and people get richer. Suppose incomes grow at 3 per cent a year for the next five years. The demand for luxuries, such as restaurants, will rise strongly. In contrast, the demand for some necessities such as bread may hardly rise at all. The growth prospects of the two industries are very different.

Inflation and demand

Chapter 1 distinguished *nominal* variables, measured in prices at the time, and *real* variables, measured in constant prices to adjust for inflation. If all nominal variables double, every good costs twice as much, but all incomes are twice as high. Nothing has really changed. Quantities demanded are unaltered.

This does not contradict our analysis of price and income elasticities of demand. The former shows the effect of changing one price, holding constant other prices and nominal income. This is not relevant when all prices and incomes rise at the same rate. The latter shows the effect of higher real income. But real income does not change under pure inflation.

2·4

Demand and consumer choice

Learning outcomes

By the end of this section, you should understand:

- ◆ Substitution and income effects
- ◆ Effects of real income changes
- ◆ Tastes and marginal utility
- ◆ Diminishing marginal utility
- ◆ The market demand curve

easuring past behaviour is a good guide to the future when nothing dramatic changes. Sometimes, however, we need to think about what people might do in a future situation which is completely different from the past. To predict demand behaviour, we need a *theory* of how consumers make choices. A successful theory is consistent with past behaviour but also helps predict responses in new situations.

Effects of a price change: substitution and income effects

As the price of a good falls, people buy more of it. Demand curves slope down. Unfortunately, things are not this simple. Suppose the price of bread falls. For the rest of your life, you need to remember this has two quite different effects.

The **substitution effect** says that, when the relative price of a good falls, quantity demanded rises.

Your intuition will always discover the substitution effect, the bit that is obvious. You have to train yourself to look for, and find, the second effect.

The **income effect** says, for a given nominal income, a fall in the price of a good raises real income, affecting the demand for all goods.

If bread is a normal good, the demand for bread will rise when real income (spending power) rises. Both the income effect and the substitution effect raise the quantity of bread demanded when the price of bread falls. Bread is relatively cheaper so people buy more. Moreover, cheaper bread raises the purchasing power of the given nominal income; this also raises the demand for bread.

Hence, for normal goods, our theory says the demand curve must slope down. Price cuts lead to a higher quantity demanded. However, if bread were an inferior good, higher real income would lead to a *fall* in the quantity demanded. Now the income effect of a price cut would go in the opposite direction from the substitution effect. A fall in the price of bread makes it relatively cheaper, but also raises spending power. For inferior goods, theoretical reasoning alone cannot deduce which of the two effects is larger. We need empirical evidence to resolve the issue. In practice, demand curves for goods and services usually slope down. Inferior goods and services are rare.

In other markets, the 'perverse income effect' that outweighs the 'obvious substitution effect' is more common. Here is a quick taster of things to come. Higher interest rates increase incentives to save, don't they?

Saving means not spending all today's income, reducing consumption today to raise consumption later.

Think of the interest rate as the price of time, the cost of consuming today instead of later. When the cost of consuming today rises, you choose less of it. Surely?

Your intuition has found the substitution effect. Consuming today has got relatively more costly, and you consume less, thus saving more. Where is the income effect lurking? To afford that foreign holiday next year, you don't have to save so much if interest rates are higher and your assets cumulate more quickly! This makes you save less. Empirically, it is very hard to find whether interest rates have much effect on total saving. Politicians think higher interest rates boost saving, and are always devising schemes like PEPs and ISAs to provide tax breaks, hoping that higher after-tax interest rates will boost national saving.

Economists are pessimistic that this will work. Much of it is just a subsidy to the rich, something to remember if you become Chancellor of the Exchequer!

Effects of income changes

Real income can rise either because nominal income increases while prices are constant, or because the price of a commodity falls while nominal income is constant. The former leads to a pure income effect, the latter must be decomposed into separate income and substitution effects.

Successive rises in real income lead to large increases in the quantity demanded if the good (or service) is a luxury with a large income elasticity of demand. Quantity demanded increases less quickly for normal goods or services with smaller, but still positive, income elasticities. For inferior goods with negative income elasticities, higher income reduces quantities demanded. Poor students given up beans on toast once they become rich bankers.

Tastes and demand

Different people may have different tastes, making different choices even when facing the same prices and enjoying the same income.

Tastes describe the utility a consumer gets from the goods consumed. Utility is happiness or satisfaction.

Tastes depend on culture, history, familiarity, relationships with others, advertising, and so on. Explaining these influences is the role of other social sciences, like psychology and sociology. Economists treat them as an 'other things equal' assumption behind a particular demand curve.

However, tastes can change, with important effects. In the past few decades there have been big changes in social attitudes to organic food and the formality of dress. The demand curve for organic food shifted outwards, but the demand curve for top hats shifted inwards. We shift demand curves when there are changes in the 'other things equal'.

Marginal utility and demand

Fred goes clubbing and drinks lager. Initially, he goes to one club but has no lager. Fred is thirsty and can't enjoy himself. With a lager, he'd be a lot happier.

The **marginal utility** of a good is the *extra* utility from consuming one more unit of the good, holding constant the quantity of other goods consumed.

Fred's first lager gives him high marginal utility. A second lager gives him extra utility, but not as much extra utility as the first one did. A third and fourth lager add less and less extra utility.

Tastes display **diminishing marginal utility** from a good if each extra unit adds successively less to total utility when consumption of other goods remains constant.

Figure 2-4 shows Fred's marginal utility, which falls the more he drinks. It also shows the price of each lager. If a lager costs £4, and Fred gets £6 of marginal utility from it, he should buy another one. If he only gets £2 of marginal utility from his last lager, he has bought too many. He should buy lager up to the point the marginal cost (£4 for the last lager) equals the marginal benefit or marginal utility. Figure 2-4 shows Fred choosing point A when lagers cost £4 each.

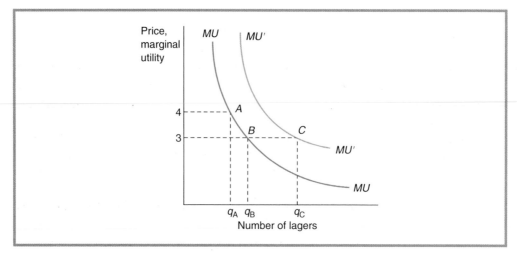

Figure 2-4 Marginal utility and lager demand

Figure 2-4 suggests that if the price of lager falls from £4 to £3 Fred will definitely buy more lager because of diminishing marginal utility. But the figure only shows the substitution effect! The marginal utility curve assumes quantities of other goods remain constant. However, as the price of lager falls, Fred can afford more club nights too. Whether this shifts Fred's marginal utility curve up or down depends on whether lager is a normal or an inferior good, which is the income effect at work.

Box 2-2   To die for

Anna Kournikova's fees from advertising dwarf the Wimbledon prize money. David Beckham's move to Real Madrid boosted the value of their football shirts as well as the skills of their football team. Thierry Henry is the suave image of the Renault Clio. Why do the manufacturers pay superfees to superstars to promote their wares? They are trying to change your tastes. There are lots of small cars, but only one has va-va-voom. It's the one to die for. No other will do.

   You could buy a car magazine and find out whether the Clio's suspension geometry really is different. But that's not the point. This advertising is about *style*. Not what you think is nice, but what *other people* think is nice. Renault is assuring you that other people, stylish people, think it's cool to drive a Clio. Do so and you can be cool too. This *interdependence* of tastes is what opens the door for so much advertising and PR.

If lager is a normal good, the income effect shifts the marginal utility curve outwards to *MU'* in Figure 2-4. This also makes Fred consume more lager (point *C*). Income and substitution effects go the same way. The demand curve for lager, drawn through *A* and *C*, slopes down. If lager was an inferior good, the *MU* curve might have shifted *inwards* enough to make Fred consume less lager when its price fell.

So far, marginal utility analysis merely reinforces our earlier and simpler discussion of income and substitution effects. However, it was worth learning, as Box 2-3 confirms.

Box 2-3 The water–diamond paradox

Here's a riddle for your friends who don't study economics. Why is the price of water, essential for survival, so much lower than the price of decorative diamonds? Diamonds are scarcer than water. Yet consumers clearly get more total utility from water, without which they die.

Marginal utility solves the puzzle. The marginal benefit of the first unit of water is enormous. But we each consume lots of water. Since water is relatively abundant, the supply curve for water lies well to the right and the equilibrium price is low. Consumers have moved a long way down their marginal utility of water curve.

If water is supplied free, consumers should use water up to the point its marginal utility is zero. May as well wash the car again. Even a small rise in price may lead to a large cutback in usage – demand is very elastic in this region of the demand curve.

From individual to market demand curve

How do we aggregate individual demand curves to get the total demand in a particular market?

The **market demand curve** is the horizontal sum of individual demand curves in that market.

We always plot price on the vertical axis. All consumers in a market face the same price P. Suppose at a price of £2 the first consumer demands a quantity of A and the second consumer a quantity of B, the market demand is a quantity of $C = A + B$ when the price is £2. Repeating this procedure at each and every possible price we trace out the market demand curve. Figure 2-5 shows how two individual demand curves D_1 and D_2 are horizontally aggregated to get the market demand curve D. In most markets, where there are lots of purchasers, the market demand curve is obtained by adding horizontally the demand curves of every individual in the market.

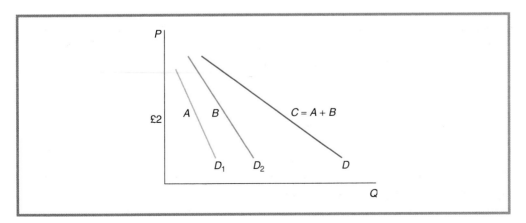

Figure 2-5 The market demand curve

The market demand curve is important because, together with the market supply curve, it determines the price that clears the market in equilibrium. Having seen how the individual demand decisions can be aggregated to derive the market demand curve, we turn next to a more detailed analysis of supply decisions.

Case study 2-3 Conspicuous consumption

This chapter has introduced the theory of demand, and examples of how the theory can be applied to real-world behaviour and the data that it generates. By now we hope you are convinced that the theory makes sense and is consistent with the facts. But are there important exceptions that we have glossed over?

Nike shoes
© Bettman/Corbis

Here is an example for you to think about. The next time a new generation of Nike trainers appear, you know that you will simply have to have them. In fact, the more they cost the more exclusive they will seem and the more you will probably be determined to have them. Your mother may feel the same about Gucci shoes and your father about the Porsche Boxster. So have economists got it wrong?

Question for discussion: *Do demand curves really slope up for such goods: the more they cost, the larger the quantity demanded?*

Try to formulate an answer before you read on. We will however give you one clue – the answer is nothing to do with income effects and inferior goods. One thing on which we can all agree is that Gucci and Porsche brands are bought only by rich people, not poor people.

The phenomenon of *conspicuous consumption* – demanding goods precisely because they are expensive and therefore exclusive – was first discussed by US economist Thorstein Veblen (1857–1929), after whom they are sometimes referred to as 'Veblen goods'. They are goods designed to create envy among others.

However, this need not pose any difficulty for our theory of demand. Indeed, Box 2-3 above already contains the beginning of the answer, the interdependence of preferences. The diagram below shows two demand curves, *MM* for a mass produced version of a good and *EE* for an exclusive version that is highly admired by the trendy elite. The elite version is more desirable for two reasons. First, it may be innately better. On most objective tests, a Boxster outperforms a Mondeo. Second, however, it is also more fashionable, more esteemed by the in-crowd, and therefore more desirable, whatever its objective characteristics. For both reasons, the demand curve EE lies above the demand curve MM. At any given quantity (a distance to the right in the horizontal

Case study 2-3   *Continued*

quantity direction), people will pay more (higher vertical distance) for the exclusive good than the mass market good.

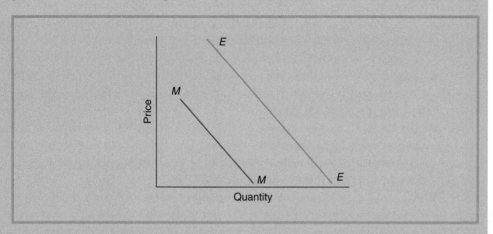

Conditional on the attributes of the exclusive good – in Nike's case how comfortable they are and how your friends think they look – the less you had to pay, the more of them you would buy. Your demand curve EE is high up because of the attributes that make them exclusive, but still slopes down – other things equal, you will buy more if they are cheaper.

Believing that Veblen goods are evidence of an upward-sloping demand curve is to make the mistake of confusing movements along a given demand curve with shifts in the demand curve itself. When a good is more exclusive, its demand curve has shifted further upwards. But the demand curve still slopes downwards. If other things remain equal, cutting the price then means sliding downwards along the given demand curve.

Recap

- The quantity demanded depends mainly on four things: the price of the good itself, the price of substitutes and complements for that good, income and spending of buyers, and tastes of buyers.
- A demand curve highlights the relation between the quantity demanded and one of these four things, namely the price of the good itself, holding constant the other three influences on quantity demanded.
- When one of the other three influences changes, we have to reflect this as a shift in the demand curve. When the price of the good itself changes, we show this as a movement along a given demand curve.
- The price elasticity of demand (sometimes simply called the elasticity of demand) is the percentage change in quantity demanded when the price of that good or service increases by 1 per cent.

- Demand is elastic (inelastic) when a 1 per cent price fall induces a rise in the quantity demanded by more (less) than 1 per cent.
- Price cuts raise (lower) total spending and producer revenue when demand is elastic (inelastic). Spending and revenue are unchanged if demand is unit-elastic.
- The income elasticity of demand shows the percentage change in quantity induced by a 1 per cent rise in income and total spending. Higher income increases demand for normal goods and reduces demand for inferior goods.
- Inferior goods have negative income elasticities; quantity demanded falls as income rises. Goods that are not inferior are normal goods, with positive income elasticities of demand.
- Luxury goods have an income elasticity above 1. Higher income increases their budget share, since demand for them rises strongly. Goods that are not luxuries are necessities, with income elasticities below 1. All inferior goods are necessities. Normal goods are necessities only if they are not luxuries.
- Doubling all nominal variables has no effect on demand since the real value of incomes and the real price of goods are unaltered.
- A price change has a substitution (relative price) effect and an income (purchasing power) effect. Intuition usually locates the substitution effect. You must also find the income effect.
- Demand curves slope down for normal goods. A sufficiently inferior good could have an upward-sloping demand curve; such goods are very rare.
- Because of the income effect, higher interest rates need not encourage more saving.
- Marginal utility is the extra benefit of consuming the last unit of a good, holding constant consumption of other goods. Tastes display diminishing marginal utility. This explains the water–diamond paradox.
- At each price the market demand curve is the sum of the quantities demanded by different people facing that price.

Review questions

1 Suppose the demand for peaches is inelastic: to sell 10 per cent more you have to cut the price by 20 per cent. You are the only fruit seller in town, and your fruit stall has 100 ripe peaches that can usually be sold for £1 each. You now discover 10 of your peaches are rotten and can't be sold. (a) What quantity do you now wish to sell at once? (b) What is the new equilibrium price? (c) Do you get more or less revenue than the £100 you had originally expected to earn?

2 Two possible ways to reduce global warming are: (a) a tax on emissions of carbon dioxide from cars and power stations; and (b) a ban on driving cars except at the weekend. Which policy works by shifting the demand curve for energy to the left, and which works by moving consumers leftwards along a given demand curve for energy?

3 For vegetables, quantity demanded rises 0.2 per cent when the price falls 1 per cent, but

rises 0.9 per cent when income rises 1 per cent. For catering, quantity demanded rises 2.6 per cent when the price falls 1 per cent but rises 1.6 per cent when consumer incomes rise by 1 per cent. Are vegetables and catering luxuries or necessities, and do each of them have elastic or inelastic demand?

4 During 1975–2004, UK households' spending on bread and cereals rose from £1.5 million to over £5 million. Does this mean bread is a normal good? Could it be an inferior good? Which seems more likely to you?

5 Why is demand more elastic in the long run than in the short run?

6 Why are these statements wrong? (a) Because cigarettes are a necessity, tax revenue on cigarettes must rise when the tax rate is raised. (b) Farmers should insure against bad weather that might destroy half the crops of all farmers. (c) Farmers should not insure against events that affect their crops alone.

7 Do higher consumer incomes always benefit producers?

8 'A higher hourly wage makes people want to work longer by making work more attractive than leisure.' 'A higher wage makes people better off, raising the quantity of leisure demanded, and thereby reducing the length of time people wish to work.' Which is the income effect, and which is the substitution effect?

9 Suppose Glaswegians have a given income, and like weekend trips to the Highlands, a three-hour drive. (a) If the price of petrol doubles, what is the effect on the demand for trips to the Highlands? Discuss both income and substitution effects. What do you expect to happen to the price of Highland hotel rooms?

10 Explain the concepts of utility, marginal utility, and diminishing marginal utility.

11 Name a good for which your marginal utility falls so much that you get negative marginal utility when you consume too much of this good.

12 Why are these statements wrong? (a) Inflation reduces demand since prices are higher and goods are more expensive. (b) Abolishing income tax on the income from saving must make people save more.

Answers on page 342

3

Supply

3-1

The supply curve

Learning outcomes

By the end of this section, you should understand:

- ◆ That supply describes the behaviour of sellers
- ◆ The effect of price on quantity supplied
- ◆ How supply curves depict this relationship

M uch of the world's cocaine began as a coca plant in Columbia, and poppies in Afghanistan are the source of most of the heroin that finds its way into European countries. American and European governments keep pressurizing politicians in Columbia and Afghanistan to eradicate the problem by stopping their farmers producing the raw materials for the drugs trade. From time to time the BBC and CNN show flaming hillsides as helicopters attack peasant farmers. But the following year, the same crops are back in bloom. Why is the supply of coca and poppies so hard to stamp out?

An economist's answer is that the incentive to produce this crop is large. When poor farmers get much higher prices for one crop than for the alternative crops that they could produce instead, they will be very keen to supply. French farmers could also produce poppies, but, within the Common Agricultural Policy, they have other crops which also yield them high returns.

Frozen out of the markets of G8 countries by high external tariffs, farmers in Third World countries do not have profitable opportunities to engage in legal trade with the world's rich countries. Illegal trade is relatively more attractive to farmers. The quantity supplied is high because farmers get a high price for their crops. As international travel has become easier, transporting drugs has become easier too. In turn, this has raised the price that drug traffickers will pay poppy growers, making poppy growing even more attractive to farmers.

Moreover, in comparison with the government of Afghanistan, the French government has more incentive and greater ability to stamp out illegal crop production. It has more incentive because, as a member of the G8 and EU, it has more to lose by upsetting its partner countries. It has greater ability because it is richer and technically more sophisticated. Identifying and eradicating illegal crops is easier.

This example illustrates many of the themes of this chapter. What determines the incentive to produce and supply to the market? How sensitive is production to the price being offered? Must prices be reduced in order to diminish the incentive to supply or can supply be reduced through other means?

Supply is the quantity producers wish to offer for sale at each conceivable price.

Supply is not a particular quantity but a full description of the quantity producers would sell at each and every possible price. We can show this relationship between price and quantity demanded as a *supply curve*, SS in Figure 3-1.[1] The vertical distance measures the price of the good or service. The horizontal distance measures the corresponding quantity supplied. Thus, each point on SS indicates a price and corresponding quantity supplied at that price.

A **supply curve** shows the quantity supplied at each possible price, other things equal.

When the price of poppies is zero, nobody will bother to grow them for sale. As the price of poppies rises, the quantity supplied rises, other things equal. In Figure 3-1 this corresponds to moving *along* the line SS — rightwards and upwards — offering more and more poppies for sale as the price is increased, until every Afghan hillside is saturated with poppies and no more can be produced. In Figure 3-1 the maximum possible supply is Q^*, and any price above P^* has no further effect in raising the quantity supplied.

---

[1] As with demand curves, supply curves may be a straight line or a curve, but in either case must slope upwards as we move to the right. If, unlike Figure 3-1, the supply curve was a straight line this would imply that the quantity supplied could be increased without limit provided the price was high enough.

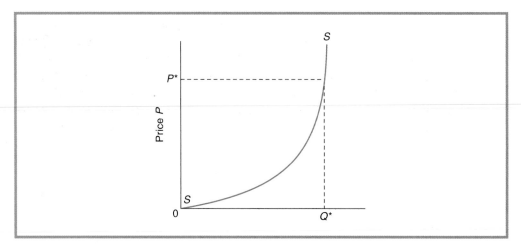

Figure 3-1   The supply of poppies

We can use a similar figure to think about the clean UK energy from wind power in the early twenty-first century. At a low price, it is not worth UK producers producing energy from wind farms (which are not very efficient and, being noisy and ugly, cause a lot of local resentment that is not worth incurring for low levels of energy production). If energy prices were to rise a lot, it would then become worth bearing these costs and producing more UK energy in wind farms. But there is only so much physical wind in the UK in any one year. Beyond some output Q^*, the UK cannot currently produce any more energy from wind no matter how high the price. The supply curve becomes vertical at that point.

Figure 3-2 shows what happened to poppy production when the advent of cheaper and faster travel made smuggling easier, raising the price that smugglers were prepared to pay for poppies. Initially, the poppy market was at point A, with a price P_0 and quantity Q_0 supplied. Once smuggling became easier, the price rose to P_1 and farmers responded by raising quantity supplied to Q_1. They moved upwards along a given supply curve, from A to B, in response to the higher price they were being offered.

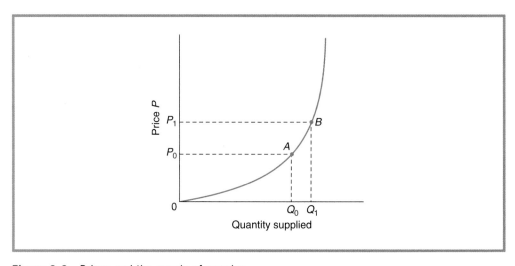

Figure 3-2   Prices and the supply of poppies

Conversely, if Western countries adopt better surveillance techniques that eradicate smuggling, the prices being offered to Afghan poppy growers will fall: only a few flower shops will want to buy poppies. In Figure 3-2 we can imagine that we begin at point B, with a price P_1 and quantity Q_1. The consequence of eradicating drug smuggling is to reduce the price to price P_0 and poppy farmers respond by reducing the quantity supplied to Q_0.

If changes in prices make suppliers move *along* a given supply curve, how then do we represent more effective policing of illegal poppy production by the Afghan government?

3-2

Behind the supply curve

Learning outcomes

By the end of this section, you should understand:

- ◆ Other determinants of supply
- ◆ When supply curves shift

Recall our discussion of demand curves in Chapter 2, in which price changes moved demanders along a given demand curve but changes in the prices of related goods, changes in incomes, or changes in tastes led to shifts in the demand curve. In exactly the same way, movements in price move suppliers along a given supply curve, but changes in any of the 'other things equal' have to be depicted as *shifts* in the supply curve.

The three principal 'other things' that affect supply are technology available to producers, the cost of inputs (labour, machines, fuel, and raw materials), and government regulation. Holding these three things constant, movements *along* a particular supply curve show the effect of prices on quantity supplied. A change in any of these 'other things equal' shifts the supply curve, changing the amount producers want to supply at each price.

Technology

Better knowledge of fertilizers or improvements in irrigation technology make it profitable to supply more poppies than before at any particular price being offered, just as electronic or information technology have made it possible to supply more televisions and computers at any price than was the case ten years ago.

As a determinant of supply, technology must be interpreted broadly. A technological advance is any improvement in knowledge that allows more physical output from the same quantity of physical input as before. It is this productivity increase that means that producers are willing to supply more than before at any particular price. This improvement might come from better science, but it might also arise from better psychology.

When Japanese car producers first established car plants in the UK, they achieved much higher productivity levels than traditional car producers. This was due in part to workforce motivation and organization. Rather than take lunch alone in a directors' dining room, those running the company ate in the same cafeteria as workers, making the workers feel more valued and allowing insights from the factory floor to be fed into senior management.

Technical progress can reflect better teamwork as well as better science. Either way, a supplier gets more output from given input quantities, and hence can supply more at any particular price. The supply curve shifts to the right (because we measure quantities in the horizontal direction, a rightward shift implies a greater quantity supplied at each price). Conversely, if we ever had a collective memory lapse and forgot how to do something, the supply curve would shift to the left.

Input prices

A particular supply curve is also drawn for a given level of input prices. Lower input prices (lower wages, lower fuel costs) induce firms to supply more at each price, shifting the supply curve to the right. When world oil prices fell to $10/barrel for several years in the late 1980s and early 1990s, the airline business was profitable and lots of new airlines sprung up supplying more airline flights than before. The supply curve for flights shifted to the right. Conversely, when oil prices rose to over $50/barrel, the cost of running an airline increased dramatically, and the supply curve for flights shifted sharply to the left. Some airlines even went bankrupt and quit the industry entirely.

Government regulation

Given a free choice, suppliers choose the lowest-cost production method from their viewpoint. If regulations make suppliers use a different production method, this must be more costly for suppliers. It shifts the supply curve to the left, reducing the quantity supplied at each price. More stringent safety regulations prevent chocolate producers using the most productive process because it is dangerous to workers. Anti-pollution devices raise the cost of making cars. More effective prosecution of poppy growers raises the cost of supplying poppies. When regulation prevents producers (legal or illegal) from selecting the cheapest production method, regulation shifts the supply curve to the left.

Event	Supply curve for UK university places	
	Shifts right	Shifts left
1 UK top-up fees abolished		
2 UK lecturers get big pay rise		
3 New law requires wheelchair access to every classroom		
4 Young people lose faith in education, volunteer instead for a lifetime of service in Africa		
5 Bill Gates donates E-learning packages to all UK universities		
6 An earthquake destroys five UK universities		

Table 3-1   Shifts in the supply curve (tick the appropriate box in each line)

(answers on page 59 but complete the table before skipping to the answers!)

3-3

Measuring supply responses

Learning outcomes

By the end of this section, you should understand:

- ◆ The price elasticity of supply
- ◆ The revenue effect of a price change

The price responsiveness of supply

When a price rise has a large effect on quantity supplied, we say that the supply of the good is *elastic*. Suppliers are very responsive to prices. When the same size of price rise has a small effect on quantity supplied, we say that supply is *inelastic*. Sellers are not very responsive to prices.

The **elasticity of supply** measures the *responsiveness* of quantity supplied to the price that suppliers receive.

When supply is elastic (inelastic), a 1 per cent price rise increases quantity by more than (less than) 1 per cent.

In the previous chapter, whether demand was elastic or inelastic affected whether revenue (price times quantity) fell or rose when the price increased. Because demand curves slope down, prices and quantities change in opposite directions, which is why it is important to know which effect dominates the other. For supply, there is no such conflict. Supply curves slope up not down. Prices and quantities always change in the same direction: high prices go with high quantities, low prices with low quantities. Hence, a price increase always raises the total revenue received by sellers (both price and quantity increase), and a price fall always reduces the revenue of sellers since both price and quantity are lower. In Figure 3-2 a price increase from P_1 to P_0 increases total revenue received by suppliers from OP_0AQ_0 to OP_1AQ_1.

Box 3-1   What determines supply elasticities?

The elasticity of supply is determined by how profitable it is for suppliers to increase quantity supplied when they are offered higher prices for their output. In part, this reflects technology. With a mass production line, it may be relatively easy to respond to opportunities to sell at higher prices, but doubling the prize money for golf tournaments is no guarantee that another Tiger Woods will emerge.

As with demand, we need to distinguish between supply to the market as a whole and the behaviour of individual suppliers. If prices rise, a particular supplier may already be near full capacity, and have little ability or willingness to increase the quantity supplied. But higher prices may entice new suppliers into the market, thereby enlarging total supply. Total supply is then more elastic than the supply of individual producers. In the 1990s, the airline boom reflected the arrival of EasyJet and Ryanair, rather than a major expansion of British Airways and Air France.

As with elasticity of demand, elasticity of supply is higher in the long run than the short run. Given more time, it is easier for producers to respond to a price change. It may take time to build new production capacity to respond to a price increase. Similarly, closing factories or laying off workers is not something producers undertake on the first day that prices fall. They wait a bit to see if the price reduction is permanent, and even then it takes time to organize a production response. Overnight, supply can be pretty inelastic. Supply curves are often steep in the short run, showing that price changes have only small effects on quantity supplied. In the longer run, supply is more elastic and supply curves become flatter, indicating that quantity supplied varies more with price changes.

Event	Supply curve for UK university places	
	Shifts right	Shifts left
1. UK top-up fees abolished	Alters the price and moves universities along a given supply curve. No shift.	
2. UK lecturers get big pay rise		Lower quantity supplied at each level of fees
3. New law requires wheelchair access to every classroom		Lower quantity supplied at each level of fees
4. Young people lose faith in education, volunteers instead for a lifetime of service in Africa	Affects demand not supply	
5. Bill Gates donates E-learning packages to all UK	Makes supplying universities easier and cheaper; hence entire supply curve shifts right	
6. An earthquake destroys five UK universities		Lower capacity to supply, so supply curve shifts left

Answers to Table 3-1 (page 56)   Shifts in the supply curve

3-4

Introducing the theory of supply

Learning outcomes

By the end of this section, you should understand:

- ◆ Revenue, economic cost, and economic profit
- ◆ Stocks and flows
- ◆ Whether profit maximization is plausible
- ◆ How a firm chooses the output to supply

S o far, we have described supplier behaviour, but in order to develop a better simulation model that allows us to predict how suppliers respond in hypothetical situations, we need to develop an explicit theory of supply. For each possible output level, a firm compares what this output costs to make and what revenue it earned from sales. Profits are the excess of revenue over costs. Our theory of supply assumes each firm chooses the output level that maximizes its profit. This is the key to our theory of supply.

A firm's accounts

Although illegal poppy growers may not bother to keep accounts, legitimate businesses are required to keep and submit accounts. Moreover, once a business attains any level of sophistication, those running it will want to know all the details of how it is operating, in order to take the best decisions possible.

In modern economies, firms report two sets of accounts, one for stocks and one for flows.

Stocks are measured at a point in time; flows are corresponding measures over a period of time.

The water flowing out of a tap is different per second and per minute. The measurement requires a time interval to make sense. The stock of water in the basin at any instant is a number of litres, and requires no time dimension. A firm reports profit-and-loss accounts per year (flow accounts) and a balance sheet showing assets and liabilities at a point in time (stock accounts). The two are related, as they are for the basin of water. The inflow from the tap is what changes the stock of water over time, even though the latter is only measured in litres at each point in time.

Flow accounts (profit and loss)

A firm's revenue is income from sales during the period, its costs are expenses incurred in production and sales during the period, and its profits are the excess of revenue over costs.

This sounds very easy, but there are a few tricky complications. Economists and accountants adopt different definitions because they are interested in different things. Accountants have to certify that nobody is stealing cash from the business. They care about cash flow.

Cash flow is the net amount of money received by a firm during a given period.

Economists care about what, how, and for whom goods are produced. Accountants keep track of actual cash spent. Economists focus on opportunity cost.

Opportunity cost is the amount lost by not using resources in their best alternative use.

You quit a job as a teacher of ICT and start an Internet business, paying out £5000 in the first year as you camp in an Internet cafe, whose facilities are used as your office. An accountant treats your costs as £5000. An economist stresses that your time was not free – you could have earned £20 000 a year teaching ICT. It only makes sense to switch your labour resources into the Internet job if you can earn at least £25 000. For an economist, interested in incentives to allocate resources, a revenue of £25 000 is merely break-even; for an accountant it is £20 000 profit after paying the Internet cafe.

Normal profit is the accounting profit to break-even after all economic costs are paid. **Economic (supernormal) profits** in excess of normal profit are a signal to switch resources into the industry. **Economic losses** mean that the resources could earn more elsewhere.

Here is a second case in which economists and accounting definitions are different. The Internet start-up also requires the ICT teacher to use £2000 of her savings to cover everyday expenses. The accountant treats this personal financial injection by the owner as free, but an economist recognizes the opportunity cost. If the money could have earned £100 in interest during the year, that is another economic cost to deduct in calculating economic profit.

Suppose the Internet start-up company does so well that it buys its own office.

Physical capital is any input to production not used up within the production period. Examples include machinery, equipment, and buildings. *Investment* is additions to physical capital.

This capital is a stock and not a flow, but we cannot exclude it entirely from the firm's flow accounts. The capital becomes less valuable during the period for which flow accounts are drawn up. This depreciation is a proper charge on the flow accounts.

Depreciation is the cost of using capital during the period.

It reflects both wear and tear, and gradual obsolescence. Capital has a second economic cost in flow accounts: the money tied up when the capital was bought. The interest this could have earned is an economic cost to the flow accounts of the firm.

Stock accounts (balance sheet)

The balance sheet shows at a point in time the assets and liabilities that the firm has built up as a result of flows in all preceding periods.

Assets are what the firm owns. **Liabilities** are what it owes. **Net worth** is assets minus liabilities.

Assets include cash in the bank, money owed by customers, inventories, and physical capital such as plant and machinery. Liabilities are debts the firm still has to repay to suppliers and its bankers. Net worth includes not just these tangible assets minus liabilities, but should also include an estimate for the value of its reputation, customer loyalty, and a host of intangible assets that economists call *goodwill*.

Box 3-2   The value of a good name

Goodwill affects the ability of the firm to make money in the future and is just as valuable an asset as physical assets cumulated from past behaviour. The consultancy Interbrand tries to calculate goodwill by comparing the stock market value of companies with the identifiable physical and financial assets they own. US giants such as Coca-Cola top the worldwide list. Microsoft, Nokia, and Yahoo! are well up the list. So are Nike and Adidas. Interestingly, the big banks perform poorly in this rating.

Box 3-2 *Continued*

Rank	Company	Industry	Brand value ($bn)
1	Coca-Cola	Drinks	71
2	Microsoft	Software	65
3	IBM	Computers	52
5	Intel	Computers	31
6	Nokia	Mobile phones	29
7	Disney	Entertainment	28
10	Mercedes	Cars	21
20	Sony	Electronics	13
33	Nike	Sports goods	8
43	Ikea	Furniture	7
67	Adidas	Sports goods	4

Source: www.interbrand.com

You are considering switching resources between uses. Should you study the flow accounts for the year, or the stock accounts at the time of your decision? The former shows recent behaviour, the latter shows the long-run position. If you can afford to take a long-run view, you may be more interested in the stock accounts. If you have to worry about short-term considerations, the flow accounts may be more informative.

Do firms really maximize profits?

Economists assume that firms make supply decisions to maximize profits. Some business executives, and even some economists, question this assumption. A sole owner is account-able only to herself and may have other aims (nice location, popularity with the local com-munity, doing good). However, most business is done by large companies.

Companies are not run directly by their owners. Company directors have day-to-day discretion and only account formally to shareholders at the annual shareholders' meeting. In practice, shareholders rarely dismiss the directors, who have inside information about the true prospects of the firm. It is hard for shareholders to be sure that new directors could do better.

Given this separation of ownership and control, shareholders want maximum profits but directors have some scope to pursue their own agenda. This may include executive perks, such as nice cars and a company jet. If status depends on size, directors may pursue size rather than profits, advertising too much or holding prices lower than is ideal for profits and shareholders' interests.

Even so, profit maximization is a good place to start in developing a theory of supply. First, even if shareholders are kept partly in the dark, other firms in the industry are better informed. Companies not pursuing profits have low profits, and hence low share prices. A takeover raider can buy the company cheaply, change the policy, make extra profits, and cash up as the share price soars. Fear of takeovers may force the directors to pursue profit maximization.

Second, shareholders provide incentives for managers to do what shareholders want. They offer directors profit-related bonuses and share options. The total value of these is small relative to company profits but big relative to what directors earn in salary alone. Directors then maximize profits, as the shareholders want.

Box 3-3   Fat-cat bosses

Many empire-building managers now indulge in takeovers in spite of, rather than because of, pressure from shareholders. *The Economist* (5/5/01)

The article cited considerable empirical evidence that shareholders in the company doing the taking over usually lose out in the process, and concluded

The takeover threat has become like a nuclear option: so disruptive that it can be used only as a last resort.

Company bosses have used this greater security to vote themselves fat-cat pay rises and ensure huge golden handshakes even if they are leaving the company because it is doing poorly. How can shareholders fight back?

Big institutional shareholders – the pension funds and insurance companies whose assets are shares held in other companies – are being more active in monitoring the companies in which they invest, using a louder voice at companies' annual general meetings. Sackings of unsuccessful bosses are at an all-time high.

3-5

An overview of the supply decision

Learning outcomes

By the end of this section, you should understand:

- ◆ Total revenue and marginal revenue
- ◆ Total cost and marginal cost
- ◆ The output level that maximizes supplier profits

W e begin with production costs. Each output level can be made in several ways. A field of wheat can be farmed by lots of workers with few tools, or by one worker with a lot of machinery.

Given the price of each input and the different production techniques available, the firm calculates the lowest cost way to make each possible output level. This may entail different techniques at different outputs.

The **total cost curve** shows the lowest cost way to make each output level. Total cost rises as output rises.

Table 3-2 shows different outputs and the corresponding total cost. At any output, the firm has a fixed cost of 10, perhaps the cost of paying interest on old debts. As output rises from 1 to 4, total cost rises from 18 to 54. Extra output incurs extra costs. The third column shows marginal cost.

Output Q	Total cost TC	Marginal cost MC	Total revenue TR	Marginal revenue MR	Economic profits	MR − MC
0	10	–	0	–	−10	
1	18	8	20	20	2	12
2	28	10	31	11	3	1
3	40	12	36	5	−4	−7
4	54	14	35	−1	−19	−15

Table 3-2   The supply decision

Source: World Bank, *World Development Report, 2003*

Marginal cost is the change in total cost as a result of producing the last unit.

The marginal cost of the first unit of production is 8, the rise in total cost from 10 to 18. Similarly, the marginal cost of producing the fourth unit of output is 14, the rise in total cost from 40 to 54. Having considered cost, now think about revenue. Column 4 shows total revenue from selling the output produced. With no output, the firm gets no revenue. One unit of output can be sold at a price of 20, giving a total revenue of 20. This is also the marginal revenue of going from zero to one unit of output sold.

Total revenue is the output price times the quantity made and sold. **Marginal revenue** is the change in total revenue as a result of making and selling the last unit.

As output and sales rise, column 4 shows that revenue rises for a bit but eventually gets smaller as sales increase. To sell more and more output, the firm has to cut prices to induce buyers to demand this output. Since all output is sold for the same price, cutting the price to sell new units reduces the revenue earned on previous units. This second effect eventually outweighs the first. Beyond three units, extra sales actually cut revenue. Column 5 does the sums for you, showing the marginal revenue from the last unit sold, which takes into account the effect on total revenue of bidding down the price that previous units have been sold for. By the bottom row of Table 3-2, marginal revenue is actually negative.

Armed with the first five columns of Table 3-2, you advise the firm what output to make and sell. One method is simply to subtract total cost from total revenue to obtain economic or supernormal profits. Column 6 shows that that profit-maximizing output is 2, at which profits are 3. This is similar to the method used by a mountaineer who checks the top has been reached by making sure he can look down on all surrounding sides.

There is another way to check you are at the top. Work out the slope you are standing on. If it is not flat, take the upwards direction. At the very top, the slope is zero. There is no direction you can move in order to get any higher. This is the marginal principle.

The **marginal principle** says that, if the slope is not zero, moving in one direction must make things better; moving the other way makes things worse. Only at a maximum (or a minimum) is the slope temporarily zero.

Economists use the marginal principle a lot. Profit is maximized at the output at which marginal profit is zero. Otherwise, a different output can add to profit. Marginal profit is simply marginal revenue minus marginal cost. Column 7 uses this decision rule. If marginal revenue exceeds marginal cost, the firm made a marginal profit on the last unit, and should make even more. If marginal revenue is less than marginal cost, the firm made a marginal loss on the last unit, and already made too much. With a marginal profit of 1, it was a good idea to make as much as 2 units. However, with a marginal loss of 7 from making a third unit, it is best to stop at 2 units. This, of course, is the same answer we got by calculating total profit from total revenue and total cost. Sometimes it is an easier method to implement.

Plotting *MC* and *MR* curves

Table 3-2 is an artificial example. Output does not have to be a whole number. Dairies can make 1284.8 litres of milk if this is the best output level. Figure 3-3 plots continuous curves for marginal cost *MC* and marginal revenue *MR*. The *MR* curve steadily falls as output rises: price cuts are needed to get customers to buy more. For most of its range, the *MC* curve rises: making the last unit gets harder and harder. For example, a coal mine has to go ever deeper to find more coal.

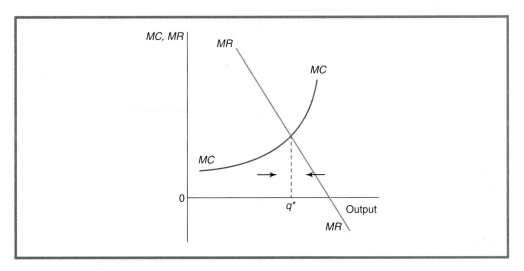

Figure 3-3   A firm's supply decision

A profit-maximizing firm chooses to supply the output q^*, at which marginal profit is zero. Marginal revenue exactly equals marginal cost. At any lower output, MR exceeds MC and the firm adds to profits by expanding. At any output above q^*, MC exceeds MR and the firm adds to profits by contracting output.

We can also use Figure 3-3 to examine changes in costs or revenue curves. Anything that shifts the MC curve up (such as wage increases, or tougher pollution controls) means that MC crosses MR at a lower output. This makes perfect sense: when costs rise, the firm supplies less. Conversely, a change in demand behaviour that shifts the MR curve up increases the output that the firm supplies: with better revenue opportunities, the firm chooses to supply more output.

You probably thought you knew that already. However, Figure 3-3 is also making a point that is less obvious. What induces a profit-maximizing firm to reduce output is an increase in *marginal* cost. If you ask your friends who are not studying economics, they might reply that it is higher average costs or higher total costs that make firms wish to cut back production. Actually, neither of these assertions need be correct.[2] But if the marginal revenue curve MR is unaltered, you now know that an upward shift in marginal cost curve MC always makes firms wish to supply less.

Do firms know their *MC* and *MR* curves?

There are two ways in which to maximize profits. The first is by having a highly professional management with access to excellent management information. Marginal cost and marginal revenue are what they are trying to discover. Alternatively, a firm may simply be run by an intuitive genius who gets things right without going through all the laborious steps above.

Competition means that most surviving bosses are good at such decisions. If they get things right, they are maximizing profit, which ensures that MC must equal MR whether anyone in the firm knows it or not. Using the marginal principle is how mere mortals keep track of what proven business leaders do instinctively.

So we've mastered the supply decision?

We have found the principle from which all else follows. There are still some details to fill in. First, both revenue and costs may differ in the short run and in the longer run. A firm may have to react to a marginal revenue schedule that changes over time. Even more important, a firm's cost curves change over time. We also have to aggregate individual supplies to get the market supply curve. This depends on how many suppliers there are, and how they react to one another. The ensuing chapters explain different forms of market structure and what this means for the supply decision.

---

[2] If you wish to show off your new economic understanding, here is a simple example. To help finance disaster relief, the government imposes a tax of £50 000 on every firm, whatever output they produce. At all positive output levels, the cost and benefit of raising output are unaffected by this tax, and hence MC and MR are unaffected. The firm will not cut back output despite the fact that average and total costs have risen. It might as well get the biggest surplus possible from production and sale, whether or not it then has to pay a disaster levy to the government.

3-6

Combining supply and demand

Learning outcomes

By the end of this section, you should understand:

- How prices reconcile demand and supply
- Equilibrium in a market
- The effect of shifts in demand or supply curves

N ow that we have developed the theories of demand and supply, and understand how to reflect behaviour in demand and supply curves, we can provide a deeper analysis of the role of markets that we introduced in Chapter 1. Prices adjust to equate the quantity people wish to buy and the quantity people wish to sell. In so doing, these prices influence what goods are produced, how they are produced, and for whom they are produced. The upward-sloping curve SS in Figure 3-4 shows how much sellers wish to sell at each price. The downward-sloping curve DD shows how much consumers wish to purchase at each price. The market is in equilibrium at point E where the two curves intersect. The equilibrium price is P^*, at which a quantity Q^* is supplied and demanded.

The **equilibrium price** clears the market. At this price, the quantity supplied equals the quantity demanded.

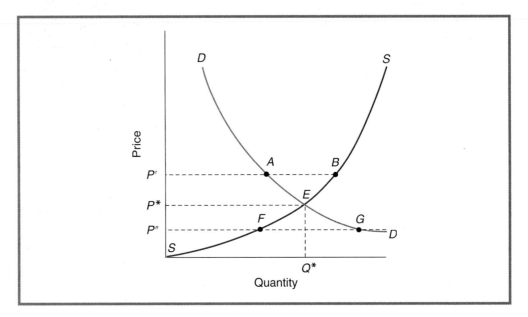

Figure 3-4   Market equilibrium

At any price P' above P^* (a higher vertical distance in the price direction in Figure 3-4), the quantity supplied exceeds the quantity demanded. There is excess supply at this price and suppliers have unsold stock. To sell this unsold stock, suppliers have to reduce the price. This keeps happening until the market returns to equilibrium at point E.

Conversely, at any price P'' below P^* (a lower vertical distance in the price direction in Figure 3-4), the quantity demanded now exceeds the quantity supplied. There is excess demand at this price, and buyers cannot find all the goods they would like to purchase. Buyers offer to pay more than suppliers are asking for, and the price is steadily bid upwards until the equilibrium is restored at point E.

Case study 3-1   The Green Revolution in Third World agriculture

Rich countries have spent years accumulating physical capital, such as factories and buildings, and human capital, the stock of knowledge and skills that makes the workforce productive. In rich countries, few people still farm the land. There are more profitable things to do. Box 1-1 in Chapter 1 showed that agriculture is now less than 2 per cent of national output in countries such as Japan, France, and the UK.

Rice fields
© Robert Essel NYC/Corbis

Poor countries are poor precisely because they have accumulated less physical and human capital. They have to make do with their labour and the land available to them. Agriculture is a much larger share of their national output. Fifty years ago many people thought that the best way to help poor countries was to provide aid and technical assistance to improve their agricultural productivity. Since this was such a large share of their output, it offered the best opportunity to increase people's living standards.

Some countries, such as Sudan, have remained ravaged by civil war and little progress has been made. But in many countries – India is a good example – there has been a Green Revolution. With better fertilizer, better irrigation, and, importantly, better varieties of crops that are faster growing and more disease resistant, agricultural output has soared. However, this has not led to the increase in national income that was expected.

The table below shows what has happened to the real (inflation-adjusted) price of the crops in the last 50 years. Prices are now only about a third of what they were fifty years ago. World markets have been flooded by extra supply, both because G8 farmers have become more productive and export to world markets, and because Third World producers have also become much more productive than they used to be.

	1955	1975	2003
Average real price of 28 crops	186	217	67
(1995 price = 100)			

However, the additional supply alone is not the whole story. It is also the fact that Third World producers are having to sell their extra supply in poor markets that have a limited capacity to absorb the extra quantity being supplied. Demand in these markets is quite inelastic. There is a limit to how much extra poor people wish to buy, no matter how much the price is reduced. If Third World producers had access to G8 markets, they would find demand was much more elastic. The two figures below illustrate the same increase in world food supply, and hence the same rightward shift in the two supply curves. However, in the left-hand figure, demand is inelastic and the demand curve is steep. Producer revenue (price times quantity) actually falls when supply increases. In the right-hand figure, demand is elastic and the demand curve is much flatter. The same increase in supply bids down the price much less in the right-hand diagram, and the rightward shift in the supply curve now increases producer revenue (price times quantity).

Case study 3-1   *Continued*

Notice finally the difference between saying that the G8 is rich and that its demand for food is more elastic than food demand of poor countries. Access to the rich markets of the G8, where demand is high because people are wealthy, would imply that the *level* of food prices is high. If poor producers could access these markets, they would get a higher price for their produce than if they have to sell in poor markets where demand curves are much lower in position.

However, this case study has been making a second point, not about levels of prices but about changes in prices in response to increases in supply. For a given rightward shift in the supply curve, the induced *change* in prices in the two diagrams below depends not on the height of the demand curves but on their *slope*. It is because the demand curve is flatter in the right-hand diagram that the same shift in supply induces a smaller fall in price (and therefore has to be reflected in a larger change in equilibrium quantity).

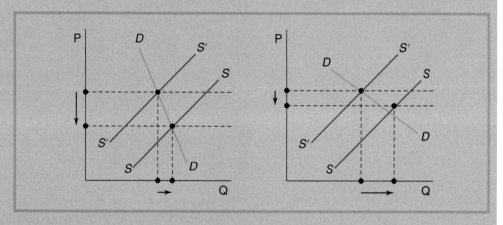

We can also consider shifts in demand rather than supply. Some countries, especially in sub-Saharan Africa, are very dependent on a single crop which, once harvested, has to be sold for whatever price it will fetch. Such countries have a very inelastic supply curve in the short run. The diagram opposite shows the consequence of shifts in demand. With a near-vertical supply curve, the effect of demand fluctuations is to cause large fluctuations in the equilibrium price. When demand is *DD*, equilibrium occurs at *E*,

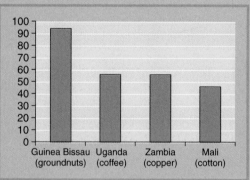

Single crop as percentage of export revenue
Source: IMF

with a price *P* and a quantity *Q*. When demand shifts to *D'D'*, the new equilibrium at *E'* entails a price *P'* and quantity *Q'*. With quantity supplied unresponsive to price, these large price fluctuations also induce large fluctuations in farmers' incomes.

Recap

- Supply describes how much producers wish to sell at each possible price.
- A supply curve plots quantity supplied against price, other things equal. Changes in price move suppliers along a given supply curve.
- The principal other things equal are technology, input price, and the extent of regulation. Technical progress makes inputs more productive and allows producers to produce more at each possible output price. The supply curve shifts to the right. Lower input prices have a similar effect. Tougher regulation makes life harder for producers and the supply curve shifts to the left.
- An increase in supply shifts supply curves to the right, which also implies downwards. This is because quantity is measured in the horizontal direction, and supply curves slope upwards. We can interpret an increase in supply either as a rightward shift (more quantity at each price) or a downward shift (do not require such a high price to produce any particular quantity). It is the same thing.
- Supply is elastic if quantity supplied is very responsive to price, inelastic if quantity supplied is not very responsive to price. Provided the supply curve remains given, revenue of suppliers always changes in the same direction as price, since price and quantity change in the same direction as we move along a given supply curve.
- Flows are measured over time, stocks at a point in time. Profit is the difference between the flow of revenue and cost.
- Economic costs include all opportunity costs. Normal profit is the accounting profit that just covers all economic costs. Supernormal profits are any profits above this level.
- Firms are assumed to maximize profits even if shareholders cannot directly observe the behaviour of directors. Maximizing profits automatically entails marginal cost equals marginal revenue.
- Marginal cost is the extra total cost entailed in producing an extra output unit. Marginal revenue is the corresponding change in revenue from selling that extra unit of output.
- An upward shift in the *MR* schedule, or downward shift in the *MC* schedule, raises the output supplied. Lower marginal revenue or higher marginal cost schedules have the opposite effect.
- The equilibrium price equates the quantity demanded and supplied. It is the point at which supply and demand curves intersect.
- Above this price, there is excess supply, which puts downward pressure on prices to restore equilibrium. Below this price, there is excess demand, which puts upward pressure on prices to restore equilibrium.
- The more inelastic the supply curve, the more a shift in demand will lead to changes in price rather than quantity. The more inelastic the demand curve, the more a shift in supply will lead to changes in price rather than quantity.

Review questions

1 Which of the following represent an increase in supply by supermarkets:
   (a) The invention of the Internet, which makes it possible for supermarkets to sell online and reduces their costs of distribution?
   (b) A reduction in the wages of supermarket workers because their trade union becomes less powerful?
   (c) Deregulation of supermarkets that ends the ban on opening on Sundays?
   (d) Higher prices for supermarket goods because families are stocking up for their annual parties?

2 Unit-elastic demand implies that price changes have no effect on the spending of buyers and revenue of sellers. Is there a corresponding interpretation of unit-elastic supply? Why or why not?

3 You are a sheep farmer in the Welsh hills. Give three examples of a change that would reduce your supply. Was one of your answers a change in the price of wool? Why or why not?

4 The table below shows two demand curves DD and D'D' and two supply curves SS and S'S'.
   Each row shows a price, and the quantities supplied or demanded at that price on each of the different curves.
   (a) What are the equilibrium price and quantity when demand is DD and supply SS?
   (b) What if demand is DD and supply S'S'?
   (c) Which of the two supply curves is more inelastic? What is the reason for your answer?
   (d) Now suppose demand increases by 3 units at each price so that DD becomes D'D'. Repeat your answers to (a) and (b).
   (e) Which of the two supply curves will be associated with smaller price fluctuations for any given shift in demand?

Price	DD Quantity demanded	D'D' Quantity demanded	SS Quantity supplied	S'S' Quantity supplied
1	7	10	4	5.5
2	6	9	6	6
3	5	8	8	6.5
4	4	7	10	7
5	3	6	12	7.5

5 Why might firms, such as accountants and lawyers, where the trust of the customer is important, choose to be partnerships with unlimited liability?

6 At the very top of a hill, what is the slope? Suppose on your walk you always move in the upward direction: will you eventually find the top of the hill? Now think of the hill as a representation of a firm's profit. Marginal profit on the next unit of output, the slope of the profit hill at this level of production, is simply marginal revenue MR minus marginal cost MC. What is marginal profit when the firm is maximizing profits? What does this tell you about MR in comparison with MC at that point?

7 A firm's consultants report that, at the current level of operations, marginal cost exceeds marginal revenue. What output decision should the firm take? What should it do if marginal cost is less than marginal revenue?

8 Which of the following are flows and which are stocks: (a) income (b) output (c) a factory building (d) labour input?

9 Why are these statements wrong? (a) Firms with an accounting profit must be thriving. (b) Firms don't know their marginal costs. A theory of supply can't assume that firms set marginal revenue equal to marginal cost. (c) The biggest profit comes from the largest sales.

10 Examine the following table and deduce what is the profit-maximizing level of output:

Output (units)	1	2	3	4	5	6
MC	4	5	6	7	8	9
MR	8	7	6	5	4	3

11 To check your answer to Question 10, complete the table below. Assume that it costs 5 to be in business at all, even if you produce no output, but that you get zero revenue if you produce zero output. [Hint: to get total cost of making 1 unit, take the TC of 0 units and add the marginal cost of the first unit. The TC of 2 units is simply the TC of 1 unit plus the marginal cost of the second unit, and so on.] What output maximizes total profits? Is this what you got in Question 10?

Output (units)	0	1	2	3	4	5	6
Total cost TC	5						
Total revenue TR	0						
Total profits = TR − TC							

Answers on page 343

4

Costs, supply, and perfect competition

4-1

How costs affect supply

Learning outcomes

By the end of this section, you should understand:

- ◆ Technology and production techniques
- ◆ Total, average, and marginal cost
- ◆ Returns to scale and average cost curves
- ◆ The law of diminishing returns
- ◆ A firm's supply decision, in the short run and long run
- ◆ Temporary shutdown and permanent exit

Chapter 3 introduced the bare bones of a theory of supply, which depended on both costs and revenue. Now we need to put more flesh on this theory. Chapters 4–5 deal with two ideas. First, adjusting production methods takes time. Given time, firms may be able to reduce costs by choosing more appropriate methods of production. Second, the revenue obtained from selling any particular output depends on the extent of competition in that market. This chapter deals with the special case of perfect competition. Chapter 5 examines the consequences of less competitive situations.

New companies, such as Orange and Amazon, lost a lot of money before eventually starting to make profits. Existing companies, such as British Airways and British Telecom, made big losses in the cyclical downturn of 2001–02, despite previous periods of healthy profits. Firms don't always close down when they are losing money. They may keep going because they expect demand to rise, or costs to fall. We need to distinguish between the *short-run* and the *long-run* supply decisions of firms. In the short run, a firm can't fully adjust to new information. In the long run, full adjustment is possible. In this section, we focus on how costs affect the supply decision. We then turn to the influence of demand and revenue on supply decisions.

Inputs are labour, machinery, buildings, raw materials, and energy. An *input* (sometimes called a *factor of production*) is any good or service used to make output. A technique is a particular way of using inputs to make output.

A technique is said to have **technical efficiency** if no other technique could make the same output with fewer inputs. **Technology** is all the techniques known today. **Technical progress** is the discovery of a new technique that is more efficient than existing ones, making a given output with fewer inputs than before.

Box 4-1   Britannica shelved

Serious parents used to purchase their children a bookshelf filled with *Encyclopaedia Britannica* (www.britannica.co.uk). This prestige reference work was the market leader for two centuries after its launch in 1768, despite commanding a premium price, which peaked at £1000. Annual sales reached £450 million in 1990. After 1990, sales revenue collapsed. The CD-ROM destroyed the printed encyclopaedia: it was technically more efficient, doing the old job at a fraction of the price. The marginal cost of making a CD-ROM is about £1. The marginal cost of *Encyclopaedia Britannica* had been about £150 for the books, plus all that commission for the doorstep salesforce.

The main challenge came when Microsoft decided to produce software for an encyclopaedia, called Encarta, at a thirtieth of the price of Britannica. Encarta was not only cheaper but also easier to carry around. Being shorter, it fitted on a single CD-ROM. Britannica was not brought down by a new entrant to the 24-volume book business but by a new technology that changed the nature of the niche.

Britannica gradually figured out how best to respond to Encarta's entry. It produced its own CD-ROM. The door-to-door salesforce got fired. Those using computers pay more attention to website advertising than doorstep sales patter. Britannica has tried to emphasize that, now with similar technology to Encarta, it remains longer and therefore more informative. Encarta is trying to get bigger to undermine the new niche that Britannica is hoping to create.

Sources: P. Evans and T. Wurster, *Blown to Bits*, Harvard Business School Press, 1999; R. Melcher, 'Dusting off the Britannica', *Business Week*, 20 October 1997

Technology relates volumes of inputs to volume of output. But costs are values. To deduce the cheapest way to make a particular output, the firm needs to know input prices as well as what technology is available. At each output level, the firm finds the lowest-cost technique. When labour is cheap, firms choose labour-intensive techniques. If labour is expensive, the firm will switch to more capital-intensive techniques that use less labour.

Long-run costs

Faced with higher demand, the firm will want to expand output, but adjustment takes time. In the long run, the firm can adjust all input quantities and the choice of technique. In the short run, the firm can't change all inputs, and may also be unable to change technique. It may be years before a new factory is designed, built, and operational.

Long-run total cost *LTC* is the total cost of making each output level when a firm has plenty of time to adjust fully and produce this output level by the cheapest possible means. **Long-run marginal cost** *LMC* is the rise in total cost if output permanently rises by one unit. **Long-run average cost** *LAC* is *LTC* divided by the level of output *Q*.

In the long run, most firms face the U-shaped average cost curve shown in Figure 4-1. At higher output levels, the firm achieves efficiency gains and average costs (sometimes called unit costs) fall. However, beyond some output level Q^*, life gets more difficult for the firm, and its average costs increase if output is higher. This is a common pattern of average costs in the long run.

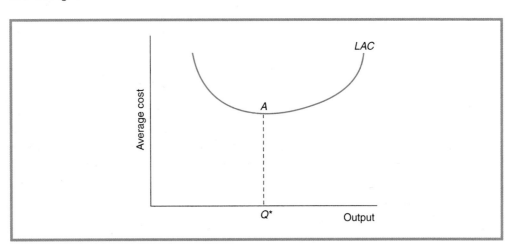

Figure 4-1   The U-shaped *LAC* curve

There are **economies of scale** (or increasing returns to scale) if long-run average cost *LAC* falls as output rises, **constant returns to scale** if *LAC* is constant as output rises, and **diseconomies of scale** (or decreasing returns to scale) if *LAC* rises as output rises.

The U-shaped average cost curve in Figure 4-1 has scale economies up to point *A*, where average cost is lowest. At output levels above Q^*, there are decreasing returns to scale. Since *LAC* is horizontal at point *A*, there are constant returns to scale when output is close to Q^*.

Other shapes of cost curve are possible. Later, we shall see that in some industries with large-scale economies, *LAC* may fall over the entire output range. Conversely, the output Q^* may be so tiny that the *LAC* curve slopes up over most normal output ranges.

Scale economies

There are three reasons for economies of scale. Production may entail some *overhead costs* that do not vary with the output level.[1] A firm requires a manager, a telephone, an accountant, a market research survey. It can't have half a manager and half a telephone if output is low. From low initial output, rises in output allow overheads to be spread over more units of output, reducing average cost. Beyond some output level, the firm needs more managers and telephones. Scale economies end. The average cost curve stops falling.

A second reason for economies of scale is *specialization*. At low output levels, each of the few workers has to do many jobs and never becomes very good at any of them. At higher output and a larger workforce, each worker can focus on a single task and handle it more efficiently. The third reason for economies of scale is that large scale is often needed to take advantage of better machinery. Sophisticated but expensive machinery also has an element of indivisibility. A farmer with a small field may as well dig the field by hand. With a larger field, it becomes worth buying a tractor.

Diseconomies of scale

The main reason for diseconomies of scale is that management is hard once the firm is large: there are *managerial diseconomies of scale*. Large firms need many layers of management, which themselves have to be managed. Co-ordination problems arise, and average costs begin to rise. Geography may also explain diseconomies of scale. If the first factory is sited in the best place, a second factory has to be built in a less advantageous location, and the third in a less advantageous location still.

The shape of the average cost curve thus depends on two things: how long the economies of scale persist, and how quickly the diseconomies of scale occur as output rises.

The lowest output at which all scale economies are achieved is called minimum efficient scale.

In heavy manufacturing industries economies of scale are substantial. At low outputs, average costs are much higher than at minimum efficient scale. High fixed costs of research and development need to be spread over large output to reduce average costs. Hence, large markets are needed to allow low costs to be attained.

High transport costs used to mean that markets were small. For industries with large fixed costs, this meant that average costs were high. Globalization is partly a response to a dramatic fall in transport costs. By selling in larger markets, some firms can enjoy big-scale economies and lower average costs.

In other industries, minimum efficient scale occurs at a low output. Any higher output raises average cost again. There is a limit to a hairdresser's daily output. A larger market makes little difference. Globalization has not had a big impact on hairdressing; but the Internet has always been global – admitting another user to Google hardly costs anything at all. Almost all the costs are fixed costs, the cost of setting up the website in the first place. Marginal cost is very low. And average cost falls as more users are admitted and the fixed costs are spread across more and more users.

[1] Some textbooks refer to these as fixed costs, because they must be paid anyway. We prefer to call them overhead costs, reserving the 'fixed costs' for those which cannot be varied in the short run but could be altered if there is sufficient time to adjust production methods. In contrast, overhead costs have to be paid by any firm that remains in business, no matter how long it has to adjust.

Box 4-2 The Rolls-Royce treatment

Rolls-Royce cars, once the badge of Britishness, are now made by BMW. But the Rolls-Royce aero engine business is booming, and the company's market share has risen from 20 per cent to over 30 per cent within the last decade, making it the second largest aero engine manufacturer in the world. How was this success achieved? By recognizing the crucial role of scale economies. Aircraft engines have huge costs in research and development, requiring large production runs to recover this initial investment. The company's change in strategy reflected two key insights.

First, it extended its initial investment so that its engines could service a wide range of aircraft, thereby increasing the chances of building up long-term relationships with particular aircraft manufacturers and the airlines that they supply. Second, by signing fixed-price agreements for the subsequent repair and maintenance of their engines, Rolls-Royce effectively insured the user against defective quality, thereby signalling their commitment to excellence and safety.

As a result, companies ordered Rolls-Royce engines in greater numbers and over longer time periods, creating the volume business necessary to recoup the large costs of research and development.

Adapted from http://news.bbc.co.uk/1/hi/business/3673477.stm

We begin by discussing the output decision of a firm with a U-shaped average cost curve. Then we show how this analysis must be amended when firms face significant economies of scale.

Average cost and marginal cost

As output rises, average cost falls whenever marginal cost is below average cost; average cost rises whenever marginal cost is above average cost. Hence average cost is lowest at the output Q^* at which LAC and LMC cross. Figure 4-2 illustrates.

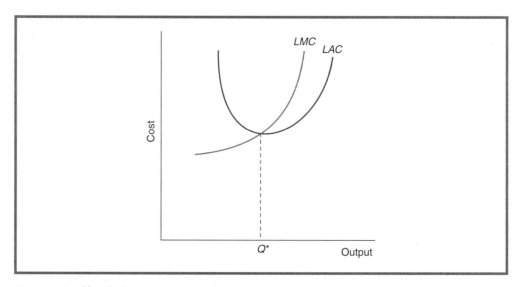

Figure 4-2 Marginal and average cost

This relation between average and marginal is a matter of arithmetic, as relevant to football as to production. Suppose Wayne Rooney scores 3 goals in his first 3 games, thus averaging 1 goal a game. Two goals in the next game, implying 5 goals from 4 games, raises the average to 1.25 goals a game. In the fourth game the marginal score of 2 goals exceeded the average score of 1 goal in previous games, thus raising the average. But if Wayne had not scored in the fourth game (a marginal score of 0) this would have dragged down his average per game from 1 (3 goals in 3 games) to 0.75 (3 goals in 4 games).

Similarly, when the marginal cost of making the next unit of output exceeds the average cost of making the existing units, making another unit *must* raise average cost. Conversely, if the marginal cost of the next unit is below the average cost of existing units, another unit *must* reduce average cost. When marginal and average cost are equal, making another unit leaves average cost unchanged.

Hence in Figure 4-2, average and marginal cost curves cross at minimum average cost. At outputs below Q^*, LMC is below LAC, so average cost is falling. Above Q^*, LMC is above LAC so average cost is rising. At output Q^*, average costs are at a minimum. As in Wayne's world, this relation rests purely on arithmetic.

The firm's long-run output decision

We can now describe how a firm chooses its output level in the long run. This is a two-part decision. First, the firm evaluates its marginal cost and marginal revenue, thereby telling the firm the best output at which to produce in the long run. It should produce the output at which $LMC = MR$. If marginal revenue exceeds marginal cost at any particular output, the firm is still making a marginal profit by producing more, and should therefore raise production. If marginal cost exceeds marginal revenue, the firm has made a marginal loss on the last unit of production and should produce less. Only when marginal revenue equals marginal cost is there no scope to increase operating profits by changing the output level. The marginal condition tells us the best positive output level for maximizing profit, namely where marginal revenue equals marginal cost.

However, the firm also has to check that it should be in business at all. Given that it has chosen the most advantageous output level, is it making profits at this output? Or does it make losses at every output level, in which case the marginal condition has merely identified the least bad output to produce. It might be even better to give up completely and eventually make zero rather than lose money for ever.

Suppose Q^{**} is the output at which $LMC = MR$. If, at this output, the price for which this output can be sold (which we deduce from the demand curve) exceeds the average cost LAC of making this output, the firm is making permanent profits and should remain in the industry. However, if at the 'best' output Q^{**}, the firm is losing money because LAC exceeds the price for which Q^{**} can be sold, the firm is better off by closing down completely.

Notice the two-stage argument. First we use the *marginal condition* ($LMC = MR$) to find the best output, *then* we use the *average condition* (comparing LAC at this output with the price or average revenue) to determine whether the best output is good enough for the firm to stay in business in the long run. If the firm's best output yields losses, it should close down.

It is important to realize that the best output Q^{**} is not in general the same as the output Q^* in Figure 4-2 at which long-run average costs are minimized. Figure 4-2 is purely an analysis of costs. What the firm wishes to do depends both on costs and revenues. If demand is strong enough, it will be profitable to produce more than the minimum efficient scale Q^* because at this output level there are still further profits to be exploited by producing even more. Conversely, demand may be so weak that the firm chooses to produce less than minimum efficient scale. Any attempt to produce more would drive prices down too much. The firm would lose more from lower prices than it would gain from being able to reduce average costs. This completes our analysis of the long-run production decision.

Short-run costs and diminishing returns

In the short run, the firm has some fixed inputs.

A **fixed input** can't be varied in the short run. A **variable input** can be adjusted, even in the short run.

The short run varies from industry to industry. It may take ten years to build a new power station, but it took Jamie Oliver only weeks to open new restaurant premises. The existence of fixed inputs in the short run has two implications. First, in the short run the firm has some fixed costs, which must be paid even if output is zero. It has to honour the rental agreement for its premises even if it decides not to produce anything this month. Second, because the firm cannot make all the adjustments it would like, its short-run costs must exceed its long-run costs. If it behaves differently in the long run, this can only be because it prefers to switch to a cheaper production method once this opportunity arises.

Box 4-3   Sunk costs

If certain costs have *already* been incurred and can't be affected by your decision, ignore them. They shouldn't influence your future decisions. In deciding how much to produce in the short run, the firm ignores its fixed costs which must be incurred anyway.

It may seem a pity to abandon a project on which a lot of money has already been invested. Poker players call this throwing good money after bad. If you don't think it will be worth reading the rest of this book, you should not do it merely because you put a lot of effort into the first three chapters.

Variable costs are the costs of hiring variable factors, typically labour and raw materials. Although firms may have long-term contracts with workers and material suppliers, in practice most firms retain some flexibility through overtime and short time, hiring or non-hiring of casual and part-time workers, and raw material purchases in the open market to supplement contracted supplies.

Fixed costs don't vary with output levels. **Variable costs** change with output.

The short-run marginal cost curve *SMC* has the same general shape as the long-run marginal cost curve in Figure 4-2, but for a different reason. In the short run, there is at least one fixed factor, probably capital. As output rises – a firm moves along its *SMC* curve – it is adding ever-increasing amounts of labour to a given amount of plant and machinery.

The **marginal product** of a variable input (labour) is the *extra* output from *adding* 1 unit of the variable input, holding constant the quantity of all other inputs (capital, land, energy) in the short run.

The first worker has a whole factory to work with and has too many jobs to produce much. A second worker helps, a lot, and so does a third. Suppose the factory has three machines and the three workers are now specializing in each running one of the factory's machines. The marginal product of a fourth worker is lower. With only three machines, the fourth worker gets a machine only when another worker is resting. A fifth worker only makes tea for the other four. By now there are diminishing returns to labour.

Holding all factors constant except one, the **law of diminishing returns** says that, beyond some level of the variable input, further rises in the variable input steadily reduce its marginal product of that input.

Diminishing returns refer to adding a variable factor to fixed factors in the short run. *Decreasing* returns refer to diseconomies of scale when *all* factors are varied together in the long run.

Output is varied by using more labour input. Changes in the marginal product of labour affect the marginal cost of making output. The more productive a worker, the lower is the cost of making output. Figure 4-3 shows that, as output rises, short-run marginal costs initially fall as we move to the right along *SMC*; however, beyond some output, diminishing returns set in, additional workers add less and less to extra output, and hence marginal cost becomes higher and higher as the firm raises output further by adding to its variable labour input, but then rise. While the marginal product of labour is rising, each worker adds more to output than the previous workers, and marginal cost is falling.

Short-run marginal cost *SMC* is the extra cost of making one more unit of output in the short run while some inputs are fixed.

Once diminishing returns to labour set in, the marginal product of labour falls and *SMC* starts to rise again. It takes successively more workers to make each extra unit of output.

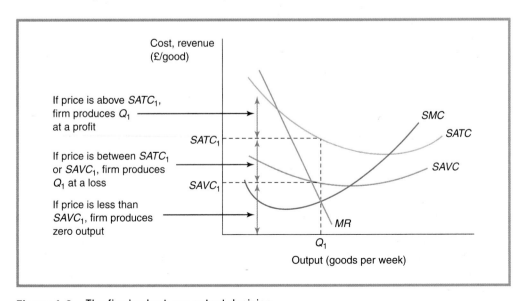

Figure 4-3 The firm's short-run output decision

Short-run average costs

Short-run **average fixed cost** is short-run fixed cost divided by output. **Short-run average variable cost** is short-run variable cost divided by output. **Short-run average total cost** is short-run total cost divided by output.

$$\begin{matrix} \text{Short-run} & & \text{short-run} & & \text{short-run} \\ \text{average total cost} & = & \text{average fixed cost} & + & \text{average variable cost} \\ (SATC) & & (SAFC) & & (SAVC) \end{matrix}$$

In Figure 4-3 the shape of the SMC curve reflects the behaviour of marginal labour productivity: beyond some output, diminishing returns to additional labour input make marginal cost rise as output rises. The usual arithmetic between marginal and average explains why SMC passes through the lowest point on the short-run average total cost curve. To the left of this point, SMC is below $SATC$, dragging it down as output expands. To the right of A, the converse holds.

Variable costs are total costs minus fixed costs. Fixed costs don't change with output, so marginal costs also show how much total *variable* costs are changing. The usual reasoning implies that SMC goes through the lowest point on $SAVC$. To the left of this point, SMC is below $SAVC$, so $SAVC$ is falling. To the right, $SAVC$ is rising. Total costs exceed variable costs, so $SAVC$ is below $SATC$.

A firm's supply decision in the short run

Figure 4-3 shows a firm's output choice in the short run. Profits are maximized by equating short-run marginal cost and marginal revenue at the output Q_1.

Next, the firm decides whether or not to stay in business in the short run. Profits are positive at the output Q_1 if the price p for which this output is sold covers average total costs. If p exceeds $SATC_1$, the firm makes profits in the short run and produces Q_1. To deduce the price p for which this output is sold, we need also to draw the demand curve in Figure 4-3. Exactly how demand curves relate to marginal revenue MR is the subject of the next chapter and a half. For the moment, just imagine that we could draw a demand curve in Figure 4-3 and hence deduce the price when output is Q_1.

Suppose this price p is less than $SATC_1$, average total cost at the best output the firm can choose. The firm loses money because p does not cover costs. In the long run a firm closes down if it keeps losing money. However, even at zero output the firm must pay the fixed costs in the short run. The firm thus has to calculate whether losses are bigger at an output of Q_1 or at zero output. If revenue exceeds *variable* cost, the firm earns something towards its fixed costs. The firm then makes Q_1 even if this may involve losses. If p is less than $SAVC_1$, the firm does not even recoup variables costs. It is then better to make zero.

A firm's short-run supply decision is to make Q_1, the output at which $MR = SMC$, provided the price covers short-run average variable cost $SAVC_1$ at this output. If the price is less than $SAVC_1$ the firm produces zero.

Table 4-1 summarizes the short-run and long-run output decisions of a firm.

Output decision	Marginal condition: output at which	Produce this output unless
Short-run	$MR = SMC$	$P < SAVC$; if so, shut down temporarily
Long-run	$MR = LMC$	$P < LAC$; if so, quit permanently

Table 4-1 A firm's supply decisions

Short-run and long-run costs

Even if losing money in the short run, a firm will stay in business if it at least covers its variable costs. In the long run it must cover all its costs to stay in business. A firm may reduce its costs in the long run, converting a short-run loss into a long-term profit. Figure 4-4 shows a U-shaped *LAC* curve. Each point on the curve shows the least-cost way to make that output once all factors of production can be varied.

Suppose 'plant' is the fixed factor in the short run. Each point on the *LAC* curve involves a particular input of plant. For that plant size, we can draw the short-run average total cost curve. The $SATC_1$ curve corresponds to a plant size at *A* on the *LAC* curve. The $SATC_2$ and $SATC_3$ curves correspond to the plant size at *B* and *C* on the *LAC* curve. We could draw an *SATC* curve for the plant size at each point on the *LAC* curve.

Since the *LAC* curve is the least-cost way to make each output, point *B* shows the minimum average-cost way to make an output Q_2. Hence it *must* be more costly to make Q_2 using the wrong input of plant. For the plant size at *A*, $SATC_1$ shows the cost of making each output including Q_2. Hence $SATC_1$ lies above *LAC* at every point except *A*, the output at which this plant size is best.

This argument can be repeated for any other plant size. Hence $SATC_3$ and $SATC_4$, corresponding to plant sizes at *C* and at *D*, must lie above *LAC* except at points *C* and *D* themselves. In the long run the firm can vary all inputs and can generally make a particular output

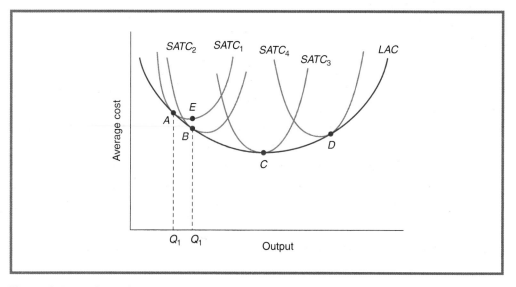

Figure 4-4 *LAC* and *SATC*

more cheaply than in the short run, when it inherits quantities of some fixed factors from previous decisions. A firm currently making losses because demand has fallen may be able to anticipate future profits once it can adjust plant size to its new output.

Case study 4-1   Steel here?

Twenty-five years ago, British Steel was a state-owned monopoly, selling largely in the UK. Since then, three things have happened. First, the firm was privatized. Second, its market became global, in which British Steel was a relatively small player. Third, it decided to merge with a Dutch steel maker to form a new company, Corus. Even so, its UK plants continued to lose money. Partly, this reflected a continuing decline in UK demand for steel, shrunk as UK manufacturing as a whole has contracted. UK labour costs are now six times those in Brazil and ten times those in India, both countries now being capable of producing steel for the world market. If the UK wishes to be a high-wage producer within the global economy, it needs either to have massive investment to make UK factories ultramodern and technically sophisticated or else recognise that more basic production will be undertaken in lower-wage countries than the UK. Corus had to move upmarket into the niche of providing hi-tech steel that drew on the UK's science and technology base. But this entailed shutting down more basic capacity that was being outcompeted by cheaper producers abroad.

Steel factory
© Royalty-free/Corbis

As competitive pressures mounted, loss-making Corus faced the classic choice: undertake expensive investment to restore competitiveness, shut down temporarily and hope for better demand conditions in the future, or exit the industry in order to avoid making permanent losses. If you had been a shareholder, would you have thought it worth contributing more money in the hope of saving the business, or concluded that it was more prudent to allow Corus to contract, saving your money for other, more profitable ventures with a greater prospect of international success?

In 2001, Corus announced plans for 6000 job losses and the closure of 3 million tonnes of steel capacity. It was beginning to exit the industry. The UK government offered to pay half the wage bill of these workers for a year if their jobs could be saved. Effectively, the government was betting either that costs could be reduced if the company had longer to adjust, or that demand would somehow improve within a year. In retrospect, this optimism was unjustified. Corus continued to lose money and further job losses ensued.

Sometimes, the firms that survive are not those with the lowest costs but those with the deepest financial pockets and the best relationships with the shareholders and bankers. As China has continued its rapid industrialization, it is now buying vast quantities

Case study 4-1 *Continued*

of raw materials to fuel its continuing development. The result has been a dramatic upward shift in demand, and a corresponding rise in commodity prices, including the price of steel. Once Corus survived the tough years of 2000–03, its fortunes began to revive. Its uncompetitive capacity had been streamlined and reduced, it was focused increasingly on specialist steel, and it was able to raise prices by 10–20 per cent both because it was making higher-quality products and because the Chinese boost meant that world demand for steel rose by 8 per cent per annum during 2003–05. The table below shows the turnaround in output and profits.

Corus (£ billion)	2001	2002	2003	2004
Output and sales	7.7	7.2	8.0	9.3
Net profits	−0.4	−0.4	−0.2	0.4

Source: www.corus.group.com

4-2

Perfect competition

Learning outcomes

By the end of this section, you should understand:

- ◆ The concept of perfect competition
- ◆ Why a perfectly competitive firm's output equates price and marginal cost
- ◆ Incentives for entry and exit
- ◆ The supply curve of a perfectly competitive industry
- ◆ The effect of shifts in demand or costs

We now switch our attention from costs to revenue and demand, for which we need to know about the structure of the industry in which the firm operates. An industry is the set of all firms making the same product. The output of an industry is the sum of the outputs of its firms. Yet different industries have very different numbers of firms. The UK has thousands of florists but only one producer of nuclear energy.

We begin with perfect competition, a hypothetical benchmark against which to assess other market structures.

In **perfect competition**, actions of individual buyers and sellers have no effect on the market price.

This industry has many buyers and many sellers. Each firm in a perfectly competitive industry faces a horizontal demand curve, shown in Figure 4-5. Whatever output q the firm sells, it gets exactly the market price P_0, and the tiny firm can sell as much as it wants at this price. If it charges more than P_0, the firm loses all its customers. If it charges less than P_0, it attracts all the vast number of customers of other firms. This horizontal demand curve is *the* crucial feature of a perfectly competitive firm. We sometimes say such a firm is a *price taker*. It has to treat the market price as given, independent of any decisions made by the individual firm. Next time you visit a fruit market, in which there are many stalls selling identical onions, you can think of each stall as a price taker in the market for onions.

For each firm to face a horizontal demand curve, the industry must have four characteristics. First, there must be many firms, each trivial relative to the industry as a whole. Second, the firms must make a standardized product, so that buyers immediately switch from one firm to another if there is any difference in the prices of different firms. Thus, all firms make essentially the same product, *for which they all charge the same price*.

Why don't all the firms in the industry do what OPEC did, collectively restricting supply to raise the market price of their output? A crucial characteristic of a perfectly competitive industry is *free entry and exit*. Even if existing firms could organize themselves to restrict total supply and drive up the market price, the consequent rise in revenues and profits would attract new firms into the industry, raising total supply and driving the price back

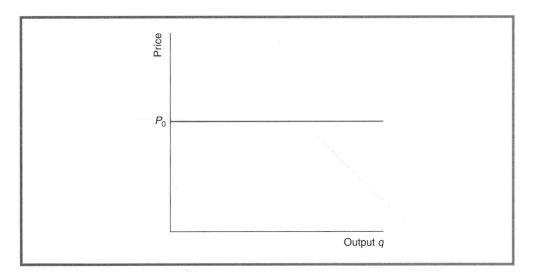

Figure 4-5 A horizontal demand curve

down. Conversely, when firms in a perfectly competitive industry are losing money, some firms close down. This reduces total supply and drives the price up, allowing the remaining firms to survive.

The firm's supply decision

We have already developed a general theory of the supply decision of a firm. First, the firm uses the marginal condition ($MC = MR$) to find the best positive level of output; then it uses the average condition to check whether the price for which this output is sold covers average cost. *The special feature of perfect competition is the relationship between marginal revenue and price.* Facing a horizontal demand curve, a competitive firm does *not* bid down the price as it sells more units of output. Since there is no effect on the revenue from existing output, the marginal revenue from an additional unit of output *is* its price: $MR = P$.

The firm's short-run supply curve

Firms in any industry choose the output at which short-run marginal cost *SMC* equals marginal revenue *MR*. In perfect competition, *MR* always equals the price *P*. Hence, a competitive firm produces the output at which price equals marginal cost, then checks whether zero output is better.

Figure 4-6 illustrates the firm's supply decision in the short run. P_1 is the shutdown price below which the firm fails to cover variable costs in the short run. At all prices above P_1, the firm chooses output to make $P = SMC$.

A competitive firm's **short-run supply curve** is that part of its short-run marginal cost curve above its shutdown price.

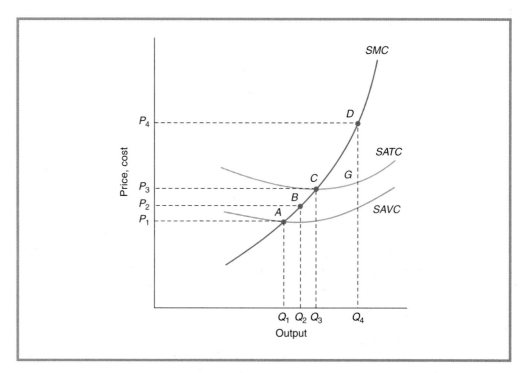

Figure 4-6   Short-run supply by perfectly competitive firm

This shows how much the firm wants to make at each price it might be offered. For example, at a price P_4, the firm chooses to supply Q_4.

The firm's long-run supply curve

Similar reasoning applies in the long run. Figure 4-7 shows the firm's average and marginal costs in the long run. Facing a price P_4, equating price and long-run marginal cost, the firm chooses the long-run output Q_4 at point D. In the long run, the firm exits from the industry only if, at its best positive output, price fails to cover long-run average cost LAC. At price P_2, the marginal condition leads to point B in Figure 4-7, but the firm is losing money and leaves the industry in the long run.

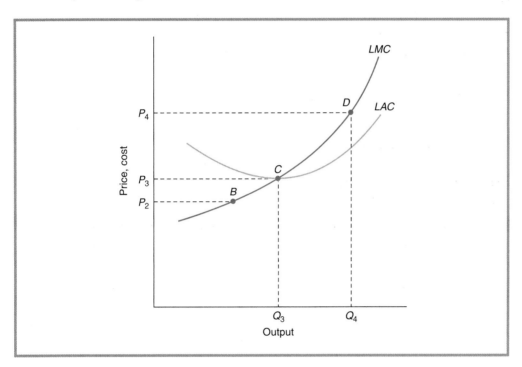

Figure 4-7 Long-run supply by perfectly competitive firm

A competitive firm's **long-run supply curve** is that part of its long-run marginal cost *above* minimum average cost. At any price below P_3, the firm leaves the industry. At price P_3, the firm makes Q_3 and just breaks even after paying all its economic costs.

Entry and exit

The price P_3 corresponding to the minimum point on the LAC curve is called the *entry or exit price*. There is no incentive to enter or leave the industry. The resources tied up in the firm are earning just as much as their opportunity costs — what they could earn elsewhere. Any price less than P_3 will induce the firm to exit from the industry in the long run.

Entry is when new firms join an industry. **Exit** is when existing firms leave.

We can also interpret Figure 4-7 as the decision facing a potential entrant to the industry. At a price P_3, an entrant could just cover its average cost if it produced an output Q_3. Any price above P_3 yields economic profits and induces entry by other firms in the long run.

Industry supply curves

A competitive industry comprises many firms. In the short run, two things are fixed: the quantity of fixed factors used by each firm, and the number of firms in the industry. In the long run, each firm can vary all its factors of production, but the number of firms can also change through entry and exit.

The short-run industry supply curve

Just as we can add individual demand curves by buyers to get the market demand curve, we can add the individual supply curves of firms to get the industry supply curve. In Figure 4-8, at each price we add together the quantities supplied by each firm to get the total quantity supplied at that price. In the short run the number of firms in the industry is given. Suppose there are two firms, A and B. Each firm's short-run supply curve is the part of its SMC curve above its shutdown price. Firm A has a lower shutdown price than firm B, perhaps because it has modern machinery. Each firm's supply curve is horizontal up to its shutdown price. At a lower price, no output is supplied.

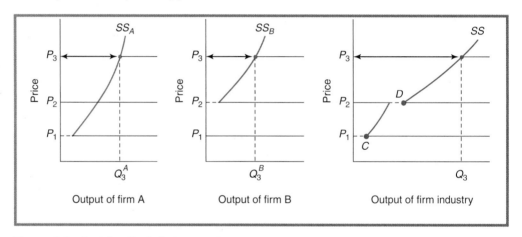

Figure 4-8 Deriving the industry supply curve

The industry supply curve is the horizontal sum of the separate supply curves. Between P_1 and P_2 only the lower-cost firm A is producing. At P_2, firm B starts to produce too. When there are many firms, each with a different shutdown price, there are many small discontinuities as we move up the industry supply curve. Since each firm in a competitive industry is trivial relative to the total, the industry supply curve is effectively smooth.

The long-run industry supply curve

As the market price rises, the total industry supply rises in the long run for two distinct reasons: each existing firm moves up its long-run supply curve, and new firms find it profitable to enter the industry. Thus, total quantity rises both because each existing firm makes additional output and because new firms enter the industry and produce. Conversely, at lower prices, all firms move down their long-run supply curves, producing less output because prices are lower, and some firms may also leave the industry because they can no longer break even at the lower prices.

At any price, the industry supply is the horizontal sum of the outputs produced by the number of firms in the industry at that price. Hence, the long-run supply curve is flatter than the short-run supply curve for two reasons: each firm can vary its factors more appropriately in the long run; and higher prices attract *extra* firms into the industry. Both raise the output response to a price increase.

For each firm, the height of the minimum point on its *LAC* curve shows the critical price at which it can just survive in the industry. If different firms have *LAC* curves of different heights, they face different exit prices. At any price, there is a marginal firm only just able to survive in the industry, and a marginal potential entrant just waiting to enter if only the price rises a little.

The *long-run* industry supply curve normally slopes up, but in one special case it is horizontal. Suppose all existing firms and potential entrants have *identical cost curves*. In particular, they have the same long-run average cost curves *LAC* and thus the same price, shown as P_3 in Figure 4-7, at which they will enter or exit the industry in the long run. In this special case, if the market price ever exceeds P_3, new firms will enter the industry since they can make profits at any price above P_3. This flood of new entrants creates extra output, reduces scarcity, and bids down equilibrium prices until the price reverts to P_3, at which price there is no longer any incentive for firms to enter the industry. Conversely, if the price ever falls below this critical price, firms leave the industry, which makes output scarcer and raises the equilibrium price, until prices rise again to P_3, at which price there is no longer any pressure on firms to leave the industry.

Thus, in the long run, if all firms face identical cost curves, industry supply entails each individual firm producing at the output corresponding to the bottom of its average cost curve, and changes in industry output would be entirely accomplished by changes in the number of firms, via entry and exit. The industry supply curve in the long run is then *horizontal* at price P_3 corresponding to minimum average cost.

But this is a very special case. Normally, firms will have slightly different cost curves from one another for a whole host of reasons – differences in location, in expertise and knowledge, in materials. Perfect competition does not require that firms are identical, merely that each firm is tiny relative to the market as a whole. Once firms are different, there is no possibility of expanding industry output indefinitely merely by attracting yet more of these identical firms.

On the plausible assumption that the lowest-cost producers are *already* in the market, inducing a rise in the quantity that an industry supplies generally requires higher prices, for two reasons: to induce existing firms to move along upward-sloping *LMC* curves and to attract new firms able at least to break even now that prices are higher than previously. Saying that higher prices are needed to induce the industry to supply more output is just to say that the industry supply curve slopes upwards.

Equilibrium in a competitive industry

Although each individual firm faces a horizontal demand curve for its output, the industry as a whole faces a downward-sloping demand curve for its total output. People will only buy a larger quantity if the price is lower. To induce people as a whole to buy more flowers from flower stalls, the price of flowers needs to fall. Only then will romantic partners buy fewer boxes of chocolates and instead take home more roses for Valentine's Day.

Industry demand obeys the general laws of demand that we discussed in Chapter 2. Having now also discussed the industry supply curve, we can examine how supply and demand determine equilibrium price in the short run and the long run in a perfectly competitive industry.

In short-run equilibrium, the market price equates the quantity demanded to the total quantity supplied by the given number of firms in the industry when each firm produces on its short-run supply curve. In long-run equilibrium, the market price equates the quantity demanded to the total quantity supplied by the number of firms in the industry when each firm produces on its long-run supply curve. Since firms can freely enter or exit from the industry, the marginal firm must make only normal profits so that there is no further incentive for entry or exit.

Figure 4-9 shows long-run equilibrium for the industry. Demand is *DD* and supply is *SS*. At the equilibrium price P^*, the industry as a whole produces Q^*. This is the sum of the output of each tiny producer. At price P^*, the marginal firm is making q^* at minimum LAC and just breaks even. There is no incentive to enter or exit.

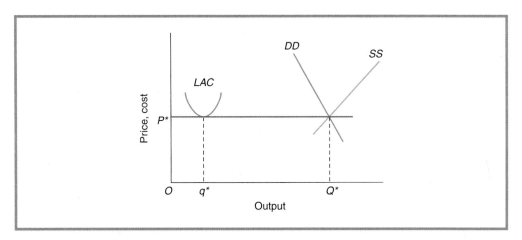

Figure 4-9 Long-run equilibrium

A rise in costs

Beginning from this equilibrium, suppose a rise in the price of raw materials raises costs for all firms in the industry. The average cost curve of every firm shifts up. The marginal firm is now losing money at the old price, P^*. Some firms eventually leave the industry. With fewer firms left, the industry supply curve SS shifts to the left. With less supply, the equilibrium price rises. When enough firms have left, and industry output falls enough, higher prices allow the new marginal firm to break even, despite an upward shift in *LAC*. Further incentives for entry or exit disappear.

Notice two points about the change in the long-run equilibrium that higher costs induce. First, the rise in average costs is eventually passed on to the consumer in higher prices. Second, since higher prices reduce the total quantity demanded, industry output must fall.

A rise in industry demand

The previous example discussed only long-term effects. We can of course discuss short-run effects as well. And we can examine changes in demand as well as changes in cost and

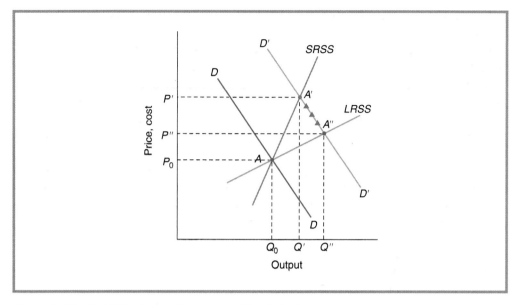

Figure 4-10 A shift in demand in a competitive industry

supply. Figure 4-10 illustrates the effect of a shift up in the industry's demand curve from DD to $D'D'$.

The industry begins in long-run equilibrium at A. Overnight, each firm has some fixed inputs, and the number of firms is fixed. Horizontally adding their short-run supply curves (the portion of their marginal cost curves above the shutdown price), we get the industry supply curve $SRSS$. The new short-run equilibrium is at A'. When demand first rises, it needs a big price rise to induce individual firms to move up their steep short-run supply curves, along which some inputs are fixed.

In the long run, firms adjust all factors and move on to their flatter long-run supply curves. In addition, economic profits attract extra firms into the industry. The new long-run equilibrium is at A''. Relative to A' there is a further expansion of total output, but, with a more appropriate choice of inputs and the entry of new firms, extra supply reduces the market-clearing price.

Case study 4-2   Globalization, potential competition, and price taking

The key feature of perfect competition is that each individual producer understands that it cannot affect the price by its production decisions. So what are these industries populated by trivially small firms? Some service industries provide good examples. There are no haircut hypermarkets. Most hairdressers are small because the technology does not yield large-scale producers any cost advantage. Because

Combine harvester
© Tom Bean/Corbis

Case study 4-2 *Continued*

each operates on a small scale, but the market in the aggregate is large, each is therefore small relative to the market as a whole.

Perfect competitors can be producers of goods as well as services. There are also lots of small sheep farmers, each with a small patch of hillside, and lots of car washes, each having to charge similar prices.

Farms cultivating wheat usually operate on a much larger scale nowadays. If there were only 100 UK wheat farmers, would this mean that they would no longer be price takers? Each is surely large enough to affect the price of UK wheat. Does this mean that wheat should not be viewed as a perfectly competitive industry? This argument would make sense if the UK did not trade with the rest of the world. But international trade is increasing all the time, as shown in the table below.

Imports as percentage of national output	1967	2003
Belgium	36	85
Netherlands	43	67
UK	18	28
France	14	29

UK firms have to compete not just with other UK firms but also with foreign firms who actually export to the UK or would like to do so. Potential entrants to the UK market are not merely UK firms but foreign firms that can sell to UK consumers not merely by building factories in the UK but simply by exporting goods from their factories abroad.

In theory, we could have a situation in which the entire UK market is supplied by a single UK firm but that firm is still a price taker, and has no effect on UK prices at all. Suppose the whole of Norfolk became a giant wheat field supplying wheat to every UK bakery. If this superfarm thinks it faces no competition, it will be tempted to raise prices in order to make larger profits. It will try to do to wheat what OPEC did to oil: harvest a little less, make the good more scarce, force up the price (as with oil, the demand for wheat is inelastic – we all need our daily bread). So the superfarm has a small bonfire of its wheat crop to make the remaining wheat scarce. Imagine its disappointment when it subsequently discovers that high wheat prices then induce a flood of wheat imports as French and German farmers see profitable opportunities to sell their wheat in the UK!

Perhaps in the original situation, the UK superfarm faced only slightly cheaper costs of supplying the UK market than the costs faced by French and German farmers. For example, the only difference arose from the slightly higher transport costs of bringing wheat through the Channel Tunnel. Once UK wheat prices rise by more than the initial cost advantage of UK producers, suddenly there is a flood of new supply from abroad.

The more globalization takes place – national markets are increasingly integrated into a single world market – the more the relevant definition of the market is that global market itself and the prices that prevail in that market. We may therefore see situations

Case study 4-2   *Continued*

in which even large UK firms have little ability to affect the price of their output because these firms are tiny *relative to the world market that sets the price.*

The fact that a UK firm looks large relative to the size of the UK market may not be an indication that the industry cannot be perfectly competitive. When products are standardized and can be shipped relatively easily (and therefore cheaply) from one country to another, national prices may in fact be set by international market forces.

Recap

- In the long run, a firm can adjust all its inputs. In the short run, some inputs are fixed.
- The production function shows the most output obtained from particular quantities of inputs.
- The total cost curve reflects technology and input prices. The long-run total cost curve is the cheapest way to make each output level, when all inputs and the production technique are adjusted.
- Average cost is total cost divided by output. The long-run average cost curve *LAC* is typically U-shaped. There are economies of scale on the falling bit of the U. The rising part reflects diseconomies of scale.
- When marginal cost is below average cost, average cost is falling. When marginal cost is above average cost, average cost is rising. Average and marginal cost are equal only at the lowest point on the average cost curve.
- In the long run, the firm supplies the output at which long-run marginal cost *LMC* equals *MR* provided price covers *LAC* at that output. If price is lower, the firm goes out of business.
- The short-run marginal cost curve (*SMC*) rises because of diminishing returns to the variable input as output rises.
- Short-run average cost *SATC* is short-run average fixed costs (*SAFC*) plus short-run average variable costs (*SAVC*). The *SMC* curve cuts both the *SATC* and *SAVC* curves at their minimum points.
- The firm sets output in the short run to equate *SMC* and *MR*, provided price covers short-run average variable cost. In the short run the firm may produce at a loss if it recoups part of its fixed costs.
- The *LAC* curve is always below the *SATC* curve, except at the point where the two coincide. Hence, a firm can reduce costs in the long run if its inherited plant size in the short run is no longer appropriate.
- In a competitive industry, each buyer and seller is a price-taker, and cannot affect the market price.
- Perfect competition is most plausible when a large number of firms make a standard product, there is free entry and exit to the industry, and customers can easily verify that the products of different firms really are the same.

- For a competitive firm, marginal revenue and price coincide. Output is chosen to equate price to marginal cost. The firm's supply curve is its *SMC* curve above *SAVC*. At any lower price the firm temporarily shuts down. In the long run, the firm's supply curve is its *LMC* curve above its *LAC* curve. At any lower price the firm exits the industry.
- Adding, at each price, the quantities supplied by each firm, we get the industry supply curve. It is flatter in the long run both because each firm can fully adjust all factors and because the number of firms in the industry can vary.
- A rise in demand leads to a large price increase, but only a small rise in quantity. Existing firms move up their steep *SMC* curves. Price exceeds average costs. Profits attract new entrants. In the long run, output rises further but the price falls back a bit. In the long-run equilibrium, the marginal firm breaks even and there is no further change in the number of firms in the industry.
- A rise in costs for all firms reduces the industry's output and raises the price. In the long run, a higher price is needed to allow the firm that is now the marginal firm to break even. The price rise is achieved by exit from the industry, and a reduction in industry supply.

Review questions

1 (a) What does the production function tell a firm? (b) What other information is needed to run a firm?
2 (a) Why might scale economies exist? (b) The table shows some production techniques. The cost of a worker is £5. A unit of capital costs £2. Complete the table and calculate the least-cost way to make 4, 8, and 12 units of output. (c) Are there increasing, constant, or decreasing returns to scale in this output range? Which applies where?

Units of	Method 1	Method 2	Method 3	Method 4	Method 5	Method 6
Labour input	5	6	10	12	15	16
Capital input	4	2	7	4	11	8
Output	4	4	8	8	12	12
Total cost						
Average cost						

3 Suppose the cost of capital rises from 2 to 3 in the question above: (a) Would the firm change its method of production for any levels of output? Say which, if any. (b) How do the firm's total and average costs change when the cost of capital rises?
4 From the total cost curve shown below, calculate marginal and average cost at each output. Are these short-run or long-run cost curves? How can you tell?

Output	0	1	2	3	4	5	6	7	8
Total cost	12	25	40	51	60	70	84	98	120

5 Why does a marginal cost curve always pass through the minimum point on the average cost curve?

6 Why are these statements wrong? (a) Firms making losses should quit at once. (b) Big firms can always produce more cheaply than smaller firms. (c) Small is always beautiful.

7 The domestic economy has only one firm, but faces a flood of imports from abroad if it tries to charge more than the world price. Is this firm perfectly competitive?

8 Suppose an industry of identical competitive firms has a technical breakthrough that cuts costs for all firms. What happens in the short run and the long run? Explain for both the firm and the industry.

9 If every firm is a price-taker, who changes the price when a shift in demand causes initial disequilibrium?

10 Which industry has a more elastic long-run supply curve: coal mining or hairdressing? Why?

11 Since Ford and Vauxhall are very competitive with one another, should we view them as perfectly competitive firms?

12 Why are these statements wrong? (a) Since competitive firms break even in the long run, there is no incentive to be a competitive firm. (b) Competition prevents firms passing on cost increases.

Answers on pages 343–345

5

Market structure and imperfect competition

5-1

Pure monopoly

Learning outcomes

By the end of this section, you should understand:

- ◆ How a monopolist chooses output
- ◆ How this output compares with that in a competitive industry
- ◆ How a monopolist's ability to price discriminate affects output and profits

Having discussed perfect competition, we turn next to the opposite extreme, pure monopoly. Then we discuss other forms of imperfect competition. These are all different types of market structure. As you will see, the extent of competition between firms has a big effect on how firms behave and the decisions that they make.

The perfectly competitive firm is too small to worry about the effect of its own decisions on industry output. In contrast, a pure monopoly *is* the entire industry.

A monopolist is the sole supplier or potential supplier of the industry's output.

A sole national supplier need not be a monopoly. If it raises prices, it may face competition from imports or from domestic entrants to the industry. In contrast, a pure monopoly does *not* need to worry about competition from either existing firms or from firms that could enter.

Profit-maximizing output

To maximize profits, a monopolist chooses the output at which marginal revenue *MR* equals marginal cost *MC* then checks that it is covering average costs. Figure 5-1 shows the average cost curve *AC* with its usual U-shape.

Marginal revenue *MR* lies below the downward-sloping demand curve *DD*. The monopolist recognizes that, to sell extra units, it has to lower the price, even for existing customers. The more units the firm is already making and selling, the more any price reduction to sell a new unit has the effect of depressing revenue earned on existing units produced. Hence, as we move to the right and output increases, the marginal revenue schedule lies increasingly below the demand curve. Indeed, marginal revenue can become negative. In cutting the price to sell an additional output unit, the firm can lose more revenue on existing units than it gains in revenue by being able to sell an extra unit.

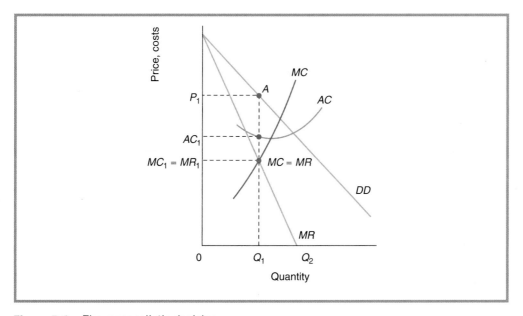

Figure 5-1 The monopolist's decision

It is implicit in this argument that the firm has to charge a single price to all purchasers, and therefore has to reduce the price for which existing units are sold in order to sell an extra unit by inducing buyers to move downwards along their demand curve. Later, we analyse what happens when the monopolist can charge different prices to different customers. Initially, however, we assume that this is impossible.

Any firm maximizes profits choosing the output at which marginal revenue MR equals marginal cost MC. In Figure 5-1 the monopolist thus chooses the output Q_1. The demand curve DD implies that the monopolist sells Q_1 at a price P_1 per unit. Profit per unit is thus $[P_1 - AC_1]$, price minus average cost at the output Q_1. Total profit is the area $(P_1 - AC_1) \times Q_1$.

Even in the long run, the monopolist *continues* to make these monopoly profits. By ruling out the possibility of entry, we remove the mechanism by which profits are competed away in the long run by additional supply.

Price-setting

A competitive firm is a *price-taker*, taking as given the price determined by supply and demand at the industry level. In contrast, the monopolist is a *price-setter*. Having decided to make Q_1, the monopolist quotes a price P_1 knowing (from the demand curve) that the output Q_1 will be bought at this price.

When demand is elastic, lower prices increase revenue by raising quantity demanded a lot. When revenue rises, the marginal revenue from the extra output is positive. Conversely, when demand is inelastic, marginal revenue is negative. To raise output demanded, prices must be cut so much that total revenue falls.

To maximize profits, a monopolist sets $MC = MR$. Since MC is always positive, MR must also be positive at the profit-maximizing output. But this means that demand is elastic at this output. Hence, in Figure 5-1, the chosen output must lie to the left of Q_2. *A monopolist will never produce on the inelastic part of the demand curve where* MR *is negative, for then* MR *could not equal* MC*, which can never be negative.*

Monopoly power

At any output, price exceeds a monopolist's marginal revenue since the demand curve slopes down. In setting $MR = MC$, the monopolist sets a price above marginal cost. In contrast, a competitive firm equates price and marginal cost, since its price is also its marginal revenue. A competitive firm cannot raise price above marginal cost. It has no monopoly power.

Monopoly power is measured by price *minus* marginal cost.

Changes in profit-maximizing output

Figure 5-1 may also be used to analyse the effect of changes in costs or demand. Suppose higher input prices shift the MC and AC curves up. The higher MC curve must cross the MR curve at a lower output. The cost increase must reduce output. Since the demand curve slopes down, lower output induces a higher equilibrium price.

Similarly, with the original cost curves, an upward shift in demand and marginal revenue curves means that MR now crosses MC at a higher output. The monopolist raises output.

Monopoly versus competition

We now compare a perfectly competitive industry with a monopoly. Facing the same demand and cost conditions, how would the *same* industry behave if it organized as a competitive industry or as a monopoly. Cost differences are often the reason why some industries become competitive while others become monopolies. Only in special circumstances could the same industry be either perfectly competitive or a monopolist.

One case in which the comparison makes sense is when an industry has lots of *identical* firms. From Chapter 4 we know that, as a competitive industry, its long-run supply curve *LRSS* is then horizontal. It can always expand or contract output by changing the number of firms, each producing at the bottom of its long-run average cost curve. If run as a competitive industry, long-run equilibrium occurs where this horizontal supply curve crosses the industry demand curve. In Figure 5-2 this occurs at A, where output is Q_C and the price P_C.

Now suppose two things happen. The different firms come under a single co-ordinated decision maker, and all future entry is prohibited. Perhaps the industry is nationalized (but told to keep maximizing profits). Long-run costs, both marginal and average, are unaffected, but now the industry supremo recognizes that higher output bids down prices for everyone.

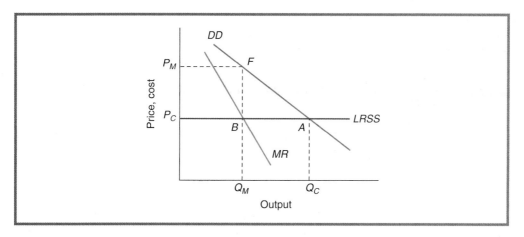

Figure 5-2 Comparing monopoly and perfect competition

In the special example, *LRSS* is also the marginal cost of output expansion by the multi-plant monopolist. In the long run the cheapest way to raise output is to build more of the identical plants, each operated at minimum average cost. Hence, equating marginal cost and marginal revenue, the multi-plant monopoly produces at B. Output Q_M is lower under monopoly than competition, and the price P_M is higher than the competitive price P_C.

The monopolist cuts output in order to create scarcity and raise the equilibrium price. In Figure 5-2 average cost and marginal cost are equal, since each plant is at the bottom of its *LAC* curve, where it crosses *LMC*. Hence, the monopolist's profits are the rectangle $P_M P_C BF$.

Without fear of entry, the consequent profits last forever. Notice the crucial role of blocking competition from entrants. Without this, the attempt to restrict output to raise prices is thwarted by a flood of output from new entrants.

Box 5-1 Barriers at the checkout

In 2004, the Morrisons supermarket chain finally completed its takeover of rival Safeways. At a stroke, Morrisons was catapulted from the supermarket minnow, with a 6 per cent market share, to a big league player with 17 per cent of the UK market; only marginally less than Sainsbury's, one-time leader of the supermarket industry.

The takeover of Safeways was contested, with Tesco, Asda, and Sainsbury's all mounting rival bids to Morrisons. At one stage, Philip Green, the owner of high-street retailer British Home Stores, also registered an interest in Safeways. Safeways was such an attractive target because it provided the last chance to enter the supermarket industry. Without access to land, and facing difficulty getting planning permission for new supermarkets, the only way in which to become a successful supermarket chain was to enter the industry by taking over a chain that already had all the distribution outlets required. With Safeways now in the hands of Morrisons, and the industry consolidated into large players, the next takeover is that much more difficult. The entry barriers are firmly up.

Discriminating monopoly

Thus far, all consumers were charged the same price. Unlike a competitive industry, where competition prevents any individual firm charging more than its competitors, a monopolist may be able to charge different prices to different customers.

A **discriminating monopoly** charges different prices to different buyers.

Consider an airline monopolizing flights between London and Rome. It has business customers whose demand curve is very inelastic. They have to fly. Their demand and marginal revenue curves are very steep. The airline also carries tourists whose demand curve is much more elastic. If flights to Rome are too dear, tourists can visit Athens instead. Tourists have much flatter demand and marginal revenue curves.

The airline will charge the two groups *different* prices. Since tourist demand is elastic, the airline wants to charge tourists a low fare to increase tourist revenue. Since business demand is inelastic, the airline wants to charge business travellers a high fare to increase business revenue.

Profit-maximizing output will satisfy two separate conditions. First, business travellers with inelastic demand will pay a fare sufficiently higher than tourists with elastic demand that the marginal revenue from the two separate groups is equated. Then there is no incentive to rearrange the mix by altering the price differential between the two groups. Second, the general level of prices and the total number of passengers are chosen to equate marginal cost to both these marginal revenues. This ensures that the airline operates on the most profitable scale as well as with the most profitable mix.

When a producer charges different customers different prices, we say it *price discriminates*. There are many examples in the real world. Rail operators charge rush-hour commuters a higher fare than midday shoppers whose demand for trips to the city is much more elastic.

Price discrimination often applies to services, which must be consumed on the spot, rather than to goods, which can be resold. Price discrimination in standardized goods won't work. The group buying at the lower price resells to the group paying the higher price, undercutting the price differences. Effective price discrimination requires that the submarkets can be isolated from one another to prevent resale.

Figure 5-3 illustrates *perfect price discrimination*, where it is possible to charge every customer a different price for the same good. If the monopolist charges every customer the same price, the profit-maximizing output is Q_1 where MR equals MC and the corresponding price is P_1.

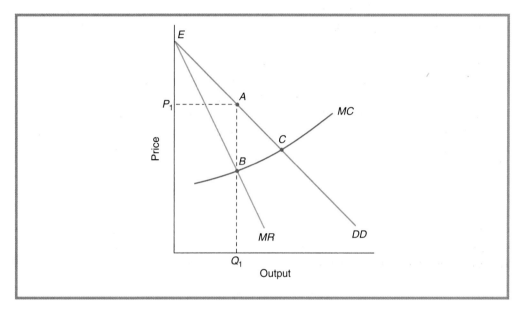

Figure 5-3   Perfect price discrimination

If the monopolist can perfectly price discriminate, the very first unit can be sold for a price E. Having sold this unit to the highest bidder, the customer most desperate for the good, the next unit is sold to the next highest bidder, and so on. In reducing the price to sell that extra unit, the monopolist no longer reduces revenue from previously sold units. The demand curve *is* the marginal revenue curve under perfect price discrimination. The marginal revenue of the last unit is simply the price for which it is sold.

A perfectly price discriminating monopolist produces at C where $MC = DD$, which is now marginal revenue. Price discrimination, if possible, is always profitable. In moving from the uniform pricing point A to the price discriminating point C, the monopolist adds the area ABC to profits. This is the excess of additional revenue over additional cost when output is higher.

The monopolist makes a second gain from price discrimination. Even the output Q_1 now brings in more revenue than under uniform pricing. The monopolist also gains the area EP_1A by charging different prices, rather than the single price P_1, on the first Q_1 units. Economic consultants often earn their fees by teaching firms new ways in which to price discriminate.

Notice too that whether or not the firm can price discriminate affects its chosen output by affecting its marginal revenue. In the extreme case, perfect price discrimination leads to the same price and output as under perfect competition, since in both cases the firm then sets $MC = MR = P$.

Monopoly and technical change

Joseph Schumpeter (1883–1950) argued that, even with uniform pricing, a monopoly may not produce a lower output and at a higher price than a competitive industry because the monopolist has more incentive to shift its cost curves down.

Technical advances reduce costs, and allow lower prices higher output. A monopoly has more incentive to undertake research and development (R&D), necessary for cost-saving breakthroughs.

In a competitive industry a firm with a technical advantage has only a temporary opportunity to earn high profits to recoup its research expenses. Imitation by existing firms and new entrants soon compete away its profits. In contrast, by shifting down all its cost curves, a monopoly can enjoy higher profits forever. Schumpeter argued that monopolies are more innovative than competitive industries. Taking a dynamic long-run view, rather than a snapshot static picture, monopolists may enjoy lower cost curves that lead them to charge lower prices, thereby raising the quantity demanded.

This argument has some substance, but may overstate the case. Most Western economies operate a *patent* system. Inventors of new processes acquire a *temporary* legal monopoly for a fixed period. By temporarily excluding entry and imitation, the patent laws increase the incentive to conduct R&D without establishing a monopoly in the long run. Over the patent life the inventor gets a higher price and makes handsome profits. Eventually the patent expires and competition from other firms leads to higher output and lower prices. The real price of copiers and micro computers fell significantly when the original patents of Xerox and IBM expired.

Case study 5-1   The value of a good patent

Why have food giants Unilever and Proctor & Gamble withdrawn from the espresso coffee business? Not because they don't know where to find good coffee or how to manufacture home espresso machines. Rather, they have been defeated by the series of patents taken out by Nestlé.

The best cup of coffee requires that all coffee grounds are the same size, are stored in containers that do not allow the coffee to oxidize before it is used, and that it is brewed in hot water of exactly the optimal temperature and pressure. Nestlé's patents

Espresso machine
© Royalty-free/Corbis

for grinding, packaging, and delivering coffee through their famous Nespresso system (now licenced and retailed by other brand names) have effectively wiped out the competition. Nestlé's patent lawyers managed to preempt the key processes so accurately that Nestlé's competitors gave up trying to challenge the Nestlé monopoly. Now they are simply waiting for the patents to expire. Patents have become a key part of competitive strategy in the knowledge economy.

Case study 5-1 *Continued*

You are probably aware of two other hotly contested patent issues in today's global economy.

The first is the patents of music companies such as EMI, who argued, successfully eventually, that Napster and other free Internet download music services were infringing the patent (usually called a copyright when it applies to music, writing, and the arts) that EMI held over the artistes that it had produced. Without such protection, there is no incentive to remain in the industry if all expensive investment never has any payback since Internet companies subsequently compete away all the profits. Foreseeing this, recording studios would go bankrupt and there would be no music for the Internet to download. This issue has now been resolved, and the music industry has received sufficient protection that it can now coexist with Napster and iPods, which have to pay a fee for the music to which they have access.

Another contentious issue is the price of drugs that combat HIV/Aids. Global pharmaceutical companies, such as GSK, Pfizer, and Merck, always argue that drug development is hugely costly, and that many drugs fail to succeed in the testing phase, so that the occasional winner has to earn lots of money to cover the cost of all the ones that fail, just as successful gamblers recognize that their winnings on the occasional horse that they pick has to cover all the losses on the plausible horses that nevertheless failed to win as expected. Yet poor countries, such as those in sub-Saharan Africa where HIV/Aids is a major social and economic problem, argue that they should not be forced to pay drug prices considerably in excess of current production costs merely so that pharmaceutical companies can repay their failed investment in other drugs that did not work out as planned.

Both sides of course are simultaneously correct. If pharmaceutical companies are deprived of profits on their winners, they will have to exit the industry since they will no longer be able to pay for their inevitable losers. Since the latter lose big, it also takes big winnings just to keep pharmaceutical companies in the industry. However, if they charge prices that poor Africans cannot afford, not only do many people find this ethically unattractive, it may even diminish the profits of drug companies themselves. You already know enough economics to appreciate that, if the world price of drugs is substantially above the current production cost, then even a lower price would yield a profit. If Africans could then afford to buy at this lower price, total drug company profits would rise *provided they did not have to reduce the price for which the drugs were sold in rich countries*. Hence, if all countries support this form of price discrimination – and if those allowed to import at lower prices undertake not to attempt to resell to richer countries at higher prices – poor countries will get the cheaper drugs that they need, and drug producers will find that they get the same revenue as before from the rich countries (where prices have not changed), plus some new sales to poor countries that were not taking place before because poor countries could not afford the high prices previously charged to them.

5-2

Imperfect competition and market structure

Learning outcomes

By the end of this section, you should understand:

- ◆ Imperfect competition and market power
- ◆ How differences in cost and demand affect market structure
- ◆ Monopolistic competition
- ◆ The tension between collusion and competition within a cartel
- ◆ Oligopoly and interdependence
- ◆ Games
- ◆ Commitment and credibility
- ◆ Why there is little market power in a contestable market
- ◆ Innocent entry barriers and strategic entry barriers

Perfect competition and pure monopoly are useful benchmarks of extreme kinds of market structure. Most markets lie between these two extremes. What determines the structure of a particular market? Why are there 10 000 florists but only a handful of chemical producers? How does the structure of an industry affect the behaviour of its constituent firms?

A perfectly competitive firm faces a horizontal demand curve at the going market price. It is a price-taker. Any other type of firm faces a downward-sloping demand curve for its product and is an *imperfectly competitive* firm.

An **imperfectly competitive** firm recognizes that its demand curve slopes down.

For a pure monopoly, the demand curve for the firm is the industry demand curve itself. We now distinguish two intermediate cases of an imperfectly competitive market structure.

An **oligopoly** is an industry with only a few, interdependent producers. An industry with **monopolistic competition** has many sellers making products that are close but not perfect substitutes for one another. Each firm then has a limited ability to affect its output price.

Table 5-1 offers an overview of market structure. As with most definitions, the distinctions can get a little blurred. How do we define the relevant market? Was British Gas a monopoly in gas or an oligopolist in energy? Similarly, when a country trades in a competitive world market, even the sole domestic producer may have little influence on market price.

Competition	Number of firms	Ability to affect price	Entry barrier	Example
Perfect	Many	Nil	None	Fruit stall
Imperfect:				
Monopolistic competition	Many	Small	None	Corner shop
Oligopoly	Few	Medium	Some	Cars
Monopoly	One	Large	Huge	Post Office

Table 5-1 Market structure

Why market structures differ

We now develop a general theory of how the economic factors of demand and cost interact to determine the likely structure of each industry. The car industry is not an oligopoly one day but perfectly competitive the next. It is long-run influences that induce different market structures. In the long run, one firm can hire another's workers and learn its technical secrets. In the long run, all firms or potential entrants to an industry essentially have similar cost curves.

Chapter 3 discussed minimum efficient scale MES, the lowest output at which a firm's long-run average cost curve bottoms out. When MES is tiny relative to the size of the market, there is room for lots of little firms, each trivial relative to the whole, a good approximation to perfect competition. Conversely, when MES occurs at an output nearly as large as the entire market, there is room for only one firm. A smaller firm trying to squeeze into the remaining space would be at too great a cost disadvantage because it enjoys inadequate scale economies.

A **natural monopoly** enjoys sufficient scale economies to have no fear of entry by others.

When *MES* occurs at, say, a quarter of the market size, the industry is an oligopoly, with each firm taking a keen interest in the behaviour of its small number of rivals. Monopolistic competition lies midway between oligopoly and perfect competition.

Monopolistic competition

The theory of monopolistic competition envisages a large number of quite small firms, each ignoring any impact its own decisions might have on the behaviour of other firms. There is free entry and exit from the industry in the long run. In these respects, the industry resembles *perfect* competition. What distinguishes monopolistic competition is that each firm faces a *downward*-sloping demand curve in its own little niche of the industry.

Different firms' products are only limited substitutes. An example is the location of corner grocers. A lower price attracts some customers from other shops, but each shop has some local customers for whom local convenience matters more than a few pence on the price of a jar of coffee. Monopolistically competitive industries exhibit *product differentiation*. For corner grocers, differentiation is based on location. In other cases, it reflects brand loyalty or personal relationships. A particular restaurant or hairdresser can charge a slightly different price from other producers in the industry without losing all its customers.

Monopolistic competition requires not merely product differentiation, but few economies of scale. Hence there are many small producers, ignoring their interdependence with their rivals. Many examples of monopolistic competition are service industries.

Each firm produces where its marginal cost equals marginal revenue. If firms make profits, new firms enter the industry. That is the competitive part of monopolistic competition. As a result of entry, the downward-sloping demand curve of each individual firm shifts to the left. For a given market demand curve, the market share of each firm falls. With lower demand but unchanged cost curves, each firm makes lower profits. Entry stops when enough firms have entered to bid profits down to zero for the marginal firm.

Figure 5-4 shows long-run equilibrium once there is no further incentive for entry or exit. Each individual firm's demand curve *DD* has shifted enough to the left to just be tangent to its *LAC* curve at the output q^* the firm is producing. Hence, it makes zero economic profits. Price P^* equals average cost. For a perfectly competitive firm, its horizontal demand curve would be tangent to *LAC* at the minimum point on the average cost curve. In contrast, the tangency for a monopolistic competitor lies to the left of this, with both demand and *LAC* sloping down. The firm chooses output such that marginal revenue equals long-run marginal cost. That is the monopolistic part of monopolistic competition.

Notice two things about the firm's long-run equilibrium. First, the firm is *not* producing at the lowest point on its average cost curve. It could reduce average costs by further expansion. However, its marginal revenue would be so low as to make this unprofitable.

Second, the firm has some monopoly power because of the special feature of its particular brand or location. Price exceeds marginal cost. Hence, firms are usually eager for new

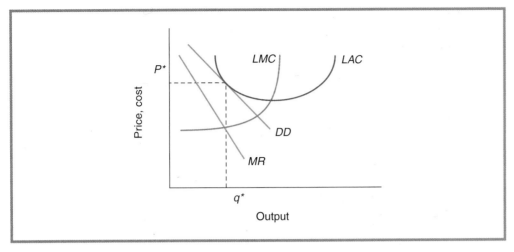

Figure 5-4 Tangency equilibrium in monopolistic competition

customers prepared to buy more output at the *existing* price. It explains why we are a race of eager sellers and coy buyers. It is purchasing agents who get Christmas presents from sales reps, not the other way round.

Oligopoly and interdependence

Under perfect competition or monopolistic competition, there are so many firms in the industry that no single firm need worry about the effect of its own actions on rival firms. The essence of an oligopoly is the need for each firm to consider how its actions affect the decisions of its relatively few rivals. The output decision of each firm depends on its guess about how its rivals will react. We begin with basic tension between competition and collusion in such situations.

Collusion is an explicit or implicit agreement between existing firms to avoid competition.

Initially, for simplicity, we ignore entry and exit, studying only the behaviour of existing firms.

The profits from collusion

The existing firms maximize their *joint* profits if they behave like a multi-plant monopolist. A sole decision-maker would organize industry output to maximize total profits. By colluding to behave like a monopolist, oligopolists maximize their *total* profit. There is then a backstage deal to divide up these profits between individual firms.

Having cut back industry output to the point at which $MC = MR < P$, each firm then faces a marginal profit $(P - MC)$ if it can expand a little more. Provided its partners continue to restrict output, each individual firm now wants to break the agreement and expand!

Oligopolists are torn between the desire to collude, thus maximizing joint profits, and the desire to compete, in the hope of increasing market share and profits at the expense of rivals. Yet if all firms compete, joint profits are low and no firm does very well.

Box 5-2 Double album

Sony Corporation and Bertelsmann unveiled plans for a joint venture to create one of the world's largest recorded music corporations. *Financial Times*, November 2003

Sony have 14 per cent of the global recorded music market, which added to Bertelsmann's 11 per cent means a quarter of the total. Only Universal Music (29 per cent), EMI (12 per cent), and Warner (12 per cent) have double-digit market shares. One reason for mergers is the pressure created by a shrinking global market, caused principally by Internet piracy. Sony and Bertelsmann hope that, by combining, they will not merely have opportunities to rationalize production and achieve greater scale economies, thereby lowering average costs, but also that their greater market power may allow them higher prices and profit margins too.

Cartels

Collusion between firms is easiest when formal agreements are legal. Such *cartels* were common in the late nineteenth century. They agreed market shares and prices in many industries. Such practices are now outlawed in Europe, the US, and many other countries. However, secret deals in smoke-filled rooms are not unknown even today.

The kinked demand curve

In the absence of collusion, each firm's demand curve depends on how competitors react. Firms must guess these reactions. Suppose that each firm believes that its own price cut will be matched by all other firms in the industry but that an increase in its own price will induce no price response from competitors.

Figure 5-5 shows the demand curve DD each firm then faces. At price P_0 the firm makes Q_0. Since competitors do not follow suit, a price rise leads to a big loss of market share to other firms. The firm's demand curve is elastic above A at prices above P_0. However, a price cut is matched by its rivals, and market shares are unchanged. Sales rise only because the industry as a whole moves down the market demand curve as prices fall. The demand curve DD is much less elastic for price reductions from the initial price P_0.

Thus, marginal revenue MR is discontinuous at Q_0. Below Q_0 the elastic part of the demand curve applies, but at Q_0 the firm hits the inelastic portion of its kinked demand curve and marginal revenue suddenly falls. Q_0 is the profit-maximizing output for the firm, given its belief about how competitors will respond.

The model has an important implication. Suppose the MC curve of a single firm shifts up or down by a small amount. Since the MR curve has a discontinuous vertical segment at the output Q_0, it remains optimal to make Q_0 and charge a price P_0. The kinked demand curve model may explain the empirical finding that firms do not always adjust prices when costs change.

It does not explain what determines the initial price P_0. It may be the collusive monopoly price. Each firm believes that an attempt to undercut its rivals induces them to cut

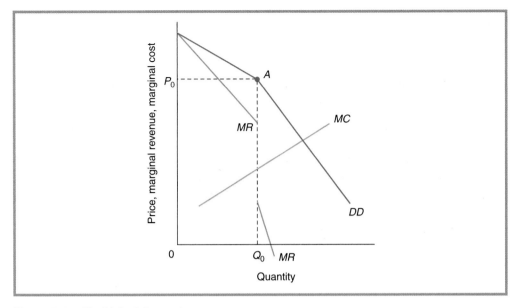

Figure 5-5   The kinked demand curve

prices to defend market share. However, its rivals are happy for it to charge a higher price and lose market share.

There is a difference between the effect of a cost change for a single firm and a cost change for all firms together. The latter shifts the marginal cost curve up for the industry as a whole, raising the collusive monopoly price. Each firm's kinked demand curve shifts up since the monopoly price P_0 rises. Thus, we can reconcile the stickiness of a single firm's prices with respect to changes in its own costs alone, and the speed with which the entire industry marks up prices when all firms' costs are increased by higher taxes or wage rises in the whole industry.

Game theory and interdependent decisions

A good poker player sometimes bluffs. Sometimes you make money with a bad hand that your opponents misread as a good hand. Like poker players, oligopolists have to try to second-guess their rivals' moves to determine their own best action. To study how interdependent decisions are made, we use *game theory*.

A **game** is a situation in which intelligent decisions are necessarily interdependent.

The *players* in the game try to maximize their own *pay-offs*. In an oligopoly, the firms are the players and their pay-offs are their profits in the long run. Each player must choose a strategy.

A **strategy** is a game plan describing how the player will act or **move** in each situation.

Being a pickpocket is a strategy. Lifting a particular wallet is a move. As usual, we are interested in equilibrium. In most games, each player's best strategy depends on the strategies chosen by other players. It is silly to be a pickpocket in a police station.

In **Nash equilibrium**, each player chooses his best strategy, *given* the strategies chosen by other players.

This description of equilibrium was invented by John Nash, who won the Nobel Prize for Economic Science for his work on game theory, and was the subject of the film *A Beautiful Mind*, starring Russell Crowe. Sometimes, but not usually, a player's best strategy is independent of those chosen by others. If so, it is a *dominant strategy*. We begin with an example in which each player has a dominant strategy.

Box 5-3   War games

Nintendo, Sony, and Microsoft have pitted their video game consoles against each other, fighting for a global industry now worth £12 billion a year. Sony spent £500 million in 2002 protecting its huge PlayStation franchise. Microsoft spent even more launching its Xbox. Merrill Lynch estimates that Nintendo's 2001 profits fell by a quarter because of money spent launching the GameCube. In the end Sony's PlayStation 2 won out, selling about 70 million units. While the battle has been interesting, the next generation of gaming (console and business based) is beginning. Sony has begun development of PlayStation 3 and is expected to sell 30 million units by 2010, a figure which should be more than the combined sales of XBox and Nintendo's Cube. Sony and Microsoft are rich and can afford price wars and software developments. Nintendo, with less financial muscle, is looking to stress the quality of its gaming experience.

Source: BBC Online, 9 March 2004

Collude or cheat?

Figure 5-6 shows a game[1] that we can imagine is between the only two members of a cartel like OPEC. Each firm can select a high-output or low-output strategy. In each box, the first number shows firm A's profits and the second number, firm B's profits for that output combination.

When both have high output, industry output is high, the price is low, and each firm makes a small profit of 1. When each has low output, the outcome is more like collusive monopoly. Prices are high and each firm does better, making a profit of 2. Each firm does best (a profit of 3) when it alone has high output; for, then, the other firm's low output helps hold down industry output and keep up the price. In this situation we assume the low-output firm makes a profit of 0.

Now we can see how the game will unfold. Consider firm A's decision. If firm B has a high-output strategy, firm A does better also to have high output. In the two left-hand boxes, firm A gets a profit of 1 by choosing high but a profit of 0 by choosing low. Now suppose firm B chooses a low-output strategy. From the two right-hand boxes, firm A still

---

[1] The game is called the Prisoners' Dilemma, because it was first used to analyse the choices facing two people arrested and in different cells, each of whom could plead guilty or not guilty to the only crime that had been committed. The penalties were such that each prisoner would plead innocent if only he or she knew the other would plead guilty.

		Firm B output	
		High	Low
Firm A output	High	1 1	3 0
	Low	0 3	2 2

Figure 5-6 The Prisoners' Dilemma game

does better by choosing high, since this yields it a profit of 3, whereas low yields it a profit of only 2. Hence firm A has a dominant strategy. Whichever strategy B adopts, A does better to choose a high-output strategy. Firm B also has a dominant strategy to choose high output. Check for yourself that B does better to go high whichever strategy A selects. Since both firms choose high, the equilibrium is the top left-hand box. Each firm gets a profit of 1.

Yet both firms would do better, getting a profit of 2, if they colluded to form a cartel and both produced low – the bottom right-hand box. But neither can afford to take the risk of going low. Suppose firm A goes low. Firm B, comparing the two boxes in the bottom row, will then go high, preferring a profit of 3 to a profit of 2. And firm A will get screwed, earning a profit of 0 in that event. Firm A can figure all this out in advance, which is why its dominant strategy is to go high.

This is a clear illustration of the tension between collusion and competition. In this example, it appears that the output-restricting cartel will never get formed, since each player can already foresee the overwhelming incentive for the other to cheat on such an arrangement. How then can cartels ever be sustained? One possibility is that there exist binding commitments.

A **commitment** is an arrangement, entered into voluntarily, that restricts one's future actions.

If both players could simultaneously sign an enforceable contract to produce low output they could achieve the co-operative outcome in the bottom right-hand box, each earning profits of 2. Clearly, they then do better than in the top left-hand box, which describes the non-cooperative equilibrium of the game. Without any commitment, neither player can go low because then the other player will go high. Binding commitments, by removing this temptation, enable both players to go low, and both players gain. This idea of commitment is important, and we shall meet it many times. Just think of all the human activities that are the subject of legal contracts, a simple kind of commitment simultaneously undertaken by two parties or players.

This insight is powerful, but its application to oligopoly requires some care. Cartels within a country are illegal, and OPEC is not held together by a signed agreement that can be upheld in international law! Is there a less formal way in which oligopolists can commit themselves not to cheat on the collusive low-output solution to the game? If the game is played only once, this is hard. However, in the real world, the game is repeated many times: firms choose output levels day after day. Suppose two players try to collude on low output. Furthermore, each announces a *punishment strategy*. Should firm A ever cheat on the low-output agreement, firm B promises that it will subsequently react by raising its output. Firm A makes a similar promise.

Suppose the agreement has been in force for some time, and both firms have stuck to their low-output deal. Firm A assumes that firm B will go low as usual. Figure 5-6 shows that firm A will make a *temporary* gain today if it cheats and goes high. Instead of staying in the bottom right-hand box with a profit of 2, it can move to the top right-hand box and make 3. However, from tomorrow onwards, firm B will also go high, and firm A can then do no better than continue to go high too, making a profit of 1 for evermore.

However, if A refuses to cheat today it can continue to stay in the bottom right-hand box and make 2 forever. In cheating, A swaps a temporary gain for permanently lower profits. Thus, punishment strategies can sustain an explicit cartel or implicit collusion even if no formal commitment exists.

It is easy to say that you will adopt a punishment strategy in the event that the other player cheats; but this will affect the other player's behaviour only if your threat is credible.

A **credible threat** is one that, after the fact, it is still optimal to carry out.

In the preceding example, once firm A cheats and goes high, it is then in firm B's interest to go high anyway. Hence B's threat to go high if A ever cheats is a credible threat.

Entry and potential competition

So far we have discussed imperfect competition between existing firms. What about potential competition from new entrants? Three cases must be distinguished: where entry is trivially easy, where it is difficult by accident, and where it is difficult by design.

Contestable markets

Suppose we see an industry with few incumbent firms. Before assuming it is an oligopoly, we must think about entry and exit.

A **contestable market** has free entry and free exit.

Free exit means that there are no *sunk* or irrecoverable costs. On exit, a firm can fully recoup its previous investment expenditure, including money spent on building up knowledge and goodwill. A contestable market allows *hit-and-run* entry. If the incumbent firms, however few, are pricing above minimum average cost, an entrant can step in, undercut them, make a temporary profit, and exit. If so, even when incumbent firms are few in number, they have to behave as if they were perfectly competitive, setting $P = MC = AC$.

The theory of contestable markets is controversial. There are many industries in which sunk costs are hard to recover, or where expertise takes an entrant time to acquire. Nor is it safe to assume that incumbents will not change their behaviour when threatened by entry. But the theory does vividly illustrate that market structure and incumbent behaviour cannot be deduced by counting the number of firms in the industry. We were careful to stress that a monopolist is a sole producer *who can completely discount fear of entry*.

Innocent entry barriers

Entry barriers may be created by nature or by other rivals.

> An **innocent entry barrier** is one made by nature.

Absolute cost advantages, where incumbent firms have lower cost curves than entrants, may be innocent. If it takes time to learn the business, incumbents have lower costs in the short run.

Scale economies are another innocent entry barrier. If minimum efficient scale is large relative to market size, an entrant cannot get into the industry without considerably depressing the price. It may be impossible to break in at a profit. The greater the innocent entry barriers, the more we can neglect potential competition from entrants. The oligopoly game then reduces to competition between incumbent firms as we discussed in the previous section.

Where innocent entry barriers are low, incumbent firms may accept this situation, in which case competition from potential entrants prevents incumbent firms from exercising much market power, or else incumbent firms will try to design some entry barrier of their own.

Strategic entry deterrence

The word 'strategic' has a precise meaning in economics.

> Your **strategic move** influences the other player's decision, in a manner helpful to you, by affecting the other person's expectations of how you will behave.

Suppose you are the only incumbent firm. Even if limited scale economies make it feasible for entrants to produce on a small scale, you threaten to flood the market if they come in, causing a price fall and big losses for everyone. Since you have a fat bank balance and they are just getting started, they will go bankrupt. Entry is pointless. You get the monopoly profits. But is your threat credible? Without spare capacity, how can you make extra output to bid down the price a lot.

Seeing this, the potential entrant may call your bluff. Suppose, instead, you build a costly new factory which is unused unless there is no entry. If, at some future date, an entrant appears, the cost of the new factory has largely been paid, and its marginal cost of production is low. The entrant succumbs to your credible threat to flood the market and decides to stay out. Provided the initial cost of the factory (spread suitably over a number of years) is less than the extra profits the incumbent keeps making *as a result of having deterred entry*, this entry deterrence is profitable. It is strategic because it works by influencing the decision of *another* player.

> **Strategic entry deterrence** is behaviour by incumbent firms to make entry less likely.

Is spare capacity the only commitment available to incumbents? Commitments must be irreversible, otherwise they are an empty threat; and they must increase the chances that the incumbent will fight. Anything with the character of fixed and sunk costs may work. Fixed costs artificially increase scale economies, and sunk costs have already been incurred.

Box 5-4   Freezing out new entrants?

Unilever is a major player in many consumer products from toothpaste to soap powder. One of its big winners is Wall's ice cream, which has two-thirds of the UK market and generates profits of £100 million a year; retailers' mark-ups can also be as high as 55 per cent. In addition to established rivals such as Nestlé (www.nestle.com) and Haagen Dazs, Unilever has faced new challenges from frozen chocolate bars such as Mars.

A critical aspect of these 'bar wars' is the freezer cabinets in which small shops store ice cream. As the leading incumbent, Unilever 'loaned' cabinets free of charge to small retailers. Unilever contended that its high market share reflected its marketing expertise (just one Cornetto); Mars argued that Unilever erected strategic barriers to entry, particularly effective in small shops with space for only one freezer cabinet, by requiring that only Unilever products were stocked in the cabinet they loaned to retailers. In January 2000, the UK government ordered Unilever to stop freezing out competitors.

Advertising to invest in goodwill and brand loyalty is a good example. So is product proliferation. If the incumbent has only one brand, an entrant may hope to break in with a different brand. If the incumbent has a complete range of brands or models, however, an incumbent will have to compete across the whole product range. Sometimes deterring entry costs incumbents too much money. Entry will then take place, as in the example of monopolistic competition.

Summing up

Few industries in the real world closely resemble the textbook extremes of perfect competition or pure monopoly. Most are imperfectly competitive. Game theory in general, and notions such as commitment, credibility, and deterrence, let economists analyse many of the practical concerns of big business.

What have we learned? First, market structure and the behaviour of incumbent firms are determined *simultaneously*. At the beginning of the section, we argued that the relation between minimum efficient scale and market size would determine market structure, whether the industry was a monopoly, oligopoly, or displayed monopolistic or perfect competition. However, these are not merely questions of the extent of innocent entry barriers. Strategic behaviour can also affect the shape of cost curves and the market structure that emerges.

Second, and related, we have learned the importance of *potential* competition, which may come from domestic firms considering entry, or from imports from abroad. The number of firms observed in the industry today conveys little information about the extent of the market power they truly exercise.

Finally, we have seen how many business practices of the real world – price wars, advertising, brand proliferation, excess capacity, or excessive research and development – can be understood as strategic competition in which, to be effective, threats must be made credible by commitments.

Case study 5-2   Why advertise so much?

Evan Davis is the BBC's Economics Correspondent. John Kay writes a fortnightly column on corporate strategy for the *Financial Times*. This case study is based on work they did together at the London Business School over 15 years ago, but still just as relevant today.

Advertising is not always meant to erect entry barriers to potential entrants. Sometimes, it really does aim to inform consumers by revealing inside information that firms have about the quality of their own goods.

When consumers can tell at a glance the quality of a product, even before buying it, there is little gain from advertising. Black rotten bananas cannot convincingly be portrayed as fresh and delicious. Information is freely available and attempts to deceive consumers are detected rapidly. However, for most goods, consumers cannot detect quality before purchase, and gradually discover quality only after using the good for a while.

The producer then has inside information over first-time buyers. A conspicuous (expensive) advertising campaign *signals* to potential buyers that the firm believes in its product and expects to make enough repeat sales to recoup the cost of the initial investment in advertising. Firms whose lies are quickly discovered by consumers do not invest much in advertising because they never sell enough to recoup their outlay on adverts. Consumers discover the poor quality and refrain from repeat purchasing. Foreseeing this, the firm that knows it will be quickly discovered never wastes money on expensive advertising in the first place.

What about one-off purchases, such as refrigerators, that usually last a decade or more. Consumers would really benefit from truthful advertising but producers of high-quality goods have no incentive to advertise. It would pay producers of low-quality refrigerators to advertise too since it would be ages before gullible consumers needed to return for a repeat purchase. A willingness to advertise no longer signals how much the firm believes in its own product. Since high-quality firms do not bother advertising, and since low-quality firms mimic the behaviour of high-quality firms, low-quality firms do not advertise either.

The table below shows advertising spending as a fraction of sales revenue for the three types of good identified above. The theory fits the facts well.

Quality detected	Time till buy again	Example	Advertising as percentage of sales revenue
Before buy	Irrelevant	Bananas	0.4
Soon after buy	Soon	Biscuits	3.6
Long after buy	Much later	Refrigerator	1.8

Source: E. Davis, J. Kay, J. Star 'Is Advertising rational?', *Business Strategy Review*, 1991, Oxford University Press

Recap

- A pure monopoly is the only seller or potential seller in an industry.
- To maximize profits, it chooses the output at which $MC = MR$. The relation of price to MR depends on the elasticity of the demand curve.
- A monopolist cuts back output to force up the price. The gap between price and marginal cost is a measure of monopoly power.
- A discriminating monopoly charges higher prices to customers whose demand is more inelastic.
- Monopolies have more ability and incentive to innovate. In the long run, this is a force for cost reduction. Temporary patents achieve some of the same effect even in competitive industries.
- Imperfect competition exists when individual firms face downward-sloping demand curves.
- When minimum efficient scale is very large relative to the industry demand curve, this innocent entry barrier may produce a natural monopoly in which entry can be ignored.
- At the opposite extreme, entry and exit may be costless. The market is contestable, and incumbent firms must mimic perfectly competitive behaviour, or be undercut by a flood of entrants.
- Monopolistic competitors face free entry and exit, but are individually small and make similar though not identical products. Each has limited monopoly power in its special brand. In long-run equilibrium, price equals average cost. Each firm's downward-sloping demand curve is tangent to the downward-sloping part of its LAC curve.
- Oligopolists face a tension between collusion to maximize joint profits and competition for a larger share of smaller joint profits. Without credible threats of punishment by other collusive partners, each firm is tempted to cheat.
- Game theory describes interdependent decision making. In the Prisoners' Dilemma game, each firm has a dominant strategy but the outcome is disadvantageous to both players. With binding commitments, both are better off by guaranteeing not to cheat on the collusive solution.
- In Nash equilibrium, each player selects her best strategy, given the strategies selected by rivals.
- Innocent entry barriers are made by nature, and arise from scale economies or absolute cost advantages of incumbent firms. Strategic entry barriers are made in boardrooms and arise from credible commitments to resist entry if challenged.

Review questions

1 A monopolist produces at constant marginal cost of £5 and faces the following demand curve:

Price (£)	9	8	7	6	5	4	3	2	1	0
Quantity	0	1	2	3	4	5	6	7	8	9

Calculate the MR curve. What is the equilibrium output? Equilibrium price? What would be the equilibrium price and output for a competitive industry? Why does the monopolist make less output and charge a higher price.

2 In addition to the data above, the monopolist also has a fixed cost of £2. What difference does this make to the monopolist's output, price, and profits? Why?

3 Now suppose the government levies a monopoly tax, taking half the monopolist's profit. (a) What effect does this have on the monopolist's output? (b) What was the marginal profit on the last unit of output before the tax was levied? (c) Does this help you answer (a)?

4 Why do golf clubs have off-peak membership at reduced fees?

5 Why might a monopoly have more incentive to innovate than a competitive firm? Could a monopoly have less incentive to innovate?

6 Why are these statements wrong? (a) By breaking up monopolies we always get more output at a lower price. (b) A single producer in the industry is a sure sign of monopoly.

7 An industry faces the demand curve:

Q	1	2	3	4	5	6	7	8	9	10
P	10	9	8	7	6	5	4	3	2	1

(a) As a monopoly, with MC=3, what price and output are chosen? (b) Now suppose there are two firms, each with MC=AC=3. What price and output maximize joint profits if they collude? (c) Why do the two firms have to agree on the output each produces? Why might each firm be tempted to cheat?

8 With the above industry demand curve, two firms, A and Z, begin with half the market each when charging the monopoly price. Z decides to cheat and believes A will stick to its old output level. (a) Show the demand curve Z believes it faces. (b) What price and output would Z then choose?

9 Vehicle repairers sometimes suggested that mechanics should be licensed so that repairs are done only by qualified people. (a) Evaluate the arguments for and against licensing car mechanics. (b) Are the arguments the same for licensing doctors?

10 A good-natured parent knows that children sometimes need to be punished, but also knows that, when it comes to the crunch, the child will be let off with a warning. Can the parent undertake any pre-commitment to make the threat of punishment credible?

11 Why are these statements wrong? (a) Competitive firms should collude to restrict output and drive up the price. (b) Firms would not advertise unless it increased their sales.

Answers on pages 345–346

6

Input markets and income distribution

6-1

The labour market

Learning outcomes

By the end of this section, you should understand:

- ◆ The demand for labour
- ◆ Labour supply and work incentives
- ◆ Why poverty traps arise
- ◆ What determines wages and employment
- ◆ Why David Beckham and Robbie Williams earn so much

We turn now from markets for output to markets for the inputs from which output is produced. With a few minor modifications, the tools we have developed over the last four chapters can be used to analyse input markets too.

In winning a tournament, Tiger Woods earns more in a weekend than a professor earns in a year. Students studying economics can expect to earn more than students studying philosophy. An unskilled worker in the EU earns more than an unskilled worker in India. Each of these outcomes reflects the supply and demand for that particular type of labour.

The demand for labour

By a single firm, in the long run

A firm's demand for inputs depends on the technology it faces, the price of each input, and demand for its output. Technology and input prices determine its costs. Demand determines the revenue from sales. The chosen output equates marginal cost and marginal revenue. In so doing, it determines the inputs that the firm demands.

In the long run a firm can adjust its inputs and the technique it uses to produce output. If the wage rises, the firm substitutes away from labour towards capital that is now relatively cheaper than before. Mechanized farming economizes on costly workers in the UK. However, with cheap abundant labour but scarce and expensive capital, Indian farmers use labour-intensive techniques.

At a given output, a higher wage makes a firm demand less labour and more of its other inputs. However, by raising the cost of making output, a higher wage also reduces the firm's chosen output level. This reduces the firm's demand for *all* inputs. In the long run, both effects reduce the quantity of labour demanded when the wage rises.

The effect of a higher wage on the demand for *other* inputs is ambiguous. The demand for capital rises as firms substitute away from labour, but lower output reduces the demand for capital input.

Similarly, a higher price of capital reduces the demand for capital. Firms substitute away from capital, and lower output also reduces the demand for capital. However, if the substitution effect is strong, the demand for labour may rise, despite lower output.

In the short run

In the short run, the firm has some fixed inputs. Suppose capital and land are fixed, and we view labour as the input that can be varied.

The **marginal product of labour** *MPL* is the extra physical output when a worker is added, holding other inputs constant.

Beyond some point, the *diminishing marginal productivity* of labour sets in. With existing machines fully utilized, there is less and less for each new worker to do, and the marginal product of labour falls. However, profits depend on revenue not just on physical output.

The **marginal revenue product of labour** *MRPL* is the change in sales revenue when an extra worker's output is sold.

Thus, *MRPL* is the marginal benefit of hiring an extra worker. If the firm is perfectly competitive, it can sell more output without affecting its output price. *MRPL* is then simply *MPL* multiplied by the output price. Figure 6-1 shows the marginal revenue product of labour for a competitive firm. It slopes down because of diminishing marginal productivity. The wage is the marginal cost of hiring another worker. The firm expands workers until the marginal cost of another worker equals the marginal benefit. At a wage W_0, the firm hires N_0 workers. At a wage W_1, the firm hires N_1 workers.

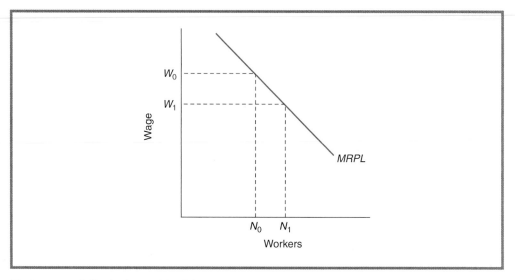

Figure 6-1   A firm's demand for labour

Thus, $MRPL$ is the demand curve for labour for a competitive firm, showing how many workers it hires at each wage. It measures the marginal benefit of having another worker. Moving down this schedule shows how the desired quantity of employment by the firm rises as the wage falls.

This theory is easily amended when the firm has *monopoly power* in its output market (a downward-sloping demand curve for its product) or *monopsony power* in its input markets (an upward-sloping supply curve for inputs because the firm's large scale affects the price of inputs).

A **monopsonist** must raise the wage to attract extra labour.

The marginal cost of an extra worker exceeds the wage paid to that worker: if all workers must get the same wage, extra hiring also bids up the wage paid to the existing labour force.

Similarly, for a firm with monopoly power in its output market, the $MRPL$ schedule is no longer the marginal product of labour multiplied by the output price. To sell extra output, facing a downward-sloping demand curve the firm must cut its output price, even on existing output. To calculate the marginal revenue product of labour, it finds the marginal product of labour MPL, then calculates the change in total revenue when it sells the extra output.

Figure 6-2 shows the schedules $MRPL_1$ and $MRPL_2$ for two firms with the same technology. Both schedules reflect diminishing marginal productivity – a property of technology – but $MRPL_2$ is steeper because an imperfectly competitive firm must also cut its price to sell more output. The marginal benefit of another worker is lower on $MRPL_2$ than on $MRPL_1$. Similarly, although W_0 is the marginal cost of labour for a competitive firm taking the wage as given, a monopsonist faces a marginal cost of labour MCL in Figure 6-2.

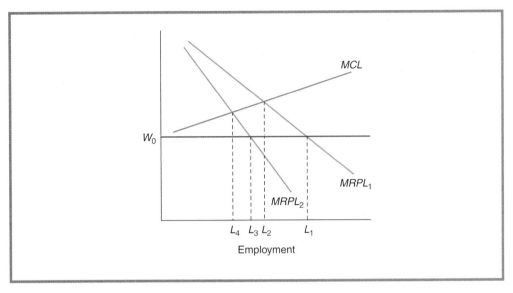

Figure 6-2 Monopoly and monopsony power

Profit is maximized when the marginal revenue from an extra worker equals its marginal cost. Otherwise, the firm's hiring is inappropriate. A firm that is a price-taker in both its output and input markets hires L_1 workers in Figure 6-2. A firm with market power in its output market hires L_3 workers. A firm with market power in hiring labour input hires L_2 workers. And a firm with market power in both markets hires L_4 workers. For the rest of this chapter we assume both output and input markets are competitive. The analysis is easily amended for other cases.

Box 6-1   Good economists in short supply

The Bank of England warned that it was having difficulty recruiting staff with good post-graduate degrees in economics. British students account for only 10 per cent of PhD students in economics in leading UK universities. Why so low? Partly because a good undergraduate economics degree is now worth so much to banking and consulting firms in the City of London. Professor Andrew Oswald of Warwick University has estimated that economics undergraduates earn about £35 000 a year in their mid-twenties, rising to over £100 000 a year by retirement. The Bank of England cannot match these salaries. Nor, incidentally, can universities. Some of us have to write textbooks to make a decent living!

Changes in a firm's demand for labour

A higher wage moves a firm *along* its *MRPL* schedule, reducing the quantity of labour demanded. If the marginal cost of a worker is higher, the firm has to adjust employment until the marginal benefit of a worker is also higher. Lower employment means that labour encounters fewer diminishing returns when working with a given quantity of other inputs.

At this lower level of employment, the marginal benefit of a worker is higher. By reducing employment enough, the firm can raise the marginal benefit of a worker in line with the higher marginal cost of a worker when the wage rises. The firm moves leftwards and upwards along a given *MRPL* schedule.

However, a rise in the output price raises the marginal benefit of labour at any particular wage. It *shifts* the entire *MRPL* schedule upwards, raising its demand for labour. For a given output price, two other things raise a firm's demand for labour. Technical progress makes labour more productive and raises its marginal benefit. So does a greater quantity of other inputs with which labour can work. When a firm gets more capital, this raises the demand for labour by shifting the *MRPL* schedule up. At any wage, the firm hires more workers than before.

For the special case of a perfect competition, a firm hires labour until $W = MRPL = [P \times MPL]$. Hence, the marginal product of labour *MPL* equals the real wage W/P. If nominal wages and output prices both double, real wages and employment are unaffected. Nothing real has changed.

Demand for labour by an industry

Since all firms in the industry face the same wage as each other, you might think that we simply add each firm's labour demand schedule horizontally to get the industry demand schedule. This is nearly correct but not quite. At a lower wage, each firm wants to hire more labour. This expands industry output, bidding down the output price. Even a competitive industry must cut its price to induce people to buy its higher total output.

This fall in the output price shifts to the left each individual firm's demand curve for labour. The marginal benefit of a worker is lower. We thus conclude that the industry demand curve for labour, relating the wage and the quantity of labour demand, is *steeper* than the horizontal sum of firms' individual labour demand curves.

Although each firm takes its output price as given, the entire industry bids down its output price when lower wages induce it to expand hiring and output. At industry level, this reduces the sensitivity of labour demand to the wage. Indeed, the more inelastic is the demand for the industry's output, the more inelastic will be the industry's demand for labour, because any given expansion will reduce prices by more, reducing the marginal benefit of hiring workers.

Labour supply

Labour supply depends both on how many people work and on their hours of work. To analyse labour supply, we ask how many hours do people in the labour force wish to work, and what makes people join the labour force at all?

The labour force is everyone in work or seeking a job.

Hours of work

How many hours a person in the labour force wants to work depends on the *real* wage, W/P, the nominal wage divided by the price of goods, which measures the amount of goods that can be bought as a result of working.

People not working can stay at home and have fun. Each of us has only 24 hours a day for work and leisure. More leisure is nice but, by working longer, we can get more income with which to buy consumer goods.

We can use the model of consumer choice in Chapter 2. The choice is now between goods as a whole and leisure. A higher real wage raises the quantity of goods an extra hour of work will buy. This makes working more attractive than before and tends to increase the supply of hours worked. But there is a second effect. Suppose you work to get a target real income to finance a summer holiday. With a higher real wage, you don't have to work so long to meet your target.

These two effects are the *substitution and income effects* of Chapter 2. A higher real wage raises the relative return on working, a substitution effect or pure relative price effect that makes people want to work more. But a higher real wage also makes people better off, a pure income effect. Since leisure is a luxury good, the quantity of leisure demanded rises sharply when real incomes increase. This income effect tends to make people work less. Lottery winners quit their jobs.

The income and substitution effects pull in opposite directions. We need empirical evidence to see whether higher wages make people supply more hours of work. For most developed economies, this evidence says that, for men and women with full-time careers, the two effects largely cancel out. A change in the real wage has little effect on the quantity of hours supplied.

This conclusion applies to relatively small changes in real wage rates. In most Western countries, the large rise in real wages over the past 100 years has been matched by reductions of ten hours or more in the working week. The income effect has outweighed the substitution effect.

Workers care about take-home pay after deductions of income tax. A reduction in income tax rates thus raises after-tax real wages. Hence, the same empirical evidence implies that lower income tax rates will not lead to a big rise in the supply of hours worked! Tax cuts are not a magic solution to work incentives, and moderate tax rises should not be expected to have a major disincentive effect on hours of work.

Labour force participation

The effect of real wages on the supply of hours is smaller than often supposed. Real wages also affect labour supply by changing incentives to join the labour force.

The **participation rate** is the fraction of people of working age who join the labour force.

Table 6-1 presents UK data on participation rates. Most men are in the labour force, though nowadays when older men lose their jobs they often give up completely and leave the labour force. A smaller but still quite stable percentage of unmarried women are in the

	1971	1985	2003
Men	92	89	84
Women: unmarried	72	74	77
: married	50	62	76

Table 6-1   UK participation rates (%)

Source: General Household Survey

labour force. There has been a big rise in the number of married women in the labour force, a trend continuing steadily since 1951 when only 25 per cent of married women were in the UK labour force. By 2003, over 75 per cent of all women were in the labour force.

Someone not in the labour force has lots of leisure, but how does she afford consumer goods? She may have inherited wealth, won the Lottery, be supported by her working boyfriend, or get income support and housing benefit from the government.

If she joins the labour force and gets a job, she loses an hour of leisure for every hour she works. However, for every pound she initially earns she loses over 90 pence in withdrawal of government benefits. Since the Treasury coffers are not limitless, governments help the very poor but claw as much money back as they can once people's circumstances improve a little. Moreover, going out to work entails several costs – the right clothes, commuting to work, and paying for child care. It may simply not be worth it.

The **poverty trap** means that getting a job makes a person worse off than staying at home.

Suppose the real wage rises. It may now be possible to pole vault over the poverty trap into work that pays. Conversely, lower real wages make the poverty trap worse. Hence, higher real wages increase the incentive to join the labour force.

What happened to income and substitution effects here? These tools compare two situations in which an individual can adjust their behaviour at the margin. The poverty trap is a high wall that entrants must clear to get into the labour force. Analysis of small changes is not the right procedure. Beginning from a low wage, a small rise in the wage makes no difference. As wages keep rising, eventually a person can soar over the wall and wants to join the labour force. Different people face walls of different heights. As wages in the economy rise, the aggregate labour supply response is continuous. A few more people join with each rise in real wages.

Box 6-2   Boosting UK labour supply

Under New Labour, current UK policies fall under two main headings, 'Welfare to Work' and 'Making Work Pay'. Both reflect a belief that work allows people to acquire skills and new opportunities: work is a ladder allowing people gradually to climb out of poverty. 'Welfare to Work' has two elements, more help in finding a job and more pressure (threat of loss of social security benefits) on those thought to be making little effort to find work.

Both raise the incentive to participate in the labour force. 'Making Work Pay' deals with incomes of people once they are in the labour force. The 'Working Family Tax Credit' gives money to workers with children, provided the parent works a minimum number of hours a week (the limit being set roughly to make it possible for mothers to work while their children are at school).

Both measures attack the poverty trap. To pay for these schemes, the government could have taxed much richer people. Instead, part of the cost is being recouped by faster withdrawal of social security benefits just above the range of the poverty trap. Critics say this is still not a very good answer to the 'for whom' question.

Why does Table 6-1 show much more labour force participation by married women in recent decades? First, there was a social change in attitudes to married women working. Second, pressure for equal opportunities has raised women's wages. Third, the opportunity cost of working has fallen. Dishwashers and vacuum cleaners, and some limited assistance from men, has made it easier for women to go out to work.

To sum up, social influences matter and are one of the 'other things equal' that can change. For given attitudes, labour supply to the economy rises with the level of real wages, but not by a lot. It is rather inelastic. Many people are already in the labour force. Offsetting income and substitution effects means that further changes in wages have a small effect on hours worked. The main reason aggregate supply of person-hours rises when real wages rise is that extra people can leap over the wall and join the labour force.

Labour supply to an industry

Suppose the industry is small relative to the economy, and wishes to hire workers with common skills. It must pay the going rate, adjusted only for the particular non-monetary characteristics of that industry. The *equilibrium wage differential* across two industries offsets differences in the desirability of jobs to workers, removing any incentive for workers to move between industries. Nasty and dangerous jobs have to pay more.

A small industry faces a horizontal labour supply curve at the appropriate wage. Paying this going rate, it can hire as many workers as it wants. In practice, few industries are this small. The construction industry is a significant user of roofers, and the haulage industry a significant user of lorry drivers. When an industry expands, it usually bids up wages for those skills by raising the whole economy's demand for a skill that, in the short run, is in limited supply. In the short run, an industry faces an upward-sloping labour supply curve.

In the long run, the industry's labour supply curve is flatter. When short-run expansion bids up the wages of computer programmers, more school-leavers train in this skill, enhancing the long-run supply of programmers. With more programmers available, an individual industry does not have to raise the wage so much to attract extra workers with this skill.

Box 6-3 Premiership wages

Premiership footballers earn breathtaking amounts of money. The wage bill in UK Premier League football rose from £50 million in the 1992–93 season to £500 million in the 2002–03 season, while income of the clubs rose from £150 million to £950 million. Hence, of £800 million extra revenue from selling the output of football clubs, the best players (the inputs to football clubs) got their hands on an extra £450 million.

Spiralling club incomes reflect not only increasing demand as satellite TV retails football to ever wider (and more profitable) audiences, but also greater proficiency in marketing ancillary products like replica shirts. Manchester United is estimated to earn around 40 per cent of its income from games, 33 per cent from TV rights, and 27 per cent from commercial activities. Such breadth and depth to football teams' revenues has led to players trying to get their hands on all of the club's additional revenue.

Labour market equilibrium in an industry

Figure 6-3 shows labour supply and demand for an industry. In equilibrium, the real wage is W/P_0 and employment is N_0. Shifts in these supply or demand curves change this equilibrium. In the market for Premier League footballers, the labour supply curve LS is steep since it is hard to find more good footballers no matter how much the industry offers to pay.

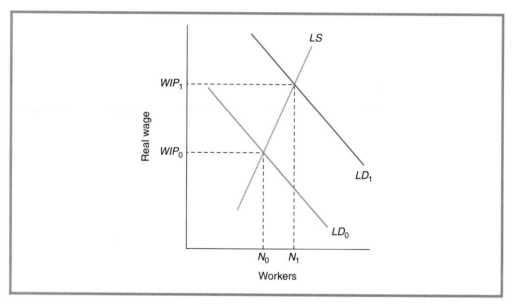

Figure 6-3   Industry labour market equilibrium

Football clubs' revenue from TV depends in turn on the revenue that TV can earn from advertising. If the global economy slows down, firms cut back their spending on advertising. When they do, even David Beckham feels the effects.

The arrival of Sky TV, paying vast sums to show games on TV, raised the demand for footballers from LD_0 to LD_1, causing a large rise in their wages. Thus, Premier League footballers get high wages for two reasons. First, the derived demand curve for their labour is high because football clubs can earn massive revenue from the success of their talented footballers.

Second, the labour supply curve for people with these skills is very steep. Even by paying a lot more, it is hard to attract many more Beckhams into the football industry. Beckham and Owen have few adequate substitutes. Thus, supply and demand explain the high wages of top stars.

Conversely, football matches in the lower divisions were first shown live on ITV Digital. When this channel went bankrupt, revenues of football clubs outside the Premier League fell sharply, reducing the demand for players in the lower divisions. Their equilibrium wage fell. As you would expect, since Sky TV has begun televising games from the Championship division as well as the Premier League, demand curves for players in the Championship division have started shifting upwards again. These fluctuations illustrate vividly that the demand for footballing labour is derived from the demand for the output of the football clubs, which nowadays depends significantly on whether the games get access to TV revenues.

6-2

Different kinds of labour

Learning outcomes

When you have finished this section, you should understand:

- The many different kinds of labour
- How human capital adds to skills
- When investment in education and training makes sense
- The role of trade unions
- How globalization affects trade unions

In most European countries men earn more than women, and whites earn more than non-whites. Is this discrimination, or do different workers have different productivity? Workers differ not merely in sex and race but in age, experience, education, training, innate ability, and in whether or not they belong to a trade union.

Figure 6-4 shows that UK women earn only about 80 per cent as much as men, though the gender gap is closing steadily. Table 6-2 highlights other sources of pay differentials.

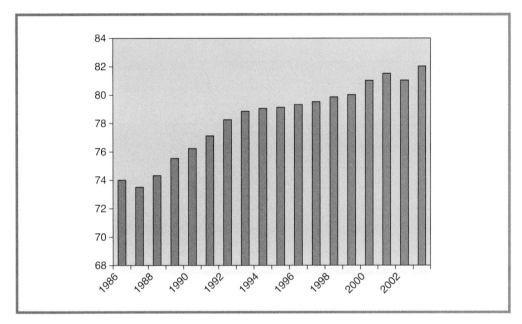

Figure 6-4   UK women's pay as percentage of men's pay
Source: www.statistic.gov.uk/cci

People with more education and training earn more, whether or not they are in a trade union. Work experience adds to earnings, though at a diminishing rate, especially in manual work, where older workers cannot match their strong, young colleagues. But experience still matters, even in manual work. Job characteristics also affect pay. Manual workers, perhaps with fewer skills, earn less than non-manuals. Firms in the busy (and expensive) South East region, including London, have to pay workers more.

Human capital

Human capital is the stock of accumulated expertise that raises a worker's productivity.

Human capital is the result of past investment in workers. It enhances their productivity and thus their current and future incomes. Education and training involve current sacrifices – both direct costs, and giving up opportunities to earn immediate income – but yield the benefit of higher future incomes because productivity is higher. In long-run equilibrium, the extra benefit of acquiring skills must just cover the extra cost of acquiring them. Table 6-2 suggests that the pay-off to education can be large. Don't quit now!

% extra pay for	Union	Non-union
Education and training		
GCSE	+5	+13
A-levels	+16	+21
University degree	+32	+47
Postgraduate degree	+50	+50
Other higher education	+18	+21
Apprenticeship	+11	+9
Personal		
Ethnic minority	−1	−5
Years experience		
5	+13	+10
10	+23	+20
15	+30	+28
30	+35	+32
Job character		
South East	+15	+16
London	+23	+15
Manual	+17	−21
Shift work	+12	+8

Table 6-2 UK pay differentials

Source: A. Booth, 'Seniority, Earnings and Unions', *Economica*, 1996

On-the-job training

Human capital can also be accumulated after people get a job. *Firm-specific skills* raise a worker's productivity only in that particular firm. A worker knows how that factory works and what makes these particular teams of workers function effectively. These skills may be worthless in another firm. In contrast, *general skills*, such as knowing how to use Windows or Excel, can be transferred to work in another firm.

A firm will pay for training in firm-specific skills. Its workers' productivity rises, but they are unlikely to move to other firms where their productivity (and hence wages) will be lower. Conversely, the more general or transferable the skill, the more a firm will want the worker to pay the cost of training. No firm will invest in training workers who then move to other firms.

An apprentice works for less than his immediate marginal product, thus paying for his own training. This investment raises his future productivity, raising his future income wherever he works. Firms do not mind if the worker quits, since the worker bore the cost of the training.

Trade unions

Trade unions are worker organizations that affect pay and working conditions. UK union membership was almost 40 per cent of the workforce in 1929, then collapsed in the depression of the 1930s, before climbing to almost 50 per cent in 1979. Since then it has been in constant decline, in part because the industrial economy is giving way to the service economy, and because the public sector has shrunk significantly. Table 6-3 examines various ways to disaggregate the employed population, shedding light on various possible causes of the decline of unionized workers.

	1990	2003	Change
Male	43	29	−14
Female	32	29	−3
Full-time	43	32	−11
Part-time	22	21	−1
Manual	42	26	−16
Non-manual	35	29	−6
Industry	44	27	−17
Services	37	30	−7
Public	65	58	−7
Private	24	11	−13

Table 6-3   Union membership (percentage of employees), 1990–2003
Source: ONS, *Labour Market Trends*

The traditional view of unions is that they offset the firm's power in negotiating wages and working conditions. A single firm has many workers. The firm is in a strong bargaining position if it can make separate agreements with each of its workers. By presenting a united front, the workers can impose large costs on the firm if they *all* quit. The firm can replace one worker but not its whole labour force. The existence of unions evens up the bargaining process.

A successful union must be able to restrict the firm's labour supply. If the firm can hire non-union labour, unions find it hard to maintain the wage above the level at which the firm can hire non-union workers. Hence, unions are keen on closed-shop agreements with individual firms.

A closed shop means that all a firm's workers must be members of a trade union.

By restricting supply and making workers scarce, a union can raise wages for the workers who still have jobs. How far will a union swap lower employment for higher wages in an industry? And what determines union power to control the supply of labour to particular industry?

The more the union cares about its *senior* members, the more it will raise wages by restricting employment. Senior workers are the least likely to be sacked. Conversely, the more a union is democratic, and the more it cares about potential members as well as actual members, the less it restricts employment to force up wages.

The more inelastic the demand for labour, the more a given restriction in jobs raises the wage. The incentive to unionize the labour force is strong when big wage rises are achieved with little loss of employment. Conversely, when labour demand is elastic, forcing up wages costs many jobs. Unions are then less attractive to their members.

Unions and globalization

On the first of May each year, union members are well represented in the big marches against capitalism and globalization. Now you understand why. In a small country, big firms may have significant monopoly power. This makes their demand for labour inelastic. Taking on extra workers and producing more output quickly bids down the output price, reducing the marginal benefit of another worker.

Conversely, at lower employment and output, the firm's output price rises since it no longer floods the small domestic market. With a higher output price, workers are more valuable and earn a higher wage. Thus, the demand for labour: lower employment is accompanied by much higher wages, which is good news for the union. Restricting labour supply forces up the wage a lot.

Globalization makes domestic firms swim in a much bigger pond with many foreign competitors. Facing this extra competition, the output price is much less sensitive to the output of domestic firms. Hence, when unions restrict labour supply, they scarcely manage to force up the wage. Globalization thus weakens the power of domestic trade unions, which is why they mind about it.

Other effects of unions

Union wage differentials arise not only from the successful restriction of labour supply. Union work has certain characteristics – a structured work setting, inflexibility of hours, employer-set overtime, and a faster work pace – a whole set of conditions that might be regarded as unpleasant. Higher wages in such industries are partly *compensating wage differentials* for these non-monetary aspects of the job.

Thus, unions tend to emerge in industries where large productivity gains would result from the introduction of unpleasant working conditions. The union exists not to restrict labour supply in total, but to negotiate productivity gains, ensuring that workers receive proper compensating differentials for the unpopular changes in working practices that firms find it profitable to introduce. On this view, the unions do not make separate deals for pay and working conditions; rather, their role is to secure pay increases *in exchange for* changes in working conditions.

From this perspective, unions play an important role in allowing firms to commit to what they promise. Without unions, there is the danger that workers would agree to new technologies and changes in work conditions but then find that the firm failed to honour its promise to offer higher wages in return. The existence of unions helps their members believe that firms will stick to their half of the bargain.

Case study 6-1   Higher education pays off

Nowadays many students have to contribute to the cost of their own education, and emerge from college and university with the debt millstone round their neck. Of course, compared with 30 years ago, borrowing in general has become a lot easier. Some of the debt millstone of graduates is probably accounted for by a few shopping sprees too many and a rather nice lifestyle while in higher education. Even so, we all know that education has become expensive and most of the debt burden was incurred in the good cause of acquiring a proper education.

Student graduation ceremony
© Patrik Giardino/Corbis

But this raises some obvious questions. Why has education become more expensive? Are the gains to having a university education sufficient to justify actually paying for one? And are some subjects better investments than others?

The main reasons that university education has become more expensive are (a) as a society we have decided that many more young people should go to university, which is no longer something that only the privileged think of doing, and (b) as taxpayers we have been unwilling to raise state support for university education in line with our targets for getting a much higher percentage of the population through university. If the state won't pay, the rest has to be borne by private individuals.

The fairness of who pays for what is not independent of the benefits that education confers. If students are subsequently going to earn enormous salaries, it is not unreasonable that they bear a part of the cost of their own education. If higher education makes hardly any difference to lifetime income, the case for charging students in some form is correspondingly reduced. We know from Table 6-2 that people with university degrees earn at least a third more than people without such degrees. This may overstate the effect of the degree itself – some people get well rewarded because they are smart and happened to go to university rather than because they went to university.

What about the particular subject that you are studying? Are some better passports to a job than others? The table below shows the results of a major empirical study on determinants of people's wages by the time they are 33 years old. Women who studied humanities at undergraduate level on average gain only 5 per cent on the salary they are subsequently earning at the age of 33. In contrast, if they were studying economics, they would on average add 24 per cent to their salary at age 33. Men also add 20 per cent to their salary by studying economics rather than the arts – in the latter case, a humanities degree is actually associated with below-average salaries at age 33.

Just be glad you are reading *Foundations of Economics*, rather than *Foundations of English*. Notice too how poorly chemistry is treated in the market place.

Case study 6-1 *Continued*

% extra wage in Britain at age 33 for	Men	Women
First degree	+15	+32
Postgraduate degree	+15	+35
Extra effect by subject:		
Arts	−10	+5
Economics	+10	+24
Chemistry/biology	−17	−11
Maths/physics	+9	+16

Source: R. Blundell et al. 'Returns to higher education in Britain', *Economic Journal*, 2000

6-3

Other input markets

Learning outcomes

By the end of this section, you should understand:

- ◆ The markets for capital and land
- ◆ Flows over time, and stocks at a point in time
- ◆ The markets for renting capital services and for buying new capital assets
- ◆ The required rental on capital
- ◆ How land rentals are determined

Wₑ now examine other inputs used with labour in the production process. Having completed this analysis of factor markets, we discuss the *income distribution* in an economy. The price of an input, multiplied by the quantity used, is the income of that input. We need to know the prices and quantities of all inputs to understand how the economy's total income is distributed.

Physical capital is the stock of produced goods used to make other goods and services. **Land** is the input that nature supplies.

Physical capital includes machinery used to make cars, railway lines that produce transport services, and school buildings that produce education services. Land is used in farming, and in the supply of housing and office services. The distinction between land and capital is blurred. By applying fertilizer to improve the soil balance, farmers can 'produce' better land.

Capital and land are both assets. They do not completely depreciate during the time period in which we study output decisions by firms.

Physical capital

Fixed capital is plant, machinery, and buildings. Inventories are stocks of working capital, goods awaiting further production or sale. Over time, the economy is becoming more *capital-intensive*. Each worker has more capital with which to work. Because capital depreciates, it takes some investment in new capital goods merely to stand still.

Gross investment is the production of new capital goods and the improvement of existing capital goods. **Net investment** is gross investment minus the depreciation of the existing capital stock.

If net investment is positive, gross investment more than compensates for depreciation and the capital stock is growing. However, very small levels of gross investment may fail to keep pace with depreciation; the capital stock then falls.

Rentals, interest rates, and asset prices

Table 6-4 stresses two distinctions: between *stocks* and *flows*, and between *rental payments* and *asset prices*. The hourly wage is the *rental payment* to hire an hour of labour. There is no asset price for the asset called a 'worker' because we no longer allow slavery! However, for capital there are markets both to buy and sell capital goods and to lease capital services from other firms.

A **stock** is the quantity of an asset at a point in time (eg 100 machines on 1/1/06). A **flow** is the stream of services that an asset provides in a given period. The cost of using capital services is the **rental rate** for capital. The **asset price** is the sum for which the stock can be bought, entitling its owner to the future stream of capital services from that asset.

	Capital	Labour
Flow input to hourly production	Capital services	Labour services
Payment for flow	Rental rate (£/machine hour)	Wage rate (£/labour hour)
Asset price	£/machine	£/slave, if purchase allowed

Table 6-4 Stock and flow concepts

Buying a factory for £10 000 entitles the owner to a stream of future rental payments on the capital services that the factory provides. What will a purchaser pay for a capital asset?

If you borrow £10 000 to buy the machine, you face two costs. First, the opportunity cost of the funds tied up, which could instead have earned interest. If the interest rate is 10 per cent a year, this costs you £1000 a year in lost interest. Second, the value of the machine falls each year as its wears out with use and becomes obsolete. Suppose this depreciation is £500 a year. Although it cost £10 000 to buy the asset outright, it is effectively costing you £1500 a year then to use the flow of capital services that it generates during its lifetime.

If you enter the leasing business, you will buy the machine only if you can rent it for at least £1500 a year. The required rental is the price that connects the market for capital assets, in which capital goods are bought and sold, and the market for capital services, in which capital is hired out for use. Even where a business buys an asset for its own use, it should calculate whether the asset is covering its economic cost.

The **required rental** is the income per period that lets a buyer of a capital asset break even.

The required rental can change for three reasons. First, a higher price of new capital goods means that required rentals must rise: with more funds tied up, there is more interest and depreciation to offset. Second, a higher interest rate raises the required rental, since the interest foregone by owning the asset has risen. Third, a higher depreciation rate raises the cost per period of holding the asset, and hence the return it must earn to cover its costs.

The demand for capital services

The firm's demand for capital services is very like its demand for labour services. The rental rate for capital replaces the wage rate as the cost of hiring factor services. We emphasize the *use* of *services* of capital. The example to bear in mind is a firm renting a vehicle or leasing office space.

The **marginal revenue product of capital** *MRPK* is the extra revenue from selling the extra output that an extra unit of capital allows, holding constant all other inputs.

The marginal revenue product of capital *MRPK* falls as more capital is used. First, physically there are diminishing marginal returns to adding more and more capital with other inputs held constant. Second, the firm may have to cut its output price to sell the extra output. The firm rents capital up to the point at which the rental rate equals its marginal revenue product. A lower rental rate makes the firm demand more capital services.

This entire demand curve for capital services shifts up if there is (a) a higher output price, making the extra physical output more valuable, (b) a rise in the quantity of other inputs that makes capital more productive, or (c) a technical advance that makes capital more productive.

Box 6-4 The future's orange, but the past was in the red

How would you like to start a company, lose £229 million pounds in your first year of trading, and watch your share price rise on the stock market? Not a bad beginning for Orange, the mobile phone operator. Because telecommunications was a growth area, stock market analysts forecast profits in the future even when the young company made massive losses in its early years. Orange's stock market value reflected guesses about the stream of future profits that shareholders expected to receive.

Even after the 1997 announcement of a £229 million loss that year, Orange total share value was £2.6 billion. Shareholders were banking on some pretty big profits in the future. Nor were they disappointed. By October 1999, Orange was worth £20 billion after a takeover by German competitor Mannesmann. After its subsequent sale to France Telecom, Orange's market value reached £21.6 billion, more than that of the whole of its new French parent company.

Because capital lasts a long time, the price of a capital asset has to value the stream of income that it will earn throughout its lifetime, not just the rentals that it is earning today. By 2002, people were much more pessimistic about future profits in telephony, and Orange's share price fell back sharply. Then, like other hi-tech stocks, its share price grew substantially during 2003–05. Asset prices are volatile because they depend on beliefs about the asset's income over its entire future life.

The industry demand curve for capital services

As with labour, the industry demand for capital services adds together how much each individual firm demands at each rental rate. Again, the industry demand is less elastic than those of individual firms. Even if each firm thinks it has no effect on the output price, the industry as a whole must cut the price to sell more output. This reduces the marginal benefit of more capital, making demand less responsive to a fall in the rental rate on capital.

The supply of capital services

Capital services are produced by capital assets. In the short run, the total supply of capital assets (machines, buildings, and vehicles), and thus the services they provide, is fixed to the economy as a whole. New factories cannot be built overnight. The economy's supply curve of capital services is vertical at a quantity determined by the existing stock of capital assets.

Some types of capital are fixed even for the individual industry. The steel industry cannot quickly change its number of furnaces. However, by offering a higher rental rate for delivery vans, the supermarket industry can attract more vans from other industries, even in the short run, and thus faces an upward-sloping supply curve.

In the long run the total quantity of capital in the economy can be varied. New machines and factories can be built. Conversely, with no new investment in capital goods the existing capital stock will depreciate and its quantity will fall. Similarly, individual industries can adjust their stocks of capital.

Long-run equilibrium

The inherited stock of capital determines the vertical supply curve for capital services in the short run. Given the industry demand for capital services, this determines the equilibrium rental on capital services in the industry. If this matches the required rental on capital, this is a long-run equilibrium. Users of capital services are equating their marginal benefit and marginal cost. Owners of capital services are earning streams of income that just cover the cost of buying the capital asset. Likewise, producers of capital assets – the construction and machine tool industries – are selling new assets at a price that just covers the cost of making them.

Adjustment to changes

In Figure 6-5 greater import competition reduces the demand for domestic textiles. Beginning in long-run equilibrium at A, a lower output price shifts the derived demand curve for capital services to the left in the textile industry, from DD to $D'D'$. Overnight, the supply of capital services SS is vertical, determined by previous investment in capital assets.

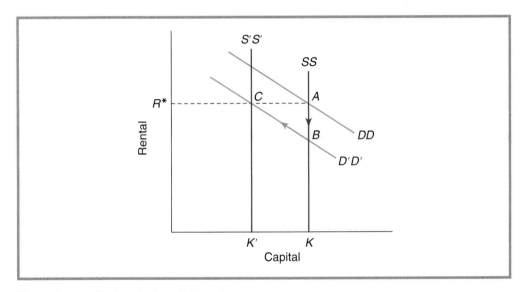

Figure 6-5 Adjustment of capital services

The immediate effect is a big drop in rentals on textile machinery. The industry moves from A to B. Machine owners no longer get the required rental R^*, and stop building new machines. Depreciation gradually reduces the stock of existing machines. This makes capital services scarcer, and bids up the rental. When capital has fallen to K', the rental returns to the required rental R^* and long-run equilibrium is restored at C. Producers of new machines make just enough new machines to cover depreciation of existing machines, and the capital stock remains constant.

Land

Since land is the input supplied by nature, we often treat its supply as constant, since it cannot be augmented by economic activity. This is not literally true. We can drain marshes, and improve land with fertilizer. However, it is much harder to add to the total supply of land than that of machines or buildings. We capture the key feature of land by treating its total supply as fixed.

Box 6-5   The best address

Since land is in fixed supply, land prices are dearest where demand is greatest. Here are the ten dearest places to buy a two-bedroom apartment.

Rank and city	Area	Price (£)
1 London	Eaton Square	1 500 000
2 San Francisco	Pacific Heights	1 400 000
3 Hong Kong	Barker Road	1 300 000
4 New York	Fifth Avenue	1 200 000
5 Amsterdam	R. Wagnerstraat	1 200 000
6 Stockholm	Strandvagen	1 100 000
7 Sydney	Circular Quay	900 000
8 Chicago	Michigan Ave	800 000
9 Zurich	Zurichberg	700 000
10 Singapore	Scotts 28	700 000

Source: BA Business Life, August 2001

Figure 6-6 shows the derived demand curve DD for land services. With a fixed supply, the equilibrium rental is R_0. A rise in the derived demand, for example because wheat prices have risen, leads only to a rise in the rental to R_1. The quantity of land services is fixed by assumption.

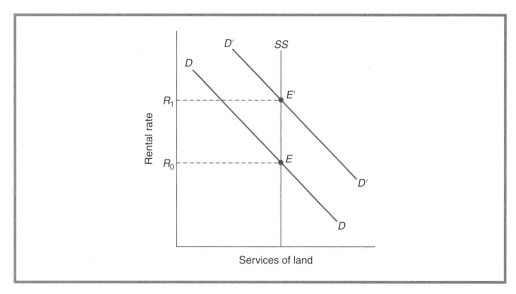

Figure 6-6   The market for land services

Consider a tenant farmer who rents land. Suppose the EU's Common Agricultural Policy (CAP) offers better prices for wheat. Since the demand for using land rises, this will bid up rents, as in Figure 6-6. Despite receiving more for the wheat crop, the tenant farmer is also paying higher rent and may not be better off, complaining that high rentals make it hard to earn a decent living. As in our discussion of footballers' wages, it is the combination of a strong derived demand and inelastic supply that leads to a high price for the input's services. Figure 6-6 implies that farm subsidies earned through the CAP benefit the owners of land, for whom rentals rise, but may not benefit those who rent land in order to farm it.

Long-run trends explained

Modern economies are becoming more capital-intensive in production techniques. Why is capital intensity rising in the long run? First, in the long run we can raise the supply of capital more easily than that of labour or land. Hence, rising demand bids up wages more than rental rates for capital. Firms substitute away from labour as it gets relatively more expensive than capital. Second, firms then look for inventions that economize on expensive labour. Hence, new technologies often favour more capital-intensive methods.

Why does the price of a house in London keep rising, even after adjusting for inflation? The supply of land close to the city centre is fixed. As households and businesses get richer, their demand for land rises. With a fixed supply, the price has to rise to ration scarce land in London. So, low-paid nurses complain that they cannot find affordable accommodation close to their job in hospitals located in central London.

6-4

Income distribution

Learning outcomes

When you have finished this section, you should understand:

- ◆ The functional distribution of income
- ◆ The personal distribution of income
- ◆ Their relation to input markets

The income of an input is simply its rental rate multiplied by the quantity of the factor employed. We now use our discussion of input markets to analyse the distribution of income in the UK.

The **functional income distribution** is the division of national income between the different production inputs.

Table 6-5 shows the income shares of the different inputs in the UK in 2002 and compares these shares of national income with their shares during the 1980s. The functional income distribution has been quite stable over time. As national income rose, the total income of each production input broadly kept pace, though advances in IT made it easier for large companies to outsource specialist activities to small suppliers, which helps explain the rise in self-employment and the decline in the share of capital and land.

Input	(% of national income)	
	1981–89 average	2002
Employment	64	67
Self-employment	6	9
Capital and land	30	24

Table 6-5   UK functional income distribution
Source: ONS, *UK National Accounts*

The **personal income distribution** shows how national income is divided between people, regardless of the inputs from which these people earn their income.

The personal income distribution is relevant to issues such as equality and poverty within a country. Table 6-6 excludes the very poor, showing data only for those whose incomes are large enough to have to submit a tax return. Even within this group, pre-tax income is quite unequally distributed in the UK. The richest 20 per cent of taxpayers earn over half the total UK income, whereas the poorest 20 per cent earn only 3 per cent of total income. Why do some people earn so much while others earn so little?

Household group	Average income (£ 000)
Poorest 20%	3
Next 20%	7
Next 20%	17
Next 20%	27
Richest 20%	51

Table 6-6   UK personal income distribution, 2000
Source: ONS, *Social Trends*

Unskilled workers have little training and low productivity. Workers with high levels of training and education earn much more. Some jobs, such as coal mining, pay high compensating differentials to offset unpleasant working conditions. Pleasant, but unskilled, jobs pay much less since many people are prepared to do them. However, talented superstars in scarce supply but high demand earn big money.

Another reason for the disparities in Table 6-6 is that personal income is not just labour income but also income from owning capital and land. This wealth is even more unequally divided than labour income. In 2001, the richest 1 per cent of the UK population owned 23 per cent of the nation's wealth, and the poorest 50 per cent of the population owned only 5 per cent of this wealth. Large disparities in income from capital and land help explain the disparities in personal income in Table 6-6.

Case study 6-2   The invisible helping hand

After Labour lost the 1979 general election, it moved to the left. This pleased party activists but took the party too far away from the preferences of most voters. The Conservatives were in power for the next 17 years. After heavy defeat in 1983, successive Labour leaders slowly moved the party back to the middle ground. New Labour focus groups interviewed people directly to clarify the majority view on different issues. The result? Labour victories in 1997, 2001, and 2005.

Did Labour abandon its principles to win and keep office? Initially, it gave up old traditions of high welfare spending and high, visible taxes. But Chancellor Gordon Brown helped the poor a lot without frightening the middle classes. As a result of his first four budgets, the post-tax income of the poorest 10 per cent of people rose by 9 per cent, the post-tax income of the next poorest 10 per cent rose by 8 per cent. He did this without raising income tax or VAT.

Some of it was financed by stealth taxes, such as the tax treatment of pension funds, which ordinary voters did not notice or understand. Some was financed by making transfer payments more selective. Instead of a universal benefit, scarce resources were concentrated only on those who really needed them. Some of it was financed by economic growth: as incomes grew, given tax rates yielded more tax revenue, which was mainly given to the poor. What is politically interesting about the Blair–Brown strategy is that they have redistributed spending power substantially towards the poor, but have not trumpeted their achievement, preferring to continue to make steady cumulative changes without scaring off the floating middle-income voters on whom election results depend.

Recap

- In the long run, a firm will choose the lowest cost way of producing its chosen output level. A higher wage has a substitution effect (a switch out of labour into other inputs) and an output effect (higher costs reduce output and the need for inputs). Both reduce the demand for labour.

- In the short run, the firm has some fixed inputs, and varies output by varying its variable input, labour. Labour faces diminishing returns when other factors are fixed. Its marginal physical product falls as more labour is used.

- A profit-maximizing firm produces the output at which marginal output cost equals marginal output revenue. Equivalently, it hires labour up to the point where the marginal cost of labour equals its marginal benefit (its marginal revenue product).

- A firm's *MRPL* schedule shifts up if its output price rises, if its capital stock rises, or if technical progress makes labour more productive. All raise the demand for labour by raising its marginal benefit. The converse changes shift the *MRPL* schedule downwards.

- For someone already in the labour force, a higher real wage has a substitution effect that raises the supply of hours worked, but an income effect that reduces the supply of hours worked. The two roughly cancel out.

- Participation rates rise with higher real wage rates, lower fixed costs of working, and changes in tastes in favour of working rather than staying at home. All three have raised labour force participation, especially by married women.

- Equilibrium wage differentials are monetary compensation for different non-monetary characteristics of jobs across industries.

- When demand is high and supply is scarce, equilibrium wages will be high. Firms can still make profits provided demand continues to be high.

- Different workers get different pay. This reflects personal characteristics such as education, job experience, gender, race, and union status.

- Skills or human capital are the most important source of wage differentials. Human capital formation includes both formal education and on-the-job training. Workers with more education and training earn higher lifetime incomes.

- Skilled labour is relatively scarce because it is costly to acquire human capital. Workers acquire human capital if the benefit exceeds the cost. Firms pay for training if there is then little danger of the worker leaving the firm; otherwise, the worker has to pay for it.

- Under 30 per cent of the UK labour force now belongs to a trade union. Unions restrict the labour supply to firms or industries, thereby raising wages but lowering employment. Unions move firms up their demand curve for labour.

- Unions achieve higher wages the more inelastic the demand for labour and the more they are willing or able to restrict the supply of labour. Globalization makes labour demand more elastic and reduces unions' incentive to raise wages.

- Unions also raise wages by negotiating compensation for changes in work practices that raise productivity but reduce the pleasantness of the job. Without unions, workers might never agree to such changes, believing that firms would not honour their promise to raise wages after conditions were irreversibly altered.

- Stocks are measured at a point in time. Flows are measured during periods of time. Flows are the rate of change of the corresponding stock, and a stock is the cumulation of the relevant flows.

- A firm demands capital services up to the point at which the rental equals the marginal revenue product of capital. The latter rises if the output price rises, if capital has more of other inputs with which to work, or if technical progress makes capital more productive.

- In the short run, the supply of capital services is fixed. In the long run, it can be adjusted by producing new capital goods or allowing the existing capital stock to depreciate.

- The required rental allows a supplier of capital services to break even in buying a capital asset. The required rental is higher the higher is the interest rate, the depreciation rate, or the purchase price of the capital good.

- In long-run equilibrium, the asset price of a capital good is both the price at which suppliers of capital goods are willing to make new goods and the price at which buyers can earn the required rental.

- Land is the special capital good whose supply is fixed even in the long run.

- The functional distribution of income across different inputs reflects equilibrium prices and quantities in input markets. Each input's share of national income is quite stable over time.

- The personal distribution of income shows how income is distributed across individuals, through whichever input supply they earn this income.

- High incomes reflect ownership of attributes or assets in scarce supply and high demand. Markets do not produce equality across individuals.

- The bequest of wealth across generations perpetuates advantage and disadvantage. Across individuals, wealth is even more unequally distributed than income.

Review questions

1 Why is a firm's output supply decision the same as its labour demand decision?
2 (a) Why does the marginal product of labour eventually decline as more labour is hired?
  (b) A firm builds a new factory, adding to its capital stock and the flow of capital services thereby provided. What happens to the firm's demand for labour as a result?
3 Over the last 100 years, the real wage rose but the working week got shorter.
  (a) Explain this result using income and substitution effects.
  (b) Could labour input have risen despite shorter working hours per person?
4 A film producer says that the industry is doomed because Russell Crowe and Julia Roberts are paid too much. Evaluate the argument.
5 When might an industry face a horizontal supply curve for labour?

6 Why are the following statements wrong? (a) There is no economic reason why a sketch that took Picasso one minute to draw should fetch £100 000. (b) Higher wages must raise incentives to work.

7 Suppose going to university adds nothing to productivity but reveals that you were simply born clever and determined. Would graduates earn more than non-graduates? Would it matter if you studied philosophy or economics? What can be deduced from the fact that arts graduates earn less than economics graduates?

8 A worker can earn £20 000 a year for the next 40 years. Alternatively, the worker can take three years off to go on a training course whose fees are £7000 per year. If the government provides an interest-free loan for this training, what future income differential per year would make this a profitable investment in human capital?

9 Suppose economists form a union and establish a certificate that is essential for practising economics. Would this raise the relative wage of economists? How would the union restrict entry to the economics profession?

10 Young hospital doctors complain that the long hours they have to work are not adequately compensated by their initial salaries. Use the material of this section to discuss two theories of what is going on.

11 Why are trade unions highly visible in industries with monopoly power in their output market but not in competitive industries? What is the likely consequence of globalization for the future of trade unions?

12 Why are these statements wrong? (a) Free schooling from 16 to 18 ensures that the poor can stay on in education. (b) Many low-paid workers belong to a trade union. Hence unions do not improve pay and conditions.

13 Classify each as a stock or a flow: (a) a four-bedroom house, (b) the annual output of the UK house-building industry, (c) a painting by Picasso, (d) a training video.

14 Discuss the main determinants of the firm's demand curve and the industry's demand curve for capital services. How do these determinants affect the way a tax on the industry's output will shift the industry demand for capital services?

15 The interest rate falls from 10 to 5 per cent. How does this affect the rental on capital services and the level of the capital stock in an industry in the short and long run?

16 A plot of land is suitable only for agriculture. Can the farming industry go bankrupt if there is a rise in the price of land? How would your answer be affected if the land could also be used for housing?

17 How fixed is the supply of land?

18 Why are these statements wrong? (a) If the economy continues to become more capital-intensive, eventually there will be no jobs left for workers. (b) Land is freely supplied by nature, and hence land rentals should be zero.

19 Name three taxes that help equalize the after-tax personal income distribution. Do any taxes have the opposite effect? Did you remember inferior goods?

20 If land is fixed in quantity and quality, can land rentals keep pace with other factor incomes in a growing economy?

21 Brazil has an unequal personal income distribution. Suggest at least three reasons.

Answers on pages 346–348

7

Governing the market

7-1

Equity, efficiency, and market failure

Learning outcomes

By the end of this section, you should understand:

- ◆ Horizontal equity and vertical equity
- ◆ Efficiency
- ◆ When markets are efficient
- ◆ Sources: of market failure
- ◆ Externalities and public goods
- ◆ Informational problems in markets
- ◆ Moral hazard and adverse selection

A re markets a good way to allocate scarce resources? What does 'good' mean? Is it fair that some people earn much more than others in a market economy? These are not positive issues about how the economy works, but normative issues based on value judgements by the assessor.

Left-wing and right-wing parties disagree about the market economy. The right believes the market fosters choice, incentives, and efficiency. The left stresses the market's failings and how government intervention can improve market outcomes. Generally, outcomes are judged against the criteria of equity and efficiency.

Horizontal equity rules out discrimination between people with similar characteristics and performance. Vertical equity is the Robin Hood principle, taking from the rich to give to the poor.

Horizontal equity is the identical treatment of identical people. **Vertical equity** is the different treatment of different people in order to reduce the consequences of these innate differences.

An economy's *resource allocation* describes who does what, and who gets what. Equity always entails value judgements but Vilfredo Pareto suggested a definition of efficiency that might be free of value judgements.

For given tastes, inputs, and technology, an allocation is **efficient** if no one can then be made better off without making at least one other person worse off.

Suppose we have 10 apples to give Stan and Rudi. Failure to hand out all 10 apples is inefficient. A free lunch is available. Stan can get more apples without Rudi having fewer. Giving Stan and Rudi 5 apples each is efficient. None are wasted. However, giving all 10 to Rudi is also efficient, but many would think this unfair; 8 for Stan and 2 for Rudi is still efficient, but fairer.

Taxation and subsidies can redistribute apples, but may waste some in the process. If a free market yields 7 for Rudi and 3 for Stan, suppose by redistribution we could then gain 1 more for Stan but only at the cost of losing 2 for Rudi. Reasonable people will disagree whether this is desirable. It is a pure value judgement.

The invisible hand

Adam Smith suggested that a market economy is efficient 'as if by an Invisible Hand'. Perfect competition may do the job. Each consumer buys goods until his marginal cost (the price of the good) equals the marginal benefit of the good to him. The demand curve shows how much consumers buy at each price. Thus at each quantity in Figure 7-1 the demand curve DD is also the marginal benefit to consumers of getting that quantity of films.

Perfectly competitive producers equate price to marginal cost. At each output in Figure 7-1 the supply curve SS thus shows the marginal cost of making that amount of the good. At Q_1 films, the marginal benefit to consumers is P_1, above the marginal cost to producers. Society should make more films than Q_1. Where supply and demand intersect, the social marginal benefit P^* of using resources to make films equals the social marginal cost P^* of films. No free lunch is available by reallocating resources. The allocation is efficient.

No government decided this. Each consumer and each firm pursued their self-interest, buying and selling what made sense to them. Prices co-ordinated their decisions. Because

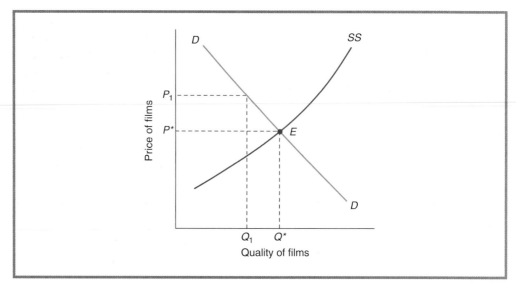

Figure 7-1   Competitive equilibrium and Pareto-efficiency

every buyer and seller faced the *same* price, marginal benefits equalled marginal costs. Society got the efficient quantity produced and consumed.

Even so, the resulting allocation may well be very unequal, as the talented are rewarded more highly than the disadvantaged. The Invisible Hand applies to efficiency but not to equity. Quite often, it does not deliver efficiency either.

Market failures

A **distortion** or **market failure** exists if society's marginal cost of making a good does not equal society's marginal benefit from consuming that good.

There are four principal sources of market failure.

Taxation

Governments levy taxes to finance public spending. A tax creates a gap between the price the buyer pays and the price the seller receives. If there is car tax of £2000, car buyers equate the marginal benefit of cars to the gross price, but car producers equate the marginal cost of cars to the lower net price received by producers. Hence the marginal cost of cars is £2000 less than the marginal benefit of cars. This is inefficient. Society should make more cars. Government spending is needed to offset other distortions in the market economy, and to redistribute income, but taxation itself usually creates a distortion.

Imperfect competition

Facing down-sloping demand curves, imperfect competitors set marginal cost equal to marginal revenue, which is less than the price they charge. Thus, price exceeds marginal cost, like a privately imposed tax. Again, such industries produce too little from the social viewpoint: in equilibrium, the marginal benefit of more output exceeds its marginal cost.

Externalities

Externalities are spillovers, such as pollution, noise, and congestion. A person's decision ignores her effect on other people. There is no market for externalities like noise, secondary cigarette smoke, or induced congestion on roads. Without a market in noise, prices cannot equate the marginal benefit of making a noise and the marginal cost of that noise to other people.

Other missing markets

People cannot always insure against the risks that they face, or find a loan on reasonable terms. Like externalities, these are examples of missing markets. The problem is often the fear market participants have of being exploited by others with superior information. Again, with no market, price cannot equate society's marginal costs and benefits of these activities.

We now discuss market failures in more detail, and how policy might solve them. The rest of this section discusses externalities and other missing markets. The next two sections discuss taxation and imperfect competition.

Externalities

An **externality** arises if a production or consumption decision affects the physical production or consumption possibilities of other people.

A chemical firm pollutes a lake, imposing an extra production cost on anglers (fewer fish) or a consumption cost on swimmers (dirty water). The firm pollutes until the marginal benefit of polluting (a lower cost of making chemicals) equals its marginal cost of polluting, which is zero. It ignores the marginal cost its pollution imposes on anglers and swimmers.

Conversely, you paint your house but ignore the consumption benefit to your neighbours, who now live in a nicer street. You paint up to the point where your own marginal benefit equals your marginal cost, but society's marginal benefit exceeds yours. There is too little house painting.

In both cases, the private costs or benefits differ from social costs or benefits. Figure 7-2 shows the marginal private cost MPC of making chemicals. For simplicity, we assume it is constant. The marginal social cost MSC of chemical production is the marginal private cost plus the *marginal externality* from pollution at each output of chemicals. As chemical production rises, each extra unit of chemical output causes more pollution damage.

The curve DD shows the demand for chemicals. At the equilibrium output is Q, the marginal social cost MSC exceeds the marginal social benefit of chemicals (the private demand curve DD, since there are no consumption externalities). The output Q is inefficient. By reducing chemical production, society saves more in social cost than it loses in social benefit. Society could then make some people better off without making anyone worse off.

The efficient output is Q', at which the marginal social benefit and cost of the last output unit are equal. By producing at the market equilibrium E, not the efficient point E', society wastes the triangle E'EF, the excess of social cost over social benefit when output rises from Q' to Q.[1]

---

[1] Beneficial production externalities help other producers. Pest control by one farm reduces pests on nearby farms. The marginal social cost of farm output is then *below* the marginal private cost. We could re-label the MSC curve as MPC in Figure 6-2 and re-label MPC as MSC. Free market equilibrium is at E' but E is now the efficient point.

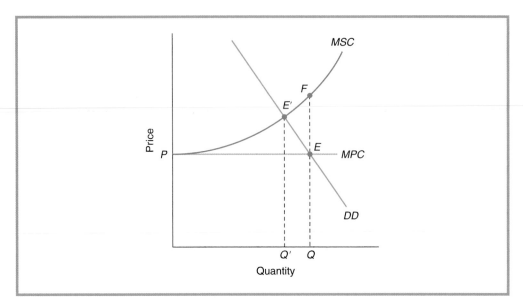

Figure 7-2 The social cost of a production externality

Production externalities make private and social cost diverge. Consumption externalities make private and social benefit diverge. Again, free market equilibrium is inefficient. Output is too low if externalities are beneficial, as with planting roses in your garden, but is too high if externalities are adverse, as with smoking in restaurants.

Box 7-1   Atmosphere of pollution

Chlorofluorocarbons (CFCs), gases used in things like aerosols, are destroying the ozone layer. Without this sunscreen, more people get skin cancer. Organizing international cutbacks in atmospheric pollution is difficult: each country wants to free ride, enjoying the benefits of other countries' cutbacks but making no contribution of its own. The Montreal Protocol was signed by nearly 50 countries in 1987. Before the Protocol, projected ozone depletion was 5 per cent by 2025 and 50 per cent by 2075. In the Protocol, countries agreed to take steps to reduce ozone depletion to 2 per cent by 2025 with no further deterioration thereafter. Dream on.

A second type of atmospheric pollution is the greenhouse effect from emissions of CFCs, methane, nitrous oxide, and, especially, carbon dioxide. Greenhouse gases are the direct result of pollution and the indirect result of the atmosphere's reduced ability to absorb them. Plants convert carbon dioxide into oxygen. Chopping down forests to clear land for cattle, as global demand for hamburgers rises, has accelerated the greenhouse effect.

The consequence is global warming. People in London and Stockholm get better suntans; people in Africa face drought and famine. As icecaps melt, the sea rises, flooding low-lying areas. By 2070, the temperature will have risen by 4 °C, and the sea by 45 centimetres. Again, organizing collective international cutbacks has been difficult.

In 1997, the Kyoto Protocol agreed national targets for lower emissions of green-

Box **7-1** *Continued*

house gases. Becoming binding in 2008–12, the Kyoto deal would have cut emissions by 5 per cent relative to the 1990 level, but by much more relative to the growth that a do-nothing policy would have allowed. The table shows 1990 levels, actual behaviour in the 1990s, and the target for 2012.

	1990 emission (million tonnes)	2012 target (% change from 1990 level)
Japan	1190	−6
USA	5713	−7
Germany	1204	−21
UK	715	−12
Italy	532	−6
France	498	0
Spain	301	+15

In 2001, US President George W. Bush announced that the US would not ratify the Kyoto Protocol because it did not force poorer countries such as India and China to do their share of pollution reduction. In July 2001, after a meeting in Bonn, 178 countries decided to proceed with a weaker version of the Kyoto Protocol, despite the refusal of the US to participate.

Property rights and externalities

Can we set up a market in pollution? By pricing pollution itself, people could trade it until private marginal costs and benefits were equal. With nobody now ignored, private and social costs or benefits are the same again. Notice, in passing, that this implies that the efficient quantity of pollution is not zero. Eliminating the last little bit has a huge marginal cost and only a small marginal benefit. It is not worth cutting back to zero.

Why do we not have a market in pollution? Someone at your door says: 'I am collecting money from people who hate factory smoke in their gardens. We'll pay the factory to cut back. Will you contribute? I'm visiting 5000 houses nearby.' Even though you hate smoke, you pretend not to care and do not contribute. If everybody else pays, the factory cuts back and you get the benefit. If nobody pays, your small payment makes little difference. Whatever others do, you do not pay: you are a *free rider*. Everyone else reasons similarly. Nobody pays, even though you are all better off paying to get the smoke cut back.

A **free rider**, knowing he cannot be excluded from consuming a good, has no incentive to buy it.

Taxing externalities

Cigarette smokers cause bad consumption externalities for those nearby. Figure 7-3 shows the supply curve *SS* of cigarette producers, which also shows marginal social cost. *DD* is the

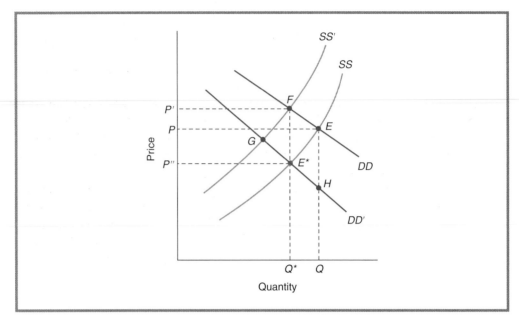

Figure 7-3   Taxes to offset externalities

private demand curve, showing the marginal private benefit of cigarettes to smokers. The marginal social benefit *DD'* of cigarette consumption is lower than *DD*.

Free market equilibrium is at *E*, but the efficient point is E^*. The government now levies a tax E^*F per packet of cigarettes. With the tax-inclusive price on the vertical axis, the demand curve *DD* is unaffected, but the supply curve shifts up to *SS'*, which, subtracting the tax E^*F from each price, returns producers to the original supply curve *SS*.

A tax rate E^*F leads to market equilibrium at *F*. The efficient quantity Q^* is produced and consumed. Consumers pay *P'* and producers get P_0 after tax is deducted at E^*F per unit. The tax rate E^*F is exactly the marginal externality on the last unit when the efficient quantity Q^* is produced. Consumers behave as if they took account of the externality, though they look only at the tax-inclusive price. Taxes that offset externalities *improve* efficiency. The fact that alcohol and tobacco have harmful externalities is a reason to tax them heavily.

Box 7-2   Keeping pollution in check

Environmental protection has been a mixed success in the last 30 years. Smog has gone, and fish are back in many rivers. But coal-fired power stations still emit sulphur dioxide, and Greenpeace activities highlight many other examples that still cause concern. If we want to reduce pollution further, should we use quotas or taxes?

Facing the same pollution tax rate, each firm would adjust until the marginal cost of cutting pollution is the same across firms, a necessary feature of the efficient solution. However, in an uncertain world, the government might miscalculate, and set the wrong tax rate. If pollution beyond a certain critical level is disastrous, for example irreversibly damaging the ozone layer, direct regulation of the quantity of pollution is safer, even if it fails to cut pollution in the least-cost way. However, a clever compromise is possible.

Box 7-2 *Continued*

The US Clean Air Acts include an *emissions trading programme* and *bubble policy*. The Acts specify a minimum standard for air quality, and impose pollution emission quotas on individual polluters. Any firm below its pollution quota gets an *emission reduction credit* (*ERC*) that can be sold to other polluters wanting to exceed their pollution quotas. Total pollution is regulated, but firms that can cheaply cut pollution do so, selling their *ERC* to firms for which pollution reduction is costlier. This reduces the total cost of pollution reduction.

When a firm has many factories, the *bubble policy* applies pollution controls to the firm as a whole, not to individual factories. A firm can cut back most in the plants where pollution reduction is cheapest. US policy combines 'control over quantities' for aggregate pollution where the risk and uncertainty are greatest, with 'control through the price system' for allocating efficiently the way these overall targets are achieved.

Public goods

Public goods are like a very strong externality. Most goods are private goods. The ice cream in your throat is now unavailable for eating by other people. Not so with public goods, such as clean air and national defence.

A **public good** is necessarily consumed in equal amounts by everyone.

Public goods have this special feature in consumption, in whichever sector they are produced. If the Navy patrols coastal waters, your consumption of national defence does not affect our quantity of national defence. We get different amounts of utility from it if our tastes differ, but must all consume the same quantity. Nobody can be excluded from consuming a public good once it exists, and the act of consumption does not deplete the quantity left for other people.

Public goods supplied in private markets are wide open to the free-rider problem. Since you get it, *whether or not you pay for it*, you never buy a public good that already exists. Private markets do not produce the efficient quantity. We need government intervention. The efficient quantity of a public good equates the marginal cost of making it to the marginal social benefit of having it, which is simply the *sum* of the marginal private benefit of each person consuming that quantity.

Democracies resolve this problem through elections. By asking 'How much would you like, given that everyone will be charged for the cost of providing public goods?', society tries to identify the efficient quantity of a public good. This may then be produced by the public sector, or contracted out to private suppliers.

Other missing markets

Information is not always free to acquire. People often know more about their own behaviour than others can easily find out. Fear that people will exploit this informational advantage may then prevent markets from developing. Here are two problems that crop up regularly.

Moral hazard

Insurance companies calculate the odds of various risks occurring. Is this how they calculate what premium to charge for house insurance? Sitting in a restaurant, you remember you left some chips frying in a pan. Why leave your nice meal to go home to switch the cooker off? You are fully insured against fire. Similarly, with full health insurance you may not bother with precautionary check-ups. The act of insuring raises the likelihood of the thing you are insuring against.

Moral hazard exploits inside information to take advantage of the other party to the contract.

With complete information, the insurance company could refuse to pay out if you do not take proper care. With costly information, it is hard for the company to discover this key fact.

Actuarial calculations for the whole population, many of whom are uninsured, are now a poor guide to your behaviour once insured. Moral hazard makes it harder to get insurance and costlier if you get it. Insurance firms at best offer partial insurance, leaving you to bear part of the cost if the bad thing happens. This gives you an incentive to take care, reducing the odds of the bad outcome. Hence, insurance firms pay out less often and can charge you a lower premium.

Adverse selection

People who smoke are more likely to die young. Individuals know if they themselves smoke. If an insurance firm cannot tell who smokes, it must charge everyone the same price.

Box 7-3   Economics: A Nobel Science

The 2001 Nobel Prize for Economic Science was shared by three economists who pioneered the analysis of inside information.

George Akerlof first analysed *adverse selection* in the used car market, where sceptical buyers know sellers may try to offload useless cars about which the seller has much more information than the buyer. Akerlof showed that, in market equilibrium, buyers assume all cars are bad. Sellers of good cars cannot get a fair price. The same analysis helps us understand loan sharks, junk bonds, and street traders offering supposedly genuine Armani perfume at silly prices.

Michael Spence showed that this problem is partly solved if those with good characteristics take costly actions to reveal credibly that they must be the good guys. Higher education can *signal* that you are smart and determined, valuable things in a worker. Investment banks hire history as well as economics graduates because they value these attributes, not because they want to know more about Queen Elizabeth 1.

Joseph Stiglitz, former Chief Economist of the World Bank, developed another solution to adverse selection, relying on *screening* by the buyer rather than signalling by the seller. Offering lower initial wages but correspondingly higher salaries later in life is attractive only to those workers who plan to remain with the firm in the long run. It allows the firm then to invest in training, knowing that their workers will not then take years out to surf in Australia.

Suppose this reflects mortality rates for the whole country. Non-smokers, with above-average life expectancy, find the price too dear. Smokers, knowing their looming health problems, realize that the price is a bargain.

Adverse selection means individuals use their inside information to accept or reject a contract. Those accepting are no longer an average sample of the population.

The insurance firm cannot distinguish the two groups, but knows that a price based on the national average will attract only smokers, a loss-making proposition. Instead, the firm assumes that all its customers smoke, and charges a suitably high price. It defends against the worst. Non-smokers cannot get insurance at a fair price.

To check the difference between moral hazard and adverse selection, which is which in the following examples? (1) A person with a fatal disease signs up for life insurance. (2) Already having insured his kids, a person then becomes unexpectedly depressed and commits suicide. (The first is adverse selection, the second moral hazard.)

Similarly, borrowers know if they are safe or risky, but this is hard for lenders to discover. Suppose a bank should charge safe borrowers an interest rate of 5 per cent, but risky borrowers an interest rate of 15 per cent. An accountant may tell the bank to charge something in between, like 10 per cent. An economist knows this will attract only risky borrowers. The only equilibrium is for the bank to charge 15 per cent, attracting only risky borrowers. Safe borrowers are fed up because they cannot get a loan on decent terms. Adverse selection prevents a market for safe borrowers.

Moral hazard and adverse selection prevent some markets developing properly. Without markets, the Invisible Hand cannot equate marginal social benefit and marginal social cost.

7-2

Taxation

Learning outcomes

By the end of this section, you should understand:

- ◆ Average and marginal tax rates; direct and indirect taxes
- ◆ Fair and unfair taxes
- ◆ Tax incidence
- ◆ Taxation, efficiency and waste

Table 7-1 shows UK government spending over nearly 50 years. Governments buy goods and services – schools, defence, the police, and so on – which directly use resources that could have been used in the private sector. Governments also spend on *transfer payments* – subsidies such as social security, state pensions, and debt interest – that do not directly use scarce resources. Rather, they transfer purchasing power to people who then buy goods and services.

	1956	1976	2003
Total spending	34	47	42
Goods and services	21	26	23
Transfer payments	13	21	21

Table 7-1 UK government spending (percentage of GDP)

Sources: ONS, *UK National Accounts: HM Treasury, Budget*

Between 1956 and 1976, the scale of government got bigger. Since then, the trend has been reversed. One reason has been the desire of governments to make tax cuts.

If T is the amount paid in tax, and Y is income, then T/Y is the **average tax rate**. The **marginal tax rate** shows how total tax T increases as income Y increases.

Taxable income	Marginal tax rate (%)	
(2001 £)	1978/79	2004/05
2000	34	10
5000	34	22
20 000	45	22
40 000	70	40
80 000	83	40

Table 7-2 UK income tax rates, 1978–2004

Sources: ONS, *Financial Statement & Budget Report*

Note: Taxable income after deducting allowances. In 2004/05 a single person's allowance was £4745

Taxes are *progressive* if the average tax rate rises as income rises, taking proportionately more from the rich than from the poor. Taxes are *regressive* if the average tax rate falls as income level rises, taking proportionately less from the rich. Table 7-2 shows that the UK, like many other countries, has cut tax rates in the last two decades, especially for the very rich.

UK government spending, and the taxes that finance it, are now about 40 per cent of national output. Nearly half government spending goes on transfer payments such as pensions and debt interest. Just over half goes to buy goods and services, especially health, defence, and education. Most government spending is financed by taxation, mainly *direct taxes* related to income (income tax itself, national insurance contributions, and corporation tax paid by firms) and *indirect taxes* on expenditure (value added tax (VAT) and excise duties on fuel, alcohol, and tobacco).

Direct taxes are taxes on income; indirect taxes are taxes on spending.

We now assess the UK tax system against our two criteria: equity and efficiency.

How to tax fairly

In taking proportionately more from the rich than from the poor, income tax reflects the principle of *ability to pay*, based on a concern about vertical equity. In contrast, the *benefits principle* argues that people who get more than their share of public spending should pay more than their share of tax revenues. Car users should pay more than pedestrians towards public roads.

The benefits principle often conflicts directly with the principle of ability to pay. If those most vulnerable to unemployment must pay the highest contributions to a government unemployment insurance scheme, it is hard to redistribute income, wealth, or welfare. If the main objective is vertical equity, the ability to pay principle must take precedence.

Two factors make the tax and benefit system more progressive than income tax alone. First, transfer payments actually give money to the poor. The old get pensions, the unemployed get jobseeker's allowance, and the poor get income support. Second, the state supplies some public goods available to the poor even if they do not pay taxes. The rich sunbathe in their own gardens, but the poor sunbathe in public parks.

There are some *regressive* elements that take proportionately more from the poor. Beer and tobacco taxes, and the National Lottery, are huge earners for the government. Yet the poor spend much more of their income on these goods than do the rich. These things effectively redistribute from the poor to the rich!

Tax incidence

The ultimate effect of a tax can be very different from its apparent effect.

Tax incidence is the final tax burden once we allow for all the induced effects of the tax.

Figure 7-4 shows labour demand DD and labour supply SS. With no tax, equilibrium is at E. Now an income tax is introduced. If we measure the gross wage on the vertical axis, the demand curve DD is unaltered since the gross wage is the marginal cost of labour to the firm.

However, it is the wage net-of-tax that induces workers to supply labour. SS still shows labour supply in terms of this net wage, so we must draw the higher schedule SS' to show the supply of labour in terms of the gross wage. The vertical distance between SS' and SS is the income tax on earnings from the last hour of work.

The new equilibrium is E'. The gross wage is W' at which firms demand L hours. The vertical distance $A'E'$ is the tax paid on the last hour of work. At the net wage W_0, workers supply L' hours. Relative to the original equilibrium, a tax on wages raises the gross wage to W', but cuts the net wage to W_0. It raises the wage firms pay, but cuts the wage workers get.

The **tax wedge** is the gap between the price paid by the buyer and the price received by the seller.

The incidence of the tax fell on *both* firms and workers even though, for administrative convenience, the tax was collected from firms. The incidence or burden of a tax does not depend on who hands over money to the government. Taxes alter equilibrium prices and

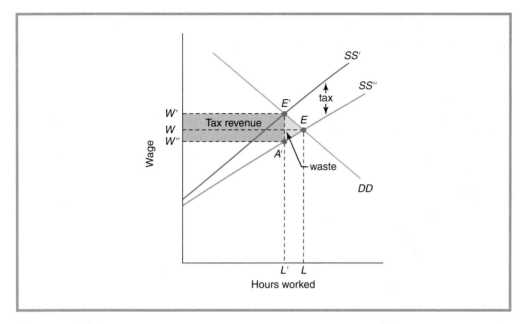

Figure 7-4 A tax on wages

quantities. These induced effects must also be taken into account. However, we can draw a general conclusion. The more inelastic the supply curve and the more elastic the demand curve, the more the final incidence will fall on the seller rather than the purchaser.

Figure 7-5 shows the extreme case of a vertical supply curve. Without a tax, equilibrium is at E and the wage is W. A vertical supply curve SS implies that a quantity of hours L are supplied whatever the net wage. A tax on wages leads to a new equilibrium at A'. Only if the gross wage is unchanged will firms demand the quantity L that is supplied. The entire incidence falls on the workers. To check you have got the idea of incidence, draw for yourself a market with a horizontal supply curve but down-sloping demand curve. Show that the incidence of a tax now fall only on consumers.

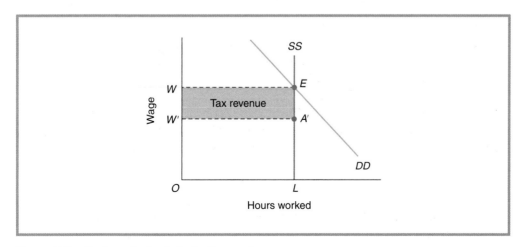

Figure 7-5 Taxing a factor in inelastic supply

Taxation, efficiency, and waste

Having examined taxation and equity, we now look at taxation and efficiency. We can use Figure 7-4 again. Before the tax, labour market equilibrium is at E. The wage W is both the marginal social benefit of the last hour of work and its marginal social cost. The demand curve DD shows the marginal benefit of labour, the value of extra output. The supply curve SS shows the marginal social cost of work, the value of leisure sacrificed to work another hour. At E, marginal social cost and benefit are equal, which is socially efficient.

A tax shifts equilibrium to E'. The tax $A'E'$ raises the gross wage to firms to W' but cuts the net wage for workers to W_0. The triangle $A'E'E$ is a deadweight loss or pure waste. By cutting hours from L to L', the tax stops society using hours on which the marginal social benefit, the height of the demand curve DD, exceeds the marginal social cost, the height of the supply curve SS. By driving a wedge between the wage firms pay and the wage workers get, the tax makes market equilibrium inefficient.

Box 7-4   Betting tax scrapped early

'The tax on punters will be abolished three months ahead of schedule on the first weekend in October', the Financial Secretary Paul Boateng announced today (13/7/01). Gordon Brown announced in his March Budget that by January 1, 2002, the current tax on betting stakes would be replaced with a tax on bookmakers' gross profits, a radical reform which means Britain's bookmakers will end the deductions they currently charge punters, and look to grow their domestic and international business from a UK base. *Source*: www.hm-treasury.gov.uk

This example illustrates the limits to government sovereignty. Betting tax had been a big earner for the Treasury. Competition from offshore bookies offering online betting put an end to this. The government was forced to change betting tax to stop onshore bookies being wiped out. How the Internet and globalization are changing the nation state is a key issue of the new millennium. Economics helps you understand better what is going on.

Must taxes distort?

Most taxes do, but Figure 7-5 showed a tax when supply is completely inelastic. With equilibrium quantity unchanged, there is no distortion triangle. This is a general principle. If either the supply or the demand curve is inelastic, a tax induces a small change in quantity. Hence the deadweight loss triangle is small. Since the government needs some tax revenue, the smallest waste occurs if the goods most inelastic in supply or demand are taxed most heavily. Another reason for high taxes on alcohol and tobacco is that they have inelastic demand.

Finally, Section 7–1 showed that taxes actually improve efficiency if they offset externalities. By building marginal externalities into the prices to which private individuals react, such pollution taxes and congestion charges make people 'internalize' externalities.

7.3

Dealing with monopoly power

Learning outcomes

By the end of this section, you should understand:

- ◆ The social cost of monopoly power
- ◆ UK competition policy in theory and practice
- ◆ Mergers
- ◆ Regulation of natural monopolies

Imperfectly competitive firms with some monopoly power must cut their price to sell more output. Since marginal revenue is less than the price for which the last good is sold, marginal cost is less than price and marginal consumer benefit. Such firms make less than the efficient quantity.

Moreover, when a competitive firm gets lazy it loses market share and may go out of business. When a monopoly gets lazy, it simply makes less profit. From the social viewpoint, its cost curves are then unnecessarily high.

Social cost

There are two **social costs of monopoly power**. The first is too little output, the second is wastefully high cost curves.

Society may not worry just about the inefficiency of imperfect competition. It may also care about the *political* power that large firms exert, and the *distributional* issue of the fairness of large monopoly profits.

Taxing monopoly profits

The way to maximize after-tax profits is to maximize pre-tax profits. Thus, for *given* cost curves, a monopolist's output is unaffected by a tax on monopoly profits. Since the demand curve for its output is unaffected, making the same output means charging the same price. Governments can tax away monopoly profits. High profits are not directly a social cost of monopoly power.

Must liberalization help?

Is more competition always better? Suppose there are big economies of scale and a steadily downward-sloping average cost curve. Suppose the government insists on more competition, say entry of a second producer. Greater competition reduces profit margins, but, with lower output, the firms cannot enjoy scale economies and have high average costs. Society may lose more from the cost increase than it gains from greater competition.

We thus discuss two approaches to policy. Where scale economies are not too big, promoting competition is indeed the answer. But where scale economies are vast, it is better to keep the monopoly but regulate its behaviour.

Competition policy

What do Durex, Valium®, and cornflakes have in common with household gas supplies and mobile phones? All were investigated by the Competition Commission, which monitors the behaviour of big firms and checks for the possible abuse of monopoly power.

Competition policy tries to promote efficiency through competition between firms. The **Competition Commission** examines whether a monopoly, or potential monopoly, is against the public interest.

UK businesses operating internationally are increasingly subject to EU competition law, but many businesses still operate primarily within the UK. The latter are governed by UK competition law, chiefly the Competition Act of 1998 and the Enterprise Act of 2002, which made it a criminal offence, punishable by a jail sentence, to engage in a dishonest cartel.

The **Office of Fair Trading** is responsible for making markets work well for consumers, by protecting and promoting consumer interests while ensuring that businesses are fair and competitive.

In particular, the OFT has the power to refer cases to the Competition Commission for a detailed investigation in cases in which existing monopoly power may be leading to a 'substantial lessening of competition'.

For UK companies with substantial business within the EU, EU competition law takes precedence over UK law. Article 81 of the Treaty of Amsterdam prohibits anti-competitive agreements that have an appreciable effect on trade between EU Member States and which prevent or distort competition within the EU. Article 82 prohibits the abuse of any existing dominant position.

Responsibility for enforcement of these Articles lies with the European Commission. Since 1999, the Commissioner specifically responsible for competition policy has been Mario Monti, a former economics professor in Italy. The case study at the end of the chapter discusses how Monti took on software giant Microsoft.

For UK companies operating principally within the UK, it is UK competition policy that matters. Prior to the Enterprise Act of 2002, the Commission evaluated whether or not a monopoly was acting 'in the public interest', with no presumption that monopoly was bad. Many previous judgements of the Commission concluded that companies were acting in the public interest – for example, because they had an excellent record of innovation and cost reduction that outweighed the fact that their monopoly position also allowed them to reduce output and raise prices.

The 2002 Enterprise Act focuses more narrowly on competition itself and made the Competition Commission more accountable by defining its objectives more clearly. This also brought UK law more clearly into line with EU competition law, by placing measures of competition at the centre of the evaluation of competition policy.

UK competition policy in practice

The Competition Commission has wide powers, yet few firms have been penalized after its investigation. The Commission has often relied on informal assurances that bad behaviour would stop.

For example, after examining charges from fixed phones to mobile phones, it concluded that emerging competition in telecommunications was not yet sufficient to discipline the top suppliers, whose charges were too high. The Commission recommended that top suppliers such as Vodafone and O_2 reduce their prices considerably.

Other recent cases include the 2004 investigation of whether 'store cards' issued by particular retailers were substantially reducing competition, and the 2003 report on the extended warranties that retailers often offer when you buy a new camera or TV. Annual UK sales of domestic electrical goods are nearly £20 billion, and consumers spend nearly £1 billion a year buying extended warranties (multi-year insurance and service agreements) usually purchased from the retailer of the goods at the time the goods are bought. If you are buying a new camera in one shop, it is difficult for a different supplier simultaneously to be offering you a warranty.

The Commission concluded that this monopoly power led to prices on warranties being up to 50 per cent higher than they would have been in a competitive market. To remedy this, the Commission demanded that retailers provide consumers with much more transparent written information about the cost of warranties, and that consumers should be allowed to cancel warranties (with a full refund) for up to 45 days after their initial purchase.

This judgement illustrates what has long been a distinction between the US and UK approaches to competition policy. US competition law often seeks a structural change in the industry to *prevent* the potential for monopoly power. UK competition law has more frequently sought to *control* behaviour of those with monopoly power rather than to restructure the industry altogether.

Market structure often reflects the tension between the output required for minimum efficient scale and the size of the market as given by demand for the product. Large countries, facing large demand, may have room for many firms operating at minimum efficient scale. Small countries, with smaller markets, have room for fewer firms at minimum efficient scale.

Hence, large countries can break up monopolies more easily, since subdivided firms may still enjoy substantial scale economies. In smaller countries, with smaller markets, breaking up monopolies may sacrifice scale economies and simply raise costs. Developing policies to contain monopoly behaviour may then be preferable to policies that outlaw monopoly itself.

Merger policy

Competition policy also scrutinizes the formation of large new companies.

A **merger** is the union of two companies where they think they will do better by amalgamating.

A *horizontal merger* is the union of two firms at the same production stage in the same industry. A *vertical merger* is the union of two firms at different production stages in the same industry. In *conglomerate mergers*, the production activities of the two firms are essentially unrelated.

A horizontal merger may allow more scale economies. One large car factory may be better than two small ones. Vertical mergers may assist co-ordination and planning. It is easier to make long-term decisions about the best size and type of steel mill if a simultaneous decision is taken on car production for which steel is an important input. Conglomerate mergers involve companies with completely independent products, and have less scope for a direct reduction in production costs.

Merger policy must thus compare the social gains (potential cost reduction) with the social costs (larger monopoly power). Table 7-3 shows merger activity involving UK firms. It shows dramatic merger booms in the late 1980s and again in the late 1990s.

	Number	Value (1998 £bn)
1972–78	640	1
1979–85	490	4
1986–89	1300	43
1990–94	590	10
1995–98	580	31
1999–00	540	61
2001–03	490	26

Table 7-3 UK mergers (annual averages), 1972–2003

Source: ONS, *Mergers and Acquisitions*

Merger booms would have been impossible if policy had opposed them. Individual cases were again examined case by case. There are currently two grounds for referring a prospective merger to an investigation by the Competition Commission: (1) that the merger creates market share of at least 25 per cent, or (2) that the company taken over has an annual turnover of at least £70 million.

Since 1965, only 4 per cent of merger proposals have been referred to the Competition Commission. UK policy has largely consented to mergers, reflecting two assumptions. First, cost savings from scale economies are big. Second, as part of an increasingly competitive world market, even large UK firms have little monopoly power.

Regulating natural monopolies

Sometimes, large domestic firms face little foreign competition, and the size of scale economies makes them natural monopolies.

A **natural monopoly**, having vast scale economies, does not fear entry by smaller competitors.

The government can nationalize them, to control their behaviour in the public interest, or can leave them as private firms but appoint independent regulators to supervise their behaviour. After 1945, most European countries chose nationalization. Since 1980, they have increasingly reverted to regulation of private monopolies.

To limit the exercise of monopoly power, regulators sometimes impose a price ceiling. For many years after its privatization in 1984, BT had an '$RPI - X$' price ceiling. Its *nominal* prices could rise with the retail price index, minus X per cent. X is the annual fall in its *real* price that the regulator demands. Since BT enjoyed rapid technical progress, it should have been able to cut costs year after year. And it did: during its first ten years as a private company, BT's real prices fell by 43 per cent.

Telecoms is an interesting industry because competition has increased substantially in the last decade. BT now faces competition from mobile phones, cable TV companies, and local providers. For calls made from land lines, regulators have now concluded that it is no longer necessary to place so much emphasis on regulating the price of phone calls themselves. Competition may be adequate provided that other entrants can access the infrastructure of BT's phone lines. Regulation has shifted back up the vertical chain, from regulation of the final price to regulation of access to intermediate networks that then facilitate competition in the final output market.

Unlike telecoms, where greater competition has altered the need for regulation, some industries will always exhibit significant monopoly power. Because transporting water is very expensive, there is always likely to be only one local water company. To contain this monopoly power, the water regulator OFWAT has adopted an annual price ceiling of '$RPI + K$', letting the real price of water *rise* a K per cent a year to finance much needed investment in pipes and water purification. Conversely, after criticizing the termination charges that mobile phone companies imposed on calls to other networks, the Competition Commission imposed a price ceiling of '$RPI - 15$' for industry giants Vodafone and O_2, and slightly smaller rates of real price reduction for Orange and T-Mobile.

Box 7-5   Off the rails

In 1997, rail privatization broke up British Rail into many train operators with one company, Railtrack, to supply the track infrastructure. Railtrack's share price soared as investors expected it to prosper. By October 2001, Railtrack was bankrupt. What are the lessons of its failure?

After decades of under-investment in rail infrastructure, a change of ownership was not enough. Massive investment was needed. Since both Railtrack and train operators were regulated, they were not allowed to raise fares enough to earn the revenue needed for this investment. Politicians were sensitive about the level of rail fares and unwilling to inject much public money.

Two things made a bad situation worse. First, everyone underestimated the cost of upgrading the track, notably the line from London to Glasgow. Second, rail accidents, especially at Hatfield where the track was to blame, led to expensive and unanticipated programmes to improve safety rapidly.

The table shows the cumulative investment planned during 2001–10. With the Treasury refusing more help, the private sector was reluctant to invest £34 billion in an industry subject to outside regulation, with no guarantee of enough revenue to repay the investment with interest.

	Public	Private
Rail infrastructure	3.5	25.5
New trains	11.5	8.5
Total	15.0	34.0

Planned Rail investment, cumulative funding (£ billion, 2000 prices), 2001–10

When the government refused to inject any more money into this private company, Railtrack was bankrupt. The government took over control again. Some private investors claimed that this would make future partnerships between public and private sectors more difficult and a court case was fought in 2005 over whether the government had knowingly misled investors in order to renationalize on the cheap. Yet the private sector is happy to keep the profits when things go well. It is unclear that they have grounds for complaint when things happen to go the other way.

Source: The Economist, 20/10/01

Case study 7-1   The full Monti

After more than five years of investigation, the European Commission has fined Microsoft almost €500m for monopolistic abuses and given it four months to make life easier for competitors in the server and media-player markets. *The Economist*, 2/3/04

The success of Microsoft is partly built on the way it bundles products together, making it hard for competitors to compete on individual components without offering the entire package. If you buy Windows, you get Internet Explorer, Windows Media Player, and perhaps even Microsoft Office. Each program works effectively with the rest of the Windows family. Rival producers complain that their products do not interface easily with the Windows family, which deters customers from buying elsewhere. By refusing to disclose access codes for interoperability in workgroup servers, Microsoft makes it harder for non-Windows programs run on office networks to access Windows systems. Similarly, RealPlayer, offered by RealNetworks, claimed to be disadvantaged in comparison with Windows Media Player.

In March 2004, EU Competition Commissioner Mario Monti ruled (a) that Microsoft had illegally refused to supply the proprietary information needed for interoperability and (b) that Microsoft had illegally tied Media Player to the Windows operating system. Microsoft was fined €497m, and ordered to remedy these deficiencies. During 1998–2002, similar issues (for example, the monopoly position of Windows' Internet browser) were examined by the US Department of Justice, though the case was finally settled out of court.

Microsoft continues to appeal against this judgement, which is not finally settled. The Microsoft case demonstrates why firms operating in global markets need to face competition authorities that operate on a similar scale. Imagine if Microsoft had been investigated separately by national authorities in the UK, France, Germany, Sweden, and Ireland, each with its own national rules, and all frightened to be tough in case they lost market share to more lenient regulators in other countries. When global giants deal with fragmented national regulators, it may be impossible for the latter to discharge their responsibility effectively.

Indeed, EU Commissioner Monti revealed that he had been in close discussion with his US counterpart throughout the investigation of Microsoft and subsequent appeal negotiations. Monti noted that the EU had consulted the US authorities more than had been the case in reverse when the US was deciding its attitude to Microsoft, and that the EU happened to be more united than the United States, in the sense that this decision had the unanimous support not only of the EU Commission, but also of the individual competition authorities of each of the EU Member States. The EU judgement – a record fine of €497m ($611m), together with an order to Microsoft to unbundle Windows Media Player from Windows – nevertheless attracted wide criticism from members of the US Congress and Senate!

Mario Monti
© Reuters/Corbis

Recap

- Horizontal equity is the equal treatment of equals, and vertical equity is the deliberately unequal treatment of unequals.

- A resource allocation says who makes what and who gets what. It is efficient if no reallocation of resources could then make some people better off without making others worse off.

- For given inputs and technology, there are many efficient allocations, differing in fairness.

- If there are no market failures, free markets are efficient. Producers and consumers equate marginal costs and marginal benefits to the same price, and thus to each other.

- Governments face a conflict between equity and efficiency. Redistributive taxes drive a wedge between prices to buyers and sellers, undermining the Invisible Hand.

- Distortions occur if market equilibrium does not equate marginal social cost and benefit, an inefficiency, or market failure. Distortions arise from taxation, imperfect competition, externalities, and other missing markets reflecting informational problems.

- Externalities imply one agent's decisions have direct but neglected effects on others. The free-rider problem usually inhibits markets in pollution or congestion. Imposing taxes (subsidies) to reflect the marginal adverse (beneficial) externality makes people act as if the market existed, restoring efficiency.

- Public goods are a strong externality in which everyone consumes the same amount and cannot be prevented from doing so. Markets cannot handle this well. Having elections to decide the level of public goods is a possible solution.

- Inside information inhibits markets through moral hazard and adverse selection. Where markets are missing, prices cannot equate marginal social cost and benefit.

- Government revenues come mainly from direct taxes on personal incomes and company profits, and indirect taxes on purchases of goods and services. Government spending is partly purchases of goods and services, and partly transfer payments.

- A progressive tax and transfer system takes most from the rich and gives most to the poor. The UK tax and transfer system is mildly progressive.

- By taxing or subsidizing goods that involve externalities, the government can induce the private sector to behave as if it takes account of the externality, raising efficiency.

- Except for taxes designed to offset externalities, taxes are generally distortionary. By driving a wedge between the selling price and the purchase price, they stop prices equating marginal cost and marginal benefit. The higher the marginal tax rate and the more elastic supply and demand, the greater the size of the deadweight burden.

- The incidence of tax is who ultimately pays the tax. The more inelastic is demand relative to supply, the more a tax falls on buyers not sellers, and vice versa.

- The social costs of monopoly power are too little output and high cost curves that waste resources.
- Competition policy tries to promote competition to discipline monopoly power. In the UK, where the Office of Fair Trading believes that competition is being substantially reduced, it can refer the case to the Competition Commission. The Commission weighs the costs of monopoly power against possible gains from larger scale.
- Anti-competition agreements between firms, such as collusive price-fixing, are illegal.
- Mergers may be horizontal, vertical, or conglomerate. Conglomerate mergers have the smallest scope for economies of scale. The recent merger boom consisted largely of horizontal mergers to take advantage of larger markets caused by globalization, European integration, and deregulation.
- In principle, mergers can be referred to the Competition Commission if they will create a firm with a 25 per cent market share or the company taken over has a turnover of at least £70 million.
- For both monopolies and mergers, EU competition law takes precedence over UK law if the firms operate within the EU on a significant scale.
- Natural monopolies enjoy such scale economies that effective competition is impossible.
- Governments can nationalize such firms or regulate them as private monopolies. In the latter case, price ceilings help limit the abuse of monopoly power.
- Sometimes, by breaking up companies or by requiring that the owner of a large infrastructure network makes access available to smaller competitors, it is possible to stimulate adequate competition in the final output market.

Review questions

1 An economy has 10 goods to share between two people. (x, y) denotes that the first person gets x and the second person y. For allocations (a) to (e), say if they are efficient, equitable, or neither: (a) $(10, 0)$, (b) $(7, 2)$, (c) $(5, 5)$, (d) $(3, 6)$, (e) $(2, 8)$. Would you prefer allocation (d) or (e)?

2 Driving your car in the rush hour, you slow down other drivers. Is this an externality? How might it be offset efficiently? Discuss the merits of fuel taxes that also penalize rural drivers on deserted roads.

3 Should it be compulsory to wear seat belts in cars?

4 Which of the following are public goods: a privatized coastguard system, a tolerant society, a state-owned post office? In each case explain your answer.

5 Why are these statements wrong? (a) Society should ban all toxic discharges. (b) Railways must be made completely safe. (c) Anything the government can do the market can do better.

6 Which of the following are public goods? (a) the fire brigade; (b) clean streets; (c) refuse collection; (d) cable television; (e) social toleration; (f) the postal service. Explain and discuss alternative ways of providing these goods or services.

7 Classify the following taxes as progressive or regressive. (a) 10 per cent tax on all luxury goods; (b) taxes in proportion to the value of owner-occupied houses; (c) taxes on beer; (d) taxes on champagne.

8 There is a flat-rate 30 per cent income tax on all income over £2000. Calculate the average tax rate (tax paid divided by income) at income levels of £5000, £10 000, and £50 000. Is the tax progressive? Is it more or less progressive if the exemption is raised from £2000 to £5000?

9 (a) Suppose labour supply is completely inelastic. Show why there is no deadweight burden if wages are taxed. Who bears the incidence of the tax? (b) Now suppose labour supply is quite elastic. Show the area that is the deadweight burden of the tax. How much of the tax is ultimately borne by firms and how much by workers? (c) For any given supply elasticity, show that firms bear more of the tax the more inelastic is the demand for labour.

10 Why are these statements wrong? (a) Taxes always distort. (b) If government spends all its revenue, taxes are not a burden on society as a whole.

11 With constant $AC = MC = 5$, a competitive industry makes 1 million cars. Taken over by a monopolist, output falls to 800 000 cars, and the price rises to £8. AC and MC are unchanged. By calculating an inefficiency triangle analogous to those in Section 6−1, quantify the social cost of monopoly in this case.

12 A regulator now imposes a price ceiling of 6. What happens to the social cost of monopoly? Could the regulator impose a ceiling of 5? Would this be efficient?

13 Now draw AC and MC for a natural monopoly that continues to enjoy scale economies as its output rises. What is the socially efficient output if cost curves do not shift? Could the regulator set a price ceiling that would achieve this?

14 Does globalization always reduce the case for merger control?

15 Why are these statements wrong? (a) Monopolies make profits and must be well-run companies. (b) Mergers are beneficial; otherwise companies would not merge.

Answers on pages 348−349

8

The income and output of nations

8-1

Macroeconomic data

Learning outcomes

By the end of this section, you should understand:

- ◆ Measures of national income and output
- ◆ The circular flow of resources and payments
- ◆ Why leakages must equal injections
- ◆ What national income fails to measure

icroeconomics magnifies the detail in order to analyse particular markets. In contrast, macroeconomics simplifies the building blocks in order to focus on how they fit together as a whole. The media are always discussing problems of slow growth, inflation, unemployment, and future of national currencies. These issues help determine the outcome of elections, and make some people interested in learning more about macroeconomics.

Macroeconomics studies the economy as a whole.

Table 8-1 shows both national income and income per person in the Group of Seven or G7, the largest of the rich industrial countries.[1] In total, Americans earned $9.6 trillion (ie $9600 billion) in 2000, or about $34 000 a person. Japanese national income was $3.3 trillion, about $26 000 a person. Although China, India, and Russia are much less developed, and thus have lower incomes per person, they have such large populations that their total incomes are large. China now has the second largest national income in the world, although its citizens each earn only a tenth as much as the average American. What do we mean by the concepts of national income and national output, and how are they measured?

		National income (US$ trillion)	Income per citizen (000's of US$)
G7:	US	9.6	34
	Japan	3.3	26
	Germany	2.1	25
	France	1.4	24
	UK	1.4	24
	Italy	1.3	23
	Canada	0.8	27
Other:	China	4.9	4
	India	2.4	2
	Russia	1.2	8

Table 8-1   National income and income per citizen, 2000
Source: World Bank, *World Development Report, 2002*

Households and firms

Households own land, labour, and capital, whose services they rent to firms as production inputs. Households spend this income buying the output of firms.

The **circular flow** is the flow of inputs, outputs, and payments between firms and households.

In Figure 8-1, the inner loop shows the flows of real resources between the two sectors, and the outer loop shows the corresponding flows of payments.

[1] The G7 are the US, Japan, Germany, UK, France, Italy, and Canada. When Russia is also included, this becomes the G8.

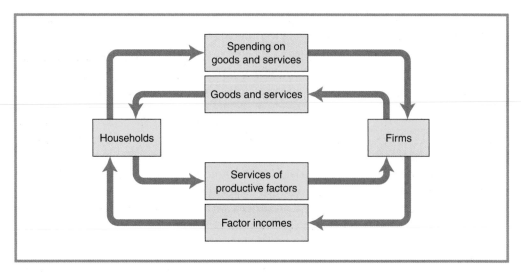

Figure 8-1 The circular flow between firms and households

This suggests three ways to measure the amount of economic activity in an economy: (a) the net value of goods and services produced, (b) the value of household earnings, and (c) the value of spending on the final output of firms. Whether we measure net output, incomes (including profit), or final spending, we get the same answer for GDP.

Gross domestic product (GDP) measures an economy's output.

However, there are several complications. First, the output of firms is not all sold to households. The concept of value added avoids double the output that some firms buy from other firms.

Value added is net output, after deducting goods used up during the production process.

From gross output we deduct the use of raw materials and partly finished goods, but not the cost of labour or capital. The steel in a car door was *already* counted as the output of the steel producer, and must not be counted again as part of the output of the car producer.

We do not deduct the labour of car workers from car output, since car workers were not produced and measured elsewhere in the economy. Nor do we deduct the cost of using the assembly line that made cars. Provided this capital input does not depreciate, it is available next period to make yet more cars, and hence was not used up.

Total value added is the net output of the economy. One way or another, this is paid to households as income and profits, and this income is spent buying the final output that firms sell to end users. So far, households are the only end users.

Leakages and injections

Saving S is the part of income not spent buying output. **Investment** I is firms' purchases of new capital goods made by other firms.

If households earn £7000 but spend only £5000 on consumption C, they must save the other £2000. To pay out incomes of £7000, firms must have value added of £7000 which is sold to end users. If £5000 is sold to households for consumption, the other £2000 must have been sold to firms buying new capital goods. These firms are end users because this capital is *not* then used up as a production input.

Saving is a **leakage** from the circular flow, money paid to households but *not* returned to firms as spending. Investment is an **injection** to the circular flow, money earned by firms but *not* from sales to households. Leakages always equal injections, as a matter of definition.

The *only* way to measure saving is the part of income not spent on output, since income equals output, which is either goods for households or investment goods for firms. Saving must equal investment. By definition.

Similarly, suppose firms do not sell all their output. We treat the flow of unsold goods as temporary *investment* by firms to add to their stock of working capital. Household consumption plus *total* investment still equal output and spending. When stocks are run down, this is negative investment, again keeping the accounting straight.

Adding the government and foreign countries

The government is also an end user, buying the output of firms (education, health, tanks). Governments also spend money on welfare benefits B for things like pensions, jobseeker's allowance, and income support. Not being physical output, these subsidies or *transfer payments* are not part of GDP. They get counted later when spent on household consumption. However, government purchases G of final output are part of GDP. Government spending, both on physical goods and services and on monetary transfer payments, are financed by taxes T.

Finally, we add trade with the rest of the world. Net exports add to GDP.

Exports X are made at home but sold abroad. **Imports** Z are made abroad but bought at home.

Domestic output is bought for consumption C, investment I, government spending G, and exports X. Subtracting the import content Z in these goods, GDP is $[C+I+G+X-Z]$. This is paid out as incomes and profits to households, who use it for consumption, saving, or paying taxes net of benefits received. Thus GDP is also $[C+S+T-B]$. These two measures of GDP must be equal. Deducting consumption from both measures, $[I+G+X-Z]=[S+T-B]$. Hence

$$\begin{array}{cc} \textit{Total leakages} & \textit{Total injections} \\ S+[T-B]+Z & = \quad I+G+X \end{array}$$

Total leakages from the circular flow (savings, net tax payments, and imports) are money from domestic firms that households do not recycle to domestic firms again. Total injections (firms' investment, government purchases, and exports) are sources of firms' revenue not originating from households. Total leakages still equal total injections.

Saving needs no longer equal investment if other elements ensure that total leakages and injections remain equal. But when we remove the government and the foreign sector, we recover the special case that saving must equal injections.

Box 8-1   How big is the hidden economy?

The gangster Al Capone, never charged with murder or gun running, was eventually convicted of income tax evasion. Taxes are evaded not only by smugglers and drug dealers but also by gardeners, plumbers, street vendors, and others working 'for cash'. Since estimates of GNP are derived from tax statistics, the 'hidden' economy is omitted from GNP.

To estimate the size of the hidden economy, we can keep track of what people spend. Maria Lacko used the stable relationship between household consumption of electricity and its two main determinants – income and weather temperature – to estimate incomes by studying available data on electricity consumption and the weather. The hidden economy is large both in the former communist economies, where the new private sector is not yet part of official statistics, and in several Mediterranean countries with a long history of tax evasion.

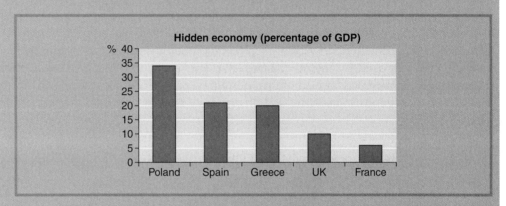

Source: M. Lacko, *The Hungarian Hidden Economy in International Comparisons*, Institute of Economics, Budapest, 1996

From GDP to GNP

To complete the national accounts, we deal with two final problems. First, foreigners own some of our capital and land, and we own some assets abroad. These assets or property earn income unconnected with domestic output.

Gross national product GNP is the total income of citizens wherever it is earned. It is GDP plus net property income from abroad.

If the UK has an inflow of £2 billion from foreign assets, but an outflow of £1 billion in property income to foreigners, UK GNP, the income of UK citizens, is £1 billion more than UK GDP, the value of output in the UK.

The final complication is depreciation.

Depreciation is the fall in value of the capital stock during the period through use and obsolescence.

Depreciation is an economic cost, reducing net output in any period. Deducting depreciation from GNP yields net national product NNP or national income.

National income is GNP minus depreciation during the period.

Our national accounts are now complete, but can you remember them? Figure 8-2 will help to keep you straight.

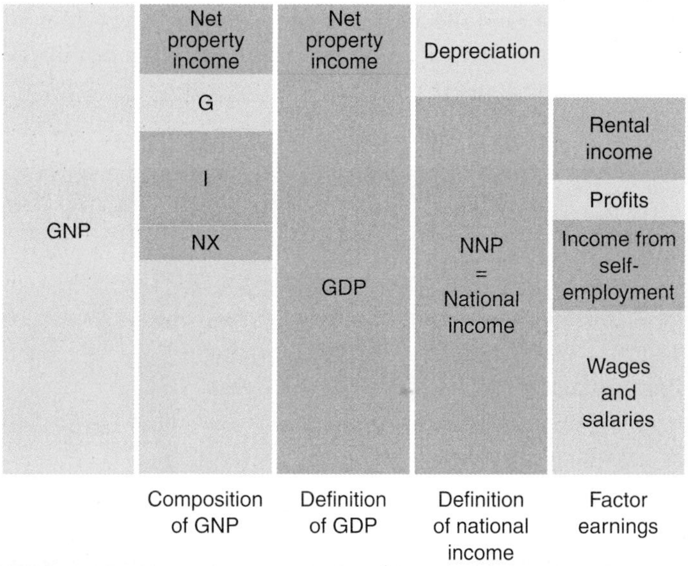

Figure 8-2 National income accounting: a summary

What GNP measures

Depreciation, being hard to measure, is treated differently in different countries. Most international comparisons use GNP, which avoids the need to argue about depreciation.

Nominal GNP is measured at the prices when income was earned. **Real GNP** adjusts for inflation by valuing GNP in different years at the prices prevailing at a particular date.

Since it is physical quantities of output that yield utility or happiness, it is misleading to judge economic performance by nominal GNP. GNP in the UK rose from £25 billion in 1960 to over £1000 billion in 2004. Yet prices in 2001 were 15 times higher than in 1960. Despite the 40-fold rise in nominal GNP, real GNP in 2004 was only about 2.7 times its level of 1960. The rest of the increase in nominal GNP was due to the effect of inflation.

What GNP omits

In practice, GNP omits some things that ideally should be included. First, some outputs, such as noise, pollution, and congestion, reduce true economic output and should be deducted from the usual GNP measure. This is logically correct but hard to implement. These 'bads' are not traded in markets, so it is hard to quantify them or value the costs they impose.

These activities include household chores, DIY activities, and unreported jobs. Moreover, deducting environmental depreciation from measures of national output and income would radically alter our view of how well different countries are doing, and might affect the political incentives to pay more attention to such issues.

Leisure is also a valuable commodity. If two countries make the same output of consumer goods but one delivers more leisure for its residents, its net output of relevant economic goodies is higher. Yet conventional measures of GNP and GDP ignore leisure completely. Standard measures are confined to what is easily measured. Often national statistics are the by-product of tax collection or other government activities. As macroeconomists, we have to deal in the statistics that we have, which are not always the ones we would like to have.

Case study 8-1   Asian tigers or Asian sloths?

'Asia propelled to brink of environmental catastrophe' reported the *Financial Times*, citing a study by the Asian Development Bank, suggesting that Asia would overtake Western economies as the world's biggest source of greenhouse gas pollutants by 2015. Environmental degradation means that almost 40 per cent of Asia's population now live in areas prone to drought, erosion, and even tsunamis. With the Asian population set to triple in the next 20 years, and half these people living in cities, air pollution will set new records. In the long run, dealing with climate change will depend even more on China and India than on the United States.

Traffic congestion in Bangkok
© Lindsay Hebberd/Corbis

Well-run firms spend serious money on information systems to let their managers make intelligent decisions. Governments often make do with economic data gathered on the cheap. Published GDP data ignores valuable commodities like leisure, and omits important harmful outputs like environmental pollution. Asian countries – China, Hong Kong, Thailand, South Korea, Singapore, Taiwan, and the Philippines – have had 40 years of rapid GDP growth, averaging 7–8 per cent, or more than double the annual growth rates achieved by Europe and the United States, and so are often called the Asian tigers to emphasize their energy and vitality.

Figure 8-2 showed that annual depreciation of the national capital stock is subtracted from GNP when calculating national income. You know how a car depreciates because there is a thriving second-hand market for cars, which are traded frequently enough to provide excellent data for car magazines to calculate depreciation rates on Minis and Mondeos. However, buildings, factories, power stations, rail networks, and other capital goods are not traded very frequently, if at all. Statisticians calculating national income have to make brave guesses about how quickly a ship or a power station

Case study 8-1 *Continued*

depreciates. These estimates underlie all national income data, and it is because different countries make different estimates that many cross-country comparisons look at GNP not national income.

There is no logical reason, however, why we will not eventually be able to estimate environmental depreciation in exactly the same way as we estimate depreciation of physical capital. Satellites and sensors will increasingly be able to measure many aspects of our environment that currently yield us services that are often untraded and unrecorded: the smell of grass and green fields, the tranquillity of unspoiled countryside, the pleasure of swimming in clean sea, and the ability to breath clean air without getting asthma attacks and other allergies.

If nations kept proper account of environmental depreciation, their growth rate of national income, properly measured, would be much less impressive than the GNP growth rates so frequently bandied about. And Asian countries might go from heroes to zeroes, because of the rate at which they are destroying their environment. Instead of calling them Asian tigers to celebrate their strength and vitality, we might have to call them Asian sloths to reflect the true pace at which their living standards, properly measured, are changing. But until we have such data, we will have to make do with comparisons based on GNP and GDP, measuring income and output before depreciation is subtracted.

8-2

Economic growth

Learning outcomes

When you have finished this section, you should understand:

- ◆ Determinants of economic growth
- ◆ Why economics was called the dismal science
- ◆ Evidence about growth rates
- ◆ The costs of growth

D uring 1870–2000, UK real GDP grew ten-fold and real income per person five-fold. We are richer than our grandparents, but less rich than our grandchildren will be. Table 8-2 shows that sustaining a slightly higher growth rate for a long time makes a huge difference. What is long-run economic growth? What causes it?

	Real GDP		Real GDP per person	
	Ratio of 2000 to 1870	Annual growth (%)	Ratio of 2000 to 1870	Annual growth (%)
Japan	100	3.7	27	2.7
USA	66	3.4	10	1.8
Australia	45	3.1	4	1.2
France	15	2.2	10	1.9
UK	10	1.9	5	1.3

Table 8-2   Long-run growth, 1870–2000

Source: Angus Maddison, 'Phases of Capitalist Development', in R. C. O. Matthews (ed.), *Economic Growth and Resources*, Macmillan, 1979; updated from IMF, *International Financial Statistics*

Economic growth is the rate of change of real income or real output.

Had we been growing for thousands of years, we would be even richer now than we are. It is only in the last 250 years that real GDP per person has been persistently increasing.

Potential output is the level of GDP when all markets are in equilibrium

Short-run shifts in demand or supply can lead to a temporary period in which output differs from potential output. However, in the long run, changes in output caused by any fluctuations around potential output are swamped by the effect of persistent growth of potential output itself.

Potential output grows either because the quantity of inputs grows, or because a given quantity of inputs makes more output. The main inputs are labour, capital, and land (the environment). How much output a given bundle of inputs produces depends on the productivity of these inputs.

Like us, our grandparents had a 24-hour day, but were probably fitter since they got more exercise. Why can we make more output than they could? We must have accumulated lasting advantages in the meantime. These cumulated advantages are physical capital, skills that we call human capital, or technical ideas that we call technology.

Technology is the current stock of ideas about how to make output. **Technical progress** or better technology needs both **invention**, the discovery of new ideas, and **innovation** to incorporate them into actual production techniques.

Major inventions led to spectacular gains in knowledge. The wheel, the steam engine, and the modern computer changed the world. Industrialized societies began only when productivity improvements in agriculture allowed some of the workforce to be freed for industrial production. Before then, almost everyone had to work the land merely to get enough food for survival.

Requirements for economic growth

Embodiment of knowledge in capital

To introduce new ideas to production, innovation usually needs investment in new machines. Without investment, bullocks cannot be transformed into tractors even when a blueprint for tractors exists. Major inventions lead to waves of investment and innovation to put these ideas into practice. The mid-nineteenth century was the age of the train. We are now in the age of the microchip.

Learning by doing

Human capital also matters. With practice, workers get better at a particular job. Difficult skills take years to master, whether the skill is bending it like Beckham, using computer software, or diagnosing and fixing a mechanical failure. Sometimes productivity and output rise even without more physical capital or new technology. However, eventually we master even difficult tasks. Further output growth then requires the use of more inputs or the application of newer technology

Growth and accumulation

In 1798, Thomas Malthus' *First Essay on Population* predicting that population growth would drive down living standards to starvation levels suggested that permanent growth in living standards was impossible. This dire prediction led to the branding of economics as 'the dismal science'.

Malthus argued that the supply of land was fixed. As the population expands, more and more labour has to work with this fixed supply of land, leading to diminishing returns to labour productivity, which would steadily fall. Hence, living standards would decline to the point at which starvation then eliminated the population growth that was causing the problem in the first place.

Some of the poorest countries today face this *Malthusian trap*. Agricultural productivity is so low that everyone must work the land to produce food. As population grows but agricultural output fails to keep pace, famine sets in and people die. If better fertilizers or irrigation raise agricultural output, population quickly rises as nutrition improves, and people are driven back to starvation.

Today's rich countries have broken out of the Malthusian trap. How did they manage it? First, by raising agricultural productivity (*without* an immediate rise in population) some workers could be shifted to industrial production. The capital goods then made included better ploughs, machinery to pump water and drain fields, and transport to distribute food more effectively. With more capital input, productivity rose further in agriculture, releasing more workers for industry to make yet more capital.

Second, rapid technical progress in agricultural production caused steady growth in productivity, reinforcing the effect of more capital input. Living standards improved steadily. Hence, even with land in fixed supply, sustained growth is possible. Accumulated capital can grow, substituting for fixed land, and technical progress keeps output growing even when inputs do not increase.

Capital accumulation

By 1960, Nobel Prize winner Robert Solow had worked out a neoclassical theory of growth used in empirical work ever since. By *neoclassical* we mean that it simply assumes that actual output equals potential output, rather than worrying also about whether this is always true in the short run.

In the long run, output, labour, and capital all grow. Since they cannot be constant, the idea of equilibrium must be applied not to levels but rather to growth rates and ratios.

Along the **long-run equilibrium path**, output, capital, and labour grow at the same rate. Hence output per worker y and capital per worker k are constant.

For simplicity, consider a closed economy isolated from the rest of the world. Suppose population growth raises labour input at a constant rate n. Assume too that a constant fraction s of income is saved; the rest is consumed. Aggregate investment (public plus private) is the part of output not consumed by either the public or private sector.

In a growing economy, **capital widening** gives each new worker as much capital as that used by existing workers. **Capital deepening** raises capital per worker for all workers.

Capital widening needs more investment per person (a) the faster is population growth n (more new workers for whom new capital is needed) and (b) the more capital per person k that new workers need to match that of existing workers. Figure 8-3 plots the line nk along which capital per person is constant.

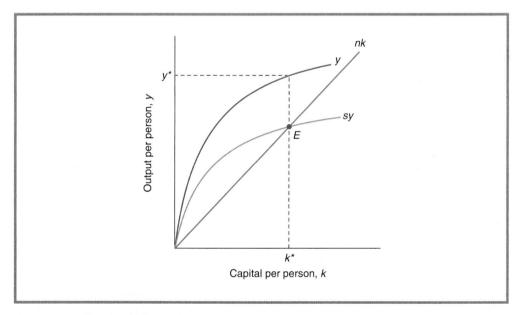

Figure 8-3   Neoclassical growth

Adding more and more capital per worker k increases output per worker y, but with diminishing returns since labour growth simply remains at n whatever the speed of capital accumulation. Hence the curve y in Figure 8-3 gets flatter as we move to the right.

If a constant fraction s of output is saved, sy is saving per person. With leakages equal to injections, saving and investment are equal, the curve sy also shows investment per person. In the steady state, the capital per person k is constant. Hence investment per person sy must equal nk, the investment per person needed to keep k constant by making capital grow as fast as labour. k^* is the long-run level of capital per person, and y^* is the long-run level of output per person. Capital and output grow at the same rate n as labour in the long run.

Figure 8-3 also shows what happens way before the economy reaches this long-run equilibrium path. If capital per worker is low, the economy begins to the left of its eventual position. Per capita saving and investment sy exceeds nk, the per capita investment that makes capital grow in line with labour. Hence, capital per person rises and we move to the right. Conversely, to the right of the steady state, sy lies below nk, capital per person falls, and we move to the left. Figure 8-3 says that, from whatever k the economy begins, it gradually converges on the (unique) long-run levels of capital per person k and output per person y.

In this long run, labour is growing at the rate n as it always does. Hence capital and output are growing at the rate n, keeping k^* and y^* constant.

A higher saving rate

Suppose people permanently increase the fraction of income saved, from s to s'. We get more saving and more investment, but *not* permanently faster growth!

Population continues to grow at the rate n. Eventually, *all* variables grow at the rate n. Hence output and capital *must* eventually grow again at n. So what happens to the extra saving? It allows capital deepening, raising capital per worker from its original level k^* to some higher level k^{**}, after which the new steady state is reached, with capital, output, and labour all growing at n. As capital per worker increases, the burden of capital widening – providing enough capital for the growing population – becomes harder. When capital per worker has risen enough, all the extra saving and investment are taken up with capital widening. Further capital deepening ceases. Only during the temporary transition from the equilibrium path to the new one has capital (and hence output) grown faster than labour (thereby increase capital per worker from k^* to k^{**}).

Thus, a rise in the saving rate does not cause a permanent increase in the growth rate, but it does cause a temporary spurt in capital accumulation, which the economy is raising capital per worker to its new equilibrium level.[2] When that is reached, all variables revert to growing at the rate n. The higher saving rate has permanently raised the *level* of capital and output, but not their eventual *rate of growth*.

Growth through technical progress

So far, the theory says that output, labour, and capital all grow at rate n. Although it is true that capital and output grow at the same rate, in practice both grow more rapidly than labour. That is why we are better off than our great grandparents. Each generation has more capital per person than the previous generation enjoyed, and hence attains a higher level of income per person than the previous generation.

Of course, capital accumulation is not the whole story. There is also technical progress. Imagine that the creation of new knowledge at the rate t lets each worker do the work of $(1 + t)$ previous workers.

Labour-augmenting technical progress increases the effective labour supply.

[2] You can also see this using Figure 8-3. A rise in the fraction of income saved will shift the sy curve closer to the output curve y. The new equilibrium state, where nk and sy intersect, will be to the right of E on the nk line, confirming that capital per person must rise. Therefore output per person also rises as workers become more productive. But in this new equilibrium, capital per worker and output per worker are constant, and hence capital and output are growing at the same rate n as labour and population.

Effective labour input grows at rate $(t+n)$ because both technical progress and population growth increase the effective labour force. Now, in the long run, capital and output each grow at the same rate $(t+n)$ as the effective labour supply. But actual people continue to grow at the rate n. Hence, capital per worker and output per worker *grow* permanently at the rate t.

With this amendment, our theory of long-run growth now fits all the important facts of the real world. The ration of capital to output is constant in the long run. Both capital and output grow at the rate $(t+n)$, which exceeds the rate n at which population and the labour force grow. Hence capital per worker and output per worker grow steadily in the long run.

Evidence about growth

The Organization for Economic Cooperation and Development (OECD) is a club of about 30 of the world's richest countries, from industrial giants like the United States and Germany to smaller economies like New Zealand, Ireland, and Turkey. Table 8-3 shows the growth of OECD countries since 1950. The table shows the sharp productivity slowdown after 1973 in all OECD countries.

	OECD	Japan	Germany	France	UK	USA
1950–1973	3.6	8.0	5.6	4.5	3.6	2.2
1973–2000	1.4	2.3	2.7	2.0	1.7	0.7

Table 8-3 Average annual growth in real output per worker (%)
Sources: S. Dowrick and D. Nguyen, 'OECD Comparative Economic Growth 1950–85', *American Economic Review*, 1989; OECD, *Economic Outlook*

Why did productivity growth slow down? First, 1973 was also the year of the first OPEC oil price shock, when real oil prices quadrupled. This had two effects. First, it diverted R&D towards very long-term efforts to find alternative energy-saving technologies. These efforts may take decades to pay off and show up in improvements in actual productivity. Second, the higher energy prices made much of the capital stock useless. Energy-guzzling factories, too expensive to operate, were scrapped. The world lost part of its capital stock, reducing output per head.

Moreover, increasing regulation and pollution control, although socially desirable, raised production costs and reduced *measured* output and hence *measured* productivity. We return shortly to the mismeasurement of output and hence of output growth.

Having discussed differences in growth across sub-periods, we now discuss differences across countries. The fact that OECD countries move together across sub-periods shows that many aspects of growth are not within a country's control. Technical progress spreads quickly wherever it originates. Countries are increasingly dependent on the same global economy.

The convergence hypothesis

Figure 8-3 has a unique steady state, to which a country converges whatever its initial level of capital per worker. When capital per worker is low, it takes little investment to equip new workers (capital-widening), so the rest of investment raises capital per worker (capital-deepening). Conversely, when capital per worker is already high, saving and investment are insufficient to give new workers the old level of capital per worker, which therefore falls.

The **convergence hypothesis** says poor countries should grow quickly but rich countries should grow slowly.

Since this seems plausible, why is sub-Saharan Africa not growing really quickly? Basically, for two reasons. First, Figure 8-3 assumed that a constant fraction of income is saved. But people with low living standards may have to consume *all* their income just to stay alive. With no saving, they then have no resources to invest at all. They are thus unable to begin the virtuous cycle of investment that generates additional output, thereby providing a surplus that can be saved and reinvested in yet more capital accumulation. Also, since a lot of technical progress is made operational through installing new capital equipment that embodies the latest ideas, countries that are not investing may also find it difficult to take advantage of technical progress as well.

Without capital accumulation or technical progress, such countries are indeed stuck in the Malthusian trap. As population expands, more labour is added to a fixed land supply and labour productivity falls. Even worse, global warming may adversely affect the land quality too, so that a growing population is having to work with a land supply that is effectively shrinking, making the Malthusian trap spring shut even more quickly.

Some of these countries also have civil wars or corrupt governments that appropriate the country's meagre wealth for the ruling elite. This reminds us that economic success depends on a flourishing civil society, good governance, and other attributes that cannot narrowly be explained by economics alone.

The costs of growth

Some people believe that the benefits of economic growth are outweighed by its costs. Pollution, congestion, and a hectic life-style are too high a price to pay for a rising output of cars, washing machines, and video games.

Since GDP is an imperfect measure of the net economic value of output made by the economy, there is no presumption that we should aim to maximize the growth of measured GDP. We discussed issues such as pollution in Chapter 7. Without government intervention, a free market economy is likely to produce too much pollution.

However, zero pollution is also wasteful. Eliminating the last little bit of pollution costs a lot and has only a little benefit. Rather, society should reduce pollution until the marginal benefit of more pollution reduction equals its marginal cost.

This is the most sensible and direct way in which to approach the problem. In contrast, the 'zero-growth' solution tackles the problem only indirectly.

The **zero-growth proposal** argues that, because higher output has adverse side effects such as pollution and congestion, we should therefore aim for zero growth of measured output.

The zero-growth approach does not distinguish between outputs that have adverse side effects and those that do not. It does not provide the right incentives. When society believes that there is too much pollution, congestion, environmental damage, or stress, the best solution is to provide incentives that directly reduce these activities. Restricting growth in measured output is a very crude alternative that is distinctly second best.

Some of these difficulties might be removed if economists and statisticians could devise a more comprehensive measure of GDP that included all the 'quality of life' activities (clean air, environmental beauty, serenity) that yield consumption benefits but at present are omitted from measured GDP. Inevitably, voters and commentators assess government performance according to published, measurable statistics. A better measure of GDP might remove some of the conflicts that governments feel between measured output and the quality of life.

Case study 8-2   The road to riches

For centuries, growth in income per person was tiny. Most people were near starvation. Now we take growth for granted. After 1750, industrialization changed everything. Capital and knowledge, accumulated by one generation, were inherited and augmented by the next generation.

Why 1750? Partly because mathematical and scientific ideas reached a critical mass, allowing an explosion of practical spinoffs. Yet many pioneers of the Industrial Revolution were commonsense artisans with little scientific training. Conversely, the ancient Greece of Pythagoras and Archimedes achieved scientific learning but not economic prosperity.

By the start of the fifteenth century, China understood hydraulic engineering, artificial fertilizers, and veterinary medicine. It had blast furnaces in 200BC, 1500 years before Europe. It had paper 1000 years before Europe, and invented printing 400 years before Gutenberg. Yet in 1600 China was overtaken by Western Europe, and by 1800 had been left far behind.

Economic historians continue to debate the root causes of progress, but three ingredients seem crucial: values, politics, and economic institutions. Growth entails a willingness to embrace change. China's rulers liked social order, stability, and isolation from foreign ideas – fine attitudes when progress was slow and domestic but a disaster when the world experienced a profusion of new technologies and applications.

Powerful Chinese rulers could enforce bans and block change in their huge empire. When individual European rulers did the same, competition between small European states undermined this sovereignty and offered opportunities for growth and change. Economic competition helped separate markets from political control. Rights of merchants led to laws of contract, patent, company law, and property. Competition between forms of institution allowed more effective solutions to emerge and evolve. Arbitrary intervention by heads of state was reduced. Opportunities for business, trade, invention, and innovation flourished.

Case study 8-2 *Continued*

Year	Income per person (1990 prices)	Inventions
1000	400	Watermills
1100	430	Padded horse collar
1200	480	Windmills
1300	510	Compass
1400	600	Blast furnace
1500	660	Gutenberg printing press
1600	780	Telescope
1700	880	Pendulum clock, canals
1800	1280	Steam engine, spinning and weaving machines, cast iron, electric battery
1900	3400	Telegraph, telephone, electric light, wireless
2000	17 400	Steel, cars, planes, computers, nuclear energy

The making of Western Europe

Source: The Economist, 31/12/99

8-3

Business cycles

Learning outcomes

By the end of this section, you should understand:

- ◆ Trend growth and cycles around this path
- ◆ Why business cycles occur

I n practice, aggregate output does not grow as smoothly as long-run growth theory might suggest. In some years output grows a lot, but in other years it actually falls.

The **business cycle** is short-term fluctuation of output around its trend path.

Is there an actual cycle? We know output fluctuates a lot in the short run, but a cycle also requires a degree of regularity. Can we see it in the data? If so, how do we explain it?

Trend and cycle: statistics or economics?

Figure 8-4 shows a business cycle. The smooth curve is the steady growth in trend output over time. Actual output follows the wavy curve. Point *A* is a *slump*, the bottom of a business cycle. At *B*, the economy enters the *recovery* phase of the cycle. As recovery proceeds, output climbs above its trend path, reaching *C*, which we call a *boom*. Then it enters a *recession* in which output is growing less quickly than trend output, and may even be falling. Point *E* shows a *slump*, after which the cycle starts again.

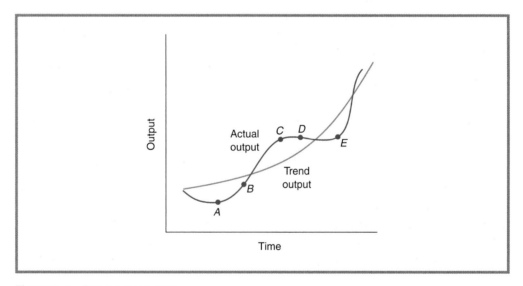

Figure 8-4   The business cycle

Figure 8-5 shows the annual growth of real GDP and of real output per worker in the UK during 1975–2004. Output and productivity grew rapidly in the late 1980s but stagnated in the early 1980s and early 1990s. The figure makes three points. First, short-run cycles *are* important. Second, in the short-run there is a close relation between changes in output and changes in labour productivity (output per worker). Third, cycles have become less pronounced since the mid-1990s. These are the facts that we need to explain.

Any series of points may be decomposed statistically into a trend and fluctuations around the trend. We begin by assuming that potential output grows smoothly. It follows the trend. Trend growth is what we studied in the previous section.

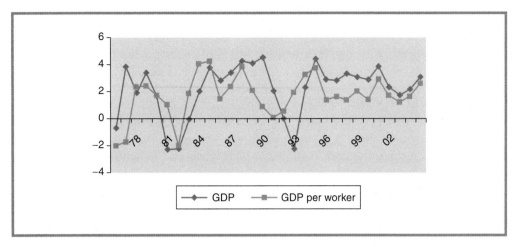

Figure 8-5 Output and productivity growth (percentage pa), 1975–2004

Political business cycles

Actual output fluctuates because it departs temporarily from the smooth trend path of potential output. But why would this happen? One possibility is a *political business cycle*. Suppose voters have short memories and are heavily influenced by how the economy is doing just before the election. To get re-elected, the government manipulates the economy into a slump, then mops up this spare capacity by using government policy to boost output and income as the election approaches, achieving a temporary period of impressive-looking growth. The voters think that the government has got things under control and votes them in for another term of office.

A **political business cycle** is caused by cycles in policy between general elections.

The theory contains a grain of truth, but it supposes that voters are pretty naive. In 1997, the Major government lost the UK election even though output was growing strongly. Voters thought Labour could do even better. Moreover, the Bank of England has now been made independent of political control precisely to take the politics out of monetary-policy decisions, and the Code for Fiscal Stability is designed to make budgetary policy more stable as well.

The period between elections is pretty fixed. In the UK it is usually four years, and a maximum of five years. The more that cycles last longer than five years, the less likely it is that politics is the main cause of the business cycle. Indeed, a lengthening of the average duration of the business cycle would be significant evidence that politics was becoming less important as a determinant of cycles.

Ceilings and floors

Cycles are likely when we recognize the limits imposed by supply and demand. The total supply of output provides an output *ceiling* in practice. Although it is possible temporarily to meet higher demand by working overtime and running down stocks of finished goods, output cannot expand indefinitely. In itself this tends to slow down growth as the economy reaches a boom. Having overstretched itself, the economy is likely to bounce back off the ceiling and begin a downturn. Conversely, there is a *floor*, or a limit to the extent to which total demand is likely to fall. Gross investment (including replacement investment) cannot actually become negative unless, for the economy as a whole, machines are being unbolted and sold to foreigners. Although falling investment is an important component of a downswing, investment cannot fall indefinitely, since it cannot fall below zero.

Fluctuations in stockbuilding

Working capital – partly finished goods or goods that have been produced but not yet sold – also plays an important role. Consider inventory investment in working capital. Firms hold stocks of goods despite the cost in interest cost forgone on the funds tied up in making goods for which no revenue has yet been received. The corresponding benefit of holding stocks is to avoid temporary changes in production levels, which can be costly. Output expansion entails overtime payments and costs of recruiting new workers. Cutting output involves redundancy payments. Holding stocks lets firms meet short-term fluctuations in demand without incurring the expense of short-run fluctuations in output.

If demand falls, firms initially build up stocks of unsold output. If demand remains low, firms gradually cut output rather than stockpile goods indefinitely. Once demand recovers again, firms are still holding all the extra stocks built up during the recession. Only by increasing output *more slowly* than the rise in aggregate demand can firms eventually sell off these stocks and get back to long-run equilibrium levels of stocks.

Thus, the evolution of stocks helps explain why output adjustment is so sluggish. Output changes more slowly than demand. This helps explain the behaviour of labour productivity in Figure 8-5. Output per worker rises in a boom and falls in a slump. This is because output adjusts more quickly than employment, since changes in employment levels themselves are costly for firms, especially if there is some prospect that these will soon be reversed again.

A fall in demand is met initially both by cutting hours of work and increasing stocks. With a shorter work week, output per worker falls. If the recession intensifies, firms undertake the costlier process of sacking workers and restoring hours to their normal level. Conversely, a boom is the time when output and overtime are high, and productivity per worker peaks.

Real business cycles

Essentially, this explanation implies that cycles in demand are the cause of cycles in actual output around a smooth trend growth path for potential output. However, there is a second possibility. Potential output may itself be subject to fluctuations. This idea is sometimes called a 'real' business cycle, since the causes arise only from changes in the real economy that affect the physical supply of inputs or the technology that affects the output derived from any given quantities of inputs.

Real business cycles are output fluctuations caused by fluctuations in potential output itself.

One source of such cycles might be shocks to technology, which affect potential output by affecting productivity. The age of the train, the car, and the microchip have required huge waves of investment, affecting not just aggregate demand but also potential output.

Some economists have been sceptical of this approach for two reasons. First, changes in aggregate supply may occur more slowly than changes in aggregate demand. Second, to provide a theory of cycles, the economy would also need to experience some periods in which productivity *fell* because technology deteriorated. Can we really forget today what we knew how to do yesterday?

Sometimes, we can get new information that causes an important change of opinion about future technology. The end of the Internet boom in 2001 had many features of a real business cycle. It was not that actual productivity fell. Rather, people were unsure about how rapidly the new technologies would increase future productivity. Initially, everyone was optimistic that growth rates would be very high indeed. Investment was very high, anticipating rapid future growth.

As evidence accumulated that that productivity growth was going to be a little slower than first imagined, suddenly everybody realized that there had already been far too much investment in some hi-tech sectors. Share prices collapsed, and further investment dried up. This reflected both a downgrading of ideas about the future level of potential output, and a fall in current aggregate demand since investment then fell.

Policy implications

Research on real business cycles has one vital message for macroeconomic policy. It is not always appropriate to try to stabilize output over the business cycle. When output falls *because* potential output has fallen, there is no longer any gap between actual and potential output that policy should be trying to close. In contrast, if cycles reflect temporary deviations of actual output from potential output, then in an ideal world policy might be trying to stabilize actual output, removing these deviations and allowing output simply to follow its smooth trend path.

Empirical research has found some evidence that technology shocks affect output in the short run. But demand shocks are usually more important. The task for stabilization policy – the headache that the Bank of England confronts once a month – is to decide whether visible changes in output have been accompanied by invisible changes in potential output, or whether the gap between actual and potential output has changed. Nobody said the Bank's job was easy.

Recap

- Macroeconomics analyses the economy as a whole.
- Households supply inputs that are used by firms to make output. Households' income from firms is used to buy firms' output. There is a circular flow between households and firms.
- GDP, the value of output made in a country, is measured in three equivalent ways: value added in production, factor incomes including profits, or spending on final output.
- Leakages from the circular flow are household income from firms not then spent on the output of firms. Savings, net taxes, and imports are leakages. Injections are revenue for firms not originating with household spending. Investment by firms, government purchases, and exports are injections. Total leakages always equal total injections.
- GNP, a country's income, is its GDP plus its net property income from abroad.
- National income deducts depreciation from GNP.

- Nominal GNP is measured at current prices. Real GNP is measured at constant prices.
- In practice, GNP and GDP omit unmarketed activities – bads like pollution, valuable activities like leisure, and work in the home – and production unreported by tax evaders. Including these would give a better measure of income and output.
- Economic growth is the percentage annual rise in real GDP or real GDP per head. It is an imperfect measure of the growth in economic well-being.
- Output rises because of larger quantities of inputs of land, labour, and capital, or because technical progress raises the output produced by given input quantities.
- Along the long-run equilibrium path, variables grow at the same rate and ratios of these variables are constant. Without technical progress, capital, output, and labour grow at the same rate. Whatever its initial level of capital, an economy tends to converge on this steady-state path. With a growing population, this theory can explain output growth but not productivity growth.
- Adding technical progress to this model explains why labour productivity and living standards can grow for ever.
- Growth rates should converge because capital-deepening is easier when capital per worker is low than when it is high. In practice, some poor countries miss out on growth either because they cannot save or because conflict, corruption, and mistrust undermine growth.
- The trend path of output is the long-run path after short-run fluctuations are ironed out. The business cycle describes fluctuations in output around this trend.
- A political business cycle means that the government ensures growth is slow immediately after the election, allowing abnormally rapid growth just before the next election.
- Full capacity and the impossibility of negative gross investment provide ceilings and floors, limiting the extent to which output can fluctuate.
- Fluctuations in stockbuilding add to the business cycle, and reflect costs of adjusting output.
- Real business cycles assume that cycles reflect fluctuations in potential output. Technology shocks can have this effect.
- Both demand and supply shocks contribute to the business cycle. Policies to stabilize output are appropriate only if cycles reflect demand shocks that create a gap between actual and potential output.

Review questions

1 The table shows final sales and purchases of intermediate goods in car production. What is the industry's contribution to GDP?

	Sales	Intermediate goods bought
Car producer	1000	330
Windscreen producer	200	10
Tyre producer	80	30
Steel producer	50	0

2 GNP is £300. Depreciation is £30 and net property income is −£3. Find the values of national income and GDP.

3 The output of the police is not marketed. GDP statistics use police wages to measure their output. If crime falls, we need fewer police. What happens to measured GDP? Is the country better off?

4 Should the following ideally be in GNP? (a) Time spent by students in lectures; (b) the income of muggers; (c) time spent watching football; (d) the salary of traffic wardens; (e) dropping litter.

5 Why are these statements wrong? (a) Unemployment benefit raises national income in years when employment is low. (b) In 2004, *Crummy Movie* earned £1 billion more than *Gone With The Wind* earned 50 years ago. *Crummy Movie* is a bigger box office success.

6 'Britain produces too many scientists but too few engineers.' What kind of evidence might help you decide if this is true? Will a free market lead people to choose the career that most benefits society?

7 Name two economic bads. Can they be measured? Are they included in GNP? *Could* they be?

8 'Because we know Malthus got it wrong, we take a more relaxed view about the fact that some minerals are in finite supply.' Is there a connection? Explain.

9 Use a diagram like Figure 8-3 to compare two economies with different rates of population growth. Which has the higher living standards in the long run? Why?

10 Why are these statements wrong? (a) Since the earth's resources are limited, growth cannot continue forever. (b) If we saved more, we would definitely grow faster.

11 Suppose higher oil prices permanently increase the costs of manufacturers, reducing supply and hence potential output. The government sees a fall in actual output. Should it take action to try to restore the former level of output? Why or why not?

12 Cycles in export demand could potentially transmit cycles from one country to another. (a) If lower transport costs make the world more integrated, would you expect national cycles to become more or less correlated with one another? (b) If all countries decided to hold their elections on the same day every five years, would this increase or reduce the scope for a political business cycle?

13 Why are these statements wrong? (a) Closer integration of national economies will abolish business cycles. (b) The more we expect cycles, the more we get them.

Answers on pages 349−350

9

Short-run fluctuations in income and output

9-1

Output and income in the short run

Learning outcomes

By the end of this section, you should understand:

- ◆ Actual output and potential output
- ◆ Aggregate demand and equilibrium output
- ◆ The consumption function
- ◆ Shifts in aggregate demand
- ◆ The multiplier
- ◆ The paradox of thrift

Wе now turn from long-run growth of national income and output to movements of income and output in the short run. Since 1960, annual real GDP growth in the UK has averaged 2.4 per cent. But there have been cycles around this trend. In some years, output actually fell, but in other years it grew strongly. What determines national output, and why does it fluctuate? We distinguish *actual* output from *potential* output.

Potential output is national output when all inputs are fully employed. The **output gap** is the difference between actual output and potential output.

Potential output tends to grow smoothly over time as inputs rise and technical progress occurs. Population growth adds to the labour force. Investment in new machinery, education, and training increase the quantity not merely of physical capital but also of human capital, the skills embodied in the current workforce. In addition to these increases in the quantity of inputs, technical progress makes any given quantity of inputs more productive. Together, these explain why the UK has grown on average by 2.4 per cent a year since 1960.

Potential output is not the maximum we could be forced to produce. Rather, it is the output when all markets are in long-run equilibrium. Potential output includes an allowance for 'normal unemployment', probably around 4 or 5 per cent in the UK today. If actual output falls below potential output, workers become unemployed and firms have spare capacity.

Figure 9-1 shows the output gap in the UK during 1985–2005. In the boom of the late 1980s, UK GDP exceeded potential output, so the output gap was large and positive. During the slump of the early 1990s, actual output fell well below potential output and the output gap was negative. However, since the late 1990s actual output has remained close to potential output. In part, this has reflected better macroeconomic policy, as we explain in the ensuing chapters. Taking the politics out of policymaking has reduced the scope for a political business cycle. Figure 9-1 is dramatic evidence of the success of this change in macroeconomic policy.

To examine how policy affects output, we first need a model of what determines movements in output and causes deviations of output from potential output. To get

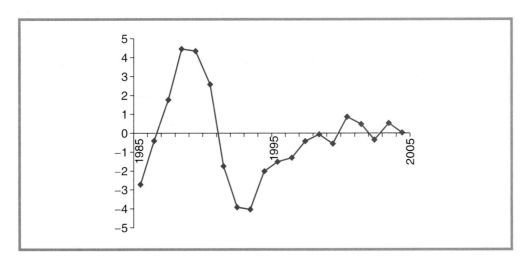

Figure 9-1　UK output gap (% actual output – potential output), 1985–2005

started, we use the model invented by the great English economist John Maynard Keynes in the 1930s. There are two key assumptions, which we shall later relax. First, all prices and wages are fixed. Second, at these prices and wages, there are workers without a job wanting to work, and firms with spare capacity they want to use. With this excess capacity, any rise in demand is happily supplied. The actual quantity of total output is then *demand-determined*. It depends only on the level of *aggregate demand*.

Aggregate demand

Initially, we ignore the government and the foreign sector. The remaining sources of demand for goods are consumption demand by households, and investment demand by firms. Aggregate demand *AD* equals *C + I*, the sum of consumption demand and investment demand, but these are determined by different economic groups, and depend on different things.

Consumption demand

Households buy goods and services, from cars and food to holidays and heating. These consumption purchases take about 90 per cent of personal disposable income.

Personal disposable income is household income from firms, plus government transfers, minus taxes. It is household income available to be spent or saved.

Given its disposable income, each household decides how to split this income between spending and saving. A decision about one is a decision about the other. Initially, we assume that consumption demand rises with personal disposable income.

The **consumption function** relates desired consumption to personal disposable income.

Our simple model has no transfer payments, or taxes. Personal disposable income is just national income. Figure 9-2 shows consumption demand *C* at each level of *national income*.

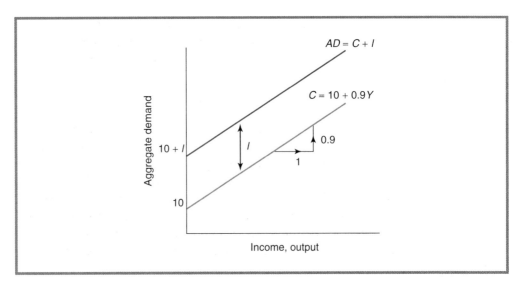

Figure 9-2   Aggregate demand

In this hypothetical example, $C = 10 + 0.9Y$. *Autonomous* consumption demand is unrelated to income. Needing to eat, households want to consume 10 even if income is zero. In Figure 8-5 the consumption function is a straight line with a constant slope. Each extra £1 of income leads to £0.9 of extra desired consumption spending. The slope of the consumption function is the marginal propensity to consume, which is 0.9 in Figure 9-2.

The **marginal propensity to consume MPC** is the fraction of each extra pound of disposable income that households wish to consume.

Investment demand

Investment demand for fixed capital (plant and equipment) and working capital (inventories) reflects firms' current guesses about how fast the demand for their output will rise in future. The current *level* of output tells us little about how output will *change*. Sometimes output is high and rising, sometimes it is high and falling. With no close connection between the output level and investment demand, we initially assume that investment demand is *autonomous*. It is independent of current output and income.

Aggregate demand

With only firms and households, aggregate demand is households' consumption demand C plus firms' investment demand I.

Aggregate demand is total desired spending at each level of income.

Figure 9-2 also shows the *aggregate demand schedule*. It adds the constant investment demand I to consumption demand C. The aggregate demand schedule is $AD = [(10 + I) + 0.9Y]$, parallel to the consumption function. The slope of both is the marginal propensity to consume, here 0.9. We now show how aggregate demand determines output and income.

Equilibrium output

When aggregate demand is below potential output, firms cannot sell all they would like. Suppliers are frustrated. But we can at least require that demanders are happy: actual output produced equals the output demanded by households for consumption and by firms for investment.

Short-run equilibrium output is where aggregate demand equals actual output.

Figure 9-3 shows income on the horizontal axis and planned spending on the vertical axis. The 45° line reflects any point on the horizontal axis into the *same* point on the vertical axis. The AD schedule crosses the 45° line only at point E. Equilibrium output and income are Y^*. At this income, the AD schedule tells us that the demand for goods is also Y^*.

At an output Y_0, less than Y^*, the AD schedule is then above the 45° line. Aggregate demand at A exceeds actual output at B. There is excess demand, which firms initially meet by an *unplanned* reduction of inventories. Soon they raise output to meet the excess demand. When output rises to Y^*, short-run equilibrium is restored. Aggregate demand again equals actual output.

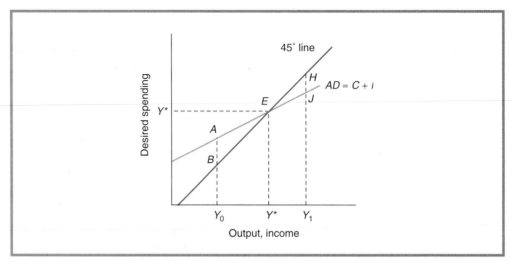

Figure 9-3 Equilibrium output

Conversely, at any output Y_1 above Y^*, the *AD* schedule is below the 45° line, desired spending at *J* is now below actual output at *H*, and firms cannot sell all their output. Initially, it piles up as *unplanned* additions to stocks. Then firms reduce their output. Once output is cut to Y^*, short-run equilibrium is restored. Aggregate demand again equals actual output.

At the short-run equilibrium output Y^*, firms sell all the goods they produce and purchasers buy all the goods they want. But Y^* may be *well below* potential output. Suppliers are still frustrated, and cannot sell what they would ideally like to make at the given wages and prices. A lack of aggregate demand prevents expansion of output to potential output. Since firms demand less labour input than at potential output, unemployment exceeds its long-run equilibrium level.

Box 9-1   Movements along the *AD* schedule versus shifts in the *AD* schedule

The aggregate demand schedule is a straight line whose height reflects total autonomous spending: autonomous consumption demand plus investment demand. Its slope is the MPC. For a given autonomous demand, changes in income lead to movements along a given *AD* schedule.

The level of autonomous demand is not permanently fixed, but is independent of income. The *AD* schedule shows the change in demand directly induced by changes in income. All other sources of changes in aggregate demand are shown as shifts in the *AD* schedule. For example, if firms decide to invest more, the new *AD* schedule is parallel to, but higher than, the old *AD* schedule.

Planned saving and investment

Equating aggregate demand and actual output is the most intuitive way to understand equilibrium output in the short run. But a second method, which turns out to be equivalent, usually gives the answer even more directly.

In short-run equilibrium, **planned leakages** must equal **planned injections**.

With no government or foreign sector, equilibrium output Y^* equals aggregate demand, which is planned investment plus planned consumption. However, income Y^* is devoted only to planned consumption or planned saving. Hence, in equilibrium, planned saving equals planned investment. For the moment, we treat planned investment as given. Hence, to understand what happens to output, we need to understand what determines saving.

The **saving function** shows desired saving at each income level. The **marginal propensity to save MPS** is the fraction of each extra pound of income that households wish to save.

If the consumption function is $C = 10 + 0.9Y$, the saving function must be $S = -10 + 0.1Y$. This ensures that desired $C + S = Y$. Households cannot plan what they cannot afford. For this saving function, the marginal propensity to save is 0.1.

Figure 9-4 shows equilibrium output Y^*, using desired saving and desired investment. The latter is constant, a horizontal line at height I. When income is zero, the saving function implies that saving is -10, the counterpart to autonomous consumption of 10 (since saving is simply the part of income not consumed). Each extra unit of income adds 0.1 to desired saving, so the saving function is an upward-sloping straight line with a constant slope of 0.1. The marginal propensity to save is 0.1. The remaining 0.9 of each extra unit of income is spent on consumption, as the marginal propensity to consume tells us.

Desired saving equals desired investment only at the income Y^*. If income exceeds Y^*, households want to save more than firms want to invest. But saving is the part of income not consumed. Saying that desired saving exceeds desired investment is the same as saying that aggregate demand is below actual output.

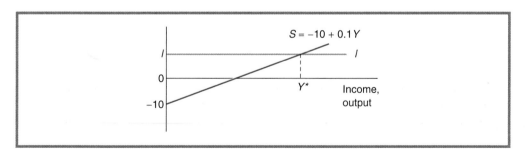

Figure 9-4 Short-run equilibrium output Y^*

Unplanned stocks pile up and firms cut output. Conversely, if income is below Y^*, desired investment exceeds desired saving. Aggregate demand for output is now too high. Firms make unplanned cuts in stocks and raise output. Again, output adjusts towards its equilibrium level Y^*. This is the same level whether we use aggregate demand and actual output in Figure 9-3, or desired investment and desired saving in Figure 9-4.

CHAPTER 9

Box 9-2 Spending like there's no tomorrow

Nowadays Nigel Lawson advertises diets. He used to be Chancellor of the Exchequer. In the Lawson boom in the late 1980s, heady optimism and easy access to credit made UK consumers spend a lot. Personal saving collapsed as people bought champagne, sports cars, and houses. The boom years did not last. As inflation rose, the government raised interest rates to slow down the economy. House prices fell. People's mortgage debt was larger than the value of their houses. To pay off this 'negative equity', households raised saving sharply in the early 1990s.

By 1997, UK households were borrowing again, as low interest rates fuelled a spending boom and a protracted rise in house prices. Reality TV shows were rivalled only by programmes showing how to decorate houses for subsequent letting or sale. The chart below shows that household saving has now fallen to the level last seen in the Lawson boom in 1987–88. In 2004, the Bank of England raised interest rates to slow down the housing market and curtail consumer credit, both of which were starting to threaten the Bank's inflation target. By 2005, the saving rate was beginning to recover. Of course, this meant that households were not spending so much on consumption and high street shops found that sales were less buoyant than in previous years. Once the Bank of England was confident that the high-interest-rate medicine had done its job, it began to reduce interest rates again in mid-2005.

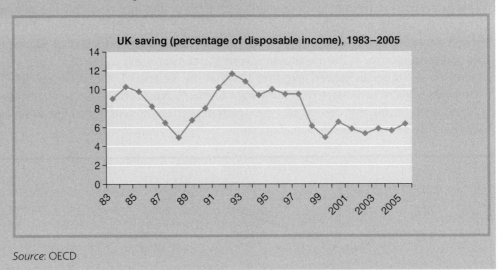

UK saving (percentage of disposable income), 1983–2005

Source: OECD

Desired versus actual

Equilibrium output and income satisfy two equivalent conditions. Aggregate demand equals actual output; and desired investment equals desired saving.[1] By definition, *actual* investment is *always* equal to *actual* saving when there is no government or foreign sector. But out of equilibrium, unplanned changes in inventories always make actual investment equal to actual saving, whatever their desired levels.

[1] We use 'desired' and 'planned' interchangeably. Both mean intentions before the fact, rather than outcomes after the fact.

A fall in aggregate demand

What alters equilibrium output? After 9/11 and the terrorist attacks on New York, firms became pessimistic about the future demand for their output. Their investment demand fell. How much should that have reduced equilibrium output?

To see the answer directly, we examine desired leakages and injections in Figure 9-5. Suppose the horizontal line showing desired investment shifts down by 20. Equilibrium moves from A to B, achieving a matching vertical fall of 20 in desired saving. Since the saving function has a slope of 0.1, it takes a horizontal leftward move of 200 in output to achieve a vertical fall of 20 in desired saving. Equilibrium output falls by 200 when desired investment falls by 20. Desired saving again equals desired investment.

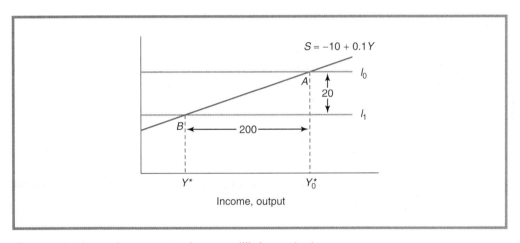

Figure 9-5   Lower investment reduces equilibrium output

Until actual output falls by this amount, desired saving exceeds the new lower level of desired investment. But *actual* leakages and injections are *always* equal. When investment demand falls, firms cannot sell their previous output and unplanned investment in stocks occurs. Firms then cut output. In the final equilibrium, desired investment and saving are equal again.

The multiplier

In this example, investment demand fell by 20 but equilibrium output fell by 200. The multiplier exceeds 1 because it takes a big change in income to alter desired saving by the amount that desired investment had changed.

The **multiplier** is the ratio of the change in equilibrium output to the change in demand that caused output to change.

Equilibrium output fell by 10 times the original change in investment demand. The multiplier was 10 in this example. Notice that this is simply $[1/(0.1)]$ or $[1/MPS]$. This is indeed the formula for the multiplier for any saving function with a constant marginal propensity to consume. If investment demand falls by 1, eventually desired saving must fall by 1. Each fall in income by 1 reduces desired saving by the smaller amount MPS, so income must fall by

[1/*MPS*] in order to reduce desired saving by 1. In the new equilibrium, desired saving is again equal to desired investment. Hence:

$$\text{Multiplier} = [1/MPS] = 1/[1 - MPC]$$

Since each extra pound of income adds either to desired consumption or desired saving, the marginal propensity to save is simply [1 − *MPC*] where *MPC* is the marginal propensity to consume. The larger the marginal propensity to consume, and hence the lower the marginal propensity to save, the larger is the multiplier.

The multiplier makes equilibrium output very sensitive to shocks to aggregate demand (changes in desired investment or desired autonomous consumption). However, if the multiplier were as large as 10 in the real world, the economy would be buffeted by every little shock that hit it. The next section explains why in practice the multiplier is lower than this section suggests.

The paradox of thrift

Suppose people want to save more at each income level, spending less at each income level. This reduces aggregate demand, shifting the *AD* schedule down because the consumption function shifts down. It also raises desired saving, shifting the saving function up.

Because aggregate demand falls, equilibrium income falls. This reduces equilibrium saving, since saving depends on income. We now have two effects: a desire to save more at each income, but lower equilibrium income, reducing desired saving. Which effect wins?

The **paradox of thrift** is that a change in the desire to save changes equilibrium output and income, but not equilibrium saving.

Think about desired investment and desired saving. Since nothing happened to desired investment, in the new equilibrium desired saving must be unaffected! A higher desire to save more, and spend less, reduces equilibrium income to the level that leaves desired saving at its original level. People save more out of any given income, but income is now lower. Desired saving stays the same.

Box 9-3   The multiplier–accelerator model of business cycles

Section 8-3 suggested some reasons why business cycles might exist. For the first time, we can now derive a cycle from a particular model. The multiplier–accelerator model distinguishes the causes and effects of a change in investment spending. In the simplest Keynesian model, the effect of higher investment is higher output in the short run. Higher investment adds directly to aggregate demand but the induced rise in income then adds further to consumption demand. We call this process 'the multiplier'.

Up till now, we have treated investment demand as given. What might cause a change in investment demand? Firms invest when their existing capital stock is smaller than the capital stock they would like to hold. The desired capital stock depends partly on the interest rate and hence the opportunity cost of the funds tied up in the capital

Box 9-3   *Continued*

goods. Changes in expectations about future profits are usually an even more important determinant of investment decisions. If interest rates and wages change only slowly, the main reason to invest in more capital capacity is because demand and output are expected to grow.

The **accelerator** model of investment assumes that firms guess future output and profits by extrapolating past output growth.

Constant output growth leads to a constant level of investment; it takes accelerating output growth to increase the desired level of investment. The accelerator model is only a simplification. Nevertheless, many empirical studies confirm that it is useful in explaining movements in investment.

We now show how a simple version of the multiplier–accelerator model can lead to a business cycle. The table below makes two specific assumptions, although the argument holds much more generally. First, we assume that the multiplier is 2. A unit of extra investment raises income and output by 2 units. Second, we assume that if last period's income grew by 2 units, firms now increase current investment by 1 unit.

Period t	Change in last period's output $Y_{t-1} - Y_{t-2}$	Investment I_t	Output Y_t
$t = 1$	0	10	100
$t + 2$	0	10	120
$t + 3$	20	20	140
$t + 4$	20	20	140
$t + 5$	0	10	120
$t + 6$	220	0	100
$t + 7$	220	0	100
$t + 8$	0	10	120
$t + 9$	20	20	140

The multiplier–accelerator model of the business cycle

The economy begins in equilibrium with output Y_t equal to 100. Since output is constant, last period's output change was zero. Investment I_t is 10, which we can think of as the amount of investment required to offset depreciation and maintain the capital stock intact.

Suppose in period 2 that some component of aggregate demand increases by 20 units. Output increases from 100 to 120. Since we have assumed that a growth of 2 units in the previous period's output leads to a unit increase in current investment, the table shows that in period 3 there is a 10-unit increase in investment in response to the 20-unit output increase during the previous period. Since the assumed value of the multiplier is

Box **9-3** *Continued*

2, the 10-unit *increase* in investment in period 3 leads to a further increase of 20 units in output, which increases from 120 to 140.

In period 4, investment remains at 20 since the output growth in the previous period was 20. Thus output in period 4 remains at 140. But in period 5 investment reverts to its original level of 10, since there was no output growth in the previous period. This fall of 10 units in investment leads to a multiplied fall of 20 units in output in period 5. In turn this induces a further fall of 10 units of investment in period 6 and a further fall of 20 units in output. But since the rate of output change is not accelerating, investment in period 7 remains at its level of period 6. Hence output is stabilized at the level of 100 in period 7. With no output change in the previous period, investment in period 8 returns to 10 units again and the multiplier implies that output increases to 120. In period 9, the 20 unit increase in output in the previous period increases investment from 10 to 20 units and the cycle begins all over again.

The **multiplier–accelerator model** explains business cycles by the dynamic interaction of consumption and investment demand.

The insight of the multiplier–accelerator model is that it takes an *accelerating* output growth to keep increasing investment. But this does not happen in Table 9-1. Once output growth settles down to a constant level of 20, investment settles down to a constant rate of 20 per period. Then in the following period, the level of investment must *fall*, since output growth has been reduced. The economy moves into a period of recession, but once the rate of output fall stops accelerating, investment starts to pick up again.

This simple model should not be regarded as the definitive model of the business cycle. If output keeps cycling, surely firms will stop extrapolating past output growth to form assessments of future profits? Firms, like economists, will begin to recognize that there is a business cycle. The less firms' investment decisions respond to the most recent change in past output, the less pronounced will be the cycle. Even so, this simple model drives home a simple result which can be derived in more realistic models. When the economy reacts sluggishly, its behaviour is likely to resemble that of a large oil tanker at sea: it takes a long time to get it moving and a long time to slow it down again. Unless the brakes are applied well before the desired level of the capital stock is reached, it is quite likely that the economy will overshoot its desired position. It will have to turn round and come back again.

9-2

Adding the government and other countries

Learning outcomes

By the end of this section, you should understand:

- How government spending and taxes affect equilibrium output
- The balanced budget multiplier
- Automatic stabilizers
- Limits to active fiscal policy
- How foreign trade affects equilibrium output

I n modern economies, governments are important and there is extensive trade with other countries. This section examines how the government and foreign countries affect aggregate demand and hence national output.

The government and aggregate demand

Figure 9-6 shows the evolution of government spending and tax revenue in the UK during 1987–2005. The gap between spending and revenue measures the budget deficit. The budget was nearly in balance in the late 1980s and again during 1999–2001. However, in the early 1990s there was a sharp increase in the budget deficit, both because government spending increased and because tax revenue fell, and the deficit increased again after 2002.

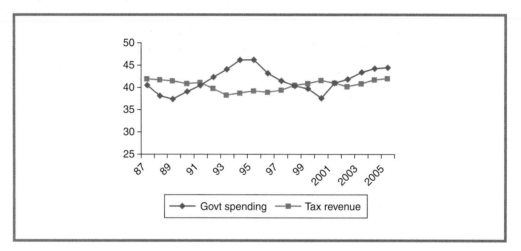

Figure 9-6 UK government spending and taxes (% of GDP), 1997–2005
Source: OECD

Figure 9-6 also shows how sharply the Labour government raised government spending after its election victory in 2001, when it committed itself to a substantial increase in spending on health and other public services. Case study 9.1 explores this fiscal expansion in more detail.

Fiscal policy is the government's decisions about spending and taxes.

We now examine the effects of fiscal policy in more detail. Government purchases G of final output add directly to aggregate demand. Hence, $AD = [C + I + G]$. The level of government demand reflects how many hospitals the government wants to build, how large it wants defence spending to be, and so on. In the short run, these decisions are not affected by changes in actual output. Planned injections also increase to $(I + G)$, which in equilibrium must equal desired leakages. How are desired leakages affected by the government?

The government levies taxes and pays out transfer benefits. At given tax rates and benefit levels, tax revenue and benefit spending both vary with output. To capture this, assume net taxes $NT = tY$, where t is the net tax rate, which in practice is around 0.5. Households' disposable income YD is now $Y(1 - t)$. Households get to keep only about 50p of every £1 of gross income. The rest goes to the government in taxes on income and spending, and because, with higher gross income, people get fewer transfer payments for income support, housing benefit, or help in paying Council Tax.

Suppose households still want to save 10 per cent of each extra pound of *disposable* income. However, with a 50 per cent net tax rate, £1 of gross income adds only 50p to disposable income, and hence only 5p to saving. This is one leakage, but the 50p paid to the government is another leakage not reverting to firms as demand for their output.

In Section 9-1 each extra £1 of national income led only to an extra leakage of £0.10 in extra saving. Now it leads to an extra leakage of £0.55 in extra net tax payments and saving. Whereas each extra £1 of output used to raise consumption demand by £0.90, now it raises it by only £0.45. That is extra desired spending by households on output after adjusting their desired saving and making their tax payments. Changes in income and output now induce much smaller changes in consumption demand. The multiplier is much smaller than in Section 9-1.

It used to be $[1/0.1] = 10$ but is now only $[1/0.55] = 1.82$. Figure 9-7 explains why. Desired injections are now $[G + I]$. Desired leakages, reflecting the need to pay taxes and the desire then to save out of remaining disposable income, are shown by the desired leakage schedule $S + NT$, whose slope is now 0.55.

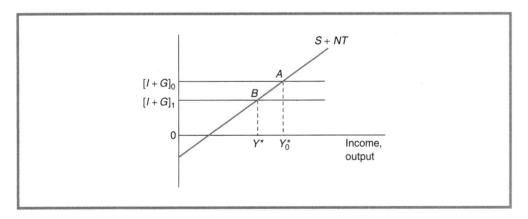

Figure 9-7 A fall in desired injections ($I + G$)

Equilibrium output is initially where the two lines cross at A. A fall in desired injections to $[I + G]_1$ has a smaller effect on equilibrium output the steeper is the desired leakages line. The multiplier is always 1/[marginal propensity to leak]. With a marginal propensity to save of 0.1 and a net tax rate of 0.5, the value of the multiplier is now $1/[0.55] = 1.82$.

This value of 1.82 is much smaller than the value of 10 in Chapter 8. Equilibrium output is much less sensitive to shocks to aggregate demand. The net tax rate acts as an automatic stabilizer. When output Y rises, the government gets more tax revenue tY, which helps dampen the expansionary effect of the rise in output. Paying more taxes, households cannot increase consumption demand so much. Conversely, when output falls, tax revenue also falls. By cushioning the disposable income of households, fiscal policy acts as a shock absorber, helping to stabilize aggregate demand and output.

Automatic stabilizers reduce fluctuations in aggregate demand by reducing the multiplier. All leakages act as automatic stabilizers.

Changes in fiscal policy

For a given investment demand, Figure 9-7 shows that lower government demand G cuts planned injections from $[I+G]_0$ to $[I+G]_1$, reducing equilibrium output from Y_0^* to Y_1^*. With less demand for goods, firms must reduce output if they are to produce and sell only the amount that is demanded.

Conversely, higher government demand raises short-run equilibrium output because firms must now produce and sell more in order to match aggregate demand. In Figure 9-7 we can view this as an increase in planned injections from $[I+G]_1$ to $[I+G]_0$.

For given government purchases G, a higher net tax rate would make the desired leakages line steeper in Figure 9-7. It must cross a given desired injections line at a *lower* equilibrium output. With higher leakages at any output, output must fall to preserve desired leakages equal to the unchanged desired injections. A higher net tax rate reduces equilibrium output.

Conversely, a tax cut raises equilibrium output. Since the level of injections is unaltered, equilibrium can be attained only if the level of leakages also remains the same. With less tax revenue leaking out of the circular flow at any particular level of output, it requires higher output to restore aggregate leakages to their former level. Equivalently, if consumers are being taxed less heavily, they have more to spend, consumption demand increases, raising aggregate demand and thereby causing a rise in equilibrium output in the short run.

Active or discretionary fiscal policy?

Although automatic stabilizers are always at work, governments may use *active* or *discretionary* fiscal policy to *alter* spending levels or tax rates to try to offset other shocks to aggregate demand. When aggregate demand is low, the government boosts demand by cutting taxes or raising spending. Conversely, when aggregate demand is high, the government raises taxes or reduces spending.

However, it is not always easy to change long-term fiscal plans quickly. Nowadays, much of the burden of stabilizing output falls not on fiscal policy but on monetary policy, the subject of the next section.

Box 9-4 The limits to active fiscal policy

Why can't shocks to aggregate demand immediately be offset by fiscal policy?

Time lags It takes time to spot that aggregate demand has changed, then time to change tax rates and spending plans, then this policy change takes time to affect private behaviour.

Uncertainty The government does not know for sure the size of the multiplier. It only has estimates from past data. Moreover, since fiscal policy takes time to work, the government must forecast the level that aggregate demand will have reached by the time fiscal policy has had its full effects. Mistakes made in forecasting can frustrate good intentions of policy makers.

Induced effects on autonomous demand Treating investment, exports, and autonomous consumption demand as fixed is only a simplification. Fiscal changes may affect private-sector confidence, or force the Bank of England to alter interest rates. If

Box 9-4   *Continued*

the government estimates these induced effects incorrectly, fiscal changes have unforeseen effects.

The budget deficit   Even if a fiscal expansion raises aggregate demand in a recession, it also adds to the budget deficit. The cure may be worse than the disease if people worry about the consequent rise in government debt or the temptation to print money to finance the budget deficit.

Foreign trade and output determination

We turn now complete our model of output determination by adding the role of other countries in aggregate demand. Figure 9-8 shows UK exports X and imports Z since 1950. Globalization means that both exports and imports have risen substantially. Like other countries, the UK now trades more than ever before. Although exports and imports are large relative to GDP, net exports $X - Z$ are usually small.

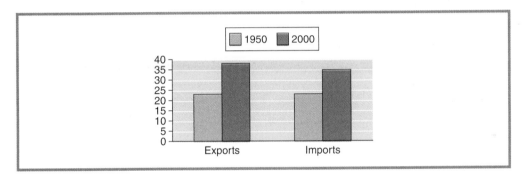

Figure 9-8   UK foreign trade (% of GDP)

The **trade balance** is the value of net exports. When exports exceed imports, the economy has a trade surplus. When imports exceed exports, it has a trade deficit.

When a household spends more than its income, it runs down its assets (bank accounts, stocks, and shares) or runs up its debts (overdrafts) to finance this deficit. Similarly, a country with a trade deficit must reduce its net foreign assets to finance this deficit.

Net exports $X - Z$ demand adds to aggregate demand, which becomes $AD = C + I + G + X - Z$. Desired injections are now $[I + G + X]$ and desired leakages $[S + NT + Z]$. Spending on imports is income for foreign producers. It leaks out of the UK circular flow between firms and households.

What determines desired exports and imports? Export demand reflects what is happening in foreign economies, which is largely unrelated to domestic output. Like other injections G and I, initially we treat export demand X as autonomous, or independent of domestic output. Imports from abroad may be raw materials for domestic production or items consumed by UK households, such as a Japanese TV or French wine. Demand for imports rises when domestic income and output rise.

The **marginal propensity to import (MPZ)** is the fraction of each extra pound of national income that domestic residents want to spend on extra imports.

Like the government budget, the trade balance varies with fluctuations in domestic income. Higher output and income raise imports, but leave exports unaffected. Hence, at low output, net exports are positive. There is a trade *surplus* with the rest of the world. At high output, there is a trade *deficit* and net exports are negative.

In Figure 9-9, the horizontal line $I+G+X$ shows desired injections. The upsloping line $S+NT+Z$ is desired leakages. Equilibrium output Y^* makes desired leakages equal to desired injections.

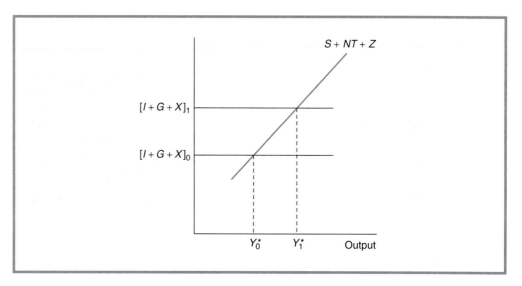

Figure 9-9 Higher desired injections raise equilibrium output

The multiplier in an open economy

By adding a third leakage through imports Z, an open economy has planned leakages $(S+NT+Z)$ that are even more responsive to output than in our previous discussion. The line for planned leakages in Figure 9-9 is steeper than for planned leakages $(S+NT)$ in Figure 9-7, which in turn is steeper than for planned saving S in Figure 9-4.

The steeper the planned leakages line, the smaller is the effect on equilibrium output of any given upward shift in planned injections. The output multiplier is large in a closed economy with no government and much smaller in an open economy with a government sector.

Even so, a rise in planned injections, from $[I+G+X]_0$ to $[I+G+X]_1$ raises equilibrium output a bit, from Y_0^* to Y_1^*. This extra output induces extra saving, extra tax revenue, and extra imports. Because of all these extra leakages, aggregate output does not increase very much.

Conversely, a higher savings rate, a higher tax rate, or a higher marginal propensity to import make the planned leakages line steeper, reducing equilibrium output. By making leakages higher than before, they lower aggregate demand and equilibrium output.

Import spending and jobs

Do imports steal domestic jobs? Cutting imports raises aggregate demand $[C + I + G + X - Z]$ and creates extra domestic output and jobs, a conclusion confirmed by Figure 9-9. A downward shift in the line for planned leakages would raise equilibrium output.

This view is correct, but dangerous. Other things equal, higher spending on domestic rather than foreign goods *will* raise demand for domestic goods. But import restrictions are dangerous because they may induce retaliation by other countries, which cuts demand for our exports, thereby reducing aggregate demand, planned injections, and equilibrium output. In the end, nobody gets more jobs, but world trade shrinks, which hurts everyone.

Case study 9-1   Gordon and Prudence

The government budget is in surplus if revenue exceeds expenditure, and is in deficit if spending exceeds revenue. Thus, the budget deficit is $G - tY$. For given levels of G, the budget varies with output Y because this automatically affects tax revenue tY. Other things equal, high output means high tax revenue and a budget surplus; low output means low tax revenue and a budget deficit. This means that it is difficult to assess whether the government's budgetary policy is prudent or reckless without knowing whether output is abnormally high or low.

Gordon Brown
© Reuters/Corbis

One solution to this problem is to examine the average level of budget over a period long enough that booms and slumps cancel out and short-run fluctuations in output can be ignored. Historically, this might mean a period of 6–7 years.

When Gordon Brown became UK Chancellor of the Exchequer in 1997, his first act was to give the Bank of England independent control of interest rates (to stop politicians being tempted to boost the economy too much in search of easy popularity with the electorate). However, similar reasoning led him to worry that fiscal policy might also be too loose most of the time. The Chancellor kept emphasizing the need to keep government spending within what could be afforded out of tax revenues. His success in sticking to this discipline gave rise to his nickname as the Iron Chancellor. To help him steer the right course, he introduced a Code for Fiscal Stability.

The Code for Fiscal Stability commits the government to a medium-run objective of financing all current government spending out of current revenues.

This commitment has two parts. First, any assessment of whether or not the government is sticking to its pledge is to be conducted over the medium run, a period long enough for short-run booms and slumps to cancel out their temporary effect on government tax revenue. Second, over this medium run, budget deficits are allowed only to pay for public-sector investment (which raises future output, and thus future tax revenues). All other government spending has to be financed by taxes.

Thus the Code for Fiscal Stability is basically a government commitment to balance

Case study 9-1   *Continued*

the budget, suitably measured, over a medium-run period of around seven years. Although the Treasury continues to insist that the UK's long-run budget position is sound, others have begun to disagree. *The Economist* ('Gordon and Prudence: it's so over', 13/13/2003; 18/04/04) argued:

Four years ago, the chancellor sanctioned an extended spending spree on the public services. Although Mr Brown put up taxes in his post-election budget in 2002, his determination to pump money into public services, especially the NHS, has driven the public finances deep into the red. A £15 billion surplus in the fiscal year 2000–01 has turned into a £38 billion deficit (3.4 per cent of GDP) in 2003–04.

By 2005, the Chancellor was in danger of failing his own test when the budget deficit was measured over the previous seven years. Rather than admit defeat, Gordon Brown argued that the economy was more stable than previously, so it now made sense to use a 9-year period as the window during which the budget had to be balanced. This gave him another two years to get things under control. Many people felt that the goalposts had shifted … .

9-3

Interest rates, aggregate demand, and output

Learning outcomes

When you have finished this section, you should understand:

- ◆ How interest rates affect aggregate demand
- ◆ How monetary and fiscal policy interact to determine aggregate demand

n this chapter, we have explained why short-run equilibrium output can fluctuate, and how fiscal policy can affect the level of output. What about monetary policy?

Monetary policy is the decision by the central bank about what interest rate to set.

In the UK, the central bank is the Bank of England, which acts on behalf of the government.

Figure 9-10 shows the behaviour of actual or nominal interest rates in the UK during 1985–2002. However, part of the interest rate is simply to allow lenders to keep pace with inflation.

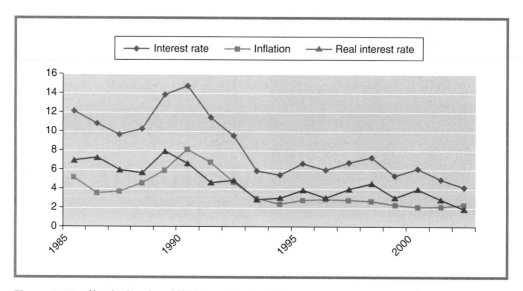

Figure 9-10   Nominal and real UK interest rates (%)

The **real interest rate**, the difference between the nominal interest rate and inflation, is what measures the real cost of borrowing and the real return on lending.

For example, if the nominal interest rate is 10 per cent and inflation is 6 per cent, the real interest rate is only 4 per cent. Figure 9-10 shows both inflation and nominal interest rates, and hence the real interest rate (the difference between the nominal interest rate and inflation).

Real interest rates were very high in the early 1990s when the UK was temporarily pegging the exchange rate against European currencies. European interest rates were high because of huge government spending by Germany on German reunification. The German central bank deliberately raised interest rates in order to prevent aggregate demand getting too far above potential output in Germany. Since then, real interest rates have returned to more normal levels.

Central banks, of course, only set the nominal or actual interest rate. They do not set the real interest rate directly. For any given inflation rate, a higher nominal interest rate implies a higher real interest rate. For simplicity, we can think of the central bank as setting the real interest rate. We now explain why higher real interest rates are likely to reduce aggregate demand.

Interest rates and consumption demand

Changes in interest rates have two effects on household decisions. The *substitution effect* makes everybody want to consume less today because the relative reward for saving has risen. The *income effect* also makes people consume less if initially they were borrowers. Higher interest rates make borrowers poorer, so that they have to consume less. Both effects reduce consumption demand by borrowers.

However, higher interest rates make lenders *richer*. For them, the income effect makes them consume *more* today, whereas the substitution effect – a more attractive return on saving than before – makes them spend *less* today. For lenders, the effect of higher interest rates on consumption demand is ambiguous. Aggregating borrowers and lenders, higher interest rates *reduce* consumption demand. Moreover, the more households have already run up large debts on mortgages and credit cards, the stronger the borrower effect will be, and the more a change in interest rates will affect consumption demand.

Interest rates and investment demand

We began this chapter by treating investment demand as given. Then we introduced the accelerator model, which argues that changes in output growth affect the level of investment demand. But interest rates also matter. Higher real interest rates raise the cost of investment by increasing the opportunity cost of the funds tied up in a new capital good. Other things equal, this reduces investment demand by firms.

At any instant there are many investment projects that a firm *could* undertake. Suppose it ranks these projects, from the most profitable to the least profitable. At a high interest rate, only a few projects earn enough to cover depreciation and the opportunity cost of funds employed. As the interest rate falls, more and more projects are profitable to undertake.

For a given rate of output growth, Figure 9-11 plots the investment demand schedule *II* showing how a lower interest rate raises investment demand. If the interest rate rises from r_0 to r_1, desired investment falls from I_0 to I_1.

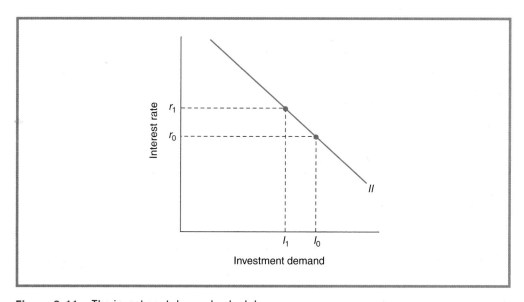

Figure 9-11 The investment demand schedule

The **investment demand schedule** shows desired investment at each interest rate.

The height of the schedule *II* depends on the cost of new capital goods, and the stream of profits to which they give rise. A higher price of new capital goods ties up more money, raising the opportunity cost of the funds employed. Investment demand is lower at any interest rate, shifting the investment demand schedule *II* downwards. Similarly, more pessimism about future demand reduces the flow of likely profits from new investment, again shifting the entire investment demand schedule downwards.

The slope of the investment demand schedule *II* depends mainly on the life of the asset. For short-lived capital goods, high rates of depreciation dominate the cost of investment. Changes in interest rates may only have a small effect on investment demand. However, for long-lived capital goods, with low depreciation rates, the interest cost of funds used is the main cost of investment, and investment demand is more sensitive to interest rates.

Hence, the *II* schedule is flatter for long-lived assets, but could be quite steep for short-lived capital assets. When the dot.com bubble burst, central banks worried that interest rate cuts might not help the sector recover quickly from excess capacity in the computer servers that handle email traffic and data transmission. With high rates of depreciation resulting from rapid technical obsolescence, changes in interest rates and the cost of funds tied up had only a small effect on demand for new computer servers.

Inventory investment

There are two reasons why firms *plan* to hold inventories of raw materials, partly finished goods, and finished goods awaiting sale.

First, the firm may be speculating, or betting on future price rises. Second, firms may plan to hold stocks to avoid costly changes in production levels. Suppose demand for the firm's output suddenly rises. A firm would have to pay big overtime payments to meet an upsurge in its order book. It is cheaper to carry some stocks in reserve with which to meet an upswing in demand. Similarly, in a temporary downturn, it is cheaper to maintain production and stockpile unsold goods than to incur redundancy payments, only to rehire workers in the next upswing.

As with physical capital, the cost of holding inventories is depreciation (and storage costs) plus the opportunity cost of the funds tied up. The investment demand schedule *II* in Figure 9-11 is thus also relevant to planned investment in stockbuilding. Other things equal, a higher interest rate raises the cost of holding inventories, and reduces desired investment in inventories.

Thus, higher interest rates reduce all types of investment demand, a move left along the investment demand schedule. A rise (fall) in the cost of capital goods or fall (rise) in expected future profit opportunities shifts this schedule down (up). Since ideas about future profits can change a lot, the investment demand schedule also shifts around quite a lot.

Interest rates and equilibrium output

By cutting interest rates, monetary policy can boost output and income. Suppose the central bank reduces interest rates. With given wages and prices, this is both a reduction in nominal interest rates and in real interest rates. Lower real interest rates raise investment demand and autonomous consumption demand (the part of consumption demand not explained by output and income). Hence, in Figure 9-12(a) aggregate demand rises, raising equilibrium output.

Equivalently, lower interest rates increase desired investment at any output, but also, by reducing desired consumption, they raise the desire to save at any output. For both reasons, desired injections exceed desired leakages at the original output level. In Figure 9-12(b) equilibrium output rises to raise desired leakages by enough to equal the new higher level of desired injections.

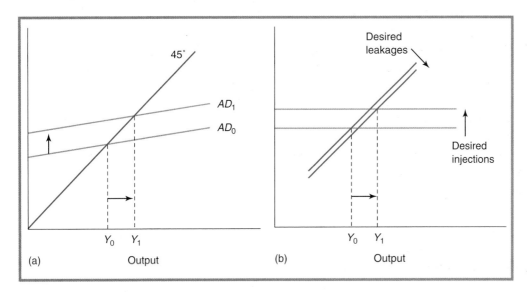

Figure 9-12 Lower interest rates raise equilibrium output

Demand management and the policy mix

Demand management is the use of monetary and fiscal policy to stabilize output near the level of potential output.

Monetary and fiscal policy are not interchangeable. First, interest rates can be changed frequently, whereas changing tax rates and spending levels is more complicated and is undertaken less frequently. Second, even in the longer run, monetary and fiscal policy affect aggregate demand through different routes and have different implications for the *composition* of aggregate demand.

A given level of aggregate demand can be achieved either by loose or expansionary fiscal policy (high government spending, low tax rates) combined with tight monetary policy (high interest rates); or by tight or contractionary fiscal policy (low government spending, high tax rates) combined with loose monetary policy (low interest rates).

Loose fiscal policy with easy monetary policy will mean that the public sector is large (high government spending) but the private sector is smaller (high interest rates reduce investment and consumption). Tight fiscal policy plus easy monetary policy will mean that the public sector is smaller but the private sector larger. With low interest rates, the level of investment may also be permanently higher. Thus, different combinations of monetary and fiscal policy affect not only the level of output and spending, but also its composition across sectors.

Recap

- The government buys some output directly. It also levies taxes and makes transfers.
- Net tax revenue rises with income, reducing the marginal propensity to consume out of national income. This acts as an automatic stabilizer by reducing the value of the multiplier.
- A rise in government purchases raises desired injections, aggregate demand, and equilibrium output. A higher tax rate raises desired leakages, reduces aggregate demand, and reduces equilibrium output.
- To stabilize aggregate demand and output, the government can set higher net tax rates, thus enhancing automatic stabilizers, or can make discretionary adjustments to government spending and tax rates to offset other shocks to aggregate demand. Discretionary changes are hard to implement quickly.
- Exports are an injection, adding to demand for domestic output. Imports are a leakage, domestic income spent on foreign output.
- Export demand is autonomous spending unrelated to domestic income. The marginal propensity to import MPZ is the amount an extra unit of national income adds to import demand.
- Imports further reduce the value of the multiplier, and are another automatic stabilizer.
- Higher export demand raises equilibrium output. Higher import demand reduces it.
- The trade surplus (net exports) falls when domestic income rises. Higher export demand raises the trade surplus, but higher import demand reduces it.
- A higher interest rate reduces consumption demand by borrowers but its effect on lenders is ambiguous. In the aggregate, consumption demand falls, especially if consumers have already borrowed a lot.
- The investment demand schedule shows how a higher interest rate reduces investment demand by raising the cost of funds for new capital goods. Higher interest rates move the economy down this schedule. Higher expected future profits, or a lower price of new capital goods, shift the investment demand schedule upwards.
- A lower interest rate raises aggregate demand and equilibrium output.
- A given output can be attained by easy monetary policy and tight fiscal policy or by the converse. In the former case, interest rates are lower and private spending higher.

Review questions

1 Consumption demand C is given by $C = 0.7Y$ and investment demand $I = 45$. (a) Draw a diagram showing the AD schedule. (b) If actual output is 100, what unplanned actions occur? (c) What is equilibrium output? (d) What is the saving function? (e) Draw a diagram showing planned injections and planned leakages. (f) Hence, find equilibrium output. How does your answer compare with your answer to (c)?

2 $I=150$. If people become thriftier, the consumption function shifts from $C=0.7Y$ to $C=0.5Y$. (a) What happens to equilibrium income? (b) What happens to the equilibrium proportion of income saved? (c) Show the change in equilibrium income in a saving-investment diagram. (d) Can you show the same change in a diagram using AD and the 45° line?

3 Which part of actual investment is not included in aggregate demand? Why not?

4 (a) Find equilibrium income when $I=400$ and $C=0.8Y$. (b) Would output be higher or lower if the consumption function were $C=100+0.7Y$?

5 Why are these statements wrong? (a) If people save more, investment will rise and hence output will increase. (b) Lower output leads to lower spending and yet lower output. The economy can spiral downwards forever.

6 Equilibrium output in a closed economy is 1000. $C=800$ and $I=80$. (a) What level is G? (b) I now rises by 50, and the MPS out of national income is 0.2. What are the new equilibrium levels of C, I, G, and Y? (c) Suppose instead G had risen by 50. Would the effect on output have been the same? (d) What level of G makes equilibrium output 1200?

7 In equilibrium, desired savings equal desired investment. True or false? Explain.

8 Why does the government tax people when it can borrow to finance its spending?

9 Suppose $MPZ=0.4$, $t=0.2$, and $MPS=0.2$. Investment demand rises by 136. (a) What happens to the equilibrium level of income and to net exports? (b) Suppose exports, not investment, rise by 100. How does the trade balance change?

10 Why are these statements wrong? (a) The budget raised taxes and spending by equal amounts. It was a neutral budget for output. (b) Countries with a trade deficit during an output boom are irresponsible.

11 Is fiscal policy a good instrument with which to fine-tune aggregate demand, maintaining it at the level of potential output? What prevents the government continuously maintaining aggregate demand at this level?

12 Recalculate the table in Box 9-3, assuming now that a 1-unit rise in I_t induces a 1-unit rise in Y_t, and a 1-unit rise in the $[Y_{t-1} - Y_{t-2}]$ induces a 1-unit rise in I_t. The economy again begins at $Y_t=100$, and the initial shock is a rise in I_t from 0 to 10.

13 People not previously allowed to borrow get credit cards with a £500 borrowing limit. What happens to the consumption function? Why?

14 Consumers tighten their belts, put in a spurt of saving, and pay off many of their credit card debts. How does this affect the effectiveness of monetary policy in future years?

15 Suppose the UK joins the euro, and that the European Central Bank raises interest rates even though UK output is already at potential output. (a) What happens to UK aggregate demand? (b) Ideally, what should UK fiscal policy then do?

16 Suppose firms expect a huge boom in a couple of years. What happens to investment and output today? How is the Bank of England likely to respond?

17 Why are these statements incorrect? (a) Consumer spending cannot rise if disposable income has fallen. (b) Whatever the monetary policy, fiscal policy can always compensate.

Answers on pages 350–351

10

Interest rates, money, and inflation

10-1

Money and banking

Learning outcomes

By the end of this section, you should understand:

- ◆ The functions of money
- ◆ How banks create money
- ◆ The money multiplier
- ◆ Different measures of money

I n the previous section, we simply assumed that the central bank can set whatever interest rate it chooses, But how does it do this? This chapter explores the financial system in more detail. In so doing, we explore what is special about a monetary economy, and discover the relation between money, growth, and inflation.

In songs and popular language, 'money' is a symbol of success, a source of crime, and makes the world go round. Dogs' teeth in the Admiralty Islands, sea shells in parts of Africa, gold in the nineteenth century: all are examples of money. What matters is not the commodity used but the social convention that it is accepted, without question, as a means of payment.

Money is any generally accepted means of payment for delivery of goods or settlement of debt. It is the **medium of exchange**.

In exchanging goods or labour services for money, we accept money not to consume it directly but for its later use in buying what we really want. Imagine an economy without money.

A **barter economy** has no medium of exchange. Goods are simply swapped for other goods.

In a barter economy, if you want an economics textbook, not only must you find someone wanting rid of one, you must have what that person wants in exchange. People spend a lot of time and effort finding others with whom to swap. Time and effort are scarce resources. Using money makes trading cheaper and more efficient. Society can use the time and effort for better purposes.

Other functions of money

British prices are quoted in pounds, American prices are quoted in dollars. However, there are exceptions. During rapid inflation, people may quote prices in foreign currency even if they still take payment in local currency, the medium of exchange.

The **unit of account** is the unit in which prices are quoted and accounts are kept.

Nobody would accept money as payment for goods today if the money was worthless when they tried to spend it later. But money is not the only store of value. Houses, paintings, and interest-bearing bank accounts all store value. Storing value is necessary but not the key feature of money, which is its role as a medium of exchange.

Money is also a **store of value**, available for future purchases.

Different kinds of money

In prisoner-of-war camps, cigarettes served as money. In the nineteenth century, money was mainly gold and silver coins. These are examples of *commodity money*, ordinary goods with industrial uses (gold) and consumption uses (cigarettes) that also serve as a medium of exchange. But society need not waste valuable commodities by using them as money.

A **token money** has a value as money that greatly exceeds its cost of production or value in consumption.

A £10 note is worth far more as money than as a 7.5 × 14 cm piece of high-quality paper. By collectively agreeing to use token money, society economizes on the scarce resources required to produce money. A token money survives only if private production is illegal. Society also enforces the use of token money by making it *legal tender*. In law, it must be accepted as a means of payment. Modern economies supplement token money by IOU money.

An **IOU money** is a medium of exchange based on the debt of a private bank.

A bank deposit is IOU money. You pay for goods with a cheque, which the bank must honour when a shopkeeper presents it. Bank deposits are a medium of exchange, a generally accepted means of payment.

Box 10-1   Travellers' tales

This contrast between a monetary and a barter economy is taken from the World Bank, *World Development Report*, 1989.

LIFE WITHOUT MONEY

'Some years since, Mademoiselle Zelie, a singer, gave a concert in the Society Islands in exchange for a third part of the receipts. When counted, her share was found to consist of 3 pigs, 23 turkeys, 44 chickens, 5000 cocoa nuts, besides considerable quantities of bananas, lemons and oranges ... as Mademoiselle could not consume any considerable portion of the receipts herself it became necessary in the meantime to feed the pigs and poultry with the fruit.'
W. S. Jevons (1898)

MARCO POLO DISCOVERS PAPER MONEY

'In this city of Kanbula [Beijing] is the mint of the Great Khan, who may truly be said to possess the secret of the alchemists, as he has the art of producing money ... . He causes the bark to be stripped from mulberry trees ... made into paper ... cut into pieces of money of different sizes. The act of counterfeiting is punished as a capital offence. This paper currency is circulated in every part of the Great Khan's domain. All his subjects receive it without hesitation because, wherever their business may call them, they can dispose of it again in the purchase of merchandise they may require.'

The Travels of Marco Polo, Book II

Modern banking

When you deposit your coat in the theatre cloakroom, you do not expect the theatre to rent your coat out during the performance. Banks lend out some of the coats in their cloak-room. A theatre would have to get your particular coat back on time, which might be tricky. A bank finds it easier because one piece of money looks just like another.

Bank reserves are cash in the bank to meet possible withdrawals by depositors. The **reserve ratio** is the ratio of reserves to deposits.

Bank assets are mainly loans to firms and households, but also financial securities (promises of future payments), such as bills and bonds, issued by governments and firms. Since many securities are very liquid – easily sellable at a predictable price – banks hold plenty of liquid securities that can be sold quickly if the bank needs money in a hurry. In contrast, many bank loans to firms and households are illiquid: the bank cannot easily get its money back quickly. Yet because there are now so many liquid securities available, modern banks get by with tiny cash reserves in the vault. Why hold cash when it is possible to hold interest-bearing liquid assets instead!

Banks' liabilities are mainly sight and time deposits. Sight deposits mean a depositor can withdraw money 'on sight' with no notice; chequing accounts are sight deposits. Time deposits, which pay higher interest rates, need a period of notice before withdrawing money. Banks have more time to organize the sale of some of their high-interest assets in order to have the cash available to meet these withdrawals. Apart from deposits, the other liabilities of banks are various 'money market instruments', short-term and highly liquid borrowing by banks, often from other banks.

The business of banking

A bank is in business to make profits by lending and borrowing. To get money in, the bank offers favourable terms to potential depositors. UK banks increasingly offer interest on sight deposits, and they offer better interest rates on time deposits. Money from these deposits is then lent by banks, either as advances (overdrafts) to other households and firms, at high interest rates, or by buying securities such as long-term government bonds. Some is more prudently invested in liquid assets, which pay less interest but can be easily sold if necessary. Some is held as cash, the most liquid asset of all.

The bank has a diversified portfolio of investments. Some of this income pays interest to depositors, the rest is for the bank's expenses and profits. Individual depositors have neither the time nor the expertise to decide which of these loans or investments to make.

UK banks' cash reserves are only about 2 per cent of the sight deposits that could be withdrawn at any time. At short notice, banks can cash in *other* liquid assets easily and for a predictable amount. The skill in running a bank is judging how much to hold in liquid assets, including cash, and how much to lend in less liquid assets that earn higher interest rates.

Box 10-2   A beginner's guide to financial markets

A *financial asset* is a piece of paper entitling the owner to a stream of income for a specified period. *Cash* is notes and coins, paying zero interest, but the most liquid asset of all. *Bills* are short-term financial assets paying no interest, but with a known repurchase date and a guaranteed repurchase price of £100. By buying it for less than £100, you earn a capital gain while holding the bill that gives a return similar to other market interest rates. Because bills have a short life, their price is never far below £100, and thus predictable. Bills are highly liquid.

Bank of England
© Royalty-free/Corbis

Box 10-2   *Continued*

Bonds are longer-term financial assets. A bond listed as Treasury 5% 2008 means that in 2008 the Treasury will buy it back for £100. Until then, the bondholder gets interest of £5 a year. Similarly, 2.5% Consolidated Stock (Consol) is a *perpetuity*, paying £2.5 a year forever. Buying it for £100, you get a return of 2.5 per cent a year. You might happily buy it for £100 if other assets yield 2.5 per cent a year. Suppose other interest rates now rise to 10 per cent. To resell your Consol, you must cut the price to £25. The new buyer then earns £2.5 a year on a £25 investment, matching the 10 per cent yield available on other assets. Bonds are less liquid than bills, not because they are difficult to buy and sell but because their future sale prices are less certain. Generally, the price of longer-term assets is more volatile.

Company shares (*equities*) earn dividends, the part of profits not retained by firms to buy new machinery and buildings. In bad years, dividends may be zero. Hence equities are risky and less liquid because share prices are volatile. Firms may even go bust, making the shares worthless. In contrast, government bonds are *gilt-edged* because the government can always pay.

Banks as creators of money

The money supply is money in circulation (cash not in bank vaults) plus bank deposits on which cheques can be written.

For simplicity, suppose banks use a reserve ratio of 10 per cent. In Table 10-1, initially citizens have £1000 in cash, which is also the money supply. This cash is then paid into the banks. Banks have assets of £1000 cash and liabilities of £1000 deposits, which is money they owe to depositors. If banks were like cloakrooms, that would be the end of the story. However, since all deposits are not withdrawn daily, banks do not need them to be fully covered by cash in the bank.

	Banks				Nonbank private sector			
	Assets		Liabilities		Monetary assets		Liabilities	
Initial		0		0	Cash	1000		0
Intermediate	Cash	1000	Deposits	1000	Deposits	1000		0
Final	Cash	1000	Deposits	10 000	Cash	0	Loans from	
	Loans	9000			Deposits	10 000	banks	9000

Table 10-1   Money creation by the banking system

In the third row, banks create £9000 of overdrafts. Think of this as loans to customers of £9000, an asset of the banks. But these are loans *of deposits*, against which cheques can be written, and hence also a liability of the banks. Now the banks have £10 000 of total deposits – the original £1000 of cash paid in, plus the £9000 deposits newly lent – and

£10 000 of total assets, comprising £9000 to keep track of the loans plus £1000 cash in the vaults. The reserve ratio is now 10 per cent. It does not matter whether this ratio is imposed by law or is merely the profit-maximizing behaviour of banks balancing risk and reward.

How did banks create money? Originally, the money supply was £1000 of cash in circulation. When paid into bank vaults, it went out of circulation as money. The public instead got £1000 of bank deposits against which to write cheques. The extra bank reserves were then used to create new loans and deposits, and the public had £10 000 of deposits in chequing accounts. The money supply rose from £1000 to £10 000. Banks created money.

The monetary base and the money multiplier

Cash is supplied by the *central bank*, which in the UK is the Bank of England. The government controls the issue of token money in a modern economy.

The **monetary base** is the supply of cash, whether in private circulation or held in bank reserves. The **money multiplier** is the ratio of the money supply to the monetary base.

In our previous example, cash was £1000 and the money supply £10 000, so the money multiplier was 10. Suppose instead that banks operate on a 5 per cent reserve ratio. When £1000 cash is paid into the banks, they now create an extra £19 000 of new loans and deposits. Banks' assets are £1000 cash + £19 000 loans, and their liabilities are £1000 deposits when the cash was paid in, plus £19 000 deposits as counterparts to new loans. Now a monetary base of £1000 leads to a money supply of £20 000. The money multiplier has risen to 20.

Hence, a lower reserve ratio means that more loans and deposits are created for any given cash in the vaults. The money multiplier is larger. Conversely, the more cash the public keeps under the bed, the less of the monetary base goes into bank vaults, and the lower is the money multiplier for any given reserve ratio. Without cash reserves, banks cannot create additional money.

Measures of money

The money supply is cash in circulation (outside banks) plus bank deposits. It sounds simple, but it is not. Two issues arise: which bank deposits, and why only bank deposits?

There is a spectrum of liquidity. Cash is completely liquid. Sight deposits (chequing accounts) are almost as liquid, and time deposits (savings accounts) only a little less liquid than that. Where people can make automatic transfer between savings and chequing accounts when the latter run low, savings deposits are as liquid as chequing accounts.

Until the 1980s everyone knew what a bank was, and whose deposits counted in the money supply. Financial deregulation has now blurred this distinction. Banks lend for house purchase, building societies (who used to lend only for house purchase) now issue cheque-books, and even supermarkets are joining the banking business.

Different measures of money draw different lines in the continuous spectrum of liquidity, and include the deposits of different institutions. The narrowest measure is M0, the *wide monetary base*. M0 measures all cash plus the banks' own deposits with the Bank of England.

Wider measures of money ignore bank reserves but add various deposits to cash in circulation outside the banks. M1 adds sight deposits of banks. M3 also adds other banks' deposits. Adding also the deposits in building societies, we get the M4 measure of broad money.

Since we can no longer distinguish between banks and building societies, routine statistics are now published only for the narrow measure M0, and for the broad measure M4. Once we leave the monetary base, the first sensible place to stop is M4.

Table 10-2 gives data for 2004. Of the £39 billion monetary base, only £5 billion was in bank reserves. Since this was multiplied up into £1087 billion of M4, the reserve ratio was below 1 per cent. Modern banks need little cash because financial markets and liquidity are so well developed. Hence, the money multiplier must be huge. In fact, Table 8-3 implies it was $1087/39 = 28$.

	Wide monetary base M0	39
−	Banks' cash and balances at bank	5
=	Cash in circulation	34
+	Banks' retail deposits	610
+	Building societies' deposits and shares	146
+	Wholesale deposits	297
=	Money supply M4	1087

Table 10-2   Narrow and broad UK money, sterling
                  (£ billion), March 2004

Source: Bank of England

10-2

Interest rates and monetary policy

Learning outcomes

By the end of this section, you should understand:

- ◆ How a central bank affects the money supply
- ◆ What determines the demand for money
- ◆ How a central bank sets interest rates

Founded in 1694, the Bank of England was not nationalized until 1947. Usually called 'the Bank', it issues banknotes, sets interest rates, and is banker to the commercial banks and the government, whose deposits are liabilities of the Bank. The Bank's assets are government securities and loans to commercial banks. Unlike commercial banks, the Bank cannot go bankrupt. It can always print more money to meet any claims upon it.

A **central bank** is responsible for printing money, setting interest rates, and acting as banker to commercial banks and the government.

The Bank and the money supply

The money supply is partly a liability of the Bank (currency in private circulation) and partly a liability of banks (bank deposits). The Bank could affect the money supply through reserve requirements, the discount rate, or open market operations.

Reserve requirements

A *required* reserve ratio is a *minimum* ratio of cash reserves to deposits that the central bank requires commercial banks to hold. Banks can hold more than the required cash reserves but not less. If their cash falls below this limit, they must immediately borrow cash, usually from the central bank, to restore their required reserve ratio.

If set above the reserve ratio that prudent banks would anyway have chosen, a reserve requirement reduces the creation of bank deposits by reducing the value of the money multiplier, reducing the money supply for any given monetary base.

The discount rate

The discount rate is the interest rate at which the Bank lends cash to commercial banks. By setting the discount rate at a penalty level above market interest rates, the Bank makes commercial banks hold larger cash reserves to reduce the risk of having to borrow from the Bank. Bank deposits are now a lower multiple of banks' cash reserves. The money multiplier is lower, reducing the money supply for any level of the monetary base.

Open market operations

The previous two policies alter the value of the money multiplier. Open market operations alter the monetary base. For a given money multiplier, this alters the money supply.

An **open market operation** is a central bank purchase or sale of securities in the open market in exchange for cash.

The Bank buys £1 billion of bonds by printing new cash, which adds £1 billion to the monetary base. Some of this ends up in circulation and some in bank reserves. The latter lets banks create new deposits. The broad money supply rises by more than the £1 billion of extra cash.

Conversely, if the Bank sells £1 billion of bonds in exchange for cash that disappears back into the Bank, the monetary base falls by £1 billion. Bank reserves fall, and commercial banks cut back on lending and deposits. The broad money supply falls by more than £1 billion.

There are three ways for a central bank to change the money supply – by changing reserve requirements, by changing the discount rate, or by open-market operations. In practice, modern central banks rely almost exclusively on open-market operations.

Box 10-3   The repo market

In American movies, people in arrears on their loans have their cars repossessed by the repo man. In the mid-1990s, London finally established a repo market, catching up with other European financial centres, such as Frankfurt and Milan. Surely central banks are not major players in dubious car loans?

A repo is a sale and repurchase agreement. A bank sells you a long-lived bond with a simultaneous agreement to buy it back soon at a specified price on a particular day. You pay cash to the bank today and get back a predictable amount of cash (plus interest) at a known future date. You effectively made a deposit in the bank, a short-term loan to the bank secured or guaranteed by the bond that you temporarily own. Repos use the stock of long-term assets as backing for secured short-term loans.

Reverse repos work the other way. Now you get a short-term loan from the bank by initially selling bonds to the bank, agreeing to buy them back at a specified date in the near future at a price agreed now. Reverse repos are secured short-term loans from the bank.

Repos and reverse repos augment short-term assets and liquidity. As the cost of lending and borrowing fell, more people made deposits to banks and borrowed from banks. The Bank of England now uses the repo market for most of its open-market operations.

Lender of last resort

Modern money is mainly bank deposits. Since banks have insufficient reserves to meet a simultaneous withdrawal of all their deposits, any hint of large withdrawals may be a self-fulfilling prophecy as people scramble to get their money out before the banks go bust. The threat of financial panics is reduced if the Bank will act as a lender of last resort.

The **lender of last resort** lends to banks when financial panic threatens the financial system.

This is useful in helping banks that face a temporary liquidity crisis but whose underlying balance sheet is perfectly sound. When the balance sheet is unsound, that particular bank is usually allowed to go bankrupt. However, the Bank will lend to other banks until confidence recovers.

Of these functions, the main role of the central bank is to affect the money supply, and hence set interest rates. To explain the connection, we need to introduce the demand for money.

The demand for money

The UK stock of money M4 was 70 times higher in 2005 than in 1965. Why did UK residents hold so much more money in 2005 than in 1965? Money is a stock, the quantity of money *held* at any given time. Holding money is not the same as *spending* it. We hold money now to spend it later. We focus on three determinants of desired money holdings: interest rates, the price level, and real income.

For simplicity, suppose money pays no interest and 'bonds' are all other assets that pay interest. How do people split their assets between money and bonds? Holding money means not earning more interest from holding bonds instead.

The **cost of holding money** is the interest given up by holding money rather than bonds.

People hold money only if there is a benefit to offset this cost. What is the benefit?

Transactions and precautionary benefits

Holding money economizes on the costs of barter. The size of money holdings to meet this *transactions motive* depends mainly on the scale of our anticipated future spending, which we can proxy by real income Y.

The **demand for money** is a demand for *real* money balances M/P.

To lubricate a given flow of real transactions, we need a given amount of real money, which is nominal money M, divided by the price level P. If the price level doubles, other things equal, the demand for *nominal* money balances doubles, leaving the demand for *real* money balances unaltered since the anticipated flow of real transactions has not changed.

People want money because of its purchasing power over goods and services. A higher real income raises the benefit of real money M/P, because more transactions occur. Having too little money raises the cost of transacting.

A second reason to hold money is the *precautionary motive*. If you see a bargain in a shop window, you need real money to grab the opportunity. Waiting while you cash in some bonds means that someone else gets the bargain. You hold money to cater for unforeseeable contingencies that require a rapid response. If these situations increase with the scale of economic activity, higher real income also strengthens the precautionary motive for holding money.

The transactions and precautionary motives are the main reasons to hold narrow money. The wider the definition of money, the less important is the role of money as a medium of exchange. We also have to take account of money as a store of value.

The asset motive to hold broad money

Forget the need to transact. Imagine someone deciding in which assets to hold wealth, to be spent at some distant date. A wise portfolio of assets will include some high-earning, but potentially risky, assets, such as company shares, but also some safer assets with a return that is lower on average but also less volatile. Holding some wealth in interest-bearing bank accounts is part of a well-diversified portfolio. Higher income and wealth gives people more to invest, raising the demand for broad money, such as M4.

Equating the marginal cost and benefit of holding money

The transactions, precautionary, and asset motives affect the benefits of holding money. The cost is the interest forgone by not holding higher-interest-earning bonds instead. People hold money up to the point at which the marginal benefit of holding more money just equals its marginal cost in interest forgone. Figure 10-1 shows how much money people want to hold.

The horizontal axis plots real money M/P. The horizontal line MC is the marginal cost of holding money, the interest forgone by not holding bonds. MC shifts up if interest rates rise.

The MB schedule is the marginal benefit of holding money, for a given real income and transactions flow. With low real-money holdings, we put lots of time and effort into

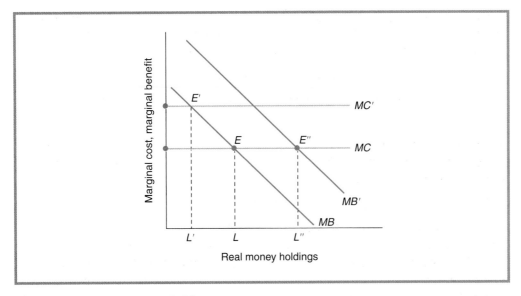

Figure 10-1 Desired money holdings

trading, being quick to invest money coming in, and alert to sell bonds just before every purchase. Also, with little precautionary money, we may miss out on unexpected chances to grab a good deal.

With low real-money holdings, the marginal benefit of money is high. More money lets us put less effort into managing our transactions, and we have more money for unforeseen contingencies. However, for a given real income, the marginal benefit of money falls as we hold more real money. Life gets easier. The marginal benefit of yet more money is lower.

Given our real income and transactions, desired money holdings are L in Figure 10-1. Only at E are the marginal cost and benefit of money equal. How do changes in prices, real income, and interest rates affect the quantity of money demanded?

Higher prices

Suppose all prices and wages double. Since interest rates are unaltered, MC stays the same. With real income unaltered, the MB schedule is unaffected. Hence, the desired holding of *real* money remains L. People hold twice as much nominal money M when prices P double. Real income and real money M/P are unaffected.

Higher interest rates

If interest rates on bonds rise, the cost of holding money rises. In Figure 10-1, this implies an upward shift in the marginal cost of holding money, from MC to MC'. Desired money holdings are now at point E', so desired real money holdings fall from L to L'. Higher interest rates reduce the quantity of real money demanded.

Higher real income

At each level of real money, higher real income raises the marginal benefit of money. With more transactions and more need of precautionary balances, it takes a greater stock of real money to simplify transacting to the same level as before. At any particular level of money holdings, the marginal benefit of money is higher than before. Hence, the MB schedule shifts up to MB' when real income rises. At the original interest rate and marginal cost MC

schedule, desired real money holdings are now L'. Higher real income raises the quantity of real money demanded.

Broad money

So far we have implicitly been discussing the demand for narrow money M0. To explain the demand for M4, which is mainly bank (and building society) deposits, we re-interpret MC as the average *extra* return from risky assets rather than safer deposits that pay a lower interest rate. MB is the marginal benefit of bank deposits in reducing the risk of the portfolio.

A rise in the average *interest differential* between risky assets and deposits shifts the cost of holding broad money from MC to MC', reducing the quantity of broad money demanded. Higher income and wealth shift the marginal benefit from MB to MB'. More time deposits are demanded.

Table 10-3 summarizes our discussion of the determinants of money demand.

Quantity demanded	Effect of rise in		
	P	Y	r
Nominal money M	Rises in proportion	Rises	Falls
Real money M/P	Unaffected	Rises	Falls

Table 10-3 The demand for money

Source: World Bank, *World Development Report, 2003*

Case study 10-1   Explaining the rise in money holdings from 1965 to 2005

To explain why nominal M4 holdings were 70 times higher in 2005 than in 1965, we need to examine changes in prices, real income, and nominal interest rates. Because of inflation, the price level was more than 13.5 times higher in 2003 than in 1965. Thus, a large part of the increase in nominal money holdings was merely to keep up with rises in prices and maintain the real value of money balances. Real money was only 5.2 times its initial level. Yet even this implies that real money demand still grew much more than real GDP, which rose only to 2.75 times its initial level. Thus, real money demand grew twice as much as real output.

Can we explain the rest by a fall in interest rates, which we know also tends to increase money demand. As the table below shows, nominal interest rates did fall, so this helps a bit. But empirical studies of the interest rate sensitivity of money demand imply that this fall in interest rates is not nearly big enough to explain why real money demand grew twice as much as real output and real income. So how do we account for the remaining discrepancy?

During the last few decades there has been a substantial increase in competition in the banking sector. In the 1960s, very few banks were licensed to accept deposits. This made it quite easy for the Bank of England to control what the banks were doing, since it always had the threat to license another bank or two, which would dilute the profits of the existing banks. In the 1970s and 1980s, successive governments came to believe

Case study 10-1   *Continued*

that it would be more advantageous to promote much greater competition in the banking sector, and many more banks were allowed to enter the industry.

This forced banks to pay higher interest rates on *deposits* in order to attract funds into their bank. For a given interest rate on bonds, a higher interest rate on bank deposits, the bulk of M4, *reduced* the cost of holding broad money, which is now *much* smaller than the 5 per cent shown in the table below. People now get interest on bank deposits, especially on savings accounts. Hence, what people sacrifice in order to hold bank deposits is only the differential between the interest rate on deposits and the interest rate on bonds. A lower cost of holding money made people hold more real money. This helps explain why real money demand in 2005 was 5.2 times its level of 1965 despite the fact that real income was only 2.75 times its 1965 level and nominal interest rates had fallen only by 2 percentage points.

	1965	2005
Index of:		
Nominal M4	1	70
Real M4	1	5.2
Real GDP	1	2.75
Interest rate	6%	4%

Holdings of M4, 1965–2005

Source: ONS, *Economic Trends*

Money market equilibrium

The money market is in equilibrium when the quantity of real money demanded equals the quantity supplied. For a given real income, Figure 10-2 shows real money demand MD. A higher interest rate raises the cost of holding money and reduces the quantity demanded.

Through open market operations, the central bank can determine the nominal money supply. If the price level is given, this also determines the real money supply. Hence the central bank can set an interest rate r_0 by supplying a quantity of real money L_0. To set an interest rate r_1, the central bank simply raises the money supply to L_1.

Changes in money demand

What would raise the demand for money at each interest rate? Either higher real income, which would raise the marginal benefit of money, or more banking competition, which would raise interest rates paid on deposits, reducing the cost of holding money at any level of interest rates on bonds and other assets.

In Figure 10-3, a rise in money demand shifts MD up to MD'. With an unchanged real money supply, interest rates rise from r to r' in order to reduce the quantity of real money demand back to the level of the unchanged real money supply.

However, if the central bank wishes to maintain the interest rate at its original level r, it

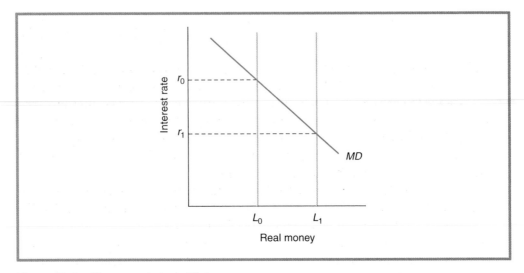

Figure 10-2 Money market equilibrium

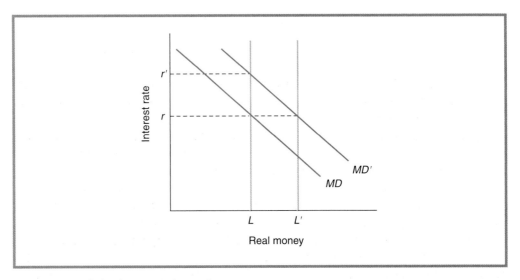

Figure 10-3 A rise in money demand

simply undertakes an open market operation to raise the real money supply from L to L'. When the central bank wants to 'set' interest rates, it therefore passively supplies whatever money is demanded at that interest rate.

Monetary policy

Interest rates are the instrument of monetary policy.

The **monetary instrument** is the variable over which a central bank exercises day-to-day control.

The *ultimate objective* of monetary policy could in principle be a combination of low inflation, output stabilization, manipulation of the exchange rate, or more stable house prices.

Box 10-4   Monetary intelligence

Good intelligence is a valuable commodity. How is the Bank of England's Monetary Policy Committee briefed, and how does it check that its briefings are not being sexed up? Teams of professional economists and statisticians scrutinize the latest data, and feed them into economic models in order to update predictions. But, as in warfare, this is usefully supplemented by human intelligence. The Bank of England has regional reps who tour the country talking to businesses and civic groups, gathering information about local economic conditions and the latest concerns.

Mervyn King, Governor of the Bank, has earned a worldwide reputation for sound judgement and good practice, making monetary policy predictable and effective. The former economics professor, and keen Aston Villa fan, has been a key player in modernizing Britain's economic policymaking since he first became chief economist at the Bank in 1991. 'Mervyn King developed the framework under which the bank gave advice to the chancellor,' says Alan Budd, chief economic adviser to the Treasury until 1997. 'When the bank was given independence, it already had a system in place.'

(adapted from 'Inside the Bank of England', *Business Week*, 12/7/04)

The Bank of England now has operational independence from government to set interest rates. But the Chancellor has decided the Bank's ultimate objective. It must set interest rates to try to keep inflation close to 2 per cent a year.

In making decisions, a central bank tries to get up-to-date forecasts of as many variables as possible. Sometimes, however, it concentrates on one or two key indicators, such as the recent behaviour of prices, the exchange rate, or the money supply.

New data on the money supply (largely bank deposits) come out faster than new data on the price level or real output. If the true, but not yet observable, behaviour of output and prices feeds reliably into money demand, then recent data on what happened to the stock of money may be a useful leading indicator of what is happening to the economy.

In the heyday of *Monetarism*, central banks responded rapidly to new data on the nominal money stock. When it rose too quickly, the central bank inferred that rises in income or prices had boosted money demand, requiring the passive supply of extra money to maintain the previous interest rate. Given this signal, the central bank then raised interest rates to prevent the economy growing too quickly and bidding up inflation.

Throughout the world, over the past decade there have been two key changes in the design of monetary policy. First, central banks have been told that their ultimate objectives should concentrate more on low inflation control and less on other things. Second, money has become much less reliable as a leading indicator. Rapid changes in the financial services sector keep changing the demand for money. When we see the money stock rising, we no longer know whether this signals imminent growth of prices and output, or whether it reflects a structural change that is making people hold more money even at constant levels of prices and output. Measures of money growth no longer have pride of place in central banks' assessments of whether to change interest rates.

Nowadays, central banks adjust interest rates to keep inflation close to its target level, and passively supply whatever quantity of money is necessary to equate money demand and money supply at the chosen interest rate. Since modern monetary policy is dedicated to the control of inflation, we now study inflation in more detail.

10-3

Inflation

Learning outcomes

By the end of this section, you should understand:

- ◆ The quantity theory of money
- ◆ How inflation affects nominal interest rates
- ◆ The costs of inflation
- ◆ Why central banks were made independent

Persistent inflation is quite a recent phenomenon. The UK price level was *the same* in 1950 as in 1920. Figure 10-4 confirms that UK inflation was negative in some of the inter-war years. Yet since 1945 annual UK inflation has never been negative. Since 1945 the price level has risen 26-fold, more than its rise in the previous 300 years. A similar story applies in most advanced economies.

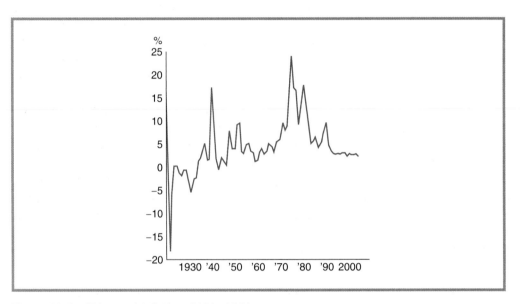

Figure 10-4   UK annual inflation, 1920–2004

Inflation and money growth

People care about real variables – the size of their house, the quantity of holidays, the number of beers. Hence, we view the demand for money as a demand for real money M/P. It rises with real income Y, but falls with the nominal interest rate r.[1] The real money supply M/P shows the quantity of goods that money will buy. If nothing in the real economy alters, real money demand is constant. Thus, nominal money M and prices P must be growing at the *same* rate as each other to keep the real money supply M/P constant. This is the quantity theory of money. It is believed to date back at least to Confucius.

The **quantity theory of money** says that changes in the quantity of nominal money M lead to equivalent changes in prices P, but have no effect on real output.

As a matter of logic, this has to be correct. If nothing real changes, and if the initial cause arises with a change in the nominal money supply M, then the consequence is an equivalent change in prices P. However, the quantity theory needs interpreting with care. First, nowa-days, central banks set interest rates in pursuit of inflation targets and then passively supply whatever money is demanded at that interest rate. Causation thus runs from prices to

---

[1] Inflation at the rate π reduces the purchasing power of money. The cost of holding money, the real interest rate $(r - \pi)$ on bonds minus the real interest rate $(-\pi)$ on money, is thus the nominal interest rate r.

money, not the other way round. It is the rate of change of prices that determines the rate at which central banks are driven to create money.

Second, real money demand is not necessarily constant. It can change either because of short-run changes in real income, or because monetary policy has changed nominal interest rates. When real money demand changes, nominal money and prices must behave *differently* in order to *alter* the real money supply in line with the change in real money demand.

In the long run, the correlation of money and prices is stronger. Eventually, output is fixed at potential output, which changes only slowly. If inflation is permanently high, nominal money must grow at a similar rate. Otherwise, the real money stock is permanently changing, which is incompatible with long-run equilibrium. Eventually we would expect real money to grow at about the same rate as real income, in other words at about 2 or 3 per cent a year.

In this sense, long-run inflation is *always* a monetary phenomenon. Take away the monetary oxygen and the inflationary fire goes out. Central banks with high inflation targets have to print lots of money to maintain the real money stock in line with real money demand. Those with low inflation targets need to print less money. If a central bank stops printing money, so that the nominal money supply is then constant, inflation eventually has to stop. Otherwise, the implication would be that ever higher prices P gradually reduce the real money stock M/P to zero. But from Section 10-1 we know that such a cut in the real money supply would cause a massive rise in equilibrium interest rates that would cause a huge slump and kill the inflation stone dead.

Hyperinflation

Ukraine's annual inflation reached 10 000 per cent in 1993. The most famous hyperinflation was in Germany during 1922–23.

Hyperinflation is high inflation, above 50 per cent *per month*.

After the First World War the German government had a big deficit, financed largely by printing money. Eventually, the government had to buy faster printing presses. In the later stages of the hyperinflation they took in old notes, stamped on another zero, and reissued them as larger-denomination notes in the morning. By October 1923, it took 192 million marks to buy a drink that had cost 1 mark in January 1922. People shopped by carrying money around in wheelbarrows. Muggers took the barrows but left the near-worthless money behind!

During hyperinflation, people try to get by with low real-cash balances to avoid their nominal cash balances being eroded by inflation. In 1923, Germans were paid twice a day so they could shop at lunchtime before the real value of their cash depreciated. Any unspent cash was quickly deposited in a bank where it could earn interest. People spent a lot of time at the bank.

Hyperinflations arise because governments can no longer raise enough taxes to finance their spending commitments, including interest on accumulated government debts. They try to print more and more money to cover the growing budget deficit. The additional money causes more and more inflation. The 'solution' often involves defaulting on the old debt, which dramatically reduces government spending, thereby removing the need to print money to finance the budget deficit.

In a modern economy, there are two ways to ensure that hyperinflations, or even moderate inflations, never arise. The first is to make the central bank independent of political control, so that it can no longer be ordered to print money to finance a budget deficit. The second is to restrict the ability of governments to run deficits in the first place. Before examining how different countries have implemented these solutions, it is important to understand why inflation should be public enemy number one as far as policy design is concerned.

The costs of inflation

Inflation illusion

Voters may suffer from inflation illusion, confusing nominal and real changes. It is wrong to say that inflation is bad *because* it makes goods more expensive. If *all* nominal variables rise together, people have larger nominal incomes and can buy the same physical quantity of goods as before. Nothing real has changed. However, if people fail to understand what is going on, they may make incorrect decisions by confusing nominal and real changes. If so, this may be a serious cost of inflation.

Assessment costs

You buy bread every day, and probably have a good idea of what is happening to bread prices in comparison to incomes and the prices of other goods. But what about some good, such as a washing machine, that a household typically purchases only every five or ten years? When inflation is significant, how do you decide what has happened to the real price of washing machines since you last bought one? Even if you remember what you paid five years ago, you have some complicated arithmetic to do in order to check whether or not the real price has risen or fallen. Wasting time on thinking and arithmetic is an important cost of inflation. When prices are stable, these calculations become trivially easy. People who avoid the costs of thinking and doing arithmetic simply by making a wild guess are likely to make mistakes and take decisions that are not in fact in their best interests. That is another way of viewing this cost of inflation.

Even if there were no assessment costs, there may be other costs. How large they are depends on whether inflation was expected and whether or not economic institutions can adapt to it.

Adaptation plus anticipation

If everyone sees inflation coming, and can adapt fully, all nominal variables should adjust in advance to restore real variables to their former levels. Nominal wages and nominal interest rates are set at appropriate levels. In that case, with unchanged real wages and real interest rates, workers and savers are protected from expected inflation. Nominal taxes and nominal government spending are adjusted regularly to maintain the real level of taxes and welfare benefits. Does inflation hurt anyone?

Cash cannot be protected from inflation since its zero interest rate cannot be adjusted. Higher inflation makes people hold less real cash, thus raising the time and effort needed for transacting.

Shoe-leather costs of inflation are shorthand for the extra time and effort in transacting when inflation reduces desired real-cash holdings.

Hyperinflation is a spectacular example of when shoe-leather costs become huge.

A second unavoidable cost arises because of the need to keep changing price labels and to keep reprinting catalogues to reflect the ever-changing price information. Higher inflation means these costs are incurred more frequently.

Menu costs of inflation are the physical resources used in changing price tags, reprinting catalogues, and changing vending machines.

Even with complete adaptation and full anticipation, we cannot avoid shoe-leather and menu costs of inflation. These are big if inflation is high, but are probably small when inflation is low.

Anticipation without adaptation

Sometimes, our institutions are not inflation-neutral. This stops full adjustment to foreseen inflation, raising the distortions that inflation creates. For example, if nominal tax allowances do not rise with prices, people are driven into higher real-tax payments. If the government taxes all interest income (only the real interest rate is a genuine profit on lending, the rest is just for keeping up with inflation), or taxes all capital gains (only the gain in excess of inflation is real profit), then higher inflation raises effective tax rates. The government gains from the failure to use proper inflation accounting, but the private sector changes its behaviour as a result. These institutional imperfections imply that even anticipated inflation has costs for society.

Unexpected inflation

Surprise inflation alters the real value of nominal contracts. Lenders lose out, having failed to charge an adequate nominal interest rate. Workers lose out, having failed to settle for an adequate nominal wage. Conversely, borrowers and firms benefit. One person's gain is another person's loss. In the aggregate these cancel out. But unexpected inflation redistributes income and wealth – for example, from lenders to borrowers. We might think this is also costly.

Uncertain inflation

Uncertainty about future inflation makes long-term planning harder. People also dislike risk itself. The extra benefits of the champagne years are poor compensation for the years of starvation. People would rather average out these extremes and live comfortably all the time. Uncertain inflation makes the real value of the contract less certain. This is a significant cost of inflation. There is some empirical evidence that inflation that is high on average also tends to be more volatile and harder to predict. One benefit of low inflation is that the institutional changes necessary to deliver it also tend to make it more predictable.

Together, these costs of inflation are significant. There is one final argument to consider. Whatever the costs of inflation itself, inflation arises usually as the symptom of some deeper problem such as the inability of the government to run a prudent budget policy. Hence, the benefits of curing inflation may not merely be avoidance of the damage that inflation does but also benefits that arise from curing the underlying problem that was giving rise to the need to print money and create inflation. Modern governments are tough on inflation and tough on the causes of inflation.

Committing to low inflation

Box 10-5 provides evidence that central bank independence is a useful commitment to tight monetary policy and low inflation. Institutional commitment has succeeded in keeping inflation up in many countries in recent years.

Box 10-5   Central bank independence

Central bankers are cautious people unlikely to favour rapid money growth and inflation. So why do these occur? Either because the government cares so much about unemployment that it never tackles inflation, or because it is politically weak and has a budget deficit which has to be partly financed by printing money. Essentially, inflation arises when governments overrule cautious bankers. Proposals for central bank independence mean independence *from the government*.

Since the aggregate supply curve and the Philllips curve are vertical in the long run, permanently lower inflation should not permanently reduce output or add to unemployment. Eventually, better institutional design yields a benefit without a cost. The two figures below confirm this reality – countries with more independent central banks have lower average inflation, but long-run output growth does not systematically suffer.

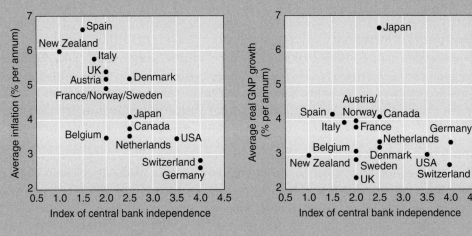

Source: Alesina and L. Summers, 'Central bank independence and macroeconomic performance: some comparative evidence', *Journal of Money, Credit and Banking*, May 1993

Case study 10-2   How governments discovered the secret of inflation control

Defeating inflation has been achieved by designing better policies, and this lesson has now been learned in over 50 countries during the last two decades. As a controlled experiment, this is as good as it gets in economics. Policy was changed, and the expected output ensued. Inflation came tumbling down permanently without causing permanent falls in output or permanent rises in unemployment. The key lay in recognizing that politicians were the problem not the solution. Reducing the scope for political control (interference?) has allowed the pursuit of better policies.

Case study 10-2   *Continued*

UK policy, 1992–97

In 1992, the UK abandoned its policy of pegging its exchange rate to European currencies, for which it had been necessary to set a similar monetary policy to that in European economies. Free to set UK monetary policy, the government first moved towards using inflation as a target for choosing interest rate policy. Although happy to receive advice from the Bank of England, the Chancellor of the Exchequer still had the final say in setting interest rates. Even so, these arrangements partially committed the government to low inflation. Minutes of the monthly meeting between the Chancellor and the Governor of the Bank of England were published a few weeks later, so any objections by the Bank were highly publicized. Moreover, the Bank was told to publish a quarterly *Inflation Report*, completely free from Treasury control. This Report soon became very influential, because it was transparent and used good economic analysis.

The *Inflation Report* includes the famous *fan chart* for inflation. A fan chart shows not just the most likely future outcome, but indicates the probability of different outcomes. The darker is the projected line, the more likely the outcome. Thus, in April 2004 the Bank was expecting UK inflation to average around 1.5 per cent in 2004, but, looking forward to 2006, the range of possible outcomes had widened to between 1.3 per cent and 3.3 per cent. The chart shows how quickly uncertainty increases as we look into the future. Notice that the Bank is also uncertain about the recent past, and has to go quite a long way back before it can be confident that the data are reliable.

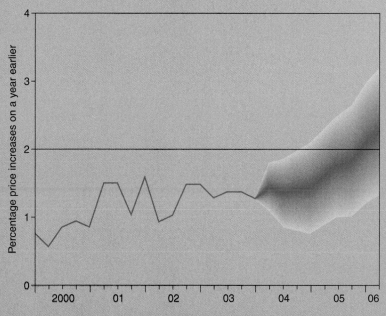

Source: Bank of England

Case study 10-2 *Continued*

UK policy since 1997

In May 1997, the new Chancellor, Gordon Brown, gave the Bank of England 'operational independence' to set interest rates in pursuit of the inflation target that he laid down. Any change in the target will be politically difficult, except in truly exceptional circumstances. Operational central bank independence is a commitment to low inflation.

UK monetary policy is now set by the Bank of England's Monetary Policy Committee, meeting monthly to set interest rates to try to hit the inflation target. Initially, the inflation data was based on the growth of the Retail Price Index, and the annual inflation target was set at 2.5 per cent, plus or minus 1 per cent. However, in December 2003 the Chancellor decided to switch to an inflation measure based on the growth of the consumer price index, a slightly different measure of inflation. Because CPI inflation is usually less than RPI inflation, the inflation target was cut to 2 per cent, still plus or minus 1 per cent.[2]

Most people give the Monetary Policy Committee high marks for its performance so far. It was prepared to change interest rates even when this was unpopular, and inflation has stayed close to target as a result. With low expected inflation, nominal interest rates are lower than for decades. The figure below shows the history of UK interest rates since 1974. Although the Bank's operational independence since 1997 has helped, the decisive break seems to have been 1992, when sterling left the Exchange Rate Mechanism and first moved towards inflation targeting.

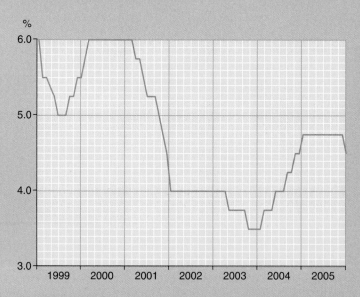

UK interest rates, 1974–2005

Source: Financial Times, 11 June 1999, Bank of England

[2] Alert readers may have noticed the discrepancy between UK inflation in Figure 10-4 and the inflation shown in the fan chart above. The former is RPI inflation, the latter CPI inflation. For example, in 2003 the RPI grew by 2.9 per cent, whereas the CPI grew by only 1.3 per cent.

Recap

- Money is the medium of exchange, for which it must be a store of value. It is usually also the unit of account.

- Bartering takes huge time and effort. Money reduces the resources used in trading. A token money's value as a money greatly exceeds its commodity value in other uses.

- Token money is used by social convention or because it is legal tender. The government has a monopoly on its supply.

- Modern banks attract deposits by offering interest and cheque-book facilities, but lend out funds at higher interest rates. If reserve ratios are below 100 per cent, banks create money by using their cash reserves to create extra loans and deposits.

- The money supply is currency in circulation plus relevant deposits. The monetary base M0 is currency in circulation and in banks. Broad money M4 is currency in circulation plus deposits at banks and building societies.

- The money multiplier is the ratio of the money supply to the monetary base. For M4 it is currently about 28. The money multiplier is larger (a) the smaller the reserve ratio and (b) the less of the monetary base is held outside banks and building societies.

- The Bank of England is the UK central bank acting as banker to the banks and to the government. Since it can print money, it can never go bust. It acts as lender of last resort to the banks.

- The Bank mainly controls the monetary base through open market operations, by buying and selling government securities. It could also change the money multiplier by imposing reserve requirements on the banks, or setting the discount rate at a penalty level.

- The demand for money is a demand for real balances. It rises if real income rises, but falls if the interest rate rises.

- To set the interest rate, the central bank passively adjusts the money supply to the level of money demand at that interest rate.

- Interest rates are the instrument of monetary policy. Nominal money is now less reliable as a leading indicator of future price and output data. Modern central banks adjust interest rates to keep inflation close to its target level.

- In the short run, there is a close correlation between nominal money and prices only if real-money demand happens to remain constant. In the long run, the correlation is closer since eventually real-money demand tends to grow slowly in line with potential output. Without rapid change in real money, any rapid growth in nominal money must be reflected in rapid growth in prices.

- Some 'costs' of inflation are illusory, but illusion can also cause costly mistakes in decision making. Assessment costs, shoe-leather costs, and menu costs are also unavoidable. Other costs of inflation depend on whether it was anticipated, and on whether an economy's institutions are inflation neutral. Uncertainty about inflation is also costly. Uncertainty may be greater if inflation is already high.

- Operational independence of central banks removes the temptation faced by politicians to boost the economy too much or to fund budget deficits by printing money.

Review questions

1 (a) Is a car taken in 'part exchange' for a new car a medium of exchange? (b) Could you tell, by watching someone buying mints (white discs) with coins (silver discs), which is money?

2 How do commercial banks create money? What happens if their reserve ratio is 100 per cent?

3 (a) Are travellers' cheques money? (b) season tickets? (c) credit cards?

4 Sight deposits = 30, time deposits = 60, banks' cash reserves = 2, currency in circulation = 12, building society deposits = 20. Calculate M0 and M4.

5 Why are these statements wrong? (a) Since their liabilities equal their assets, banks do not create anything. (b) Tax evasion raises the money supply since people keep more cash under the bed.

6 If commercial banks hold 100 per cent cash reserves against deposits, and the public hold no cash, what is the value of the money multiplier?

7 How do credit cards affect the precautionary demand for money?

8 Suppose banks raise interest rates on time deposits whenever interest rates on other assets rise. How much does a general rise in interest rates affect the demand for M4?

9 What are the desirable properties of a good leading indicator?

10 Why are these statements wrong? (a) Since higher interest rates on bank deposits make people hold less cash, they reduce the money supply. (b) Cash can never pay a decent rate of return.

11 (a) Your real annual income is constant. You borrow £200 000 for 20 years to buy a house, paying interest annually and repaying the £200 000 in a final payment at the end. In one scenario, inflation is 0 per cent and the nominal interest rate is 2 per cent a year. In a second scenario, annual inflation is 100 per cent and the nominal interest rate is 102 per cent. Are the two scenarios the same in real terms?

12 (a) Explain the following data. (b) Is inflation always a monetary phenomenon?

	Money growth	Inflation
	%	%
Euro area	3	2
Japan	12	−3
UK	6	2
USA	8	2

Source: The Economist

13 Name three groups who lose out during inflation. Does it matter whether this inflation was anticipated?

14 'The role of politicians is to make political decisions.' What do you think are the advantages and disadvantages of delegating economic policy to independent officials that are unelected? Would your answer change during wartime? Why or why not?

15 Why are these statements wrong? (a) Inflation stops people saving. (b) Inflation stops people investing. (c) Foreseen inflation is costless.

Answers on pages 351–352

11

Aggregate supply, inflation, and unemployment

11-1

Aggregate supply and equilibrium inflation

Learning outcomes

By the end of this section, you should understand:

- ◆ The classical model of output and inflation
- ◆ How inflation affects aggregate demand
- ◆ The equilibrium inflation rate
- ◆ Why wage adjustment is sluggish in the short run
- ◆ How temporary output gaps emerge
- ◆ How the economy eventually returns to potential output

Chapter 8 introduced key macroeconomics concepts and discussed the long-run growth of an economy's national output. In the long run output increases because aggregate supply increases. The economy has a greater capacity to produce.

Next, in the last three chapters, we have examined how fluctuations in aggregate demand can move the economy away from potential output in the short run, and the role of macroeconomic economic policy in stabilizing aggregate demand by the use of monetary and fiscal policy.

Initially, we analysed how aggregate demand affects output, and hence how monetary and fiscal policy can be used to change equilibrium output in the short run. But we have also seen that monetary policy nowadays is principally concerned with stabilizing inflation rather than output. Are the two connected? If so, how?

This chapter provides an answer. To do so properly, we need to analyse supply as well as demand. In so doing, we discard the simplifying assumption that the economy has spare capacity and that output is demand determined in the short run. By simultaneously analysing supply and demand, we have a better model. One benefit of this is that the relationship between inflation and output can be seen more easily. Having undertaken this analysis for output, we complete the chapter by showing what is simultaneously happening in the market for labour.

Previously, our model of output determination has treated prices and wages as given. Yet, in practice there has often been inflation, a rise in the general level of prices. Figure 11-1 shows annual inflation rates in several countries since 1990. In these countries, like many others, inflation is lower than it used to be. As explained in Chapter 10, politicians have seen the wisdom of better discipline in monetary and fiscal policy.

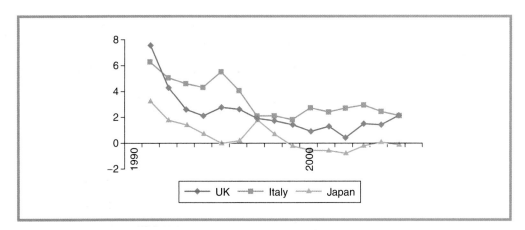

Figure 11-1 Annual inflation (%), 1991–2005

Once we stop treating prices as given, it no longer makes sense to simplify by treating output as demand determined. Higher aggregate demand does not always raise output: with finite resources, the economy cannot expand output indefinitely. We now introduce aggregate supply – firms' willingness and ability to produce – and show how demand and supply *together* determine output. And the balance of supply and demand affects what is happening to inflation.

Initially, we swap the Keynesian extreme, with fixed wages and prices, for the opposite extreme, full wage and price flexibility.

The **classical model** of macroeconomics assumes wages and prices are completely flexible.

In the classical model, the economy is *always* at potential output. Any deviation of output causes instant changes in inflation to restore output to potential output. In the short run, before prices and inflation adjust, the Keynesian model is relevant. In the long run, after all adjustment is complete, the classical model is relevant. We examine how the economy evolves from the Keynesian short run to the classical long run.

Aggregate supply

The **aggregate supply schedule** shows the output firms wish to supply at each inflation rate.

With complete flexibility, output has always adjusted back to potential output. All inputs are fully employed. This is the long-run equilibrium output of the economy. Potential output reflects technology, the quantities of available inputs in long-run equilibrium, and the efficiency with which resources and technology are exploited. Chapter 8 studied how potential output grows in the long run. In the short run, we treat potential output as given.

How does more rapid growth of prices and nominal wages affect the incentive of firms to supply goods and services? We assume that people do not suffer from inflation illusion. If wages and prices both double, real wages are unaffected. Neither firms nor workers change their behaviour. Aggregate supply is unaffected by *pure* inflation, as shown in Figure 11-2.

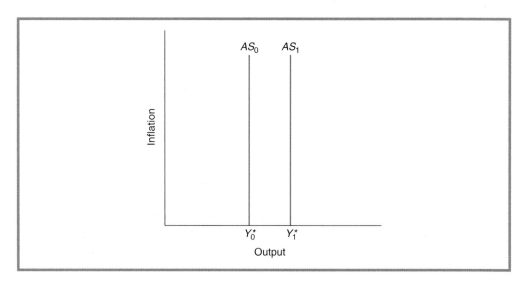

Figure 11-2 The vertical *AS* schedule

In the classical model, the **aggregate supply schedule** is vertical at potential output.

Equilibrium output is *independent* of inflation. Since nobody has inflation illusion, people adjust nominal variables to keep pace with inflation. Nothing real changes, and output is constant. If potential output increases, the aggregate supply schedule shifts from AS_0 to AS_1 in Figure 11-2.

Inflation and aggregate demand

In the classical model, inflation does not affect aggregate supply but it does affect aggregate demand. If the central bank is pursuing a given inflation target, any increase in inflation above target induces the central bank to raise *real* interest rates in order to reduce aggregate demand and make firms less eager to raise prices.

Since the real interest rate is the nominal rate r minus the inflation rate π, in order to raise *real* interest rates the central bank has to raise the *nominal* interest rate r by *more* than the increase in inflation π so that the real interest rate $(r - \pi)$ increases, thereby exerting contractionary pressure on the economy by reducing aggregate demand.

Following an **inflation target**, a central bank raises the real interest rate if it expects inflation to be too high, and cuts the real interest rate if it expects inflation to be too low.

Figure 11-3 illustrates how inflation affects aggregate demand. When inflation is high, the Bank implements its monetary policy by raising real interest rates, reducing aggregate demand and equilibrium output. The *AD* schedule slopes downwards, showing that lower inflation induces a cut in real interest rates and hence an expansion in aggregate demand.

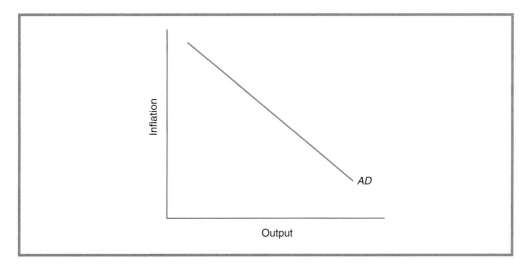

Figure 11-3 Inflation and aggregate demand, for a given monetary policy

Movements *along* the *AD* schedule reflect interest rate changes in pursuit of a given inflation target. Interest rate changes take time to affect output and inflation, so the central bank cannot keep inflation perfectly on track, though it hopes to be moving in the right direction. In contrast, *shifts* in *AD* reflect a switch to a *different* monetary policy with a *different* inflation target. If monetary policy is less tight, the central bank is prepared to accept a higher inflation target, and the AD schedule shifts upwards. Conversely, a tighter monetary policy corresponds to a downward shift in the *AD* schedule.

The equilibrium inflation rate

The equilibrium inflation rate π^* reflects the positions of the *AD* and *AS* schedules. See Figure 11-4.

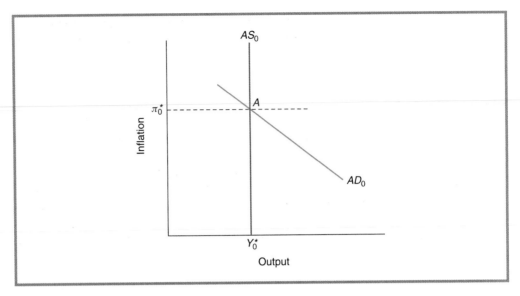

Figure 11-4 Equilibrium inflation

With aggregate supply AS_0 and aggregate demand AD_0, inflation is π_0^* and output is Y_0^*. Equilibrium is at A. Output is at potential output, and the inflation target is being achieved.

A permanent supply shock

Supply shocks may be beneficial, such as technical progress, or may be adverse, such as higher real oil prices or loss of capacity after an earthquake. Suppose potential output rises. In Figure 11-5 the AS schedule shifts to the right, from AS_0 to AS_1. To maintain the target inflation rate π_0^*, the central bank *loosens* monetary policy, setting a lower interest rate than before at any level of actual inflation. This raises demand, shifting AD_0 to AD_1, meeting the original inflation target π_0^* in long-run equilibrium at C not D.

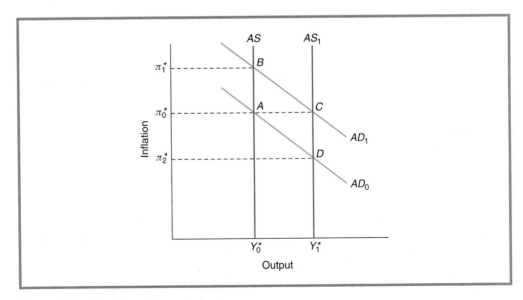

Figure 11-5 Supply and demand shocks

Monetary policy **accommodates** a permanent supply change by reducing the average level of real interest rates, thereby permanently raising aggregate demand in line with higher aggregate supply.

A demand shock

For a given aggregate supply AS_0, suppose a rise in export demand raises aggregate demand from AD_0 to AD_1 which would take the economy from A to B. Inflation π_1^* now exceeds the long-run inflation target at π_0^*. The central bank has to *tighten* monetary policy, setting a higher real interest rate at *each* possible output level. This shifts AD_1 back to AD_0 and restores equilibrium at A, letting the central bank continue to meet its inflation target.

Similarly, if the initial cause of the upward shift in demand was not a rise in export demand but a rise in government spending, there is a consequent tightening of monetary policy until private expenditure has been reduced by the same amount as government expenditure had increased. Only then is total aggregate demand restored to the level of potential output, which by assumption has not changed.

In the classical model, there is **complete crowding out**. Higher government spending causes an equivalent reduction in private spending, since total output can't change.

In other words, to keep hitting its inflation target, the central bank must raise real interest rates enough to depress consumption and investment demand so that aggregate demand remains at potential output despite higher government spending.

If government spending falls, we can use Figure 11-5 in reverse. Beginning at A, tighter fiscal policy shifts AD_1 down to AD_0. To prevent inflation falling below the target π_0^* the central bank must loosen monetary policy, which shifts demand back up to AD_1. Lower government spending then *crowds in* an equal amount of private spending because of lower real interest rates.

A rise in the inflation target

Suppose the inflation target is raised from π_0^* to π_1^*. The central bank no longer needs such high interest rates at any particular level of inflation. Real interest rates fall and the macro-economic demand schedule shifts up from AD_0 to AD_1. With an unchanged AS schedule, equilibrium moves from A to B in Figure 11-5.

Inflation is higher but real output is unaltered. Since this is a full equilibrium, all real variables, including real money M/P, are then constant. Hence, money and prices are growing *at the same rate*. In the classical model, higher inflation is accompanied by faster growth of nominal money. The idea that nominal money growth is associated with inflation, but not higher output, is the central tenet of *Monetarists*. Figure 11-5 confirms that this is correct in the classical model with full wage and price flexibility.

Sluggish adjustment in the short run

In practice, prices and wages do not instantly respond to excess supply and demand. Output can deviate from potential output in the short run. Some firms, in long-run relationships with their customers, prefer not to vary prices with short-run market conditions. It takes time and effort to decide how to react, to inform people of changes, and to alter catalogues.

Wages are even slower to adjust than prices. Since wages are the main part of costs, which in turn affect prices, sluggish wage adjustment also helps explain sluggish prices adjustment. Long-run relationships matter a lot in the labour market. Teambuilding, trust, and the acquisition of firm-specific skills take time to develop. It makes more sense for workers' pay to reflect longer-term considerations. Nor can a firm and its workforce continuously negotiate how wages should next be changed. Too much time negotiating means too little time producing. Costly negotiations are only undertaken at intervals, often once a year.

Short-run aggregate supply

In Figure 11-6 the economy is at potential output A. In the short run, the firm inherits a given rate of nominal wage growth (not shown) that had anticipated staying at A with inflation π_0. By keeping up with inflation, nominal wage growth expected to maintain the correct real wage for labour market equilibrium.

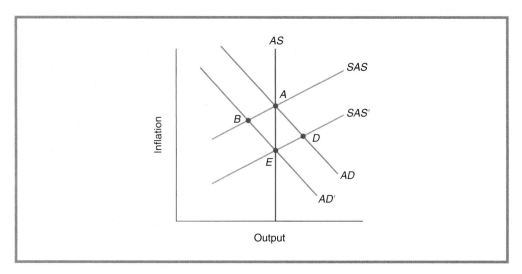

Figure 11-6   Short-run aggregate supply

If inflation exceeds the expected inflation rate π_0, firms have higher prices but nominal wages have risen less than they should. Firms take advantage of their good luck by supplying a lot more output. They pay overtime to buy workforce co-operation, and may also hire temporary extra staff.

Conversely, if inflation is below π_0, the real wage is now higher than anticipated when the nominal wage was agreed. Since labour is now costly, firms cut back output a lot. In Figure 9-5 they move along the short-run supply schedule SAS in the short run.

The **short-run supply curve SAS** shows how desired output varies with inflation, for a given inherited growth of nominal wages.

Suppose the economy begins at A, but then the central bank adopts a lower inflation target, shifting macroeconomic demand down from AD to AD'. After full wage and price adjustment, the final equilibrium is at E. Inflation is lower, but output is unchanged since nothing has happened to aggregate supply and potential output.

In the short run, firms inherit particular nominal wage settlements that were based on inflation expectations that were higher than the lower inflation that is now going to transpire. This means that real wages have actually risen, not because of what has happened to nominal wages W but because, with lower inflation, prices P are lower than would have been the case and hence the real wage W/P has gone up. Firms respond to more expensive labour by choosing to produce less. They move down their short-run supply curve for output to point B. Output is now below potential output, just as in the simple Keynesian model. Instead of *assuming* output is entirely demand determined, our model now has output jointly determined by demand and short-run supply. At B, output is below potential output. There is an output gap.

The **output gap** is actual output minus potential output.

Lower output and employment gradually bid down wages, reducing firms' production costs and shifting the short-run supply schedule down to SAS'. Eventual equilibrium at E is a point on the new demand schedule AD', but also on both the supply schedules SAS' and AS. Shifts in short-run supply reconcile it eventually with long-run supply at potential output. The output gap disappears.

Figure 11-6 can be used to examine not just a temporary slump but also a temporary boom. Beginning at E, suppose the central bank loosens monetary policy and raises the inflation target. Aggregate demand rises from AD to AD'. Given the inherited wage settlements, a higher level of output prices is needed to induce firms to produce extra output, taking the economy initially to point D. Gradually, however, workers catch on to the fact that inflation is higher, and raise wage demands. The supply curve shifts up from SAS' to SAS and long-run equilibrium is restored at point A. Inflation has risen (because the inflation target was raised, and a suitable monetary policy was adopted), but output has reverted to long-run aggregate supply.

How long it takes to make the transition from short run to long run is a key issue in macroeconomics. Some economists think it is rapid, so that the insights of the classical model quickly become relevant. Others think the Keynesian model of the previous chapter remains relevant for a long time. The mainstream view is somewhere in the middle. Within a year price adjustment has begun, but it takes probably between two and four years to get to the new long-run equilibrium.

In practice, many of the shocks that an economy experiences in the short run are demand shocks. As the aggregate demand schedule shifts, it moves the economy along the short-run supply schedule in a figure such as Figure 11-6. Since suppliers need higher prices to produce more output, this means that, in the short run, higher inflation is usually correlated with higher output. One implication of this is that stabilizing inflation will also stabilize output, provided the economy is mainly subject to demand shocks.

Case study 11-1 Economic history 1980–2005 through output gap spectacles

The output gap shows the percentage deviation of actual output from potential output. An output gap of +1 per cent thus means output is 1 per cent above potential output, which is unsustainable in the long run. People are working overtime, and firms are working machinery abnormally hard, perhaps by skipping maintenance activities for a while. Conversely, an output gap of –1 per cent means that output is below potential output and the economy has spare capacity that in the long run will be taken up as the

Case study 11-1   *Continued*

economy reverts to full capacity. The OECD produces data on the evolution of the output gap in each of the leading economies. Looking at output gaps is a good way to get a picture of the shocks that an economy is experiencing.

The figure below shows data for the UK and for Germany and helps convey a snapshot of their recent economic history. The UK began the 1980s with the Thatcher government trying to defeat high inflation. By creating a recession – the output gap was nearly 4 per cent in 1982 – the government's tough monetary and fiscal policies gradually put downward pressure on inflation.

By the mid-1980s, inflation was under control and Chancellor Nigel Lawson cut taxes and interest rates in an attempt to stimulate investment and make potential output grow more quickly. However, these policies added more to aggregate demand than to aggregate supply, leading to the famous Lawson boom of the late 1980s. In 1988, the UK's output gap peaked at over +4 per cent. As you might expect, this led to a new bout of inflation, forcing the then Chancellor John Major to put the brakes on again. The combination of tighter monetary and fiscal policy caused a sharp reduction in aggregate demand.

By 1992, the UK output gap had fallen to nearly −4 per cent again, but the UK could not respond to this by cutting interest rates because in 1990 it had joined the Exchange Rate Mechanism that pegged its interest rates and exchange rates to the levels of its European partners. In September 1992, the government abandoned the ERM, floated its exchange rate, and reduced interest rates to get the economy moving again. By 1995, the output gap had been largely eliminated.

The figure also shows that since 1995 the fluctuations in the output gap have been much smaller than in previous years. Since short-run fluctuations are more often caused by shocks to demand than supply, this largely means that macroeconomic policy has been more effective in offsetting demand shocks and maintaining aggregate demand broadly in line with aggregate supply and potential output. Making the Bank of England independent and instructing it to pursue a target of low inflation was probably the principal cause of this success. Once inflation expectations are already low, a policy of continuing to stabilize inflation is very similar to a policy of maintaining output close to potential output. The figure also shows what happened in Germany during the same period. Germans also reduced aggregate demand in the early 1980s to fight the inflation that had been caused by the second oil price shock in 1980. After 1983, the negative output gap (showing the extent of the recession) was steadily closing. In 1989, the Soviet bloc began to disintegrate and West Germany grabbed the opportunity to unify with East Germany. East German productivity was probably only a quarter of West

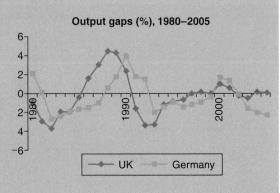

Output gaps (%), 1980–2005

Case study 11-1   *Continued*

German levels. Even unemployment benefit in West Germany exceeded the wages that could be earned by working in East Germany. To prevent East Germans all migrating westwards in search of welfare payments, the new Germany had to subsidize East Germans to remain in East Germany. Previously, the Berlin Wall had accomplished the same outcome!

This large fiscal expansion caused aggregate demand in united Germany to rise sharply (taxes could have been raised, but were not). The result was an output gap of +4 per cent by 1990 and a major boom. The Bundesbank (the German central bank) responded to emerging inflation by raising interest rates a lot, causing a big fall in demand. By the mid-1990s, this output gap was back on track and interest rates reverted to more normal levels. Germany joined the Eurozone in 1999, since when its monetary policy has been set not by the Bundesbank but by the new European Central Bank.

One final point. The figure shows that during the last ten years UK monetary policy has been more effective at stabilizing the UK economy than German monetary policy has been at stabilizing the German economy. When proponents of UK adoption of the euro talk about the trade advantages of belonging to the single European currency, opponents of UK adoption of the euro point to graphs such as the one above and note what a good job the Bank of England has done.

PS   Why do we give the credit for stabilization principally to monetary policy rather than fiscal policy? Not because fiscal policy is ineffective but because it is less easy to use flexibly. Interest-rate decisions are made once a month. Decisions on hospital building, or income tax rates, at best are made once a year. Changing fiscal policy is more costly than changing monetary policy. The latter assumes most of the role of short-run demand management.

11-2

Unemployment

Learning outcomes

When you have finished this section, you should understand:

- ◆ Classical, frictional, and structural unemployment
- ◆ Voluntary and involuntary unemployment
- ◆ Determinants of UK unemployment
- ◆ Private and social costs of unemployment

I n the early 1930s over a quarter of the UK labour force was unemployed, which was both a waste of output and the cause of misery, social unrest, and hopelessness. Postwar policy was geared to avoiding a rerun of the 1930s. Figure 11-7 shows that it succeeded.

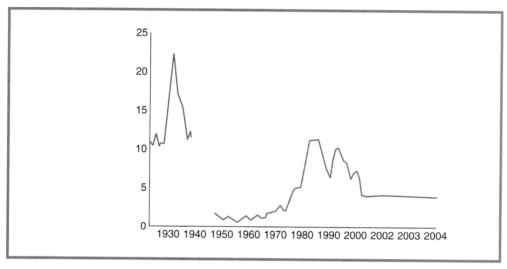

Figure 11-7   UK unemployment (%)

Sources: B. R. Mitchell, *Abstract of British Historical Statistics* and B. R. Mitchell and H. G. Jones, *Second Abstract of British Historical Statistics*, Cambridge University Press; ONS, *Economic Trends*

In the 1970s, unemployment began to rise, but boosting demand failed to help. Instead, it caused high and rising inflation. Hence, by the 1980s many governments had embarked on tighter policies to get inflation under control. The combination of tight demand policies and adverse supply shocks initially caused a dramatic rise in unemployment, shown in Figure 11-8. However, since 1990 unemployment has fallen, and in the UK is now at a very low level.

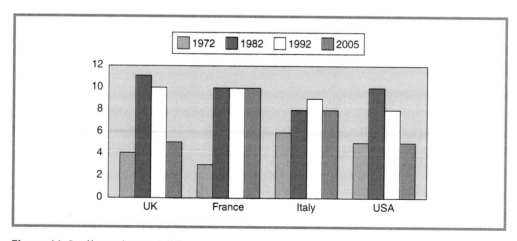

Figure 11-8   Unemployment (%)

The **labour force** is everyone who has a job or wants one. The **unemployment rate** is the fraction of the labour force without a job.

Labour force growth since 1950 conceals two opposite trends: a steady rise in women wanting to work, and a somewhat smaller fall in the number of men in the labour force.

Stocks and flows

Unemployment is a stock, measured at a point in time. Like a pool of water, it rises when inflows (the newly unemployed) exceed outflows (people getting new jobs or quitting the labour force entirely). Table 11-1 shows that the pool of unemployment is not stagnant. Even with 0.8 million unemployed, three times this many people enter and leave the pool *every* year. Most people escape quickly, though those with few skills may visit the pool many times in their working lifetime. However, some people get stuck in the pool, lose confidence, and get stigmatized as a poor bet for an employer. Sometimes this is because the labour market has identified a worker who is genuinely less willing or able, but sometimes it just reflects bad luck that then becomes self-reinforcing.

Inflow to unemployment	2.4
Outflow from unemployment	2.5
Stock of unemployed	0.8

Table 11-1 UK unemployment (millions), 2004

Source: ONS, *Labour Market Trends*

Types of unemployment

Unemployment can be frictional, structural, demand-deficient, or classical.

Frictional unemployment is the irreducible minimum unemployment in a dynamic society.

It includes some people with handicaps that make them hard to employ, but also includes people spending short spells in unemployment as they hop between jobs in an economy where both the labour force and the jobs on offer are continually changing.

Structural unemployment reflects a mismatch of skills and job opportunities when the pattern of employment is changing.

Frictional unemployment arises from temporary impediments; structural unemployment reflects medium-run forces. A skilled welder made redundant at 50 in the North of England may have to retrain or move south to find work. Firms are reluctant to take on and train older workers, and housing in richer areas may be too dear. Such workers are victims of structural unemployment.

Demand-deficient unemployment occurs when output is below full capacity.

Until wages and prices adjust to their new long-run equilibrium level, a fall in aggregate demand reduces output and employment. Some workers want to work at the going real-wage rate but cannot find jobs.

Classical unemployment arises when the wage is kept above its long-run equilibrium level.

This may reflect trade union power or minimum wage legislation. If wages cannot adjust, the labour market can restore low unemployment in long-run equilibrium.

The modern analysis of unemployment takes the same types of unemployment but classifies them differently, distinguishing between *voluntary* and *involuntary* unemployment.

11-1 Box: A weak idea

Those with no economics training often think there is an easy way to cut unemployment. Shorten the working week, so that the same amount of total work is shared between more workers, leaving fewer people unemployed. But a shorter workweek is a very weak idea. The demand for labour (in person-hours) depends on the cost of hiring workers. Shortening the working week, without cutting wages, raises the cost of labour, so firms hire fewer workers. A daily 8-hour shift probably has an hour of dead time (coffee breaks, tidying the desk, chatting up colleagues, sneaking out to the shops). With a 6-hour shift, dead time rises from 1/8 to 1/6, making labour more expensive.

Equilibrium unemployment

Figure 11-9 shows the market for labour. The labour demand schedule *LD* slopes downwards, since firms hire more workers at a lower real wage. The schedule *LF* shows how many people join the labour force at each real wage. A higher real wage makes (a few) more people want to work. The schedule *AJ* shows how many people accept a job at each real wage. It must lie left of the *LF* schedule, since the labour force is the employed plus the unemployed. The horizontal gap between *AJ* and *LF* shows voluntary unemployment at each real wage.

Voluntary unemployment is people looking for work who will not yet take a job at that real wage.

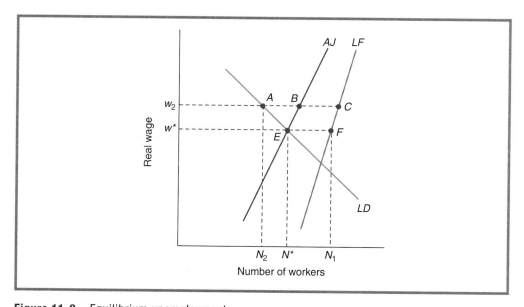

Figure 11-9 Equilibrium unemployment

People house hunting do not take the first house they see. Similarly, some people invest in searching a bit longer for a more suitable job. At high real wages, people grab job offers quickly and the *AJ* and *LF* schedules are close together. At low real wages, people are more selective about accepting offers, especially if the offer is little above the benefits available to those out of work. Hence, the *AJ* and *LF* schedules are further apart at low real wages. Labour market equilibrium is at *E*. Employment is N^* and unemployment is the distance *EF*.

Equilibrium unemployment is unemployment when the labour market is in equilibrium.

Since it is the gap between the desire to accept jobs and the desire to be in the labour force, this unemployment is entirely voluntary. At the equilibrium real wage w^*, N_1 people want to be in the labour force but only N^* want to accept job offers; the remainder do not want to work at the equilibrium real wage.

Equilibrium unemployment includes frictional and structural unemployment. What about classical unemployment: for example, if unions keep wages at w_2, above w^*? Total unemployment is now *AC*, which exceeds *EF*. At the wage w_2, *BC* workers are voluntarily unemployed, but *AB* workers are now involuntarily unemployed. Firms hire at point *A*, but individual workers want to be at point *B*.

Involuntary unemployment means the unemployed would take a job offer at the existing wage.

However, through their unions, workers collectively have chosen wage w_2 in excess w^*, thus reducing employment. For workers as a whole, this extra unemployment is voluntary. It has raised equilibrium unemployment from *EF* to *AC*.

Keynesian or demand-deficient unemployment is entirely involuntary, and arises when wages have not yet adjusted to restore labour market equilibrium. Suppose in Figure 11-9 that the original labour demand schedule goes through points *E* and *F*. Equilibrium employment is at *B*, and equilibrium unemployment is *BC*. Now labour demand falls to *LD*. Until wages adjust, *BC* remains voluntary unemployment but *AB* is involuntary unemployment, pure spare capacity. Boosting labour demand again could move the economy from *A* back to *B*. Without such a boost to demand, involuntary unemployment will slowly bid wages down, moving the economy from *A* down to *E*. If this takes a long time, policies to boost demand may be preferable.

Thus, total unemployment is equilibrium unemployment plus demand-deficient unemployment. Only the latter is spare capacity that could be mopped up by shifting demand upwards. When the labour market is already in equilibrium, shifting demand up makes hardly any difference to the gap between the nearly parallel *AJ* and *LF* schedules. We then need *supply-side policies* that can close the gap between these two schedules that together reflect labour supply to the economy.

Why was unemployment so high?

Did high unemployment reflect inadequate demand or a rise in equilibrium unemployment? Figure 11-10 shows the average unemployment rate during eight periods, from 1956–59 through to 2000–05. It shows how actual unemployment rose dramatically before eventually falling back. Clearly, most of this was explained by the rise and fall of *equilibrium* unemployment, which had many causes.

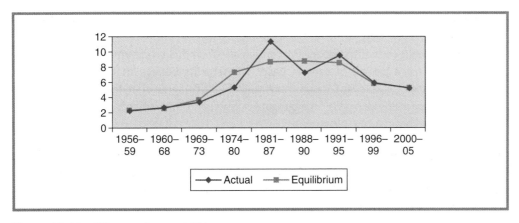

Figure 11-10 UK unemployment (%)

Unions became more powerful after the 1960s, but were then undermined by globalization, privatization, and legal legislation aimed at diminishing their power. Mismatch and structural unemployment arose in regions and skills in which manufacturing decline had severe effects. More generous welfare benefits undermined work incentives at the lower end of the wage scale, and disconnected people from the labour market.

Recent policy has laid heavy emphasis on encouraging people back into work. *Welfare to Work* seeks to help people get off benefit, and *Making Work Pay* has tried to reduce disincentives for poorer workers. People out of work but on income support, housing benefit, and council tax assistance lose benefits rapidly as they begin to earn income. The interaction of different policies used to impose effective tax rates of over 90 per cent on initial income work. Recent reforms have reduced this to below 70 per cent.

Governments need revenue to provide benefits for the very poor, including those out of work. But why do we tax the nearly poor so very heavily? We long ago abandoned 70 per cent income tax rates on the rich, who now pay 40 per cent. In practice, middle class voters are more likely to be the swing voters who decide the outcomes of elections. Hence, they have significant political power. In contrast, the poor-in-work are unlikely to vote for parties associated with support for the well-off, and hence have less political influence.

Figure 11-10 also shows a few periods when demand-deficient unemployment was important, particularly in the early 1980s, when the Thatcher government first adopted tough policies to defeat inflation, and in the early 1990s, when monetary and fiscal policy were again tightened sharply. During these recessions, Keynesian unemployment existed.

Conversely, in the 1970s, despite the rise in unemployment, the economy was actually overheating and unemployment was less than its equilibrium level. Policymakers, assuming that rising unemployment had been caused by deficient demand, boosted demand to mop up the slack. Since there was no slack, this merely added to inflation. Similarly, Figure 11-10 shows the Lawson boom at the end of the 1980s, another period of overheating, which is why the brakes had to go on in the early 1990s.

Figure 11-10 confirms again the message that policy has subsequently done better. The switch to central-bank independence and inflation targeting took the politics out of monetary policy and provided macroeconomic stability. At least since the mid-1990s, unemployment has remained quite close to its equilibrium level. The other reason is that governments gradually learned about the importance of supply-side policies to reduce equilibrium unemployment itself.

Keynesians believe that the economy can deviate from full employment for quite a long time, certainly for a period of several years. Monetarists believe that the classical full-employment model is relevant much more quickly. Both agree that the long-run performance of the economy depends on aggregate supply, and thus what happens to potential output and equilibrium unemployment.

Box 11-2 'The graphs the EU Commission dare not publish'

'Brussels riven by job market row — A controversial report linking unemployment to rigidities in the labour market has split the Commission,' reported the *Financial Times*. The first graph shows, for 14 EU members, the correlation between the degree of labour market regulation and the percentage of the labour force with jobs. The second graph shows, for some OECD countries, the correlation between the employment rate and the cost of firing a worker. The figures show a high degree of regulation, and high costs of dismissal are each associated with a lower employment rate. If correlation proved causality, this would clinch the case for deregulation.

Suppose you had to make the case for labour market regulation. If the labour market worked perfectly there would be no need for intervention. Regulations may have been designed to offset existing market failures thereby enhancing efficiency. The countries with the largest distortions have the lowest employment rates, but also the largest government intervention to ameliorate the consequences of these distortions. Of course, to be persuasive, you would have to identify exactly what these distortions were (market power of large employers, externalities in training, etc.) and explain why the particular forms of regulation made things better not worse. You might or might not be able to show this.

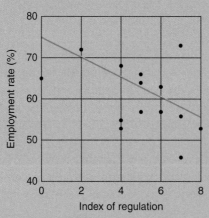 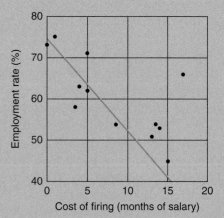

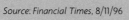
Source: Financial Times, 8/11/96

Tax cuts

Would lower tax rates improve work incentives and labour supply? Figure 11-11 again shows labour demand LD, the labour force schedule LF, and the job acceptances schedule AJ. As in Figure 11-9, the horizontal distance between AJ and LF shows voluntary unemployment, which decreases as the real wage rises relative to the given level of welfare benefits.

Now imagine an income tax equal to the vertical distance AB. Equilibrium employment is now N_1, which is both the number of workers that firms want to hire at the gross wage N_1 and the number of workers wanting to take jobs at the corresponding after-tax wage w_3. The horizontal distance BC is now equilibrium unemployment – people in the labour force, but not taking a job at the going rate of take-home pay.

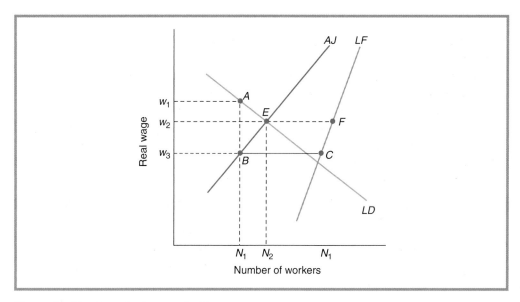

Figure 11-11 A cut in the marginal tax rate

If income tax is abolished, the gross wage to the firm now coincides with the take-home pay of a worker, and labour market equilibrium is at E. Equilibrium employment has risen, and equilibrium unemployment falls from BC to EF. Higher take-home pay, relative to unemployment benefit, reduces voluntary unemployment.

Trade unions

By restricting job acceptances and making labour more scarce, trade unions shift the AJ schedule to the left, widening the gap between AJ and LF. Imagine a new AJ' schedule through point B in Figure 11-11. Point B is now labour market equilibrium. Since labour is scarcer, the real wage has risen, but equilibrium has increased from EF to BC. Conversely, equilibrium unemployment falls if union power is weakened. Unions are less successful in restricting labour supply and forcing up wages.

Welfare to work

Recent UK policies have tried to reconnect unemployment to the labour market, both by offering assistance and by removing the option to be in permanent receipt of unemployment benefit without making an effort to look for work. In effect, this shifts the *AJ* schedule to the right, by inducing or forcing more of the labour force to take jobs.

Costs of unemployment

The private cost of unemployment

Voluntary unemployment has a private cost to those unemployed, the sacrifice of the wage they would get by taking a job. The private benefit is that they may find a better job offer by looking longer; they also get some state benefits in the meantime. Whereas the voluntarily unemployed prefer not to take a job just yet, those involuntarily out of work would prefer immediate employment and may be much worse off in unemployment. When unemployment is involuntary, people are suffering more.

The social cost of unemployment

This also varies with the nature of unemployment. Voluntary unemployment, by definition, is preferred by the individual, but should society value it too? Whereas these individuals count their benefit cheque as part of the gain from unemployment, socially this transfer payment does not contribute to national output or income.

Even so, society should not eliminate voluntary unemployment completely. First, transfer benefits may compensate for *other* market failures, such as difficulties in borrowing to acquire proper training. Second, society benefits directly from some voluntary unemployment. A changing economy needs to match up the right people to the right jobs, thus raising productivity and total output. The flow through the pool of unemployment is one way in which this is done.

Involuntary or Keynesian unemployment has a higher social cost. An economy producing below full capacity is wasting resources, which adds to the social cost of unemployment.

11-3

Inflation and unemployment: the Phillips curve

Learning outcomes

When you have finished this section, you should understand:

- ◆ The short-run Phillips curve
- ◆ The long-run Phillips curve
- ◆ The short-run correlation of inflation and unemployment
- ◆ The long-run independence of inflation and unemployment

n 1958, using UK data on inflation and unemployment, Professor A. W. Phillips of the London School of Economics discovered an empirical relationship that became famous, since it seemed also to work for other countries.

The **Phillips curve** shows that higher inflation is accompanied by lower unemployment.

The Phillips curve in Figure 11-12 shows the trade-off that people thought they faced in the 1960s. It suggested that UK inflation would fall to zero if only people would tolerate unemployment as high as 2.5 per cent. If only! Since then, we have had years when *both* inflation and unemployment exceeded 10 per cent. The simple Phillips curve ceased to fit the facts.

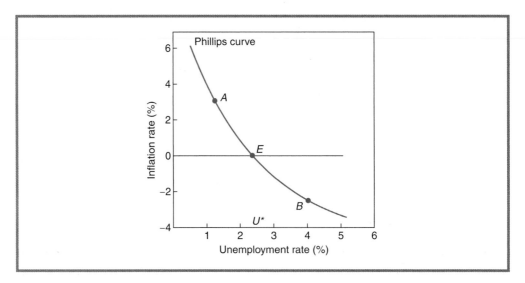

Figure 11-12   The Phillips curve

We now realize that this Phillips curve is simply the mirror image of the aggregate supply curve. The latter relates inflation to output, the former relates inflation to unemployment. The two are connected because high output goes with low unemployment.

Equilibrium unemployment U^* is the level of unemployment in long-run equilibrium.

The previous section explained why equilibrium unemployment is above zero. Once all variables can adjust, the market returns to equilibrium unemployment. There is no *long-run* trade-off between inflation and unemployment. Just as the long-run aggregate supply curve for goods is vertical at potential output, the long-run Phillips curve is vertical at equilibrium unemployment U^* in Figure 11-12. An increase in equilibrium unemployment shifts the long-run Phillips curve to the right.

The **long-run Phillips curve** is vertical at equilibrium unemployment.

The height of a *short-run* aggregate supply curve reflects the inflation expectations already built into nominal wages. The same holds in the labour market.

Each **short-run Phillips curve** is a negative relation between inflation and unemployment, given the inflation expectations already built into nominal wages.

In Figure 11-13, inflation expectations π_1 are already embodied in nominal wages and the short-run Phillips curve is PC_1. Suppose the central bank adopts a lower inflation target. Initially, this is below the previous level of expected inflation. Hence, nominal wages have been set too high. The economy moves from E to A along the short-run Phillips curve. High real wages reduce output and raise unemployment.

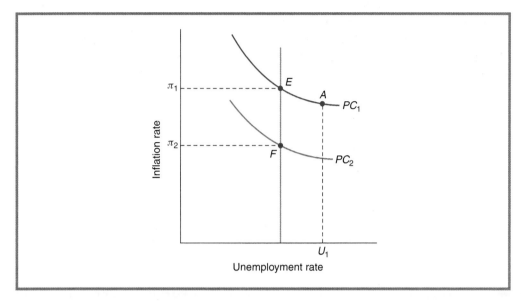

Figure 11-13 The short-run Phillips curve

If people expect lower inflation to be sustained, new wage settlements eventually embody lower inflation expectations, the Phillips curve shifts down to PC_2, and the eventual equilibrium is at F. Unemployment and output are back in long-run equilibrium, and inflation expectations have adjusted to the new policy. Since F is vertically below E, in the long run there is no trade-off between inflation and unemployment.

The original Phillips curve of Figure 11-12 was not a *permanent* trade-off between inflation and unemployment. It showed a temporary trade-off, for a given level of inherited inflation expectations and nominal wage growth. During the long historical period examined by Phillips, expected inflation happened to be low. In the second half of the twentieth century, inflation was higher on average and more variable. Hence, the short-run Phillips curve shifted up and down as inflation expectations changed.

Inflation got out of control because monetary growth was no longer tied to growth in the stock of gold, as it had been in the nineteenth century. Governments could print money. Workers, perceiving that governments were fearful of unemployment, kept raising nominal wages. Frightened to put on the monetary brakes and raise real interest rates, governments instructed their central banks to print money and accommodate nominal wage increases. The expectation of this behaviour became a self-fulfilling prophecy.

This example shows the crucial role of expectations, and explains why governments now go to such lengths to try to convince the public of their good intentions. Before discussing smart ways in which to do this, we examine why people hate inflation so much in the first place.

Recap

- Higher inflation reduces aggregate demand because the central bank raises real interest rates to get inflation back on target. The height of the aggregate demand schedule reflects the inflation target.
- In the classical model with complete wage and price flexibility, output is always potential output and the vertical long-run supply curve is valid immediately.
- The equilibrium inflation rate thus occurs at the inflation target. A rise in demand caused by fiscal expansion or private optimism induces a rise in real interest rates to reduce aggregate demand back to the level of potential output.
- The short-run supply curve shows how higher inflation temporarily raises output because inherited nominal wages have not yet had time to adjust. Over time, shifts in the short-run supply curve restore long-run equilibrium at potential output and the inflation target.
- How quickly actual output returns to potential output is a key issue in macroeconomics. If this is rapid, demand management is unnecessary. If it is slow, demand management is essential.
- Permanent supply shocks change potential output. To preserve the target inflation rate, monetary policy must accommodate the shock, thus providing the required change in aggregate demand.
- People are either employed, unemployed, or out of the labour force. Unemployment rises when inflows to the pool of the unemployed exceed outflows. Inflows and outflows are large relative to the pool of unemployment.
- Unemployment may be frictional, structural, classical, or demand-deficient. The first three types are voluntary unemployment, the last is involuntary, or Keynesian, unemployment. Equilibrium unemployment is voluntary unemployment in long-run equilibrium.
- In the long run, a sustained rise in unemployment must reflect higher equilibrium unemployment. In temporary recessions, Keynesian unemployment also matters.
- Supply-side economics aims to raise potential output, and reduce equilibrium unemployment, by improving microeconomic incentives.
- Some unemployment allows a better match of people and jobs, especially if inflows and outflows to the unemployment pool are large.
- Keynesian unemployment is involuntary, and represents wasted output. Society may also care about the human misery inflicted by involuntary unemployment.
- The Phillips curve shows the relation between inflation and unemployment. In the long run, the Phillips curve is vertical at equilibrium unemployment. There is no correlation between long-run inflation and long-run unemployment.
- The short-run Phillips curve is a negative relation between inflation and output. Given the nominal wages that firms have agreed, higher output prices induce higher output and lower unemployment. This curve shows in the labour market what the short-run supply curve shows in the output market.
- The height of the short-run Phillips curve, like the height of the short-run supply curve for output, depends on the inflation expectations that have been determined by recent nominal wage agreements.

Review questions

1 Suppose easier migration within the European Union allows large numbers of extra people to join the UK labour force. Using the framework of aggregate demand and aggregate supply, discuss the effects on output and inflation, in the short run and in the long run.

2 Suppose the Bank of England wants to keep inflation constant during this transition. How should interest rates be adjusted?

3 'Supply shocks change output, demand shocks change inflation.' Is this statement correct, in either the short run or the long run? Does the answer depend on what kind of demand shock it is?

4 Discuss the effect of a rise in export demand when wage adjustment is sluggish. What happens to (a) interest rates, (b) investment, (c) tax revenue?

5 Why are these statements wrong? (a) Higher inflation reduces output by making it more expensive for firms to produce. (b) Higher inflation reduces output because consumers demand fewer goods when prices are higher.

6 World oil prices increase permanently because of an earthquake in the Middle East that destroys oil wells. You are in charge of setting interest rates in pursuit of an inflation target of 2 per cent. What do you do? What happens to output?

7 'The microchip has caused a permanent rise in unemployment.' Discuss this assertion, showing its effects on labour demand, the labour force, and job acceptances.

8 How is high unemployment explained by (a) a Keynesian, (b) a classical economist?

9 How do lower taxes affect unemployment (a) when the economy begins at equilibrium unemployment, (b) when initially it also has Keynesian unemployment?

10 Why is unemployment among school leavers higher than that among adults?

11 Why are these statements wrong? (a) So long as there is unemployment, there is pressure on wages to fall. (b) Unemployment arises only because greedy workers are pricing themselves out of a job.

12 Would Professor Phillips have found a reliable statistical relationship between inflation and unemployment if he had happened to examine a period in which (a) equilibrium unemployment was constant and inflation expectations were high but constant, (b) equilibrium unemployment kept changing, (c) inflation expectations kept changing? Explain.

13 Is the claim that the long-run Phillips curve is vertical consistent with the claim that inflation is very damaging?

14 A newly elected government announces that it intends to run a large budget deficit, print money to pay for this, and impose laws to prevent wages and prices from being raised. (a) What do you predict will happen? Why? (b) If this government loses the next election, what policy advice would you give to the next government?

Answers on pages 352–354

12

Exchange rates and the balance of payments

12-1

Exchange rates and the balance of payments

Learning outcomes

By the end of this section, you should understand:

- ◆ The forex market
- ◆ Balance of payments accounting
- ◆ Internal and external balance

Exports and imports are each about 10 per cent of GDP in the US, but almost 30 per cent in the UK and Germany (See Figure 12.1). As transport costs fall and communications improve, the world economy is becoming more integrated and international trade is increasing. To compete within this global economy, everyone has to specialize in what they are good at. Small countries tend to export a larger fraction of their national output: once they specialize and produce on a world scale, they are making much more of particular commodities than they will ever wish to consume at home. Instead, they export a lot, and acquire most of their consumption needs by spending this income on imports.

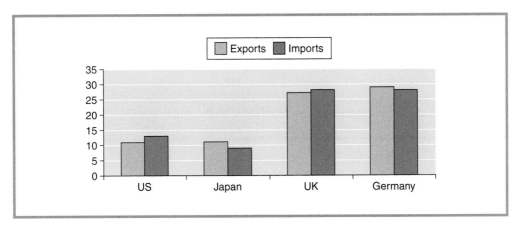

Figure 12-1   Exports and imports (% of GDP), 2000

When an economy is very open to foreign trade, the exchange rate, international competitiveness, and the trade balance with foreigners become major policy issues. We show how openness to trade and financial flows affects the domestic economy.

The foreign exchange market

The foreign exchange (forex) market exchanges one national currency for another. The exchange rate is the price at which two currencies exchange.

An exchange rate of $1.50/£ measures the international value of sterling: how much foreign currency ($) a unit of the domestic currency (£) is worth.

Who supplies $ to the forex market, wanting £ in exchange? This demand for £ arises from UK exporters wanting to convert $ back into £, and from US residents wanting to buy UK assets for which they must pay in £. Conversely, a supply of £ to the forex market reflects UK importers wanting $ to buy US goods, and UK residents wishing to buy US $ assets.

Figure 12-2 shows the resulting supply SS and demand DD for £. The equilibrium exchange rate e_1 equates the quantity of £ supplied and demanded. If the US demand for UK goods or assets rises, the demand for £ shifts right to DD_1, and the equilibrium $/£ exchange rate rises. A higher $/£ exchange rate means the £ has *appreciated*, because its international value has risen. The $ has simultaneously *depreciated*, since its international value is lower. A fall in the $/£ exchange rate has the opposite effect.

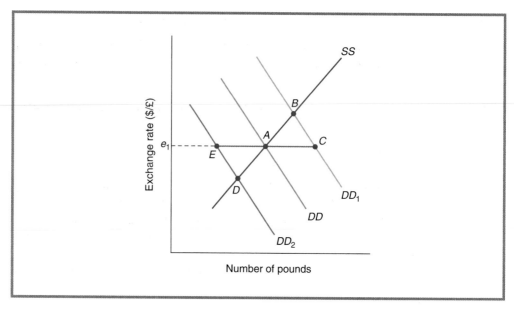

Figure 12-2 The forex market

Exchange rate regimes

An exchange rate regime describes the rules under which governments allow exchange rates to be determined.

A **fixed exchange rate** means that governments, acting through their central banks, will buy or sell as much of the currency as people want to exchange at the fixed rate.

In Figure 12-2, a fixed exchange rate e_1 is the free market equilibrium rate if the supply and demand for £ are SS and DD. The market clears unaided. Suppose the demand for pounds now shifts up to DD_1. Americans, hooked on whisky, need more £ to import from the UK. In a free market, the equilibrium is now at B and the £ appreciates against the $.

At the fixed exchange rate e_1, there is an excess demand AC for £. To meet this, the Bank of England prints AC extra £ and sells them in exchange for $[e_1 \times AC]$ of $ which are added to the UK foreign exchange reserves.

The **foreign exchange reserves** are the foreign currency holdings of the domestic central bank.

Conversely, if the demand for £ shifts down to DD_2, few foreigners now want British goods or assets. The free market equilibrium exchange rate is below e_1 unless the central bank intervenes. To defend the fixed exchange rate e_1, at which there would be an excess supply EA of £, the central bank demands EA in £, paid for by selling $(EA \times e_1)$ of $ from the foreign exchange reserves. When the central bank is forced to buy or sell £ to support the fixed exchange rate, it *intervenes* in the forex market.

If the demand for £ on average is DD_2, the Bank on average is reducing the UK forex reserves to support the £ at e_1. The £ is overvalued. As reserves run out, the government may try to borrow foreign exchange reserves from the International Monetary Fund (IMF), an international body that lends to governments in short-term difficulties. At best, this is a temporary solution. Unless the demand for £ rises in the long run, it will be necessary to *devalue* the pound.

A **devaluation (revaluation)** is a fall (rise) in the fixed exchange rate.

In November 1967, the UK government, after consultations with other governments, devalued the pound from $2.80/£ to $2.40/£. However, the UK has not always pursued a fixed exchange rate.

In a **floating exchange rate** regime, the exchange rate is allowed to find its free market equilibrium without any invervention using the foreign exchange reserves.

Thus, in Figure 12-2 the demand schedule shifts from DD_2 to DD to DD_1 would be allowed to move the equilibrium point from D to A to B.

Of course, it is not necessary to adopt the extreme regimes of pure floating or perfectly fixed exchange rates. *Dirty floating* means some intervention in the short run but allowing the exchange rate to find its equilibrium level in the longer run. By understanding the two polar cases – completely fixed and freely floating – we can see how the intermediate regimes would work.

Next, we explain balance of payments accounting, and its connection to exchange rate regimes.

Box 12-1   Effective exchange rates

Each currency has a bilateral exchange rate against each other currency. For example, we can measure the $/£ or euro/£. Sometimes it is useful to examine the average exchange rate against all countries.

The **effective exchange rate (eer)** is a weighted average of individual bilateral exchange rates.

Usually, we use the share of trade with each country to decide the weights. Important trading partners get more weight in the effective exchange rate index.

The figure shows indices of *actual* exchange rates of the UK's two main trading partners, the US and the euro zone, in each case calibrated so that the value is 100 in the year 2000. The £ has fluctuated against both. However, the £'s *effective* exchange rate against all currencies has been much more stable (again, we have measured so that its value in the year 2000 is shown as 100).

The figure makes two important points. First, the effective exchange rate, being an average, fluctuates less than its component parts. Second, since UK trade with the euro zone greatly exceeds trade with the US, the overall average is closer to the euro/£ than to the $/£.

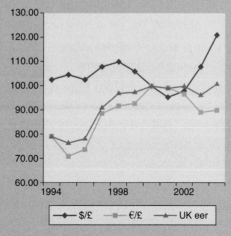

Nominal and real exchange rates

Source: OECD, *Economic Outlook*

The balance of payments

The **balance of payments** records all transactions between a country and the rest of the world.

All international transactions giving rise to an inflow of £ to the UK are credits in the UK balance of payments accounts. Outflows of £ are debits, entered with a minus sign. Table 12-1 shows the actual UK balance of payments accounts in 2003.

(1)	Current account		−19
	Of which Trade in goods	−46	
	Trade in services	14	
	Income	23	
	Current transfer payments	−10	
(2)	Capital account		1
(3)	Financial account		16
(4)	Balancing item		2
(5)	UK balance of payments (1+2+3+4)		0
(5)	Official financing (= −(4))		0

Table 12-1 UK balance of payments (£bn), 2003
Source: ONS, *Economic Trends*

The **current account** of the balance of payments records international flows of goods, services, and transfer payments.

Visible trade is exports and imports of goods (cars, food, steel). *Invisible trade* is exports and imports of services (banking, shipping, tourism). Together, these make up the trade balance or net exports of goods and services. To get the current account, we take the trade balance and add *net* transfer payments from abroad. These comprise interest income on net foreign assets, and other international transfer payments (for example, net aid to foreign countries, which is an outflow). The UK current account was £19 billion in deficit in 2003.

The **capital account** of the balance of payments shows international flows of transfer payments relating to capital items.

This covers payments received from the EU for investment in regional infrastructure projects, the transfer of capital into or out of the UK by migrants, and UK forgiveness of foreign debt. Typically, capital transfer payments are small.

The **financial account** of the balance of payments records international purchases and sales of financial assets.

Table 12-1 shows a net financial inflow of £16 billion in 2003. The inflow of money to the UK as foreigners bought UK physical and financial assets exceeded the inflow of money from the UK as residents bought assets abroad.[1]

[1] UK statistics now follow modern international practice in distinguishing the capital and financial account. Previously, rows (2) and (3) were amalgamated and simply called the 'capital account' even though all the large items were financial flows. References to international capital flows nearly always mean financial flows.

The balancing item is a statistical adjustment, which would be zero if all previous items had been correctly measured. It reflects a failure to record all transactions in the official statistics. Adding together the (1) current account, (2) the capital account, (3) the financial account, and (4) the balancing item yields the UK *balance of payments* in 2003. As it happens, it was just in balance.

The **balance of payments** records the net monetary inflow from abroad when households, firms, and the government make their desired transactions.

The final entry in Table 12-1 is *official financing*. This is always of equal magnitude and opposite sign to the balance of payments in the line above, so that the sum of all the entries is *always* zero. Official financing measures the international transactions that the government must take to *accommodate* all the other transactions in the balance of payments accounts.

Floating exchange rates

If the exchange rate is freely floating, with no central bank intervention, the forex reserves are constant, and the exchange rate equates the supply and demand for £.

The supply of £, by people needing $ to buy imports or foreign assets, measures outflows or minus items in the UK balance of payments. The demand for £, by people selling $ earned from exports and sales of assets to foreigners, measures inflows or plus items in the UK balance of payments. A freely floating exchange rate equates the quantities of £ supplied and demanded. Hence inflows equal outflows and the balance of payments is *exactly* zero. There is no intervention in the forex market, and thus no official financing.

With a zero balance of payments, under floating exchange rates a current account surplus is exactly matched by a deficit of the same size on combined capital and financial accounts, or vice versa. A current account surplus (deficit) means a country underspends (overspends) its international income. This saving (dissaving) adds to (subtracts from) its net international assets. That is precisely what the capital and financial accounts record. Since transfers on the capital account are tiny, henceforth we assume that they are zero.

Hence, under floating exchange rates, a current account surplus is exactly matched by a financial account deficit. Conversely, a current account deficit is exactly matched by a financial account surplus. The balance of payments is always in balance.

Fixed exchange rates

With a fixed exchange rate, the balance of payments need not be zero. A payments deficit means that total outflows exceed total inflows on the combined current and capital accounts. The supply of £ to the forex market, from UK imports or purchases of foreign assets, exceeds the demand for £, from UK exports or sales of assets to foreigners. The balance of payments deficit is precisely the excess supply of £ in the forex market.

To peg the exchange rate, the Bank of England must demand this excess supply of £, reducing UK forex reserves by selling $ to buy £. This is 'official financing' in the balance of payments. Hence, with a balance of payments deficit (surplus), forex reserves must be sold (bought).

The current account

UK imports depend in part on the level of UK income. Hence, UK exports, which are someone else's imports, depend partly on income in the rest of the world. The second key determinant of net exports is international competitiveness. However, we must distinguish nominal and real variables. International competitiveness depends on the real exchange rate.

The **real exchange rate** is the relative price of domestic and foreign goods, when measured in a common currency.

A higher real exchange rate, raising the price of UK goods relative to US goods measured in the same currency, makes the UK less competitive relative to the US. A fall in the UK's real exchange rate makes the UK more competitive in international markets.

The real exchange rate can thus depreciate for three different reasons: a fall in the actual or nominal $/£ exchange rate; a rise in the price of US goods; or a fall in the price of UK goods. The arithmetic does not care which it is.

Box 12-2   Calculating real exchange rates

Each row in the table below shows a different combination of the nominal exchange rate, the price of domestic goods, and the price of foreign goods. In the first row, UK shirts cost £6 and US shirts $10. At a nominal exchange rate of $2/£, a UK shirt costs $12 and is 1.2 times as expensive as a US shirt when measured in $. Since a $10 US shirt costs £5 at an exchange rate of $2/£, £6 UK shirts are also 1.2 times as expensive as US shirts if we measure them both in £. It never matters which currency we use for the comparison, but we must use the same currency for both.

In the second row, the nominal exchange rate falls by 25 per cent from $2/£ to $1/5/£, and the table shows that, other things equal, the real exchange rate also falls by 25 per cent. Nominal devaluation of the $/£ has made the UK more competitive and the US less competitive.

The third and fourth rows show that the same change in the real exchange rate can be achieved by a fall in UK prices, or a rise in US prices, without any change in the nominal exchange rate. Real exchange rates can therefore change in a monetary union even though nominal exchange rates are fixed forever.

Nominal exchange rate ($/£)	UK shirt price (£)	UK shirt price ($)	US shirt price ($)	Real exchange rate
2.0	6	12	10	1.2
1.5	6	9	10	0.9
2.0	4.5	9	10	0.9
2.0	6	12	13.3	0.9

Thus, if UK annual inflation is 10 per cent and US inflation is zero, the UK's real exchange rate depreciates by 10 per cent a year if the nominal exchange rate is fixed. However, the real exchange rate would appreciate if the nominal exchange rate fell by more than 10 per cent a year.

In summary, higher UK output raises UK imports, reducing UK net exports. Higher output abroad raises demand for UK exports, raising UK net exports. A depreciation of the UK real exchange rate makes the UK more competitive, raising UK net exports.

Other items on the current account include net government transfers to foreigners, which we treat as given. However, a country with large foreign assets has a large net inflow of property income, boosting its current account. Conversely, a country with large foreign debts has a large outflow of net property income, making its current account balance smaller than its trade balance.

Although we continue to ignore the capital account, because capital transfers are usually so small, we cannot ignore the financial account.

The financial account

Purchases and sales of foreign assets are increasingly important. Computers and telecommunications make it as easy for a UK resident to transact in the financial markets of New York, and Tokyo, as in London. Moreover, the elaborate system of controls, restricting flows of financial capital, has gradually been dismantled. There is now a global financial market in which footloose funds flow freely from one country to another in search of the highest expected return.

Huge one-way financial account flows would swamp the typical flows of imports and exports on the current account. Forex market equilibrium requires that expected returns adjust until assets in different currencies offer the *same* expected return, *removing* the incentive for vast, one-way flows of financial capital.

The return on any asset is the interest rate plus the capital gain you make while the asset is held. Exchange rate changes lead to capital gains or losses while you temporarily hold assets abroad. You have £100 to invest for a year. UK interest rates are 10 per cent, but US interest rates are zero. Keeping your funds in £, you have £110 by the end of the year. What if you lend abroad for a year?

With an initial exchange rate of $2/£, your £100 buys $200. At a zero interest rate, you have $200 at the end of the year. But if the £ falls 10 per cent in the year to $1.80/£, your $200 converts back to £110. You made 10 per cent less interest in $ but earned an extra 10 per cent capital gain while the $ rose against the £ and the £ fell against the $.

If the $/£ exchange rate falls by more than 10 per cent during the year, you do better by lending in $, since the capital gain outweighs the interest forgone. When international financial capital mobility is high,[2] massive flows are avoided only if the interest parity condition holds.

Perfect capital mobility means expected total returns on assets in different currencies must be equal if huge capital flows are to be avoided. A positive interest differential must be offset by an expected exchange rate fall of equal magnitude. This is the interest parity condition.

Internal and external balance

Internal balance means aggregate demand equals potential output. External balance means that the current account of the balance of payments is zero. Long-run equilibrium requires both.

---

[2] Because economists used to use the term 'capital account' to describe what we now call the 'financial account', the term 'perfect capital mobility' always referred to movements of *financial* capital. We still use the shorthand 'capital mobility' to refer to financial flows.

Chapter 9 explained how a closed economy eventually returns to potential output and internal balance. External balance must also hold in the long run. The current account shows a country's flow of income from abroad minus its flow of spending on foreign goods, services, and transfer payments. With a permanent current account deficit, a country goes bankrupt by overspending its foreign income indefinitely. With a permanent current account surplus, the country is saving and adding to net foreign assets forever. This makes no sense since the country could afford to import more foreign goods.

We can use internal and external balance to analyse a country's equilibrium real exchange rate in the long run. Internal balance means each country's output is at potential output. Taking this as given, the main determinant of the current account is the real exchange rate. A higher real exchange rate makes the country less competitive, reducing its net exports.

In Figure 12-3, the current account schedule CA shows how a higher real exchange rate reduces the current account balance by making the country less competitive. Only the real exchange rate R will achieve external balance in the long run. With a higher real exchange rate, competitiveness would be lower and there would be a current account deficit. A real exchange rate below R makes the country too competitive and it would have a permanent current account surplus.

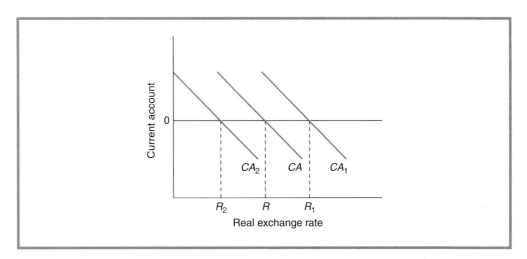

Figure 12-3   External balance

Suppose the UK discovers North Sea oil. It now has a larger current account surplus at any real exchange rate since it no longer has to import oil. The current account schedule shifts right from CA to CA_1. Only an appreciation of the real exchange rate to R_1 can restore external balance. Manufacturers complain that they are doing badly at the less competitive exchange rate, but the brutal reality is that if the UK exports more oil, it must export less of something else.

Forget North Sea oil, now think net foreign assets. A country that has previously stockpiled a lot of foreign assets now has a big current account inflow from interest, profit, and dividends. Again, its CA schedule shifts right to CA_1. Again, this induces a rise in the long-run real exchange rate. With more current account inflows from net asset income, net exports must fall if the overall current account is to remain in balance. Getting uncompetitive is what makes this happen.

Thus, countries with large foreign debts, on which they pay flows of interest on the current account, face schedule CA_2 in Figure 12-3. However, a suitably low real exchange rate makes them competitive enough to have net export surpluses large enough to finance the outflow of interest payments on the current account.

Box 12-3 Financial account flows

Financial account flows may be short term, such as putting money in a foreign bank account, or long term, such as taking a permanent stake in a foreign company.

Foreign direct investment (FDI) is the purchase of foreign firms or the establishment of foreign subsidiaries.

Has globalization made flows of financial capital bigger recently? The figure below shows the scale of average annual capital flows, relative to GDP, for 12 OECD economies in peacetime years since 1870. Capital flows dried up in the 1930s, in the Great Depression, but today we forget that the late nineteenth century was also an age of foreign investment.

Such figures need to be interpreted with care. Since official financing is usually small, our balance of payments arithmetic implies that the sum of the current and capital account must be near zero, especially if averaged over many years. If countries cannot run large current account deficits, they cannot have large capital inflows either.

Looking at the *size* of capital flows does not itself tell us about capital mobility, which relates to the *sensitivity* of capital flows to profit opportunities. If exchange rates adjust to *prevent* massive capital flows, we never see huge flows in the data whatever the degree of capital mobility.

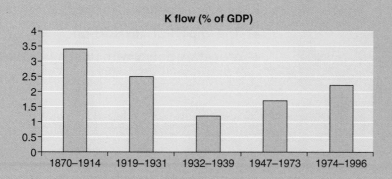

Source: M. Obstfeld, 'The global capital market: benefactor or menace?', *Journal of Economic Perspectives*, 1999

12-2

Monetary policy in open economies

Learning outcomes

By the end of this section, you should understand:

- ◆ Monetary policy with fixed exchange rates
- ◆ The impact of devaluation
- ◆ Monetary policy with floating exchange rates

Having introduced the key features of an open economy, we now ask how our previous analysis of monetary and fiscal policy must be amended once we recognize that an economy is open to international trade and financial flows. The answer is very different, depending on whether the economy has fixed or floating exchange rates, so we need to examine the two cases separately.

Fixed exchange rates

Perfect capital mobility means international lenders must get the same expected return in all currencies. Pegging the exchange rate prevents capital gains or losses on the exchange rate while holding foreign assets. Capital mobility and pegged exchange rates can be reconciled only by setting the *same* interest rate in both countries. Only then will investors expect the same return in both countries. For at least one country, this represents a loss of monetary sovereignty. It can no longer set the interest rates that it wants. Fixed exchange rates take away monetary independence.

Suppose the UK wished to peg its exchange rate against the US dollar. One possibility is that the US would meekly accept whatever interest rate the Bank of England wished to set. But this is not very likely! Given the relative size and power of the two countries, it is more likely that the Bank of England would have to match whatever interest rate the US central bank wished to set.

Suppose the UK housing market was booming and the Bank tried to raise UK interest rates above those in the US. What would happen? With a pegged exchange rate, there would be a massive inflow of financial capital to take advantage of the high interest rate. This balance of payments surplus and excess demand for pounds forces the Bank of England to print more pounds, with which it buys foreign exchange reserves. However, the rise in the UK money supply, or stock of circulating pounds, bids down UK interest rates. The attempt to raise interest rates is thwarted by the capital inflow then induced.

Adjusting to shocks

What happens if export demand falls? Interest rates cannot respond since they have to continue to match those in the partner country. Suppose fiscal policy is also unchanged. Hence, the fall in aggregate demand causes a fall in output and a rise in unemployment. Eventually, this bids down wages and prices. With a given nominal exchange rate, the real exchange rate falls and the country gets more competitive, not because its nominal exchange rate has changed but because the domestic price of its goods has fallen. This eventually restores net exports to their former level. Internal and external balance are then restored.

This confirms that market forces can adjust to shocks, even under a fixed exchange rate system. A monetary union is simply a permanent commitment to fixed exchange rates. Most of the European Union would not have embarked on a monetary union unless there was some default mechanism to restore internal and external balance. That safety valve is the response of domestic wages and prices to booms and slumps, and the consequent effect on competitiveness.

Devaluation

Countries such as Germany, France, and Italy have traditions of strong trade unions, and substantial employment protection. This tends to make wage and price adjustment slow. It may therefore take a protracted recession to achieve the required fall in domestic wages and prices when such a country becomes uncompetitive. Some people have argued this is one reason that the Eurozone countries have not grown more quickly during the past five years.[3]

For a country not committed to a permanently fixed exchange rate, devaluation immediately raises competitiveness, achieving overnight what might have taken years of domestic recession to accomplish. When a country devalues its nominal exchange, adopting a lower exchange rate peg, the real exchange rate changes because the nominal exchange rate has changed. Resources are drawn into export industries and into domestic industries that compete with imports. However, there are two points to note.

First, the initial *quantity* response may be quite slow. Demand may change slowly if there were some long-term contracts made at the old exchange rate. Supply may change slowly if it takes time to expand new production. Devaluation may not improve the trade balance in the short run. The trade balance refers to value not volume. With low initial quantity responses, cutting the $ price of UK goods may initially yield less revenue, not more. The same quantity of goods is being sold for a lower dollar price than before. However, in the longer run, quantities are more responsive and net trade revenues increase.[4]

In the medium run, the country will regain internal balance at which potential output equals aggregate demand $\{[C+I+G]+[X-Z]\}$. For a given level of potential output, net exports can respond more to devaluation the lower is the level of domestic absorption $[C+I+G]$.

If the economy returns to internal balance before net exports have increased by the desired amount, further increases in net exports raise aggregate demand above potential output. This causes inflation, reducing competitiveness at the fixed nominal exchange rate, and undoing all the good work that devaluation has accomplished. Sometimes, it is neces-

Case study 12-1   Black Wednesday, 1992

During 1990–92, the UK belonged to the exchange rate mechanism (ERM) of the European Monetary System, an arrangement to peg exchange rates between Member States but jointly float against other currencies. In 1990, German unification led to huge fiscal subsidies to East Germany and a big boost to aggregate demand in Germany, prompting a large rise in interest rates to stop German inflation getting out of control. High interest rates caused misery for Germany's partners in the ERM. In 1992, the UK and Italy left the ERM and floated their exchange rates in order to be able then to reduce interest rates and end their recessions. This immediately led to sharply lower exchange rates for Britain and Italy.

Supporters of the ERM policy called this Black Wednesday because they saw it as a defeat for government policy.

Frankfurt stock exchange
© David Pollack/Corbis

(continues on next page)

---

[3] You should not always take such arguments at face value. Recall from Chapter 8 that long-run growth is achieved by enhancing aggregate supply and potential output. The longer Eurozone stagnation continues, the more likely it is that this is because of permanently slow growth in potential output rather than because output is temporarily below potential output. Moreover, in 2005 Germany announced a record trade surplus, hardly evidence of stagnation caused by lack of competitiveness. As you master the foundations of economics, you will spot more and more fallacies in the public debate!

[4] Since devaluation causes an initial fall in the value of net exports but then a subsequent rise in export values, this response is called a J-curve. As time elapses, the current account falls down to the bottom of the J but then rises to above its initial position.

Case study 12-1   *Continued*

The Chancellor of the Exchequer, Norman Lamont, resigned and much of UK policy since 1992 has been designed to avoid another such embarrassment. Critics of the ERM policy, concerned that the UK demand was being held down by high interest rates required only because of German unification, labelled the day of the decision to float the exchange rate as Golden Wednesday. Their predictions of a subsequent recovery were correct. That is what you should have predicted too.

The figures below, showing the path of the UK's nominal and real exchange rate against its trading partners during 1992–95 and corresponding changes in the current account of the balance of payments, contain three lessons. First, the sharp fall in the nominal exchange rate was initially accompanied by a sharp fall in the real exchange rate and hence an immediate rise in competitiveness. Second, this still took a couple of years to have its full effect on the current account of the balance of payments, which improved from a deficit of £10 billion in 1992 to a deficit of only £1 billion in 1994.

Third, by 1995 all the gain in competitiveness had been lost despite the nominal exchange rate remaining well below its level of 1992. As an export boom dragged the UK out of recession, domestic wages and prices began to rise, thus offsetting the competitive edge created by the nominal devaluation.

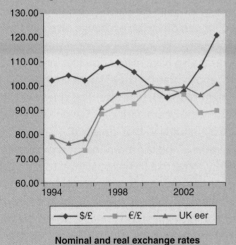

Nominal and real exchange rates

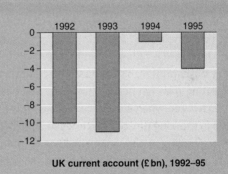

UK current account (£ bn), 1992–95

Source: OECD, *Economic Outlook*

sary to tighten *fiscal* policy, thereby reducing domestic absorption, to make sure that there are enough spare resources to produce the extra net exports required.

Taking an even longer view, in the very long run real variables determine other real variables. Changing the nominal exchange rate will not accomplish anything that adjustments of domestic wages and prices could also have accomplished. The case for devaluation is that it may speed up the process when wage and price adjustment is sluggish.

Putting this differently, devaluation, which raises the cost of imports, is eventually passed on into higher wages and prices, making no real difference. Most empirical models of the UK economy, based on past data, conclude that the effects of a nominal devaluation are offset by a rise in domestic prices and wages by the end of five years.

Having studied how macroeconomic policy works under fixed exchange rates, we now examine the same issues when a country decides to float its exchange rate.

Floating exchange rates

With a floating exchange rate, domestic monetary policy can set any interest rate that it wishes. Monetary sovereignty is restored, and may use an inflation target to decide how to set interest rates.

The long-run *real* exchange rate must be consistent with internal balance (aggregate demand equals potential output) and external balance (current account equals zero). If the nominal exchange rate is fixed, domestic prices and wages must eventually adjust to get the appropriate real exchange rate. Under a *floating* exchange rate, knowing the inflation targets at home and abroad, people can work out what path the nominal exchange rate must eventually reach to deliver the appropriate equilibrium real exchange rate in the long run. The higher a country's price level has become, relative to its competitors, the lower must be its nominal exchange rate to achieve the correct real exchange rate. Hence, in the long run, the inflation targets at home and abroad essentially determine the paths of domestic and foreign prices, from which we can deduce the path that the nominal exchange rate will have to follow to achieve the correct real exchange rate and current account balance.

Countries cannot depart from external balance in the long run, and the current account is all important. However, in the short run the role of the current account is dwarfed by the *threat* of massive financial capital movements. The forex market cannot cope with massive one-way capital flows, and must keep adjusting the exchange rate to prevent them. This implies setting the exchange rate at a level from which interest parity is expected to hold *from now on*. In the short run, the financial account can drive the exchange rate a long way away from the path that balances the current account.

In the long run, countries with high inflation rates also have higher nominal interest rates (so that their real interest rates can remain appropriate). Their long-run equilibrium exchange rate is falling steadily to preserve the right real exchange rate. This does not stimulate big capital flows because the capital losses on the depreciating exchange rate are just offsetting the high nominal interest rates earned by lending in that currency.

However, when a country has higher interest rates in the short run than it is expected to have in the long run, the currency looks temporarily attractive to financial investors. To stop them all piling in, the currency must appreciate rapidly and significantly to such a level that from now on the only way is down. The prospect of capital losses from holding the currency from now on is what offsets the attraction of high interest rates in the short run.

The upward jump in the exchange rate takes the market by surprise. Had they seen it coming, they would already have piled into the currency to get the capital gain. The exchange rate jumps up to make it credible that the foreseeable direction will be down from now on. Conversely, a temporary cut in domestic interest rates makes the exchange rate jump down, so that from now on it can offer capital gains to offset the low interest rate.

Monetary policy under floating exchange rates

Under fixed exchange rates, domestic monetary policy was powerless; under floating exchange rates, the converse is true.

A given rise in domestic interest rates does not merely depress domestic demand, it also makes the exchange rate jump up, which reduces net export demand substantially if wages and prices are sluggish and cannot respond quickly. Hence, monetary policy has a strong effect in the short run under floating exchange rates. The domestic demand effect is reinforced by the exchange rate effect on competitiveness.

Recap

■ The exchange rate is the relative price of two currencies in the forex market.

■ The demand for domestic currency arises from exports, and from sales of domestic assets to foreigners; the supply of domestic currency arises from imports and purchases of foreign assets. Floating exchange rates equate supply and demand when there is no government intervention in the forex market.

■ Under fixed exchange rates, the Bank of England intervenes to buy any excess supply of £, thus reducing its forex reserves. The Bank creates and supplies £ to meet any excess demand for £, thus raising its forex reserves.

■ The balance of payments records monetary inflows as credits and monetary outflows as debits. The current account is the trade balance plus net transfer payments from abroad, which mainly reflect income on net foreign assets. The capital account shows capital transfers. The financial account shows net sales of foreign assets. The balance of payments is the sum of the current, capital, and financial account balances (plus any balancing item to correct for mismeasurement).

■ Under floating exchange rates, the balance of payments is zero. Under fixed exchange rates, a payments surplus (deficit) is offset by official financing, raising (lowering) the domestic money supply.

■ The real exchange rate adjusts the nominal exchange rate for prices at home and abroad. It is the relative price of domestic to foreign goods, when measured in a common currency. A higher real exchange rate reduces competitiveness.

■ Higher domestic (foreign) income raises the demand for imports (exports). A higher real exchange rate reduces the demand for net exports.

■ Perfect international capital mobility implies a vast financial capital flow on the financial account if the expected return differs across countries. To prevent this, any interest differential between domestic and foreign assets must be offset by a matching expected capital gain or loss on the exchange rate while temporarily holding foreign assets.

■ At internal balance, aggregate demand equals potential output. At external balance, the current account is zero. Both are needed for long-run equilibrium.

■ Discovery of a natural resource, or higher net foreign assets, raise the long-run equilibrium real exchange rate.

■ With perfect capital mobility, monetary policy is powerless under pegged exchange rates. Domestic interest rates must match foreign interest rates. However, fiscal expansion no longer bids up domestic interest rates.

■ A devaluation lowers the fixed exchange rate. With sluggish price adjustment, it raises competitiveness and aggregate demand. With spare resources, output increases. Without spare resources, higher demand bids up prices, reducing competitiveness again.

■ In the long run, devaluing the nominal exchange rate has little real effect. But it adjusts competitiveness quickly in the short run.

■ Under floating exchange rates, domestic and foreign monetary policies determine domestic and foreign prices. Together with the real exchange rate required for external balance, this determines the eventual nominal exchange. However, in the short run the exchange rate moves around to prevent massive

- one-way financial capital flows. Temporarily, the exchange rate can deviate a lot from the level that achieves current account balance.
- Floating exchange rates magnify the effect of interest rate changes on aggregate demand, by inducing short-run changes in the exchange rate and competitiveness.

Review questions

1 A country has a current account surplus of £6 billion but a financial account deficit of £4 billion. (a) Is its balance of payments in deficit or surplus? (b) Are the country's foreign exchange reserves rising or falling? (c) Is the central bank buying or selling domestic currency?

2 For over 20 years, Japan has run a current account surplus. (a) How is this compatible with the statement that countries must eventually get back to external balance? (b) Would it be so easy to run a persistent current account deficit?

3 Which of these increase a country's competititiveness: (a) a fall in domestic wages, (b) a fall in foreign wages, (c) a fall in the foreign country's exchange rate, (d) a fall in the domestic country's wage rate, (e) a productivity increase in the domestic country?

4 In each answer to 3 above, say whether the domestic country's real exchange rate appreciates or depreciates.

5 'The exchange rate depreciated.' 'The exchange rate was devalued.' Do these statements mean the same thing? If not, why not?

6 You are running the German economy the day after unification of East and West Germany. You know East Germans will need large government subsidies to get them on their feet. (a) What happens to German fiscal policy? (b) As a result, is German aggregate demand above or below potential output? (c) If you run German monetary policy, how do you ensure your inflation target is still achieved? (d) What would have happened if Germany had revalued its exchange rate upwards?

7 Rank the following according to the ability of monetary policy to affect real output in the short run: (a) a closed economy; (b) an open economy with fixed exchange rates; (c) an open economy with floating exchange rates. Explain.

8 Newsreaders say that 'the £ had a good day' if the UK exchange rate rises. (a) When is an appreciation of the exchange rate desirable? (b) Undesirable?

9 Kuwait has a large stock of foreign assets. (a) What does this imply about its previous current account balances? (b) If Kuwait is now in external balance, is it likely to have a trade surplus or a trade deficit?

10 Victorian Britain was the workshop of the world in the early nineteenth century because of its lead in the industrial revolution. (a) Do you think Britain had a current account surplus or deficit during these years? (b) By the late nineteenth century, what do you think Britain's net foreign asset position was? (c) What would this imply about its net interest income from abroad on the current account of its balance of payments?

11 (a) If Britain was in external balance in the late nineteenth century, would it have a large trade surplus or large trade deficit? (b) What has to happen to competitiveness and Britain's real exchange rate to bring this about? (c) Do you think it surprising that late

Victorians worried about whether success and moral decay had undermined Britain's ability to compete? (d) Was their diagnosis correct?

12 Why does a floating exchange rate have to adjust continuously to prevent large one-way financial flows between one country and another? What would happen if these one-way flows were allowed to occur? Can they occur under fixed exchange rates?

13 Why are these statements wrong? (a) If global speculators have more money than central banks, central banks can no longer defend fixed exchange rates. (b) Floating exchange rates are volatile because imports and exports fluctuate a lot.

Answers on pages 354–355

13

The global economy

13-1

International trade

Learning outcomes

By the end of this section, you should understand:

- ◆ Patterns of international trade
- ◆ Comparative advantage
- ◆ Two-way trade in the same product
- ◆ The gains from trade
- ◆ When trade restrictions are beneficial

This final chapter looks at the global economy as a trading system. Why does international trade occur? Why have some countries been left behind while others prosper as never before? And what can we say about globalization, so frequently a source of fear and concern in the public debate? Is globalization a threat or an opportunity?

International trade is part of daily life. Britons drink French wine, Americans drive Japanese cars, and Russians eat American wheat. Through *exchange* and *specialization*, countries supply the world economy with things that they produce relatively cheaply, receiving in exchange things made relatively more cheaply elsewhere.

These gains from trade are reinforced by scale economies in production. Instead of each country having many small producers, different countries specialize in different things so that all countries benefit from the cost reductions that ensue. Because foreign competition may make life difficult for some voters, governments are often under pressure to restrict imports. We end the section by discussing trade policy and whether it is ever a good idea to restrict imports.

World exports are now 20 per cent of world GDP. World trade has grown by 7.4 per cent a year since 1950, as transport costs and other barriers to trade keep falling. Countries are becoming steadily more open to trade, as Figure 13-1 confirms. Events in other countries affect our daily lives much more than they did 20 years ago. Smaller countries are of course more open; when New York trades with California it does not count as *international* trade.

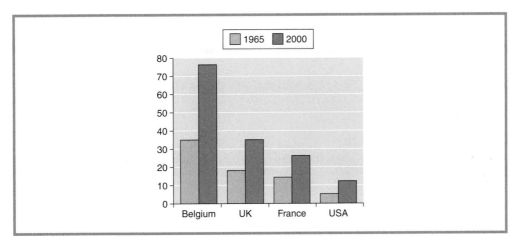

Figure 13-1 Exports (% of GDP)

Table 13-1 shows that half of world trade is trade between the rich industrial countries, and only 14 per cent of trade does not involve these countries at all. World trade and world income are organized around the rich industrial countries.

Destination country	Origin country	
	Rich	Other
Rich	37	20
Others	16	27

Table 13-1 Trade patterns (percentage of world exports), 2003

Source: WTO, *International Trade Statistics*

315

Services are over 70 per cent of GDP in rich countries, but a much smaller share of their trade. Trade in goods (merchandise trade) remains important because many countries import goods, add a little value, and then re-export them. The value added makes a small contribution to GDP but gross flows of imports and exports of goods are large.

Table 13-2 distinguishes between *primary products* (agricultural commodities, minerals, and fuels) and manufactured commodities. Although the EU is chiefly an exporter of manufactures, primary commodities account for one-fifth of exports, and although the EU has to import many raw materials, imports of wholly or partly finished manufactures account for three-quarters of EU imports. US trade exhibits the same general pattern.

	EU	North America	Asia
% of exports			
Primary products	19	23	16
Manufactures	81	77	84
% of imports			
Primary products	24	22	29
Manufactures	76	78	71

Table 13-2   Twenty-first century trade patterns

Source: WTO, *International Trade Statistics*

Having discussed trade patterns, we now examine the reasons why trade takes place at all.

Gains from trade

Comparative advantage

Trade is mutually beneficial when there are cross-country differences in the *relative* cost of making goods.

The **law of comparative advantage** says that countries specialize in producing and exporting the goods that they produce at a lower *relative* cost than other countries.

One reason why relative costs may differ is differences in technology across countries. Suppose labour is the only production and there are constant returns to scale. Table 12-3 assumes that it takes 30 hours of American labour to make a car and 5 hours to make a shirt. UK labour is less productive. It takes 60 hours of UK labour to make a car and 6 hours to make a shirt.

Suppose US workers earn $6 an hour, and British workers £2 an hour. Table 12-3 shows the *unit labour requirement* (*ULR*) or hours of work to make a unit of each good. US labour is *absolutely* more productive than UK labour in making either good. However, US labour is *relatively* more productive in cars than in shirts. UK labour takes twice as long to make a car, but only 6/5 as long as US labour to make a shirt. Different relative productivity makes trade mutually beneficial.

The *opportunity cost* (*OC*) of making a unit of one good is the quantity of the other good that must be given up to create the extra production resources. Table 12-3 shows these opportunity costs OC in each country prior to trade. Because of different relative productivity, the opportunity cost of a car is 6 shirts in the US but 10 shirts in the UK, whereas the opportunity cost of a shirt is 1/6 of a car in the US but only 1/10 of a car in the UK.

If the UK makes 60 more shirts, giving up 6 cars, the US makes these 6 cars for the loss of only 36 shirts. International trade and specialization let the world economy have 24 more shirts with no loss of cars. Similarly, if the US makes 10 more cars, giving up 60 shirts, the UK makes these extra shirts for the loss of only 6 cars, giving the world 4 more cars but no fewer shirts.

The **gains from trade** are additional output of some goods with no loss of other goods.

The market also gets the world economy to the right answer. Table 13-3 also shows the *unit labour cost (ULC)* of making each good. We assume that the hourly wage is $6 in the US and £2 in the UK. If labour is the only input, the unit labour cost is the average total cost of a good, and the price for which it is sold in a competitive market.

	ULR (hours)	Hourly wage	ULC (cost)	OC (sacrifice)
US Cars	30	$6	£180	6 shirts
Shirts	5	$6	$30	1/6 car
UK Cars	60	£2	£120	10 shirts
Shirts	6	£2	£12	1/10 car

Table 13-3 Relative costs and comparative advantage

Since the US and UK use different currencies, a foreign exchange market is set up and an equilibrium exchange rate established. Suppose the $/£ is high. This makes all UK goods, initially produced in pounds, cost a lot of dollars. The UK is uncompetitive in both goods. Now consider lower and lower values of $/£. When the exchange rate is low enough, the UK can compete by exporting one good. Which one? The one it is relatively better at making.

For example, in Table 13-3 if the exchange rate is $2/£, then UK cars can be sold for $240 and UK shirts for £24. The UK can undercut the US in shirts but not in cars. Similarly, US cars sell for £90 and US shirts for £15. Again, the UK is competitive in shirts but not in cars.

This is why absolute advantage is unimportant. The single exchange rate can adjust to make any country's goods competitive *on average*; but which goods it then imports, and which it then exports, depends on which it makes relatively better or worse than average, which is precisely what the Law of Comparative Advantage promises us.

The Law has many applications in everyday life. Suppose two students share a flat. One is faster both at making the dinner and at vacuuming the carpet. If tasks are allocated according to absolute advantage, one student does nothing. The jobs get done faster if each student does the task at which he or she is *relatively* faster.

Relative factor abundance

One country can eventually learn another country's technology. Technology differences are probably not the main explanation for comparative advantage. The main reason that a country has a relatively low price for a particular output is that it has a relatively low price for the inputs which that output uses. In turn, relatively low input prices are largely explained by having relatively abundant quantities of those inputs available.

If the UK is relatively generously supplied with human capital, it should export university places to foreign students from the Caribbean. If the Caribbean is relatively well endowed with tropical land, it exports bananas and nutmeg to the UK. Differences in relative factor supply are a vital reason for comparative advantage and the pattern of international trade.

Figure 13-2 displays evidence confirming this analysis. Countries with scarce land but abundant skills have high shares of manufactures in their exports; countries with lots of land but few skills typically export raw materials. As well as dots for individual countries, the figure also shows that the explanation works for groups of countries, represented by diamond shapes.

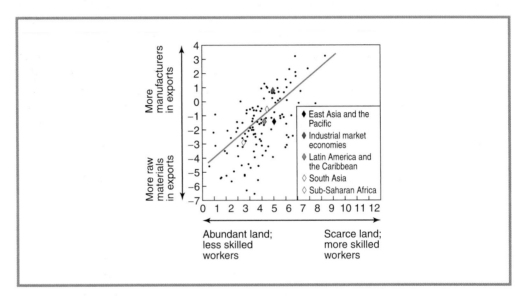

Figure 13-2   Relative factor abundance and export composition

Source: World Bank, *World Development Report, 1995*

Thus, comparative advantage reflects initial differences in relative production costs, arising from differences in technology or in relative factor abundance.

Two-way trade

Different relative factor abundance explains why OPEC exports oil, and China exports labour-intensive goods from toys to trainers. However, this approach cannot explain why the UK exports cars (Rover, Jaguar) to Germany but also imports cars (Mercedes, BMW, VW) from Germany. The UK cannot simultaneously be scarce and abundant in the inputs used to make cars.

Intra-industry trade is two-way trade in goods made by the same industry.

Two-way trade *within* the same industry occurs where consumers like a wide choice of brands that are similar but not identical. A Jaguar is not quite a Mercedes, nor is Danish Carlsberg identical to Belgian Stella. Consumers like variety.

However, we also need economies of scale. Instead of each country trying to make small quantities of each brand in each industry, the UK makes Jaguars, Germany makes Mercedes, and Sweden makes Volvos, then we swap them around through international trade. We all benefit from low cost and greater variety.

Winners and losers

Table 13-3 confirms that exploiting initial differences in relative costs allows gains from trade. The world gets more output from any given inputs. Similarly, intra-industry trade offers variety and cost reduction through scale economies. But this does not imply that *everybody* gains. Here are two examples of how some people can lose.

Refrigeration

The invention of refrigeration let Argentina supply frozen meat to the world market. Its meat exports, non-existent in 1900, were 400 000 tonnes a year by 1913. The US, with exports of 150 000 tonnes in 1900, had virtually stopped exporting beef by 1913.

Who gained and who lost? Argentinian cattle grazers and meat exporters attracted resources. Owners of cattle and land gained; other land users lost out because, with higher demand, land rents increased. Argentine consumers found their steaks became dearer as meat was shipped abroad. Argentina's GNP rose a lot, but the benefits of trade were not equally distributed. Some people in Argentina were worse off. In Europe and the United States, cheaper beef made consumers better off. But beef producers lost out because beef prices fell.

As a whole, the world gained. In principle, the gainers could have compensated the losers and still had something left over. In practice, gainers rarely compensate losers. Some people lost out.

The UK car industry

As recently as 1971, UK imports of cars were only 15 per cent of the domestic UK market, while 35 per cent of UK car output was exported. The UK was a net exporter of cars. Imports are now over 60 per cent of the UK market; however exports recovered as Nissan, Honda, and Toyota established UK plants to produce for the EU market.

UK car buyers and foreign producers like VW benefited from the rise in UK imports of cheaper foreign cars. But UK car producers like Rover had a tough time. UK governments faced repeated pressure to protect UK car producers from foreign competition. Restricting imports would help domestic producers but hurt domestic consumers by raising prices to UK car buyers.

Should the government please producers or consumers? More generally, how should we decide whether to restrict imports or have free trade in all goods? In analysing the costs and benefits of tariffs or other trade restrictions, we move from *positive economics*, why trade exists and what form it takes, to *normative economics*, what trade policy the government should adopt.

Trade policy operates through import tariffs, export subsidies, and direct quotas on imports and exports.

The economics of tariffs

An **import tariff** is a tax on imports.

If t is the tariff, the domestic price of imported goods is $(1 + t)$ times the world price of the imported good. By raising the domestic price of imports, a tariff helps domestic producers but hurts domestic consumers.

Figure 13-3 shows the domestic market for cars. Suppose the UK faces a given world price, £10 000 per car, shown by the solid horizontal line. Schedules DD and SS are the domestic demand for cars and supply of cars. Suppose brands do not matter. Domestic and foreign cars are then perfect substitutes.

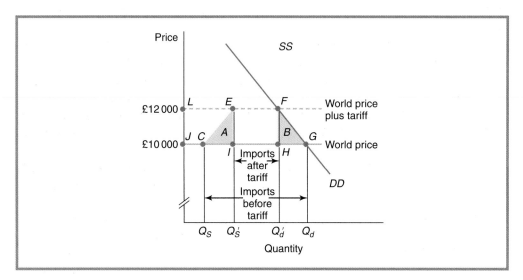

Figure 13-3   The effect of a tariff

At a price of £10 000, UK consumers wish to purchase Q_d cars, at point G on their demand curve. Domestic firms want to make Q_s cars at this price. CG shows imports, the gap between domestic supply Q_s and domestic demand Q_d.

The effect of a tariff

With a 20 per cent tariff on imported cars, car importers must charge £12 000 to cover their costs inclusive of the tariff. The broken horizontal line at this price shows that importers are willing to sell any number of cars in the domestic market at a price of £12 000. The tariff raises the domestic tariff-inclusive price above the world price.

By raising domestic car prices, the tariff boosts domestic car production from Q_s to $Q_{s'}$ and offers some protection to domestic producers. In moving up the supply curve from C to E, domestic producers with marginal costs between £10 000 and £12 000 can now survive because the domestic price of imports has been raised by the tariff.

The higher price also moves consumers up their demand curve from G to F. The quantity of cars demanded falls from Q_d to $Q_{d'}$. From the consumers' viewpoint, the tariff is like a tax. Consumers pay more for cars.

Imports fall from CG to EF both because domestic production rises *and* because domestic consumption falls. The flatter the domestic supply and demand schedules, the more a given tariff reduces imports. If both schedules are steep, the tariff-induced rise in the domestic price has much less effect on the quantity of imports.

Costs and benefits of a tariff

We need to distinguish *net costs to society* from *transfers* between one part of the economy and another. After the tariff, consumers buy Q_d', which costs them $(£2000 \times Q_d')$ *more* than buying this quantity at the world price. Who gets these extra payments, the area *LFHJ* in Figure 13-3?

Some goes to the government, whose revenue from the tariff is the rectangle *EIHF*, the tariff of £2000 times $(Q_d' - Q_s')$ imported cars. This transfer *EIHF* from consumers to the government is *not* a net cost to society. The government may use the tariff revenue to reduce income tax rates.

Some of the higher consumer payments go to firms as extra profits. The supply curve shows how much firms need to cover production costs. Hence the area *ECJL* is the rise in firms' profits, extra revenue from higher prices over and above extra production costs. Thus *ECJL* is transfer from consumers to the profits of firms, but not a net cost to society as a whole.

The shaded area *A* is part of the extra consumer payments *LFHJ* going neither to firms as extra profit nor to government as tariff revenue. It *is* a net cost to society: the cost of supporting inefficient domestic firms.

Society *could* import cars from the rest of the world in unlimited quantities at the world price £10 000, which is the true marginal cost of cars to the domestic economy. Triangle *A* is the resources society wastes by producing $(Q_s' - Q_s)$ domestically when it could have been imported at a lower cost. The resources drawn into domestic car production could be used more efficiently elsewhere in the economy, including its export sectors.

There is another net loss to society, triangle *B*. If the tariff was abolished, the quantity of cars demanded would rise Q_d. Triangle *B* is the excess of consumer benefits, as measured by the height of the demand curve showing how much consumers want the last unit demanded, over the marginal costs of expanding from Q_d' to Q_d, the world price at which imports could be purchased. Triangle *B* shows the net benefit society has lost by consuming too few cars.

To sum up, a tariff leads to a rise in the domestic price, inducing both transfers and pure waste. Money is transferred from consumers to the government and to producers. As a first approximation, the net cost of these transfers to society as a whole is zero, though there are distributional implications. Some individuals win while others lose.

In addition, a tariff involves pure waste, since post-tariff prices exceed the true marginal cost of cars to society, which remains the world price. Hence, consumers buy too few cars, and domestic producers make too many cars. Since zero tariffs avoid this waste, this is the *case for free trade*.

Should a tariff ever be adopted? Table 13-4 lists some common arguments for tariffs. The *first-best* argument is a case where a tariff is *the* best way to achieve a given objective.

	Example
First-best	Imports bid up world prices
Second-best	Ways of life, Anti-luxury,
	Infant industry, Defence, Revenue
Fallacious	Cheap foreign labour

Table 13-4 Arguments for tariffs

Second-best arguments are cases where the policy is beneficial but another policy exists that would be even better. Non-arguments are partly or completely fallacious.

The optimal tariff: the first-best argument

The case for free trade requires that an economy's imports have no effect on the world price. For a small economy, this is correct. However, a large country may affect the world price of its imports. For society, the marginal cost of the last unit of imports then exceeds the world price. Another import bids up the world price that all other importers must pay, but each small importer in the big country ignores any effect of their actions on world prices. Under free trade, the country imports too much.

For the country as a whole, the marginal cost of imports exceeds the price paid by individual importers. A tariff puts this effect back into the price, inducing individual importers to act in the way that is best for society.

When a country affects the price of its imports, the **optimal tariff** makes individual importers take account of their effect on the price that other importers must pay.

Second-best arguments for tariffs

The **principle of targeting** says that the best way to meet an aim is to use a policy that affects the activity directly. Policies with side effects are second best because they distort other activities.

The optimal tariff is an application of the principle of targeting. When the problem lies in the market for imports, a tariff on imports is the most efficient solution. Now we turn to second-best arguments for tariffs where the original problem is not directly to do with trade. The principle of targeting tells us that there are other ways to solve these problems at a lower net social cost.

Suppose society wishes to help inefficient farmers or craft industries to *preserve the old way of life*. Tariffs protect these producers from foreign competition but also hurt domestic consumers through higher prices. A *production subsidy* would still keep farmers in business but, by tackling the problem directly, would not hurt consumers. In Figure 12-3, the cost of triangle A must be incurred to prop up domestic producers so they can make Q'_s not Q_s. But a tariff unnecessarily incurs the cost of triangle B as well.

Some poor countries dislike their few rich citizens enjoying luxury yachts when society needs its resources to stop people starving. To *suppress luxury consumption*, a *consumption tax* is best. Of course, it incurs triangle B in Figure 13-3 since domestic prices rise to consumers, but it avoids triangle A. A tariff on yachts also reduces consumption, but higher domestic prices then provide an incentive for inefficient domestic firms to make yachts, incurring triangle A as well.

In case there is a future war, some countries want to preserve their *defence capability* by protecting domestic industries making food or jet fighters. Again, a production subsidy rather than an import tariff is the best way to meet this objective.

A common argument for tariffs is to let *infant industries* get started. With initial protection, they learn the business and can eventually meet foreign competitors on equal terms. If the industry is such a good idea in the long run, why however can private firms not borrow the money to see them through the early period until they can compete? If the problem lies in bank lending to small firms, the principle of targeting says that a better policy is to solve the banking problem directly. Failing this, a production subsidy in the early years is still better than a tariff, which also penalizes consumers. The worst outcome is the imposition of a *permanent* tariff, which lets the industry remain inefficient long after it is supposed to have mastered its trade.

In the eighteenth century, most *tax revenue* came from tariffs, which were administratively easy to collect. This remains in some developing countries. But modern economies can raise taxes through many channels. Administrative simplicity is no longer a pressing concern.

Fallacious arguments for tariffs

Domestic firms often complain about *cheap foreign labour*. However, the whole point of trade is to exploit international differences in the relative prices of different goods. If the domestic economy is relatively well endowed with capital, it benefits from trade because its exports of capital-intensive goods let it buy labour-intensive goods more cheaply from abroad than it could make them at home.

Over time, countries' comparative advantage evolves. Nineteenth-century Britain exported Lancashire textiles all over the world. But textile production is labour-intensive. Once Southeast Asia had the technology, their relatively abundant labour endowment gave them a comparative advantage in making textiles. The domestic producers who have lost their comparative advantage then complain about competition from imports using cheap foreign labour.

In the long run, the country as a whole benefits by facing facts, recognizing that its comparative advantage has changed, and transferring production to the industries in which its comparative advantage now lies. Our analysis of comparative advantage promises us that there *must* be some industry in which each country has a comparative advantage. In the long run, trying to use tariffs to prop up industries that have lost their comparative advantage is both futile and expensive.

In the short run, the adjustment may be painful and costly. Workers lose their jobs and must start afresh in industries where they do not have years of experience and acquired skills, but the principle of targeting tells us that, if society wants to smooth this transition, some kind of retraining or relocation subsidy is more efficient than a tariff.

Even though anti-capitalist protesters may sympathize with domestic workers who are losing their jobs and having to adjust, freezing the previous structure of employment is not merely undesirable but probably impossible. We no longer have decorators of cave dwellings or handloom weavers.

The World Trade Organization

In the nineteenth century world trade grew rapidly. The leading country, the UK, pursued a vigorous policy of free trade. Early US tariffs averaged about 50 per cent, but had fallen to around 30 per cent by the early 1920s. As the industrial economies went into the Great Depression of the late 1920s and 1930s, there was increasing pressure to protect domestic jobs by keeping out imports. Tariffs in the United States returned to around 50 per cent, and the UK abandoned the policy of free trade it had pursued for nearly a century. The combination of world recession and increasing tariffs led to a disastrous slump in the volume of world trade. Figure 13-4 shows that it took a long time for world trade to recover.

After the war, there was a collective determination to restore world trade. The International Monetary Fund and the World Bank were set up, and many countries signed

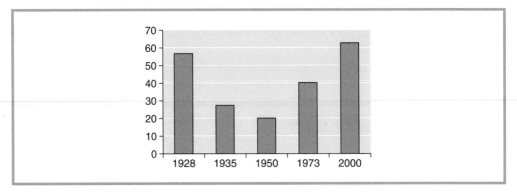

Figure 13-4 World exports (percentage of US GDP)

the General Agreement on Tariffs and Trade (GATT), a commitment to reduce tariffs successively and dismantle trade restrictions.

Under successive rounds of GATT, tariffs fell steadily. By 1960, US tariffs were only about one-fifth of their level in 1939. By 2000, Europe had completely abolished tariffs and other trade barriers for trade within the European Union, and the USA and China had reached agreement to allow Chinese membership of the WTO. Thus, tariff levels throughout the world are probably as low as they have ever been, and world trade has seen five decades of rapid growth, arising at least in part from tariff reduction.

Non-tariff barriers to trade

Domestic firms can be protected by their governments in many subtle ways. Build a railway with a different width, favour domestic firms in defence procurement, drive on the other side of the road, create paperwork to ensure major delays at the border. One reason that the European Union is keen to harmonize standards is to reduce segmentation of the European market which shelters inefficient national firms.

A more direct form of protection is a quota on imports.

A quota is a ceiling on import quantities.

Although quotas restrict the *quantity* of imports, this does not mean they have no effect on domestic prices of the restricted goods. With a lower supply, the equilibrium domestic price is higher than under free trade.

Thus quotas are rather like tariffs. The domestic price to the consumer is increased, and it is this higher price that allows inefficient domestic producers to produce a higher output than under free trade. Quotas lead to social waste for exactly the same reasons as tariffs.

Because quotas raise the domestic price of the restricted good, the lucky foreign suppliers who manage to sell goods make large profits on these sales. In terms of Figure 13-3, the rectangle *EFHI*, which would have been tariff revenue for the government, now goes in profits to foreign suppliers. It is the difference between domestic and world prices of the goods imported, multiplied by the quantity of imports allowed.

If these profits accrue to foreigners means the social cost of quotas is much bigger than the social cost of the equivalent tariff. Sometimes, however, the government can auction licences to import and thus recoup this revenue. Private importers or foreign suppliers will bid up to this amount to get their hands on a valuable important licence.

13-2

Less-developed countries

Learning outcomes

By the end of this section, you should understand:

- ◆ The handicaps with which poor countries begin
- ◆ Whether comparative advantage is a secure route to prosperity
- ◆ Industrialization and the export of manufactures
- ◆ The international debt crisis
- ◆ The importance of aid from rich countries

I n Europe or the US a drought is bad for the garden; in poor countries it kills people.

Less developed countries (LDCs) have low levels of per capita output.

Many LDCs feel that the world economy is arranged to benefit the industrial countries and to exploit poor countries. Altogether, 41 per cent of the world's people live in poor countries, with an average annual income of about £280 per person. In the rich countries, average annual income is over £18 000 per person. *Most of the world's people live in poverty beyond the imagination of people in rich Western countries.* Table 13-5 shows data on per capita income, life expectancy at birth, and adult illiteracy. The low-income countries are badly off on every measure.

Country group	Poor	Middle	Rich
Per capita GNP (£)	280	1310	18340
Life expectancy at birth (years)	59	69	78
Adult illiteracy (%)	39	15	1

Table 13-5 World welfare indicators, 2000

Source: World Bank, *Development Report* (various issues)

Nevertheless, the situation of low-income countries has improved. Table 13-5 shows a marked increase in life expectancy in low-income countries, an indication that the quality of life has improved since 1965. Per capita income grew in all groups of countries, yet, in absolute terms, poor countries fell even further behind the rest of the world.

To be so poor, these countries must have grown slowly for a long time. What special problems do they face?

LDCs' handicaps

Population growth

In rich countries birth control is widespread; in poor countries much less so. Without state pensions and other benefits, having children is one way people try to provide security against their old age when they can no longer work. With faster population growth, merely to maintain living standards poor countries grow more quickly than rich countries. However, poor countries cannot expand supplies of land, capital, and natural resources at the same rate as the labour force. Decreasing returns to labour set in: the Malthusian trap.

Resource scarcity

Dubai, generously endowed with oil, has a per capita income above that of the US or Germany. Many poor countries have not been blessed with natural resources that can profitably be exploited. And having resource deposits is not enough: it takes scarce capital resources to extract mineral deposits. Allowing foreign investors to do the job seems to let them keep most of the income too.

Capital

Rich countries have built up large stocks of physical capital which make their workers productive. Poor countries have few spare domestic resources to devote to physical investment. Financial loans and aid let poor countries buy foreign machinery and pay foreign construction firms. However, LDCs frequently complain that financial assistance is inadequate.[1]

Human capital

Without resources to devote to investment in health, education, and industrial training, workers in poor countries are less productive than workers using the same technology in rich countries. Yet, without higher productivity, it is hard to generate enough output (surplus to consumption requirements) to raise investment in people as well as in machinery.

Lack of human capital also makes it more difficult to regulate domestic markets to offset market failures such as monopoly or environmental pollution, and to achieve reliable enforcement of contracts through a transparent legal system.

Social investment in infrastructure

Developed countries achieve economies of scale and high productivity through specialization, assisted by sophisticated transport and communications. Without investment in power generation, roads, telephones, and urban housing, poor countries must operate in smaller communities, unable to exploit scale economies and specialization.

Conflict

Some of the poorest regions have been those where colonially imposed boundaries made little sense and where the end of empire left governments without wide domestic support. Both internal and international conflict has followed.

How can the world economy help? Our discussion examines all countries classified as LDCs, from the newly-industrialized nearly-rich to the very poorest countries lagging far behind.

Development through exports of primary products

Section 13-1 analysed the gains from trade when countries specialize in the commodities in which they have a comparative advantage. Relative factor abundance is an important determinant of comparative advantage. In many LDCs the relatively abundant input is land. This suggests that LDCs can best use the world economy by exporting goods using land relatively intensively.

Primary products are agricultural goods and minerals, whose output relies heavily on the input of land.

These include 'soft' commodities, such as coffee, cotton, and sugar, and 'hard' commodities or minerals, such as copper or aluminium. As late as 1960, exports of primary commodities were 84 per cent of all LDC exports. Many LDCs are now sceptical of development through specialization in production of primary products. Today, less than half of all LDC exports are primary products. Figure 13-5 shows that, except for petroleum whose supply was curtailed by OPEC, the real price of other primary products has collapsed since 1975. This reflected both greater supply and lower demand. Technical advances, such as artificial rubber and plastics, reduced the demand for many primary products. Greater supply

---

[1] At the 1996 Food Summit, Jacques Diouf, Director of the Food and Agriculture Organization, said his annual budget was 'less than what nine developed countries spend on dog and cat food in six days, and less than 5 per cent of what inhabitants of just one developed country spend on slimming products every year.' *The Times*, 14/11/96.

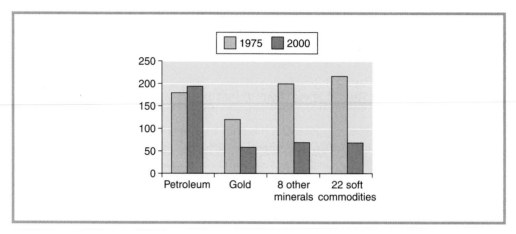

Figure 13-5   Falling prices of primary products (1990 = 100)

reflected the very success of LDCs in increasing productivity and output. With better drainage and irrigation, better seeds, and more fertilizer, agriculture was transformed by the 'green revolution'. Similarly, mineral producers, often with foreign help, developed more capital-intensive mining methods. Even where each individual LDC was small, their collective effort to raise exports induced a fall in the real price of their export commodities.

This effect has been exacerbated by extensive protection of farmers in rich countries such as the US and those in the EU. Deprived of access to these large markets, LDCs have had to sell their larger supply in smaller markets, thus depressing the price much further than would otherwise have been the case.

Allowing LDC agricultural goods into the markets of the rich countries is probably the policy change that would have the greatest benefit for LDCs as a whole. Their income from exports of primary products would soar, providing a surplus to invest in physical and human capital. Consumers in rich countries would also benefit. A rise in the supply of food would reduce the price of food in London and New York.

A second disadvantage of concentrating on the production of primary products has been the volatility of their real prices. Both supply and demand are price-inelastic in the short run. On the demand side, people need food and industrial raw materials. On the supply side, crops have already been planted and perishable output has to be marketed whatever the price. When both supply and demand curves are very steep, a small shift in one curve leads to a big change in the equilibrium price.

Reclining prices and price volatility are especially important when exports of a single crop are a large share of total export revenue. As shown in Figure 13-6, some LDCs are very vulnerable because they depend so heavily on a single export crop.

Development through industrialization

Many countries have concluded that the route to development lies not through increased specialization in making primary products but in the expansion of manufacturing industry. This has taken two very different forms.

Import substitution

When world trade collapsed in the 1930s, many LDCs found their export revenues cut in

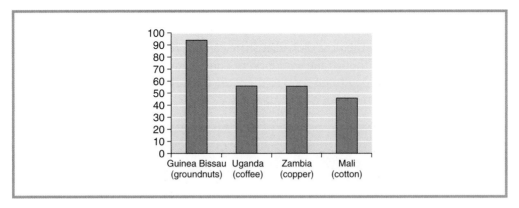

Figure 13-6 Single crop as percentage of export revenue

half. Many LDCs resolved never again to be so dependent on the world economy. After the war, they began a policy of import substitution.

Import substitution replaces imports by domestic production under the protection of high tariffs or import quotas.

Import substitution reduces world trade and suppresses the principle of comparative advantage. LDCs used tariffs and quotas to direct domestic resources away from the primary products into industrial manufacturing, where initially they had a comparative disadvantage.

International trade theory suggests that this policy is likely to be wasteful. For example, by closing itself off from the world economy, the communist bloc pursued import substitution on a grand scale, but without eventual success. Import substitution has one great danger and one possible merit.

The danger is that import substitution may be a dead end. Although domestic industry may expand quite rapidly behind tariff barriers while imports are being replaced, once import substitution has been completed economic growth may come to a halt. The country is then specialized in industries in which it has a comparative *disadvantage*, and further expansion can come only from expanding *domestic* demand.

The possible merit is that comparative advantage is dynamic not static. A tariff may help an infant industry, even though production subsidies would achieve the same outcome at lower social cost. By developing an industrial sector and learning to use the technology, LDCs may eventually acquire a comparative advantage in some industrial products. Thus, import substitution may not be an end in itself, but a prelude to export-led growth.

Export-led growth stresses output and income growth via exports, rather than by displacing imports.

Exports of manufactures

The real success story of the past three decades is the group of countries that have turned the world economy to their advantage by exporting manufactures using their relatively cheap labour. Many of these countries are in Southeast Asia. Table 13-6 shows how successful they have been. LDCs are justifiably alarmed that their strategy of economic development through industrialization and export-led growth through manufactures will also be frustrated by protection that freezes them out of markets in the rich countries. The booming industries of a middle-income country are often the declining industries of the rich countries, where a further loss of market share causes problems as workers have to be reallocated elsewhere. Although the evolution of comparative advantage says that this is efficient, politicians still have to respond to the short-run difficulties, and may be tempted to try to postpone adjustment for a little longer.

	Annual real growth of per capita GDP (%)		Percentage of manufactures in total exports	
	1965–80	1980–2002	1965	2002
Indonesia	9	5	2	89
Hong Kong	9	4	90	95
Malaysia	7	4	6	85
Singapore	10	6	34	76
South Korea	10	7	59	93
Thailand	7	5	4	78
China	–	9	47	88

Table 13-6   The Asian tigers

Source: World Bank, *World Development Report*

Development through borrowing

A third route to economic development is by external borrowing, and a third complaint of LDCs about the way the world economy works is that borrowing terms are too tough. LDCs have traditionally borrowed in world markets to finance imports of capital goods. Recall the balance of payments arithmetic:

current account deficit = trade deficit + debt interest

= increase in net foreign debt

The first line shows the sources of the current account deficit; the second reminds us that it has to be financed by selling domestic assets to foreigners or by new foreign borrowing. Table 13-7 shows debt/GDP ratios for LDCs by region. Every single region became more indebted in the last two decades. The *burden* of the debt depends not merely on the size of debt relative to GDP, but also on the interest rate that debtors must pay. When world interest rates rise, indebted countries suffer even more. Had these loans all been successfully invested in productive projects, output might now be sufficiently large to meet the interest payments with ease. Part of the problem is usually that the rate of return on large investment projects has been disappointing. Countries are then left with the cost of the debt without a corresponding benefit.

	1980	2000
All LDCs	26	41
Sub-Saharan Africa	29	69
East Europe, Central Asia	24	51
Latin America, Caribbean	35	43
East Asia, Pacific	17	34
Middle East, North Africa	31	34
South Asia	17	27

Table 13-7   LDC debt (percentage of GNP)

Source: World Bank, *World Development Report*

Box 13-1   Debt forgiveness

Bob Geldof and other famous personalities have long been campaigning for rich countries to write off the debts of the world's poorest nations. It is a laudable aim, but we have to do it correctly. One difficulty is to do so without encouraging the belief that all future debtors will be bailed out. Another problem is that the big winners could be Western banks rather than impoverished borrowers. Suppose a country owes £100 million a year, but can only pay £50 million a year. Every creditor is only getting half what they should get.

Now, suppose benevolent European governments write off the £50 million owed to them. But the country still owes £50 million to private banks in London and New York. Since the country can still afford to pay £50 million, these banks now demand to be paid in full. The country gets no relief. Instead, European taxpayers bailed out European and American banks, that now get £50 million a year instead of having to split this with other creditors.

Helping rich banks was not the intention. The message? Debt forgiveness must write off *more than* the amount the borrower was failing to pay. Remaining creditors are paid in full, but there is some left over to reduce total payments by the borrower. That is one reason why in 2005 the G8 focused their debt relief on the poorest countries. Not only are the poor countries more deserving but also spreading a given amount of debt forgiveness across many more countries would have meant that in each country the amount forgiven was less than the amount the country had been failing. In the extreme case, LDCs would not have benefited at all because the remaining creditors would have continued to press for the countries to pay what they had been paying before. By concentrating their aid on fewer countries, G8 leaders tried to make sure that the full benefit of this relief was felt in the countries that the G8 intended to help.

Aid

Aid is an international transfer payment from rich countries to poor countries.

Poor countries often argue that they should get more aid from rich countries. Many of the rich countries are also failing to honour their previous promises about the amount of aid that they will give.

Aid can take many forms: subsidized loans, gifts of food or machinery, or technical help and free advice. How much aid rich countries should give is of course a moral or value judgement. However, many of the poorest countries feel that northern prosperity was built during a colonial period when the resources of the south were exploited. Aid seems at least partial compensation. The northern countries do not share this interpretation of history.

As we indicated earlier, many LDCs believe the best contribution rich countries can make is to provide free access for the LDCs to markets in the developed countries. 'Trade, not aid' is the slogan. Just as it is better for the government to retrain a domestic worker who has become unemployed than to provide a lifetime of welfare support, LDCs want useful market access, not another culture of dependency.

The quickest way to equalize world income distribution would be to permit free migration between countries. Residents of poor countries could go elsewhere in search of higher incomes and, in emigrating, they would increase capital and land per worker for those who stayed behind.

The massive movements of population from Europe to the Americas and the colonies in the nineteenth and early twentieth centuries were an income-equalizing movement of this sort. Since 1945, migrations have been much smaller. If the gap between rich and poor widens further, rich countries may find it harder and harder to keep out economic migrants.

In this respect, one trend will eventually operate in favour of LDCs. The richest countries are getting top-heavy with old people, and have fewer and fewer young workers to pay the taxes and finance the pensions. Eventually, young labour will be in high demand, and it may have to be imported. At some future date, immigrants may be shown the red carpet, not the cold shoulder.

13-3

Globalization

Learning outcomes

By the end of this section, you should understand:

- ◆ What globalization means
- ◆ Why it is occurring
- ◆ Opportunities and threats to which it gives rise

Global brands, such as Coca Cola and McDonald's, are highly visible symbols of the increasing integration of world markets. Lower transport costs, better communications, new information technology, and deliberate policies to reduce trade barriers have all enhanced the size of the relevant economic market.

This starts to erode the sovereignty of national governments, by undermining the ability of an individual government to raise taxes, constrain firms, and regulate markets. Too much intervention and business migrates to an easier location elsewhere. In turn, perceiving the erosion of the power of their national governments to influence events, voters become apathetic and lose interest in national politics. Multinational corporations (MNCs) sometimes seem to have become more powerful than governments.

Globalization is the increase in cross-border trade and influence on the economic and social behaviour of nation states.

Section 13-1 discussed how international trade can benefit everyone, but may also create losers if the winners claim all the spoils for themselves. Section 13-2 identified the disadvantages with which poor countries begin, and why some countries have yet to share in world prosperity.

Have the benefits of globalization been outweighed by its costs? Should globalization now be resisted? The next time a hamburger outlet is being trashed by anti-globalization protesters, should you be leading the charge or explaining that there is a better way to meet their concerns? To help you make up your mind, we now discuss some of the most frequent criticisms of globalization.

Globalization is a new phenomenon, requiring a new policy response

Actually, since communications and transport have been steadily increasing for centuries, globalization is also centuries old. By many measures of trade, migration, and capital flows across borders, the period 1870–1913 was comparable to the globalization of the past few decades.

Globalization is thus neither new nor irreversible. Globalization during 1870–1913 created many winners but also some powerful losers. Cheaper grain from the US drove down grain prices and land rents in Europe, prompting agricultural protection in the 1920s. Massive migration to the US drove down wages there, leading to the introduction of immigration controls in the interwar period. History warns us that sustaining the momentum for globalization requires sufficient redistribution to ensure that powerful groups of losers do not emerge to create a backlash.

Globalization increases inequality in the global economy

A few facts are helpful. Table 13-8 summarizes the last 200 years. Globalization *did* cause a big increase in inequality during 1820–1950, when the income share of the richest 10 per cent of the world's population rose from 43 per cent to 51 per cent while the income share of the poorest 10 per cent of people fell from 5 per cent to 2 per cent. However, since 1950 it is *not* true that the income share of the poor has kept falling, nor has the income share of the rich risen much. Global inequality is acute, but not getting worse. Inequality is about relative incomes. We can also ask what is happening to the absolute incomes of the poor. Table 13-8 shows that the number of people earning less than a dollar a day (inflation adjusted, at 1990 prices) has fallen since 1950, *despite* the doubling of world population in the same period. Most of us would feel happier if the conditions of the poor were improving more rapidly. But they are improving slowly, whether measured by income, as in Table 13-8, or by life expectancy or literacy.

	1820	1910	1950	1992
Average income/person (1990 $000's)	0.7	1.5	2.1	5.0
World population (billion)	1.1	1.7	2.5	5.5
Income share: richest 10% of people	43	51	51	53
Income share: poorest 10% of people	5	4	2	2
Billion people earning < $1/day	0.9	1.1	1.4	1.3

Table 13-8 World welfare indicators, 1820–1992

Source: CEPR, *Making Sense of Globalization*, Centre for Economic Policy Research, London, 2002

Why then do people make the connection between globalization and poverty? Nowadays, we see it on the news, on documentaries, and on charity appeals. Previously, it was there, and was worse, but we were less aware of it. Similarly, people living in poor countries are much better informed about how rich the rich countries have become. Globalization of information has increased dissatisfaction about what has always existed.

Multinational corporations exploit workers and play off LDC governments against one another

Local workers employed by MNCs, whether mining minerals or producing clothes and trainers, seem to us to work for pitifully low wages and in conditions that workers in rich countries would not tolerate. However, their wages are usually higher than those earned by their compatriots in domestic industries, and working conditions in MNCs are often better than those in domestic factories, not least because MNCs care about their global image.

If workers in poor countries began with much larger quantities of physical and human capital, they would be richer and more productive. In principle, rich countries could vote for a massive transfer of aid to purchase these valuable inputs for poor countries. But they never have, and the reality is that they probably never will. Without these advantages, the equilibrium wage of the disadvantaged is low, but allowing them access to the world economy lets them gradually accumulate more of the valuable inputs that eventually enhance their own prosperity.

Well-meaning attempts to force 'improvements' in their wages and working conditions simply price them out of world markets and reduce their eventual prosperity. For an example closer to home, think of German unification in 1990. West German trade unions raised wages in Eastern Germany, but East Germans were not initially as productive as West Germans. The result was a decade of high unemployment and discontent in East Germany. So who gained? West German workers, protected from competition from cheap labour in East Germany!

What poor countries need is not less globalization but more. Here, rich countries can help a lot, principally by opening up their market in agriculture and textiles, industries in which poor countries have a natural comparative advantage. Removing tariffs would reduce prices in the rich countries but raise prices received by LDC exporters. Current estimates are that a 40 per cent reduction in agricultural tariffs would generate gains of $70 billion a year. Incidentally, it would also reduce the food bill of each EU citizen by £200 a year. Since the losers would be farmers in rich countries, the challenge for policymakers is to find a way to buy off these losers sufficiently.

What about the claim that MNCs play off one LDC against another? The trainers that you wear may have an American logo, but they were probably made in China or the Dominican Republic. MNCs effectively get each country to bid for hosting inward investment in a new factory. Does competition between countries ensure that the investment goes to the country with the lowest wages and lightest regulation?

Actually, it does not. MNCs like low wages, but they also like workers with education and skills, good transport infrastructure, and predictable legal environments. Foreign investment has flooded into Singapore not Senegal.

Moreover, competition between countries is one disciplining force on corruption in national bureaucracies that would otherwise be sheltered monopolies. The price of abuse is the failure to attract valuable inward investment. Globalization on balance is probably a force that fosters democracy, transparency, and good governance. One problem with sub-Saharan Africa is that it has been too little exposed to the global economy rather than too much.

Globalization destroys the environment

Rainforests are cut down to rear beef cows for hamburgers, oil production wipes out wildlife, and mining scars the landscape. All true. And all exacerbated by globalization. However, we need to remember the principle of targeting.

If the environment is wrongly priced, encouraging over-exploitation because producers do not pay the full social cost of what they do, the best solution is to encourage better pricing of the environment. Trying to suppress trade is a second-best solution.

Though logically correct, this is a counsel of perfection. Even countries rich in human capital have yet to implement sophisticated schemes that price and regulate use of the environment adequately. It is unrealistic to imagine that countries with fewer enforcement resources will do better in pricing their environments.

Global measures, such as a carbon tax that applies everywhere, may be a reasonable compromise. Not only could this protect the environment, it would be a useful source of tax revenue for poor countries. However, the failure of the United States to sign up to the Kyoto Agreement indicates a current unwillingness on the part of the US to play a role in such agreements. History suggests that it is wrong for the winners to believe that there is no need to heed the grievances of the losers, as the collapse of globalization in the interwar period attests. If globalization is not harnessed through better political management of the process, it may eventually be undone by conflict.

> ## Recap
> - World trade has grown rapidly in the past 50 years, and is dominated by developed industrial countries. Primary commodities are a quarter of world trade; the rest is trade in manufactures.
> - Countries trade if they can buy goods more cheaply from abroad. Cross-country differences in costs arise from differences in technology and input endowments. Economies of scale also lead to international specialization.

- Countries export the goods in which they have a comparative advantage, or make relatively cheaply. The equilibrium exchange rate offsets average differences in absolute advantage. Every country has a comparative advantage in something.
- By exploiting international differences in opportunity costs, trade leads to a pure gain. Since people share differently in the gain, some may actually lose.
- Intra-industry trade reflects scale economies plus consumer demand for variety.
- By raising the domestic price, a tariff reduces domestic consumption but raises domestic production. Hence imports fall.
- A tariff has two social costs: overproduction by domestic firms whose marginal cost exceeds the world price, and underconsumption by consumers whose marginal benefit exceeds the world price.
- When a country collectively affects the price of its imports, the optimal tariff induces individual importers to take account of their adverse effect on other importers for whom the import price is bid up.
- Other arguments for tariffs are either second-best solutions – a production subsidy or consumption tax would meet the objective at lower social cost – or are fallacious.
- Tariffs fell sharply after 1945, partly in response to the damage done by high tariffs in the 1930s. The World Trade Organization tries to negotiate further reductions and regulate existing agreements.
- World income and wealth are very unequally divided. LDCs complain that they are denied access to rich markets, that borrowing is too expensive, that past debt should be forgiven, and that aid is insufficient.
- In the poorest countries, population and labour are growing faster than other production inputs, driving down living standards and removing surplus resources to invest in sustainable growth.
- Falling real prices, price volatility, and concentration in a single commodity have made LDCs reluctant to pursue development by exporting primary products.
- LDC exports of labour-intensive manufactures are growing rapidly. Rich countries should not respond by protecting their manufacturers.
- Many LDCs have large external debts without the corresponding fruits of these investments. Token debt relief benefits Western creditors not LDC borrowers. To be successful, debt relief has to be substantial.
- Market access and trade may help the LDCs more effectively than aid, though more aid would also help. Migration would also reduce income disparities.
- Globalization is neither new nor irreversible. It is caused by cheaper transport, better communications, and policies to reduce trade protection. In the absence of other distortions, this yields gains from trade and net benefits for the global economy. However, some groups may lose out.
- In the past half century, global inequality has diminished and the number of people in absolute poverty has fallen, despite rapid population growth. Trade is usually the route to prosperity. No country ever got rich without international trade. However, better global information has made everyone aware of the extent of poverty that still exists in the world.

- Liberalizing agriculture and textile markets in rich countries would hugely benefit not only their own citizens but also potential exporters in poor countries. The gains would easily allow the losers (rich farmers and textile producers) to be bought off.
- Globalization exacerbates existing distortions, for example the over-exploitation of the environment or inadequate financial regulation in poor countries. The ideal solution is to improve these by domestic policy reform, not to curtail trade. Foreign aid could usefully be channelled into these areas.
- Taxing pollution and environmental depreciation would also generate useful tax revenue, in both poor and rich countries.
- Allowing powerful groups of uncompensated losers to proliferate is the most likely way in which globalization may eventually be arrested or even reversed. Deliberate redistribution is required to sustain the benefits of globalization. In that case, rich and poor will benefit. Aid alone will never be enough to raise the poor out of poverty.

Review questions

1 'A country with uniformly low productivity must be hurt by allowing foreign competition.' Is this true? Can you give a counter-example?

2 'Large countries gain less from world trade than small countries.' True or false? Why?

3 Cars, wine, steel: which of these do you think have high intra-industry trade? Why?

4 To preserve its national heritage, society bans exports of works of art. (a) Is this better than an export tax? (b) Who gains and who loses from the export ban? (c) Will this measure encourage young domestic artists?

5 Why are these statements wrong? (a) British producers are becoming uncompetitive in everything. (b) Free trade is always best. (c) Buy British to help Britain.

6 Discuss two forces tending to reduce the real price of food in the long run.

7 Why were LDCs so successful in exporting textiles, clothing, and leather footwear?

8 A country pays 8 per cent interest on its foreign debt, but its GDP grows by 8 per cent a year. What happens to its debt/GDP ratio if it meets all existing interest payments by new borrowing? What happens if its output growth then slows?

9 Prior to full membership of the EU, countries in Eastern Europe were allowed free trade with the EU in many products but with some notable exceptions. (a) On which products do you think the EU still applied big tariffs? (b) Were these likely to be goods in which Eastern Europe had a comparative advantage?

10 Why are these statements wrong? (a) Aid is all the help LDCs need. (b) Europe needs tariffs to protect it from cheap labour in the LDCs.

11 Could protecting the local film industry from 'cultural imperialism' from Hollywood be justified? If so, what would be the best way in which to do this?

12 Absolute poverty refers to the real amount of income or consumption that a person enjoys. Relative poverty refers to their income relative to the national or global average. (a) Can relative poverty ever be eliminated? (b) What would increase the amount of relative poverty?

13 Drug companies say that most R&D leads to failure; only the prospect of large profits on the occasional success keeps them in the industry. Poor countries in sub-Saharan Africa say it is unfair that they have to pay high prices for drugs that combat AIDS. Can an economist offer any advice?

14 Countries mainly interact with their near neighbours. There is a lot of evidence that physical distance reduces trade flows, and thus acts as a protective barrier. Do you expect New Zealand or Austria to have more scope for independent national decisions in economic policy? Explain.

15 Why are these statements wrong? (a) Globalization has now led to cross-border migration on an unprecedented scale. (b) Globalization has made the poor poorer. (c) Aid is all they need.

Answers on pages 355–356

Answers

Chapter 1

1 Sometimes by hierarchy or command (no, you can't have the car tonight!), sometimes by negotiation (I'll do the dishes if you let me go to the cinema), and sometimes using money and prices (you may get pocket money or an allowance, and have some discretion about what you spend it on).

2 All scarce except (b).

3 (a) 20 cakes (b) 15 shirts (c) 1.33 cakes.

4 (a), (c), and (e) are positive; (b) and (d) are normative.

5 Buying and selling take time, which soldiers do not have in an emergency. Certainty is also important in extreme circumstances.

6 Wages fall in jobs that students then want to do (beer tasting, modelling, sports commentating!). With lower wages, firms in these industries can cut their prices, raising the quantity sold and hence the demand for workers in doing these jobs.

7 Europeans have accumulated more human and physical capital, have longer established democracies that provide stability and continuity, have access to world markets of the rich countries. Allowing poor farmers access to rich markets is probably the most significant policy change that rich countries could make.

8 An upward-sloping line: each extra £1000 of income is associated on average with an extra seven club visits. Higher income is probably the cause of a higher demand for club visits. But if you go clubbing to network, and end up with a better job, it is just possible that more club visits also cause higher income. Of course, if you feel terrible the next day, they could also reduce income!

9 (a) Cross-section data (eg by county) for crime and unemployment. (b) Collect other data to control for income, police resources, and whether urban or rural. Sort counties by these other attributes. Comparing similar countries, examine whether there is a link between more crime and more unemployment. Even if there is, discuss which causes which.

10 Many sciences (eg astronomy) cannot conduct laboratory experiments. What matters is the formulation of testable hypothesis and careful examination of whatever relevant data can be collected.

11 Upsloping line. Rise by 1 in RPI associated with rise in house prices; time series.

12 (a) Because demand is high and the size of the ground (supply of seats) is limited. (b) No. Other things equal, higher prices reduce the quantity demanded.

13 (a) Theory organizes facts by providing a simple framework in which to interpret them. (b) Molecules are individually random but collectively predictable. People's individual whims cancel out in larger groups.

14 Equilibrium price £17; quantity 6.5.

15 (a) Excess demand = 5, and price rises. (b) Excess supply = 3, and price falls. Long queue when excess demand.

16 (a) Fall in quantity of labour demanded, so employment falls. (b) Unions might support if they think their members will not be the ones to be priced out of a job. (c) No.

17 (a) A low enough price can fill any stadium. (b) It shows the effect of a price floor for farm goods that creates excess supply.

Chapter 2

1 (a) To sell 10 per cent fewer peaches, raise the price 20 per cent to £1.20. (b) Vertical supply curve, now at 90 peaches. (c) Now earn £108, which is more than before despite the lower volume of sales.

2 (a) Moves people upwards along given demand curve. (b) Shifts demand curve to the left.

3 Vegetables: inelastic, necessity. Catering: elastic, luxury.

4 These data are for nominal not real spending on bread. In fact, the latter fell as real income rose.

5 In the short run, people may still be bound by previous contracts and by habit. It takes time to decide to do something different. In the long run, people can adapt to changes in prices more easily.

6 (a) At high enough prices, demand may be price elastic, even for tobacco. If so, raising taxes and the price of cigarettes may so reduce the quantity demanded that tax revenue then falls. When we talk about demand for particular goods being elastic or inelastic, we mean 'in the range of prices normally experienced'. Outside this range, things could be different. (b) If bad weather hits all farmers, it raises prices and helps incomes: 'good' weather needs insurance! (c) Since only

one farmer affected, will not be significant change in total supply or equilibrium price. Hence this farmer needs insurance when that farmer's quantity falls.

7 Not for producers of inferior goods, for which demand falls as income rises.

8 First statement is substitution effect, second is income effect. Since they go in opposite directions, either outcome is possible when both effects operate together.

9 (a) Both income and substitution effects reduce demand: consumer feels poorer and buys less, and trips are relatively more expensive. (b) Demand curve shifts down: equilibrium price and quantity fall.

10 Utility is the satisfaction from consuming a particular bundle of goods and services. Marginal utility is extra satisfaction when consume 1 more unit of one good, holding constant consumption of all other goods. (c) Diminishing marginal utility means that successive additions of 1 extra good yield less and less extra satisfaction, other things equal.

11 Alcohol, double cream, economics revision!

12 (a) Since both nominal income and prices rise, the previous quantities of goods are still affordable and still best of the affordable bundles. (b) There is also an income effect — since the return on saving is no higher, people are richer and do not have to save so much to get any particular level of future income. This income effect makes them save less. Substitution effect — saving is now relatively better rewarded than before — makes them save more. Empirically, the two effects largely cancel out.

Chapter 3

1 (a)–(c) all increase supply. (d) is the result of higher demand, and the higher equilibrium price moves suppliers upwards along a given supply curve.

2 Moving along a given supply curve, both price and quantity increase or decrease together. Hence any price increase raises revenue and any price cut reduces revenue. There is nothing special about unit-elastic supply.

3 Drought, sheep disease, higher wages for shepherds. Change in price of wool moves farmer along given supply curve but does not shift supply curve.

4 (a) $p = 2$, $1 = 6$; (b) $p = 2$, $q = 6$; (c) $S'S'$ is more inelastic since given price increase leads to less extra quantity supplied than on SS; (d) $p = 3$, $q = 8$; $p = 4$, $q = 7$; (e) SS.

5 Knowing that partners can lose all their personal wealth may encourage trust in the activities of the firm.

6 At the top of each hill, the slope is zero. Yes, if the hill has only one peak. A firm will maximize profit by choosing an output at which a marginal change in output has no effect on profit (otherwise it could change output to do better), which implies that marginal cost equals marginal revenue. This is the top of one hill. The other hill that it must check out is the hill corresponding to zero output.

7 Expand output a bit and see if this is still true. Reduce output a bit and see if this is still true.

8 Only the factory is a stock, the rest are all flows.

9 (a) An accounting profit may not cover the opportunity cost of the time and money tied up in the business. (b) A managerial genius may get to the right answer intuitively, but the laws of arithmetic guarantee that marginal cost will equal marginal revenue if profit maximization is achieved. (c) Sales revenue is maximized when marginal revenue is zero. Since marginal cost is usually above zero, maximizing sales revenue means an output that is too high to maximize profits.

10 $q = 3$, at which output $MC = MR$.

11 Setting $MC = MR$ leads to the optimal output choice of 3 units. The table below shows 3 units yields a profit of 2, at least as good as any other output. With discrete integers, it turns out that 2 units also yields a profit of 2. This arises because costs and revenues are discrete rather than continuous. Beginning from an output of 2, the marginal cost and marginal revenue of an extra unit are both 6, so no profit is gained or lost by raising output to 3. And beginning at an output of 3, no profit is gained or lost by cutting output to 2. With smooth cost and revenue curves, whose slope is changing continuously, setting $MC = MR$ generally yields a unique output choice.

Output (units)	0	1	2	3	4	5	6
Total cost TC	5	9	13	19	26	34	43
Total revenue TR	0	8	15	21	26	30	33
Total profits = TR − TC	−5	−1	2	2	0	−4	−10

Chapter 4

1 Production function relates output to minimum quantities of inputs required. Still need to know input prices and demand curve for output to calculate profit-maximizing output.

2 Scale economies reflect opportunities to spread fixed costs in the short run and to adopt large-scale production methods in the long run. (b) Choose methods 1, 3, and 5 rather than 2, 4, and 6 (see table at bottom of page). Average cost thus falls from 8.25 to 8 to 7.25 as output expands. Scale economies are present.

3 Methods 1 and 3 still dominate methods 2 and 4, but now method 5 has total cost of 96 and method 6 has total cost of 94, so if demand conditions make firm want to produce 12 units, will now use method 6 not 5. However, total cost (and average cost) are higher at each output when any input price is higher.

Output	0	1	2	3	4	5	6	7	8
Total cost	12	25	40	51	60	70	84	105	128
Marginal cost		13	15	11	9	10	14	21	23
Average cost		25	20	17	15	14	14	15	16

4

These are short-run costs. In the long run, the cost of producing zero output is zero.

5 If $MC < AC$, another unit can be produced more cheaply than the average for existing units, dragging down the average. Hence, to the left of minimum average cost, MC is below AC but AC is falling. Conversely, if $MC > AC$, making another unit increases average costs since the extra unit costs more than the existing average cost. Now MC lies above AC and AC is rising. Hence MC must cross AC at the point of minimum average cost.

6 (a) Given time to adjust, it may be possible to reduce costs sufficiently to stop losing money. (b) If diseconomies of scale exist, larger output raises average cost, and big firms are undercut by smaller firms. (c) If scale economies exist, a firm can reduce average cost by expanding output, thus undercutting its smaller competitors.

7 Yes, because the firm must take the price as given. The fact that a firm cannot affect the price of its output, and hence its marginal revenue is simply the price it receives, is the key feature of perfect competition.

8 In the short run, the cost curves of each firm shift down. By shifting their marginal cost curves lower, this shifts their supply curves downwards too. Industry output rises and the price falls a bit, but by less than the downward shift in supply. Existing firms are making profits. In the long run, more firms enter until economic profit is driven down to zero. Hence, the price falls further and quantity expands further.

Units of	Method 1	Method 2	Method 3	Method 4	Method 5	Method 6
Labour input	5	6	10	12	15	16
Capital input	4	2	7	4	11	8
Output	4	4	8	8	12	12
Total cost	33	34	64	68	87	96
Average cost	8.25	8.5	8	8.5	7.25	8

9 When the market is not in equilibrium, either buyers or sellers are frustrated. This creates temporary market power to change the price. For example, with excess demand, a firm raising its price will not lose all its market share to competitors, who do not have the capacity to take advantage of their relatively lower price.

10 Although each firm in both industries has a U-shaped average cost curve, it is much easier in the long run to expand the supply of new hairdressing firms than to discover new coalfields. Hairdressing has more elastic long-run supply.

11 Ford cars and Vauxhall cars are subtly different and thus not perfect substitutes for one another. Each firm has some scope to vary its price without losing all its market share to the other. Moreover, since each firm is large, each will try to anticipate the effect of its actions on the other firm. They are not price takers and not perfectly competitive.

12 (a) Opportunity cost of everything is being covered when a firm makes only normal profits, so all resources employed are earning the return they need. (b) Each firm's supply curves shift up, and the induced shift in industry supply changes the equilibrium price and quantity.

Chapter 5

1

Q	1	2	3	4	5	6
P	8	7	6	5	4	3
TR	8	14	18	20	20	18
MR	8	6	4	2	0	−2

Monopolist has $Q=2$, $P=7$. Competitive industry has $Q=4$, $P=5$. Monopolist's output lower because marginal revenue below price. With lower output, it takes a higher price to equate supply and demand.

2 No effect. MC and MR unaltered, and profits still positive.

3 (a) No effect on profit-maximizing output. Maximizing pre-tax profit is still the best way to maximize post-tax profits. (b) Marginal profit is zero on the last unit produced since $MC=MR$. (c) This is why decision about last unit is independent of the rate of profits tax. With zero profit on the last unit, the tax rate is irrelevant at that point.

4 Golf club faces two separate demand curves, from peak users who really want to play at peak times and don't mind paying for it, and off-peak users who can more easily decide when to play. Golf club wants to equate marginal revenue across the two groups (otherwise it can make more by having more of one group and less of the other). The more inelastic the demand curve, the more price exceeds marginal revenue. Hence group with the more inelastic demand curve (peak users) pays more.

5 Monopolist has greater incentive to innovate than a competitive firm because the latter knows that eventually new entrants will compete away excess profits, whereas monopolist knows these can be enjoyed forever. Conversely, those running a monopoly might decide to have an easy life and forget about maximizing profits. Competitive firms that do not stay on their toes will be outcompeted by other firms and go out of business.

6 (a) If scale economies are large, breaking up a large firm into smaller units means that each firm then produces at higher cost. This disadvantage could outweigh the benefits of more competition between the firms. (b) Raising its price above marginal cost might lead to new entry, either from new firms or in the form of competition from imports. If the threat of competition prevents a single producer raising prices, that firm is not a monopolist.

7 (a) $Q = 4$, $P = 7$; (b) same again; (c) because each firm has $MC = 3$, but will face $MR > 3$ if it alone expands: price won't fall so much since other firm not expanding too.

8 (a)

Q	1	2	3	4	5	6	7
P	8	7	6	5	4	3	2
TR	8	14	18	20	20	18	14
MR	8	6	4	2	0	−2	−4

Z makes $Q = 3$, whereas in Question 8(b) dividing the market in half, Z made $Q = 2$.

9 Certification by a reputable agency saves customers the cost of checking themselves. For mechanics, after a bad experience, you can go elsewhere. Reputation helps solve the information problem. For doctors, you might be dead after a bad experience.

10 One device is to invest in building a reputation. Much as the parent dislikes punishing the child the first time, the cost of not punishing is a loss of credibility that makes the future tougher for the parent. Recognizing this, the parent is more likely to do what was promised. Another device is to reach agreement on parenting with the other parent or with grandparents (who are usually unreliable allies in this!). Then the cost to the parent of not honouring commitments is loss of reputation with several people. Third,

do not promise what you know you won't be able subsequently to deliver.

11 (a) Can't police cheating on the collective agreement. More importantly, new firms then enter, raising output and driving the price down again. (b) If advertising raises the fixed costs of being in the industry, it deters entry and raises profits on existing output.

Chapter 6

1 Firm simultaneously chooses what output to supply and what inputs therefore to demand. Only purpose of hiring inputs is to use them to make output.

2 (a) Other inputs by assumption are fixed, so eventually adding more workers means that each worker is handicapped by having fewer other inputs with which to work. This may not happen initially if there are too many other inputs for a few workers to use effectively. (b) The downward-sloping labour demand curve shifts up. Vertical axis shows the real wage; horizontal axis shows the level of employment.

3 (a) Substitution effect means work more, but income effect means work less since leisure a normal good. (b) More people join labour force and extra bodies may compensate for fewer hours per person.

4 The only reason that film studios pay high salaries is because there is high demand for film output in which these stars appear.

5 When the industry is small relative to the whole economy and is a price-taker for workers whose wages are set by national labour market.

6 (a) Demand is high; and nobody else can supply it. (b) Only via the substitution effect. The income effect makes people want more leisure (less work) since they are richer.

7 Screening lets you get a better paid job on leaving university since firms believe they have discovered a talented worker. It would not matter what you study if all degrees are equally difficult. If economics graduates earn more this means (i) that the degree is tougher than others and screens more effectively, or (ii) that human capital from an economics training is a valuable asset.

8 Lose £30 000 while training. Future salary of £23 000 for 30 years repays this.

9 With fewer economists, their scarcity would raise wages by restricting supply. To restrict entry into economics, have tough exams and compulsory early morning lectures. Destroy all copies of *Foundations of Economics*, making study harder.

10 If screens out the good doctors of the future, maybe currently irate doctors should recognize that they will get big future salaries as compensation. Second explanation is that young doctors are implicitly paying for their training, a valuable investment in human capital from which they recoup high future incomes. Third explanation is that acts as entry deterrent, ensuring scarcity of future consultants and keeping their incomes high.

11 Unions raising wages in a single competitive firm force it out of business. In a monopoly, unions that raise wages reduce the firm's profit. Although unions could organize the whole of a competitive industry, free entry makes this extremely difficult. So does globalization and competition from foreign firms. Hence union power is likely to decline further.

12 (a) Neglects the opportunity cost of wages forgone while in education. (b) Not if the unskilled are disproportionately represented in unions in the first place. They might have got even lower wages if unions did not exist.

13 Only (b) is a flow, the rest are stocks.

14 Demand for capital input depends on demand for the firm's output, on quantities of other inputs with which capital co-operates, and on technology. Higher tax on output reduces the demand for all inputs, including capital. Demand curve for capital shifts down for both firm and industry.

15 Required rental falls, so quantity of capital goods demanded increases. Overnight, the capital stock is given, but higher investment gradually raises capital stock. In new long-run equilibrium, with permanently higher capital stock, there is more replacement investment to keep pace with depreciation. Hence price of capital goods is higher to induce capital goods suppliers to provide this replacement investment. This restores the required rental to its equilibrium level.

16 The demand for land is a derived demand. If supply is fixed, only a rise in demand for land can bid up land prices. Tenant farmers face higher rentals but extra income from their crops is what started the process. However, farmers lose out if land prices and rentals bid up by higher demand for housing.

17 Can affect land supply via fertilizers, reclaiming it from the sea, altering the level of land pollution, and many other channels. Nevertheless, the total supply of land is much harder to change than the supply of capital or labour.

18 (a) It also makes future nominal income rise, raising labour demand. (b) Competition between users is what bids up the price to ration the scarce land supply.

19 A progressive income tax, excise duties on cars (a luxury good), and inheritance tax. However, taxation of tobacco is regressive, since tobacco is an inferior good.

20 With a vertical supply curve for land, upward shifts in the demand for land raise land prices and land rentals. Since richer countries demand for land, there is no reason why land rentals should not keep pace with the other incomes.

21 Greater dispersion in educational opportunities means that there are many workers earning low wages, whereas in European countries education is more equally distributed. Nor does Brazil have high inheritance taxes as in Europe, so concentrated wealth is passed down the generations. And Brazil's welfare state provision is less generous than in Europe.

Chapter 7

1 (a) Efficient, not equitable; (b) neither efficient nor equitable; (c) both efficient and equitable; (d) not efficient nor very equitable; (e) efficient not equitable. Equitable asks 'How fair is distribution?'

2 Yes. Taxing (charging) for rush-hour road use would make drivers pay the true social cost. Since rural roads are not congested, nor urban roads at 5 a.m., a fuel tax is a blunt instrument – it may reduce rush-hour traffic but also wrongly reduces other valuable road usage.

3 Probably, since in deciding whether to fasten your seatbelt you ignore several spillovers onto others. In the event of an accident, you may not pay the full cost of treatment. You may also cause psychological damage on others if you are killed in an accident that need not have been fatal.

4 First two are public goods, since either everybody enjoys them or nobody does. Post office network has public good aspects, though individual transactions are private goods.

5 (a) For further pollution reduction, marginal cost exceeds marginal benefit once pollution already low. (b) Same applies to achieving the last little bit of safety. 100 per cent safe is too safe. (c) Monopoly, externalities, etc. are important market failures.

6 All except (d).

7 All progressive except tax on beer, which is a larger share of poor people's income.

8 18, 24, 28.8 per cent. It is progressive, and more so the higher the exemption level. With an exemption of £1 million, the tax would only hit the rich!

9 (a) No change in labour supplied, so no distortion triangle. (b) Big triangle, and firms now bear most of the tax. (c) Draw a supply curve and two demand curves of different slope. For a given vertical tax wedge, the gross-of-tax wage rises more when labour demand is steeper.

10 (a) Some taxes offset externalities. (b) Existence of marginal taxes still induces people to change the quantities that they supply and demand.

11 Competitive price is £5. Under monopoly, the social cost triangle has height of

£3 (the amount by which price exceeds £5), and length of 200 000 (the output fall). Hence cost is £300 000.

12 The triangle now has height £1 and length less than 200 000 since quantity demanded will lie between 800 000 and 1 million. So social cost less than £200 000.000. A price ceiling of £5 will achieve the efficient outcome, since monopolist will regard £5 as marginal revenue and produce as under perfect competition.

13 MC lies below MC while AC is still falling. Although efficient point is where MC crosses demand curve, setting that price as a price ceiling would entail losses since $MC < AC$. Private monopolist would rather quit.

14 Generally, the need for merger control is less when the market is larger. However, creation of a global monopoly would be worrying, for example if Boeing merged with Airbus, or if all the mobile phone companies merged.

15 (a) Profit may just reflect monopoly power. (b) Private benefit of mergers may include monopoly profits, which are a social cost.

Chapter 8

1 (a) Adding the value addeds:
670 + 190 + 50 + 50 = 960.

2 (a) GDP = 303, national income = 267.

3 GDP falls initially but country is potentially better off since labour can now be diverted to making other things.

4 (a) Leisure is lost but investment in human capital occurs. (b) No – just a transfer payment. (c) Yes. (d) Yes. (e) Pollution should ideally be subtracted from GNP.

5 (a) Just a transfer payment, not real output. (b) Only because people

compare nominal receipts. In real terms, *Gone With The Wind* wins by a mile!

6 Compare with other countries to see if factually true that we are different. For different countries, correlate long-run growth with usual explanations (labour input, capital input, etc.) and see if extra role for fraction of population who are scientists, engineers. Private and social benefits differ if there are externalities (some skills make it easier for people with other skills). Subsidies to education also imply discrepancy between private and social cost.

7 Pollution and congestion. Can quantify and value some (eg how much house prices are lower under airport flight path). As information technology lets us record data better, it will get easier to include these in GNP.

8 Despite difficulties in increasing land input, there have not been diminishing returns to increased labour input. We accumulated other factors (human and physical capital) as substitutes for land, and technical progress invented ways to economize on land. Same is already happening for other scarce inputs.

9 In terms of Figure 8-3, country with higher population growth has steeper nk line, which therefore intersects the sy curve further to the left. This implies a lower level k of capital per person, and hence a lower level y of output per person.

10 (a) Same answer as 3 above. (b) A higher saving rate makes the sy curve intersect the nk line further to the right. This raises capital per person and output per person. However, output, capital, and labour all grow at the rate n, which is independent of the saving rate s. If technical progress is also present, output and capital grow at the rate $(t + n)$, and labour grows at n, but again changes in the saving rate have no effect on long-run growth rates.

11 With aggregate supply permanently lower, aggregate demand must eventually fall too. Government may wish to smooth this fall a little, but should not seek to prevent it.

12 (a) More correlated. (b) Increase it.

13 (a) Since even a single country has a business cycle, even a single global economy would too. (b) If firms in a slump could already foresee the next boom they would be less pessimistic and investment demand would not have fallen so much in the first place. Conversely, in a boom, foreseeing a subsequent slump, firms would be less keen to invest a lot, thereby dampening the initial boom.

Chapter 9

1 Upsloping line, slope 0.7 and intercept 45. At $Y=100$, $AD=70+45=115$. Excess demand and unplanned destocking. Output then rises. Equilibrium output $=I/[1-c]=45/0.3=450/3=150$.

2 (a) Falls from 500 to 300. (b) Since $S=I$, the ratio S/Y rises from 150/500 to 150/300.

3 Unplanned inventory investment (whether positive or negative). Aggregate demand refers to plans, not outcomes after the fact.

4 (a) Equilibrium $Y=400/0.2=2000$. (b) Equilibrium $Y=[400+100]/[0.3]=1667$.

5 (a) No causal link between rise in desire to save and change in desired investment. (b) Since the marginal propensity to consume is smaller than 1, each fall in output induces a smaller fall in AD, so AD and Y converge to new lower level, as multiplier formula promises.

6 (a) $Y=1000$, $C=800$, $I=80$, so $G=120$. (b) When I rises by 50, equilibrium output must rise by 250, so C rises by 200. (c) Yes. (d) $C=0.8 \times 1200=960$, $I=80$. Hence $G=160$.

7 Desired injections must equal desired leakages in equilibrium. Desired saving and investment are equal only if the other parts of desired leakages and injections equal one another.

8 Debt would spiral, implying very high future tax payments and perhaps even bankruptcy. Long before this, people would choose to stop lending to the government.

9 (a) Multiplier $=1/[1+MPZ-(1-t)MPS]=1/[1+0.4-0.04]=1/[1.36]$. Hence when investment demand rises by 136, equilibrium output rises by 100. (b) Again, rises by 100. Hence, desired imports rise by 40. Since exports rise by 136, trade balance improves by 96.

10 (a) Aggregate demand will rise. Higher spending by 1 adds 1 to $[C+I+G+X-Z]$. Adding 1 to taxes reduces disposable income by 1 but only reduces consumption by c. Since the marginal propensity to consume is less than 1, the fall in consumption demand is less than the rise in government demand, so aggregate demand rises. (b) When domestic output falls, import demand will fall and the trade balance will improve.

11 Government spending is difficult to change quickly without disrupting planning in the public sector; frequent changes in tax rates are costly. And even when the need for change has been diagnosed, and changes in fiscal policy implemented, these still take time to affect aggregate demand. Changing interest rates is quicker and easier in the short run, but also takes time to have its

full effect on aggregate demand – anything up to two years.

12 Beginning with output of 100, a rise in investment from 0 to 10 has the following effects:

Period	Change in last period's output $Y_{t-1} - Y_{t-2}$	Investment I_t	Output Y_t
$t+1$	0	10	100
$t+2$	0	10	120
$t+3$	20	20	140
$t+4$	20	20	140
$t+5$	0	10	120
$t+6$	220	0	100
$t+7$	220	0	100
$t+8$	0	10	120
$t+9$	20	20	140

13 Initially, the consumption function shifts up (and desired saving falls) since people want to spend more at any income level. Eventually, since people having to pay interest on this new debt, income available for buying goods and services falls and the consumption function shifts down.

14 It makes consumption demand less sensitive to changes in interest rates.

15 (a) UK aggregate demand is reduced. (b) If the government wants to maintain the original level of UK demand, it should loosen fiscal policy.

16 Investment rises in advance to get new capacity in place. This raises current output, forcing monetary policy to raise interest rates in order to keep inflation on track. Higher interest rates have most effect on long-term investment. Moreover, since the Bank realized that it takes up to two years for a change in interest rates to have its full effect, it will begin raising interest rates as soon as it recognizes that a future boom is on the way.

17 (a) It could be rational if either (i) interest rates have fallen or (ii) people have raised their estimates of expected future income. (b) Fiscal policy is harder to change quickly. Moreover, monetary and fiscal policy affect different components of aggregate demand. Even if fiscal policy could achieve the same level of aggregate demand, it could not also achieve the same composition of demand as monetary policy.

Chapter 10

1 (a) No. Cannot be used directly to finance subsequent transactions. (b) Watch which is then retraded, not swallowed.

2 By simultaneously creating loans and deposits to match, without requiring a new deposit as part of the transaction. If the reserve requirement is 100 per cent, banks are unable to do this, and can no longer create money.

3 (a) They have a once-off use as money but are not subsequently retraded repeatedly. (b) No. (c) They reduce your demand for money, but do not affect supply: credit card stubs cannot be reused to purchase other goods.

4 $M0 = 12 + 2 = 14$, $M4 = 12 + 30 + 60 + 20 = 122$.

5 (a) Most of money supply is bank deposits, a liability of banks. By simultaneously expanding both sides of their balance sheet, banks increase the money supply. (b) If people put less cash in banks, banks less able to multiply up reserves into deposits.

6 The money multiplier = 1.

7 Need less money for precautionary purposes.

8 Opportunity cost of holding money is unaffected by change in interest rates.

9 Data must come out before the data on the variable one is really interested in, and must be reliably correlated with that subsequent data.

10 (a) With more cash in the banks and less with the public, banks can multiply up into more bank deposits. (b) If inflation is negative, the real value of cash is rising at the same rate at which prices are falling.

11 We say that the real interest rate is 2 per cent in both cases. Although on average the same over the life of the contract, the two scenarios are not identical. With zero inflation, your real income and real interest payments are the same year after year. Because lenders (stupidly) insist on constant annual payments even during inflation, when inflation is 100 per cent the initial payments are very high in real terms, but after a few years this constant nominal repayment has shrunk in real terms to a tiny value. If lenders wanted to make you pay a constant annual stream of payments in real terms, then in a world of inflation they would have to arrange loan contracts so that you pay higher nominal payments later in the contract.

12 Only a weak short-run correlation between money growth and inflation. Different changes in output in different countries are one possible explanation. With stock markets doing badly, large money growth in Japan and the US may also have reflected higher asset demand for money as people baled out of the stock market.

13 Surprise inflation hits people with fixed nominal incomes (lenders, holders of cash, pensioners). Bonds and pensions could have adjusted their nominal payout had inflation been correctly foreseen, but the zero nominal return on cash cannot be adjusted even when inflation is foreseen.

14 Many political questions are about redistribution from one group to another. It would not be acceptable if unelected officials made such decisions. But delegating 'technical' decisions has a long history. Recently, it has been recognized that, although monetary policy does have some distributional implications, these are probably less important than its 'technical function' in stabilizing aggregate demand, which is more effectively pursued by officials that have a clear objective set for them by the government and are then not subject today to day interference by politicians.

15 (a) Not if nominal interest rates have risen to protect real interest rates. (b) Firms' revenues will also rise in nominal terms. (c) Menu and shoe-leather costs cannot be avoided.

Chapter 11

1 Long-run aggregate supply and potential output increase. Eventually, monetary policy will accommodate this supply shock in full, allowing aggregate demand to rise by the same amount. Interest rates will be lower. In the short run, the first effect of more workers may be more unemployment. Eventually, this induces existing workers to reduce wage inflation, shifting the short run supply curve downwards.

2 Monetary policy will begin cutting interest rates since inflation is now below target and output is now below its new level of potential output. Eventually, demand and output are higher and inflation is unaltered.

3 Permanent supply shocks must eventually change the level of output. In the short run, a demand shock will affect inflation and output, moving the economy along a given short-run aggregate supply curve. In the long run, output must revert to potential output, which is unaffected. Inflation will also be unaffected if the central bank sticks to its inflation target and changes interest rates as required.

4 Aggregate demand rises so the Bank raises interest rates. Hence investment may fall if the interest rate effect outweighs the benefit of higher output. Since aggregate demand exceeds potential output (otherwise no reason to have raised interest rates), tax revenue is higher because output is higher.

5 (a) Firms' prices rise too. (b) Consumer incomes rise too.

6 With higher costs, firms' supply curves shift, shifting short-run aggregate supply curve upwards. If demand is unchanged, this causes a *fall* in output but a *rise* in inflation. Central bank raises real interest rates, and in the short run this reduces aggregate demand in line with the lower aggregate supply. The faster the central bank wants to get inflation exactly back to its inflation target, the more aggressively it has to raise real interest rates and the more output falls in the short run. Ensuring output is below potential output is what brings inflation down again. If permanently higher oil prices lead to a permanent fall in potential output, then monetary policy will have to engineer an even larger reduction of aggregate demand in

the short run in order to bring inflation down from its initially high level.

7 Reduced demand for some types of labour, raised demand for others. Temporary mismatch, but eventually skills and wages adjust. Millenia of technical progress would have driven unemployment to 100 per cent if there were any permanent relationship between technical progress and unemployment.

8 (a) Deficient demand in economy. (b) Real wage too high, for example because of union power or generous welfare benefits, so high level of equilibrium output.

9 (a) By reducing distortions, may raise equilibrium output. Also initially raises aggregate demand. Latter effect faster and probably larger, so boom and monetary policy raises interest rates to keep inflation on track. (b) Main effect is boost to aggregate demand, helping restore output to potential output.

10 Teenagers need training from scratch – lack skills and job experience; teenage wages not low enough to compensate.

11 (a) Not if equilibrium unemployment. (b) Not if Keynesian unemployment.

12 (a) yes; (b) no; (c) no. In (b) and (c), the Phillips curves are shifting around, so hard to detect in the data the downward slope of any particular short-run Phillips curve.

13 No. Since we do believe that inflation is damaging, even when foreseen, we should probably draw a long-run Phillips curve with a steep upward slope, implying higher inflation is associated with higher unemployment, even in the long run. Referring to a vertical long-run Phillips curve is a short hand, and implies that inflation is not 'very' damaging over the typical ranges of inflation that we experience.

14 (a) Wage and price controls unlikely to resist market forces for long since there will be mounting pressure to raise wages and prices. At some point, visible inflation will break out. (b) Cut budget deficit, make central bank independent, and give it a moderate inflation target.

Chapter 12

1 (a) BoP surplus £2 bn. (b) Reserves rising. (c) Selling domestic currency to buy reserves.

2 (a) Deficit countries likely to be forced by their creditors into more rapid adjustment. Surplus countries can adjust more slowly if they wish. (b) No limit to the foreign assets that a country can build up, simply that it is not optimal to save for ever if the purpose of saving is eventually to finance additional consumption.

3 (a) and (d) only.

4 Depreciates in (a) and (d), appreciates in (b) and (c). If initial exchange rate too low (high), an appreciation is good (bad).

5 Depreciates means falls, and hence becomes worth less. A devaluation entails a depreciation of the exchange rate, but we use the term to denote a decision to reduce the level of a fixed exchange rate.

6 (a) Fiscal policy is looser. (b) Aggregate demand increases. (c) Monetary policy raises interest rates to prevent inflation exceeding the target. (d) An exchange rate appreciation (the opposite of depreciation) would have reduced net exports, thereby offsetting the fiscal stimulus to aggregate demand and removing the need for higher interest rates.

7 Monetary policy is more powerful under floating exchange rates because the interest rate change induces a change in the exchange rate that reinforces the effect on aggregate demand and equilibrium output.

8 (a) Desirable if initially the exchange rate is below its equilibrium level. (b) Undesirable if exchange rate already above its equilibrium level.

9 (a) Acquired large stock of foreign assets by having previous years of current account surplus. (b) With large foreign assets, the current account will benefit from large inflow of income from these assets. If the current account is zero, the trade balance must be negative to offset the inflow of income from foreign assets.

10 (a) Large trade surplus that initially caused a current account surplus; (b) eventually built up large foreign assets; (c) from which the inflow of foreign income became large.

11 (a) Substantial trade deficit to restore external balance eventually by offsetting the inflow of income from foreign assets. (b) Loss of competitiveness (higher real exchange rate) is the market mechanism that achieves the required trade deficit. (c) Yes. (d) If they had understood economics better, they would have realized that this was inevitable and appropriate. The benefit of foreign assets is that they allow a perpetual trade deficit, enabling domestic use of goods for consumption, investment, and government spending to exceed national output.

12 A large one-way flow would mean that the traders who organize the foreign exchange market were being forced to absorb the other half of these deals, in volumes that far exceed their capacity to do so. Their only alternative is to alter the exchange rate quickly to restore two-way traffic, out of which they can take a small commission and earn large incomes because the (two-way) volume is still pretty high. Under fixed exchange rates, eventually it is the central bank that has to be the other half of one-way traffic. If the financial flow is an inflow of foreign exchange, there is no technical limit to the ability of the central bank to print domestic money with which to buy the foreign currency. If the financial flow is an outflow of foreign exchange, the central bank will run out of foreign currency reserves and have to float the exchange rate. And even an inflow cannot last, because it is another country's outflow, and their central bank will run out of foreign exchange reserves.

13 (a) They can, by setting whatever interest rates induce speculators to be content with the level of the pegged exchange rate. (b) Short-run volatility mainly reflects the need to keep restoring two-way traffic of financial flows as opinion of speculators and investors keeps changing.

Chapter 13

1 No. Equilibrium exchange rate can be low enough to offset any absolute disadvantage. To enjoy efficiency gains from comparative advantage, should allow trade. UK gains by importing cheap trainers made in China and Dominican Republic.

2 Small countries can't enjoy scale economies without international trade, and for this reason rely on it more and benefit more. Additionally, trade by large countries also bids the world price in adverse direction from their viewpoint.

3 Wine and cars have high two-way trade based on choice and differentiation;

steel b
advantag

4 (a) No. C
the tax re
buyers gain
artists lose
buyers. (c) Proba

5 (a) Changes in the
with the changes in
absolute advantage,
must then have a co
tage at something. (b) N
optimal tariff is an examp
large country gains by a departure from free trade. (c) Fails to exploit comparative advantage and the gains from trade.

6 Technical progress in agriculture (eg winter wheat). Application of machinery and fertilizer to raise land productivity. Both augmented supply a lot, driving down the equilibrium price.

7 They require intensive but low-skilled labour, which LDCS have in relative abundance, but do not need very sophisticated technology and shipping of the finished products is cheap and easy.

8 Debt/GDP ratio stays constant. If output growth then stagnates, debt/GDP ratio starts to grow because of cumulative interest so eventually the country must run a trade surplus to earn foreign exchange to pay interest to foreign creditors.

9 (a) Declining industries in Western Europe, such as shipbuilding, crude steel, and agriculture, cause political difficulties when imports flow in. (b) These are precisely the industries in which Central and Eastern Europe were likely initially to have a comparative advantage.

10 (a) LDCs often argue that aid encourages dependence. They want foreign

investment,
countries,
relief t
(b) F

...less protection by rich ...technology transfer, and debt ...o wipe out mistakes of the past. ...urope would make a net gain from greater exploitation of comparative advantage, even though vociferous particular losers have so far blocked the process.

11 Consumers like variety, but if this is the only argument they should be prepared to pay the appropriately higher price to get it. A cultural heritage may be more like a public good, however, in which case some subsidy may be appropriate. If so, it should take the form of production subsidies not tariffs (principle of targeting again).

12 (a) Suppose relative poverty defined as x per cent of the average income. By definition, there are always some people in this category, and it cannot be eliminated simply by economic growth for everyone. (b) Number in relative poverty would increase (i) if the definition was tightened (eg changed from those below 10 per cent of average income to those below 20 per cent of average income) or if the dispersion of incomes increased (in which case average unaltered but more people in the very rich and very poor groups).

13 When the market is small, it takes a big profit rate to compensate drug companies for the risks they have taken. In principle, with a larger market it now takes a smaller profit per sale to offer the same total reward. Hence, if anything, globalization eases the conflict between the need to provide adequate rewards for risky research and the need to keep the price down so that the poor can afford key drugs. Moreover, if companies making AIDS drugs had *already* been rewarded by their sales in rich markets, there may be no economic case for having to have them charge such high prices in new LDC markets.

14 Austria is very close to its major trading partners (particularly Germany) and thus faces extensive competition in deciding tax rates, interest rates, and regulations; this is why Austria was quite happy to join the EU and adopt the euro. In contrast, New Zealand is shielded by distance from both the US and the EU, and effectively has more scope to make national decisions.

15 (a) The really big migrations (to the US and Australia) took place in the nineteenth century. (b) Absolute poverty has declined, and there is quite a lot of evidence that international trade helps economic growth, which is the main solution to national poverty. (c) Trade liberalization would almost certainly be more important than any level of aid that rich countries are likely to offer.

Glossary

Chapter 1

Section 1-1

Economics is the study of how society decides what, how, and for whom to produce.

For a **scarce resource**, the quantity demanded at a zero price would exceed the available supply.

The **opportunity cost** of a good is the quantity of *other* goods sacrificed to get another unit of *this* good.

A **market** uses prices to reconcile decisions about consumption and production.

In a **command economy** government planners decide what, how, and for whom goods and services are made. Households, firms, and workers are then told what to do.

In a **free market economy**, prices adjust to reconcile desires and scarcity.

In a **mixed economy**, the government and private sector interact in solving economic problems.

Positive economics deals with scientific explanation of how the economy works.

Normative economics offers recommendations based on personal value judgements.

Microeconomics makes a detailed study of individual decisions about particular commodities.

Macroeconomics analyses interactions in the economy as a whole.

Section 1-2

A **model** or **theory** makes assumptions from which it deduces how people behave. It deliberately simplifies reality.

Data are pieces of evidence about economic behaviour.

Nominal values measure prices at the time of measurement. **Real values** adjust nominal values for changes in the general price level.

An **index number** expresses data relative to a given base value.

A **scatter diagram** plots pairs of values simultaneously observed for two different variables.

Other things equal is a device for looking at the relation between two variables, but remembering other variables also matter.

Section 1-3

Demand is the quantity buyers wish to purchase at each conceivable price.

Supply is the quantity sellers wish to sell at each conceivable price.

The **equilibrium price** clears the market. It is the price at which the quantity supplied equals the quantity demanded.

A **price control** is a government regulation to fix the price.

Chapter 2

Section 2-1

Demand is the quantity buyers wish to purchase at each conceivable price.

A **demand curve** shows the quantity demanded at each possible price, other things equal.

Section 2-2

A rise in the price of one good raises the demand for **substitutes** for this good, but reduces the demand for **complements** to the good.

For a **normal good**, demand rises when income rises. For an **inferior good**, demand falls when income rises.

Section 2-3

The **price elasticity of demand** measures the *responsiveness* of quantity demanded to price.

The **income elasticity of demand** measures the percentage increase in quantity demanded when income rises by 1 per cent, other things equal. It is positive for a **normal** good, but negative for an **inferior** good.

A **luxury good** has an income elasticity above 1, a **necessity** an income elasticity below 1.

Section 2-4

The **substitution effect** says that, when the relative price of a good falls, quantity demanded rises.

The **income effect** says, for a given nominal income, a fall in the price of a good raises real income, affecting the demand for all goods.

Saving means not spending all today's income, reducing consumption today to raise consumption later.

Tastes describe the utility a consumer gets from the goods consumed. Utility is happiness or satisfaction.

The **marginal utility** of a good is the *extra* utility from consuming one more unit of the good, holding constant the quantity of other goods consumed.

Tastes display **diminishing marginal utility** from a good if each extra unit adds successively less to total utility when consumption of other goods remains constant.

The **market demand curve** is the horizontal sum of individual demand curves in that market.

Chapter 3

Section 3-1

Supply is the quantity producers wish to offer for sale at each conceivable price.

A **supply curve** shows the quantity supplied at each possible price, other things equal.

Section 3-2

The **elasticity of supply** measures the *responsiveness* of quantity supplied to the price that suppliers receive.

Section 3-4

Stocks are measured at a point in time; **flows** are corresponding measures over a period of time.

A firm's **revenue** is income from sales during the period, its **costs** are expenses incurred in production and sales during the period, and its **profits** are the excess of revenue over costs.

Cash flow is the net amount of money received by a firm during a given period.

Opportunity cost is the amount lost by not using resources in their best alternative use.

Normal profit is the accounting profit to break even after all economic costs are paid. **Economic (supernormal) profits** in excess of normal profit are a signal to switch resources into the industry.

Economic losses mean that the resources could earn more elsewhere.

Physical capital is any input to production not used up within the production period. Examples include machinery, equipment, and buildings. *Investment* is additions to physical capital.

Depreciation is the cost of using capital during the period.

Assets are what the firm owns. **Liabilities** are what it owes. **Net worth** is assets minus liabilities.

Section 3-4

The **total cost curve** shows the lowest cost way to make each output level. Total cost rises as output rises.

Marginal cost is the change in total cost as a result of producing the last unit.

Total revenue is the output price times the quantity made and sold. **Marginal revenue** is the change in total revenue as a result of making and selling the last unit.

The **marginal principle** says that, if the slope is not zero, moving in one direction must make things better, moving the other way makes things worse. Only at a maximum (or a minimum) is the slope temporarily zero.

Section 3-5

The **equilibrium price** clears the market. At this price, the quantity supplied equals the quantity demanded.

Chapter 4

Section 4-1

A technique is said to have **technical efficiency** if no other technique could make the same output with fewer inputs. **Technology** is all the techniques known today. **Technical**

progress is the discovery of a new technique that is more efficient than existing ones, making a given output with fewer inputs than before.

Long-run total cost *LTC* is the total cost of making each output level when a firm has plenty of time to adjust fully and produce this output level by the cheapest possible means. **Long-run marginal cost** *LMC* is the rise in total cost if output permanently rises by one unit. **Long-run average cost** *LAC* is *LTC* divided by the level of output *Q*.

There are **economies of scale** (or increasing returns to scale) if long-run average cost *LAC* falls as output rises, **constant returns to scale** if *LAC* is constant as output rises, and **diseconomies of scale** (or decreasing returns to scale) if *LAC* rises as output rises.

The lowest output at which all scale economies are achieved is called **minimum efficient scale**.

A **fixed input** cannot be varied in the short run. A **variable input** can be adjusted, even in the short run.

Fixed costs do not vary with output levels. **Variable costs** change with output.

The **marginal product** of a variable input (labour) is the *extra* output from *adding* 1 unit of the variable input, holding constant the quantity of all other inputs (capital, land, energy) in the short run.

Holding all factors constant except one, the **law of diminishing returns** says that, beyond some level of the variable input, further rises in the variable input steadily reduce its marginal product of that input.

Short-run marginal cost *SMC* is the extra cost of making one more unit of output in the short run while some inputs are fixed.

Short-run average fixed cost is short-run fixed cost divided by output. **Short-run**

average variable cost is short-run variable cost divided by output. **Short-run average total cost** is short-run total cost divided by output.

A firm's **short-run supply decision** is to make Q_1, the output at which $MR = SMC$, provided the price covers short-run average variable cost $SAVC_1$ at this output. If the price is less than $SAVC_1$, the firm produces zero.

Section 4-2

In **perfect competition**, actions of individual buyers and sellers have no effect on the market price.

A competitive firm's **short-run supply curve** is that part of its short-run marginal cost curve above its shutdown price.

A competitive firm's **long-run supply curve** is that part of its long-run marginal cost *above* minimum average cost. At any price below P_3, the firm leaves the industry. At price P_3, the firm makes Q_3 and just breaks even after paying all its economic costs.

Entry is when new firms join an industry. **Exit** is when existing firms leave.

Chapter 5

Section 5-1

A **monopolist** is the sole supplier or potential supplier of the industry's output.

Monopoly power is measured by price *minus* marginal cost.

A **discriminating monopoly** charges different prices to different buyers.

Section 5-2

An **imperfectly competitive** firm recognizes that its demand curve slopes down.

An **oligopoly** is an industry with only a few, interdependent producers. An industry with **monopolistic competition** has many sellers making products that are close but not perfect substitutes for one another. Each firm then has a limited ability to affect its output price.

A **natural monopoly** enjoys sufficient scale economies to have no fear of entry by others.

Collusion is an explicit or implicit agreement between existing firms to avoid competition.

A **game** is a situation in which intelligent decisions are necessarily interdependent. The *players* in the game try to maximize their own *payoffs*. In an oligopoly, the firms are the players and their payoffs are their profits in the long run. Each player must choose a strategy.

A **strategy** is a game plan describing how the player will act or **move** in each situation.

In **Nash equilibrium**, each player chooses his best strategy, *given* the strategies chosen by other players.

A **commitment** is an arrangement, entered into voluntarily, that restricts one's future actions.

A **credible threat** is one that, after the fact, it is still optimal to carry out.

A **contestable market** has free entry and free exit.

An **innocent entry barrier** is one made by nature.

Your **strategic move** influences the other player's decision, in a manner helpful to you, by affecting the other person's expectations of how you will behave.

Strategic entry deterrence is behaviour by incumbent firms to make entry less likely.

Chapter 6

Section 6-1

The **marginal product of labour** *MPL* is the extra physical output when a worker is added, holding other inputs constant.

The **marginal revenue product of labour** *MRPL* is the change in sales revenue when an extra worker's output is sold.

A **monopsonist** must raise the wage to attract extra labour.

The **labour force** is everyone in work or seeking a job.

The **participation rate** is the fraction of people of working age who join the labour force.

The **poverty trap** means that getting a job makes a person worse off than staying at home.

Section 6-2

Human capital is the stock of accumulated expertise that raises a worker's productivity.

A **closed shop** means that all a firm's workers must be members of a trade union.

Section 6-3

Physical capital is the stock of produced goods used to make other goods and services. **Land** is the input that nature supplies.

Gross investment is the production of new capital goods and the improvement of existing capital goods. **Net investment** is gross investment minus the depreciation of the existing capital stock.

A **stock** is the quantity of an asset at a point in time (eg 100 machines on 1/1/06). A **flow** is the stream of services that an asset provides in a given period. The cost of using capital services is the **rental rate** for capital. The

asset price is the sum for which the stock can be bought, entitling its owner to the future stream of capital services from that asset.

The **required rental** is the income per period that lets a buyer of a capital asset break even.

The **marginal revenue product of capital** *MRPK* is the extra revenue from selling the extra output that an extra unit of capital allows, holding constant all other inputs.

Section 6-4

The **functional income distribution** is the division of national income between the different production inputs.

The **personal income distribution** shows how national income is divided between people, regardless of the inputs from which these people earn their income.

Chapter 7

Section 7-1

Horizontal equity is the identical treatment of identical people. **Vertical equity** is the different treatment of different people in order to reduce the consequences of these innate differences.

For given tastes, inputs, and technology, an allocation is **efficient** if no one can then be made better off without making at least one other person worse off.

A **distortion** or **market failure** exists if society's marginal cost of making a good does not equal society's marginal benefit from consuming that good.

An **externality** arises if a production or consumption decision affects the physical production or consumption possibilities of other people.

A **free rider**, knowing he cannot be excluded from consuming a good, has no incentive to buy it.

A **public good** is necessarily consumed in equal amounts by everyone.

Moral hazard exploits inside information to take advantage of the other party to the contract.

Adverse selection means individuals use their inside information to accept or reject a contract. Those accepting are no longer an average sample of the population.

Section 7-2

If T is the amount paid in tax, and Y is income, then T/Y is the **average tax rate**. The **marginal tax rate** shows how total tax T increases as income Y increases.

Direct taxes are taxes on income; **indirect taxes** are taxes on spending,

Tax incidence is the final tax burden once we allow for all the induced effects of the tax.

The **tax wedge** is the gap between the price paid by the buyer and the price received by the seller.

Section 7-3

There are two **social costs of monopoly power**. The first is too little output, the second is wastefully high cost curves.

Competition policy tries to promote efficiency through competition between firms. The **Competition Commission** examines whether a monopoly, or potential monopoly, is against the public interest.

The **Office of Fair Trading** is responsible for making markets work well for consumers, by protecting and promoting consumer interests while ensuring that businesses are fair and competitive.

A **merger** is the union of two companies where they think they will do better by amalgamating.

A **natural monopoly**, having vast scale economies, does not fear entry by smaller competitors.

Chapter 8

Section 8-1

Macroeconomics studies the economy as a whole.

The **circular flow** is the flow of inputs, outputs, and payments between firms and households.

Gross domestic product (GDP) measures an economy's output.

Value added is net output, after deducting goods used up during the production process.

Saving S is the part of income not spent buying output. **Investment** I is firms' purchases of new capital goods made by other firms.

Saving is a **leakage** from the circular flow, money paid to households but *not* returned to firms as spending. Investment is an **injection** to the circular flow, money earned by firms but *not* from sales to households. Leakages always equal injections, as a matter of definition.

Exports X are made at home but sold abroad. **Imports** Z are made abroad but bought at home.

Gross national product (GNP) is the total income of citizens wherever it is earned. It is GDP plus net property income from abroad.

Depreciation is the fall in value of the capital stock during the period through use and obsolescence.

National income is GNP minus depreciation during the period.

Nominal GNP is measured at the prices when income was earned. Real GNP adjusts for inflation by valuing GNP in different years at the prices prevailing at a particular date.

Section 8-2

Economic growth is the rate of change of real income or real output.

Potential output is the level of GDP when all markets are in equilibrium.

Technology is the current stock of ideas about how to make output. Technical progress or better technology needs both invention, the discovery of new ideas, and innovation to incorporate them into actual production techniques.

Along the long-run equilibrium path, output, capital, and labour grow at the same rate. Hence output per worker y, and capital per worker k, are constant.

In a growing economy, capital widening gives each new worker as much capital as that used by existing workers. Capital deepening raises capital per worker for all workers.

Labour-augmenting technical progress increases the effective labour supply.

The convergence hypothesis says poor countries should grow quickly but rich countries should grow slowly.

The zero-growth proposal argues that, because higher output has adverse side effects such as pollution and congestion, we should therefore aim for zero growth of measured output.

Section 8-3

The business cycle is short-term fluctuation of output around its trend path.

A political business cycle is caused by cycles in policy between general elections.

Real business cycles are output fluctuations caused by fluctuations in potential output itself.

Chapter 9
Section 9-1

Potential output is national output when all inputs are fully employed. The output gap is the difference between actual output and potential output.

Personal disposable income is household income from firms, plus government transfers, minus taxes. It is household income available to be spent or saved.

The consumption function relates desired consumption to personal disposable income.

The marginal propensity to consume MPC is the fraction of each extra pound of disposable income that households wish to consume.

Aggregate demand is total desired spending at each level of income.

Short-run equilibrium output is where aggregate demand equals actual output.

In short-run equilibrium, planned leakages must equal planned injections.

The saving function shows desired saving at each income level. The marginal propensity to save MPS is the fraction of each extra pound of income that households wish to save.

The multiplier is the ratio of the change in equilibrium output to the change in demand that caused output to change.

The paradox of thrift is that a change in the desire to save changes equilibrium output and income, but not equilibrium saving.

The **accelerator** model of investment assumes that firms guess future output and profits by extrapolating past output growth.

The **multiplier–accelerator model** explains business cycles by the dynamic interaction of consumption and investment demand.

Section 9-2

Fiscal policy is the government's decisions about spending and taxes.

Automatic stabilizers reduce fluctuations in aggregate demand by reducing the multiplier. All leakages act as automatic stabilizers.

The **trade balance** is the value of net exports. When exports exceed imports, the economy has a trade surplus. When imports exceed exports, it has a trade deficit.

The **marginal propensity to import (MPZ)** is the fraction of each extra pound of national income that domestic residents want to spend on extra imports.

Section 9-3

Monetary policy is the decision by the central bank about what interest rate to set.

The **real interest rate**, the difference between the nominal interest rate and inflation, is what measures the real cost of borrowing and the real return on lending.

The **investment demand schedule** shows desired investment at each interest rate.

Demand management is the use of monetary and fiscal policy to stabilize output near the level of potential output.

Chapter 10

Section 10-1

Money is any generally accepted means of payment for delivery of goods or settlement of debt. It is the **medium of exchange**.

A **barter economy** has no medium of exchange. Goods are simply swapped for other goods.

The **unit of account** is the unit in which prices are quoted and accounts are kept.

Money is also a **store of value**, available for future purchases.

A **token money** has a value as money that greatly exceeds its cost of production or value in consumption.

An **IOU money** is a medium of exchange based on the debt of a private bank.

Bank reserves are cash in the bank to meet possible withdrawals by depositors. The **reserve ratio** is the ratio of reserves to deposits.

The **money supply** is money in circulation (cash not in bank vaults) plus bank deposits on which cheques can be written.

The **monetary base** is the supply of cash, whether in private circulation or held in bank reserves. The **money multiplier** is the ratio of the money supply to the monetary base.

Section 10-2

A **central bank** is responsible for printing money, setting interest rates, and acting as banker to commercial banks and the government.

An **open market operation** is a central bank purchase or sale of securities in the open market in exchange for cash.

The **lender of last resort** lends to banks when financial panic threatens the financial system.

The **cost of holding money** is the interest given up by holding money rather than bonds.

The **demand for money** is a demand for *real* money balances M/P.

The **monetary instrument** is the variable over which a central bank exercises day-to-day control.

Section 10-3

The **quantity theory of money** says that changes in the quantity of nominal money M lead to equivalent changes in prices P, but have no effect on real output.

Hyperinflation is high inflation, above 50 per cent *per month*.

Shoe-leather costs of inflation are shorthand for the extra time and effort in transacting when inflation reduces desired real cash holdings.

Menu costs of inflation are the physical resources used in changing price tags, reprinting catalogues, and changing vending machines.

Chapter 11

Section 11-1

The **classical model** of macroeconomics assumes wages and prices are completely flexible.

The **aggregate supply schedule** shows the output firms wish to supply at each inflation rate.

In the classical model, the **aggregate supply schedule** is vertical at potential output.

Following an **inflation target**, a central bank raises the real interest rate if it expects inflation to be too high, and cuts the real interest rate if it expects inflation to be too low.

Monetary policy **accommodates** a permanent supply change by reducing the average level of real interest rates, thereby perma-nently raising aggregate demand in line with higher aggregate supply.

In the classical model, there is **complete crowding out**. Higher government spending causes an equivalent reduction in private spending, since total output cannot change.

The **short-run supply curve** *SAS* shows how desired output varies with inflation, for a given inherited growth of nominal wages.

The **output gap** is actual output minus potential output.

Section 11-2

The **labour force** is everyone who has a job or wants one. The **unemployment rate** is the fraction of the labour force without a job.

Frictional unemployment is the irreducible minimum unemployment in a dynamic society.

Structural unemployment reflects a mis-match of skills and job opportunities when the pattern of employment is changing.

Demand-deficient unemployment occurs when output is below full capacity.

Classical unemployment arises when the wage is kept above its long-run equilibrium level.

Voluntary unemployment is people looking for work who won't yet take a job at that real wage.

Equilibrium unemployment is unemploy-ment when the labour market is in equilib-rium.

Involuntary unemployment means the unemployed would take a job offer at the existing wage.

Section 11-3

The **Phillips curve** shows that higher inflation is accompanied by lower unemployment.

Equilibrium unemployment U^* is the level of unemployment in long-run equilibrium.

The **long-run Phillips curve** is vertical at equilibrium unemployment.

Each **short-run Phillips curve** is a negative relation between inflation and unemployment, given the inflation expectations already built into nominal wages.

Chapter 12

Section 12-1

The **foreign exchange (forex) market** exchanges one national currency for another. The **exchange rate** is the price at which two currencies exchange.

A **fixed exchange rate** means that governments, acting through their central banks, will buy or sell as much of the currency as people want to exchange at the fixed rate.

The **foreign exchange reserves** are the foreign currency holdings of the domestic central bank.

A **devaluation (revaluation)** is a fall (rise) in the fixed exchange rate.

In a **floating exchange rate** regime, the exchange rate is allowed to find its free market equilibrium without any invervention using the foreign exchange reserves.

The **balance of payments** records all transactions between a country and the rest of the world.

The **current account** of the balance of payments records international flows of goods, services, and transfer payments.

The **capital account** of the balance of payments shows international flows of transfer payments relating to capital items.

The **financial account** of the balance of payments records international purchases and sales of financial assets.

The **real exchange rate** is the relative price of domestic and foreign goods, when measured in a common currency.

Perfect capital mobility means expected total returns on assets in different currencies must be equal if huge capital flows are to be avoided. A positive interest differential must be offset by an expected exchange rate fall of equal magnitude. This is the **interest parity condition**.

Internal balance means aggregate demand equals potential output. **External balance** means that the current account of the balance of payments is zero. Long-run equilibrium requires both.

Chapter 13

Section 13-1

The **law of comparative advantage** says that countries specialize in producing and exporting the goods that they produce at a lower *relative* cost than other countries.

The **gains from trade** are additional output of some goods with no loss of other goods.

Intra-industry trade is two-way trade in goods made by the same industry.

Trade policy operates through import tariffs, export subsidies, and direct quotas on imports and exports.

An **import tariff** is a tax on imports.

When a country affects the price of its imports, the **optimal tariff** makes individual importers take account of their effect on the price that other importers must pay.

The **principle of targeting** says that the best way to meet an aim is to use a policy that affects the activity directly. Policies with side effects are second best because they distort other activities.

Section 13-2

Less developed countries (LDCs) have low levels of per capita output.

Primary products are agricultural goods and minerals, whose output relies heavily on the input of land.

Import substitution replaces imports by domestic production under the protection of high tariffs or import quotas.

Export-led growth stresses output and income growth via exports, rather than by displacing imports.

Aid is an international transfer payment from rich countries to poor countries.

Section 13-3

Globalization is the increase in cross-border trade and influence on the economic and social behaviour of nation states.

Index